Indian Diplomacy

'Rajendra Abhyankar's comprehensive survey of contemporary Indian foreign policy demonstrates that India's material weakness limited but did not extinguish its capacity to pursue a humane vision of international relations. By carefully unpacking the past against the challenges on the horizon, Abhyankar has produced a refreshingly readable guide to understanding how India's growing ability and determination to act on its vision will shape the future global system in beneficial ways.'

—**Ashley J. Tellis**, Tata Chair for Strategic Affairs, Carnegie Endowment for International Peace

'A comprehensive and interesting account of the political, economic, and strategic imperatives that have driven India's foreign and national security policies from the days of Jawaharlal Nehru to Narendra Modi. Abhyankar's narrative covers the challenges India faced through the era of decolonization and the Cold War, to contemporary times, with an interesting blend of facts, data and analysis.'

—**Ambassador G. Parthasarathy**

'Over the past seventy years India has moved from its chosen position as a nonaligned commentator on the global stage to being one of its shapers. Yet, there are very few books that explain the whys and the hows of its policy. Rajendra Abhyankar's *Indian Diplomacy* provides a much needed structured and comprehensive look. As a practitioner of long standing, Abhyankar's lucid interpretation of the Indian foreign policy should interest the curious and the serious alike.'

—**Ambassador Rajiv Dogra**

Indian Diplomacy
Beyond Strategic Autonomy

Rajendra M. Abhyankar

OXFORD
UNIVERSITY PRESS

OXFORD
UNIVERSITY PRESS

Oxford University Press is a department of the University of Oxford.
It furthers the University's objective of excellence in research, scholarship,
and education by publishing worldwide. Oxford is a registered trademark of
Oxford University Press in the UK and in certain other countries.

Published in India by
Oxford University Press
2/11 Ground Floor, Ansari Road, Daryaganj, New Delhi 110 002, India

ISBN-13 (print edition): 978-0-19-948218-4
ISBN-10 (print edition): 0-19-948218-7

ISBN-13 (eBook): 978-0-19-909176-8
ISBN-10 (eBook): 0-19-909176-5

Typeset in Bembo Std 11/14
by Tranistics Data Technologies, Kolkata 700 091
Printed in India by Replika Press Pvt. Ltd

Contents

Preface

*D*ean Acheson, the legendary US Secretary of State,[1] has written that 'the separation from high office is like the end of a great love affair – a void left by the disappearances of heightened sensitivities and focused concerns.' It succinctly encapsulates my almost four decades in the Indian Foreign Service. While no career is without its vicissitudes, it did not detract from an intensely satisfying experience. It was more than a job; equally, it was a pleasure. My experiences gained in a career spanning thirty-seven years have been truly memorable. My thirteen years as Indian Ambassador in various countries and three years as Secretary in the Ministry of External Affairs blooded me into the making of Indian foreign policy. Some of these are recounted in my book *Stuff Happens: An Anecdotal Insight into Indian Diplomacy.*[2]

Throughout the question remained: what were the principles and practice behind the formulation of India's foreign policy?

After Independence, there was a clear articulation of non-alignment as the basis of India's foreign policy during the Cold War period (1947–90) which stood India well given our meagre strengths and resources. Following the collapse of the Soviet Union, the progressive waning of non-alignment made it necessary to devise goals and the operating principle of India's foreign policy. Yet nothing has been available from the successive governments since, either in the form of a defining statement in Parliament or through White Papers, which would spell out the goals of India's foreign policy. Admittedly, some of the goals would remain immutable, while others would need review at designated intervals, either five or ten years, depending on international developments and India's capabilities.

This need is imperative, given that, over the years, the practice of diplomacy has descended from its ivory tower to the people. It is recognized for what it is: one—of the many—policy options available to the government to achieve its national goals. Yet India has contented itself to state that its foreign policy is formulated based on 'strategic autonomy', a principle of doubtful value at the best of times. Both prime ministers, Manmohan Singh and Narendra Modi, have tried to lay down the goals of India's foreign policy. There are similarities as well as differences between them. However, in neither case have these pronouncements been formalized in an authoritative document of the government or debated in Parliament.

It is from this thought that the book takes up its narrative in looking at the performance of India's diplomacy and underlines the need to go beyond the operating principle of 'strategic autonomy'. Only when the goals of the foreign policy are enunciated, does an operating principle have any value.

In writing the book, it became necessary to go into the brief history of India's major foreign policy concerns, thus some element of 'déjà vu' became unavoidable. I hope it will heighten the appeal for the lay reader, while serving as a memory check for the practitioner.

The book includes an exhaustive bibliography that will serve as a reference point for those who may wish to delve into specific strands more deeply. The data in the book is relevant up to April 2017, but that is in the nature of publishing a book.

The book aims to fulfill a lacuna in the writings on Indian foreign policy. I hope it has met this goal. Any omissions are my own.

Notes

1. Dean Acheson (1953–1971) as President Truman's Secretary of State, had a central role in defining American policy during the Cold War, designing the Marshall Plan, and was a key player in the development of the Truman Doctrine and the creation of NATO. https://en.wikipedia.org/wiki/Dean_Acheson.

2 *Stuff Happens: An Anecdotal Insight into Indian Diplomacy* (New Delhi: Har Anand Publications Pvt. Limited, 2013).

Acknowledgements

*I*n writing a book of this scope there are a number of mentors and colleagues that have given me the benefit of their wisdom in the almost forty years I spent in practicing what I learnt on the job of the principles of India's diplomacy. Among my mentors I would list Ambassadors K.B. Lall I.C.S, Naresh Chandra, and J.N Dixit. At different stages in my career, they lent guidance and a helping hand.

In the writing of this book, I had the tremendous fortune of holding a professorship at the School of Public and Environmental Affairs, Indiana University, Bloomington, now rated the top public policy school in the United States of America. In particular, the Dean John Graham and the Executive Associate Dean Michael McGuire have been magnificent in their assistance and encouragement. They have nurtured a friendly collegial atmosphere in the School that has made it a delight to pursue concentrated writing.

I would particularly like to thank my then research assistant Joao Palma Chacon, MPA and MSES, who, through the Fall 2016 semester, compiled an exhaustive bibliography. It was in keeping with desires of the publisher, to have a stand-alone bibliography that would be useful to both the practitioners and readers of the book.

I would also like to thank Farhana Khan, my research assistant, who was extremely helpful in going through the text, researching specific points, and helping to conform the manuscript to the exigent requirements of the publisher.

I would also like to acknowledge my friends and colleagues for going through the manuscript and providing brief comments,

x

acknowledgements

Professor Ashley Tellis, Tata Chair at the Carnegie Endowment for International Peace, Washington, DC; Ambassador G. Parthasarathy, Centre for Policy Research, New Delhi; Ambassador Naresh Chandra; and Ambassador Rajiv Dogra.

While I have listed only some by name, let me hasten to write that if this book ever saw the light of day much is owed to many colleagues and friends whom I have interacted with during my career and thereafter.

Needless to emphasize, its deficiencies are mine alone.

I am in eternal debt to my wife Paulomi, who has always given me the space to pursue my interests, at great cost to her own commitment to keeping alive the dying art of pottery in India, a passion she has pursued in her professional life as a studio potter. She is the most unusual person in my life.

Introduction: Setting the Stage

The Seven Year Itch (1995) was a classic American romantic comedy based on the notion that after seven years of marriage cycles of dissatisfaction in interpersonal relationships grow and lead to a decrease in happiness and satisfaction. The premise of the Marilyn Monroe film made for some great laughs and iconic images; however, this was not pure fancy. A number of studies over time have shown that the average length of a first marriage in America is about seven or eight years.

This has an interesting parallel in politics; specifically when it pertains to the lifespan of a party or long-entrenched regimes, though in this case, we might call it the '70-year itch'.

> It is impossible to create a middle-class society without eventually generating middle-class values and middle-class organizations ... With rising education and incomes and growing access to information, people become more intolerant of diversity, more demanding and assertive, and more willing to protest. Their value priorities shift from seeking material gain and security to seeking choice, self-expression, and 'emancipation from authority.... Closely intertwined with this psychological shift is the rise of a civil society—of independent organizations and flows of information, opinion and ideas. These psychological and social changes undermine the legitimacy of authoritarian rule and generate favourable conditions for a political transition....'[1]

As empirically observed, the seventh decade leads to the questioning of long-held verities in democracy, social cohesion, economic empowerment, and international outreach. The 70-year itch is attested by the end of the Russian Revolution of 1917;[2] the end of Turkey's Kemalist secularism, following the Islamist Refah Party in 1996; the fall in 2000 of Mexico's Institutional Revolutionary Party; the popular questioning of all Arab one-party regimes in the misnamed 'Arab Spring'; the changes being forced upon the ruling communist parties in China, Vietnam, and Cuba; and the challenges in the Bretton Woods institutions made inevitable by the coming together of the G-20 and setting up of new international banks such as the BRICS (Brazil, Russia, India, China, and South Africa) Bank and the Chinese-sponsored International Infrastructure Investment Bank (IIIB).

While many reasons can be adduced for such fundamental changes, perhaps, the most significant is that of generational change: 70 years represent the transition to the third generation from the so-called 'founding generation' of the prevailing political and state system. In most cases, this generation, between 15 and 35 years, often called the fast-forward generation, is the driver of change. They are young, aspirational, and fully conversant with information and communication technology (ICT) and social media. This generation is willing and able to question long-held truths, thus creating an unstoppable momentum for fundamental change leading a nation to an unstable period. Such fundamental change or the '70-year itch' equally afflicts one-party, communist, and multiparty states.

India's 70-Year Itch?

The period after the Cold War has been a testing period for Indian foreign policy and its practice. The international order remained afflicted by entropy, incapable of meeting its high expectations. In the last three decades, there has been no change in the management structure of international relationships. The single superpower, in greater or lesser degree, has imposed its stamp on all major events of the 21st century.

On 15 August 2017, India completed 70 years of existence as an independent nation. Is India, in its 70th year, on the cusp of fundamental change? Will the basis of Indian foreign policy need to be realigned?

To come to a proper understanding, we have to look into the situation leading up to India's completion of its 70 years as an independent republic and its projection since May 2014 under Prime Minister Narendra Modi. The epilogue addresses this issue in the context of India's foreign policy. There are signs of change in the country's politics, economy, and society. The landmark elections of March 2017 in Uttar Pradesh, India's largest state with a population of 200 million, was the focus of the subtle transformation. If this change becomes consolidated, it will have a profound impact on the future trajectory of the country.

The unacknowledged social story is the Bharatiya Janata Party's (BJP) rise and its transformation of the rules of caste politics aligning them to a larger narrative. Almost no other party has been able to tap into this transformative urge. Modi always had the nationalism space. He has tried to occupy the anti-corruption space citing the move of demonetization, albeit with increasing voices against its after-effects particularly on the economy's growth rate. More remarkably, he has also managed to occupy the pro-poor narrative that parties like the Congress and the Bahujan Samaj Party (BSP) thought were their natural territory. The rise of the BJP from its small beginnings in 1980 and its ascendance to overwhelming power under Modi is a remarkable development. The withering of the Indian National Congress, the party of Indian independence, may indicate a reduction in the salience of the secular ethic that was its major strength.[3] The BJP's landslide victory in March 2017 in Uttar Pradesh and Uttarakhand and the forming of governments in Goa and Tripura speaks of its better organizational structure and political receptivity. Sectarian mobilization by the polarization of voters around religious identity has also been a noticeable factor.[4]

In Uttar Pradesh, BJP won 31 of the 42 seats where the minority community comprised a third of the electorate, a strike rate of 74 per cent. Experts say the results indicate that Muslims never vote in one single wave and that the persistent focus on the minority community's influence might have consolidated the Hindu votes.[5] Interestingly, the BJP swept the polls in all six constituencies of riot-hit Muzaffarnagar, as well as Deoband in Saharanpur, Bareilly, Bijnor, and Moradabad where Muslims dominate the demography.[6] A majority of Muslims are still influenced by Islamic clerics, though a class of newly educated Muslim youth is constantly trying to think of its place in the Indian polity. However, the Muslim youth too remains caught up in the historical legacy of separatism.

> Due to the sheer logic of electoral calculations, the BJP was right not to field Muslim candidates in UP because they would have certainly lost. However, as the BJP has now emerged as a pan-India party, it must follow its policy *Sabka Saath, Sabka Vikas* [*With everyone, with progress for everyone*]—by recruiting Muslim leaders, especially women, in its organizational hierarchy at the district levels. The BJP too needs to … begin a journey that conforms to the moderate core of modern society in which everyone resides together and dreams a vision of India together.[7]

In the last seven decades three dynamic variables, and their simultaneous and continuous interaction, have determined the world that India faces.

As things stand, Prime Minister Modi has had his passage to a second term in 2019 seemingly eased. He still has around a year in which to consolidate his development programmes. In working towards these goals, India's foreign policy will bulk large, first to secure foreign direct investment (FDI) and second, to ensure that nothing disrupts the country's growth path. It would be appropriate to look at the world that faces India while keeping in view that India itself is changing.

The Global Context

International movements have been marked by contrary trends as a sign of growing discord and uncertainty:

1. The increase in world population, under 8 billion in 2016, with majority below 25 years of age, is projected to become 9.7 billion by 2050 and 11.2 billion by 2100, creating pressure on urban living space and potable water.
2. The phenomenon of unbridled globalization has lost its lustre, and the world, in the words of Rabindranath Tagore, India's first Nobel Laureate, is 'being broken up into fragments by narrow domestic walls'.[8]

3. The increase in the number of countries since World War II reflects the growing desire for self-governance but also signifies the narrowing of 'civil' space. The United Nations' (UN) current membership at 193 has not only legitimized the new states coming out of decolonization and the break-up of the Soviet Union, Yugoslavia, and Sudan but equally spurred the tendency towards sub-national distinctiveness and insularity making for fluid national boundaries.

4. Despite a globalized world, regional integration now encompasses a growing number of smaller states, demonstrating resistance against the United States' overwhelming military superiority and untrammelled partisanship in the UN; equally, it has spurred Russia to re-assert itself in the comity of nations.

5. The rush for membership with the European Union (EU), following the defeat of communism, has been tempered by the reassertion of national prerogatives, particularly on consular issues, to confront forced migration caused by the politico-religious wars in the countries on the eastern and southern Mediterranean seaboard.

6. The failure of the Bretton Woods institutions to tide over the global financial crisis of 2008–09 demonstrated the growing power of emerging economies in the G-20 group after their success in bailing out the international monetary and financial system.

7. The revolution of rising expectations is being continuously redefined. The phenomenal diversity and reach of mass communication have made possible instant comparisons of the human condition sowing seeds of civil strife.

8. The tremendous impact of science and technology in every walk of life, particularly in research and development of new products and technology, has developed a multidisciplinary approach to confronting human problems requiring higher skills but reducing employment potential.

9. The growing awareness of 'injustices' has magnified the clamour for people's participation in governance, thanks to the stellar role played by prolific social networking sites.

10. The greater salience of transnational events affecting humanity's future—nuclear threat; terrorism and its nexus with the running of arms, drugs, and human trafficking; pandemics such as acquired immunodeficiency syndrome (AIDS), severe acute respiratory syndrome (SARS), and malaria; and climate-induced disasters

like tsunami—has increased recognition that global challenges require global responses because no nation can fight these challenges alone.

11. There is far greater international concern regarding the loss of life and assault on human rights due to civil, ethnic, religious, and sectarian strife.

12. There is an increase in civil and non-governmental initiatives to bring people together, regardless of their origin or civilizational roots; yet, there prevails a growing popular appeal of conservatism in democratic societies.

13. There is the growing and malignant role of non-state actors who exploit established political, social, and economic weaknesses of national systems to achieve their purpose, making mechanisms for international cooperation imperative.

14. With the passage of time, there is recognition of the diversity of the human condition and an increasing desire to find compromises. In the new millennium, threats to established state structures have multiplied because the citizens demand democratic, inclusive societies, yet increasingly turn insular in the face of growing mobility of people across national borders.

15. The world is increasingly seeing the fragility of the rule-based order and the possibility that the US will remain the pre-eminent, though not the dominant power of the 21st century. At the same time, there is growing interest on part of China and other emerging powers to shape the world as stakeholders, since norms and standards can only be set with their engagement.

The National Context

Parallel to the changes in the international environment facing India have been changes within the country.

1. Although an 'Indian identity' which emphasizes diversity is ingrained in India's ethos, there is a growing appeal of distinctness and separatism, conforming to the global trend where a large number of people are asserting their separate identities through civil strife.

2. While Indian democracy has struck deep roots and matured with more than 700 million voters, India's secular and inclusive polity, which negated a 'clash of civilizations', is increasingly under pressure.

3. From a 'socialist pattern of society', India has moved towards free market-based economic reforms and liberalization; yet 260 million still live below the poverty line.

4. From an impoverished developing country, India is seen as an emerging global player. From India knocking on the doors of rich countries, the world now beats a path to India's door.

5. From a food-deficit country, dependent on United States' PL 480 wheat imports, India achieved self-sufficiency in one decade—a miracle in today's world. Yet the country needs a second 'green revolution' to be able to feed a population that will be nearly 2 billion in 2050.

6. While India has transcended its pre-1990 'Hindu rate of growth', never above 2 per cent per annum, it must maintain a growth rate of close to 10 per cent per annum to meet its target of an inclusive society.

7. India leads the world as much in information technology as in milk production.

8. India's growing recognition as an emerging power increasingly calls for greater commitment to the management of the international system. Yet in projecting its foreign policy, India displays 'cognitive disability' by repeating its commitment to non-alignment, without confronting the fact that a different basis is needed to take account of changing behaviours of other actors in an international system in flux.

For India, the end of the Cold War was a bittersweet augury. With remarkable resilience, the country came out of its catharsis with a new vigour to notch high economic growth in the succeeding decades. It managed major changes that it encountered:

1. Politically, 1989 was a watershed year in the country's life. It ended the dominance of the Indian National Congress at the centre and in the states. The era of coalition politics meant no single political party could get a majority in the central government. What looked then like political instability had fostered governmental stability in the ensuing 25 years, until 2014. The democratic process had become entrenched in India's body politic with three consequences:

   a. Every national party, and even some regional political parties, participated in coalitions at the centre and gained valuable experience of governance. Consequently, across the political spectrum, a better understanding existed of the parameters of government policies.

b. The importance of regional parties in coalition-building at the centre has meant a greater voice for the states in national policymaking, including in foreign policy.

c. The diversity of participation in the political process has meant that decisions are based on the interests of the widest number concerned with each issue.

2. Economically, 1991 was the watershed year when India began the process of economic reform and liberalization. It freed the energies of the Indian people to create a dynamic economy. The threshold trade turnover of USD 100 billion, seen as an indicator of an economic take-off, was crossed with ease. The economic reform process demonstrated:

a. Irrevocability: Every coalition at the central government, notwithstanding their contradictory ideologies, continued with the economic reform process.

b. Sequencing: The economic reform process focuses on improving infrastructure like roads, ports, railways, and communication systems but has suffered in the last decade due to a sluggish economy. Despite the dismantling of controls, India still remains low on the 'Ease of Doing Business' indices; equally, although in its second stage, regulatory reform was the key, the process remains incomplete largely due to the absence of mutual political accommodation in India's parliament.

c. Pace: Due to the changing political orientation of the coalitions at the centre, India has been prone to varying speeds of the economic reform process. All three stages operate in different sectors of the economy. Much is expected owing to the overwhelming mandate, after 25 years, which the BJP received in 2014.

India has always imposed itself on the world in its many incarnations, going back to civilizations that grew in the Indus Valley. It was coveted for its mineral riches and natural resources and admired for its contribution to human learning. Long before its independence in 1947 India's indispensability as the 'jewel' in the British crown made it part of the international system, not as a participant but as a recipient. In consequence, India perforce became the inheritor of every British action to preserve its hold on the country. The rapid change in India's global profile, the realignments within its polity, and its external environment today make it imperative to understand Indian diplomacy, its precepts, and current practice.

Since independence, India attracted international attention, if for no other reason than its poverty or its international stances. The country's profile as an emerging power in the global system is a development of the last 25 years, provoked by its economic reform and liberalization process.[9] It led to a major change in its political and economic trajectory. Whereas earlier international discourse was focused on India's poverty and socialist ideology, today the discourse centres on whether India will attain its promise as an economic and political powerhouse.

This broad theme underpins the narrative in the book. *Indian Diplomacy*, or India's diplomacy, is an examination of the practice of India's foreign policy. In this context, it covers the precepts or principles on which India's foreign policy is based and the manner in which it has been projected outside the country and domestically. It is axiomatic that policy once decided determines its practice, or projection, yet this is not always so. It implies looking at instances in which the practice of India's diplomacy has succeeded, failed, or caused a course correction. In this sense, the narrative operates at the level of both policy and practice.

Article 51 of the Constitution of India, Directive Principles of State Policy, Part IV, decrees that as a matter of state policy India shall 'endeavour to promote international peace and security; maintain just and honourable relations between nations; foster respect for international law and treaty obligations in the dealings of organized peoples; and encourage settlement of international disputes by arbitration'.[10]

If this is the crux of India's global mission, it incorporates the idea that India is supremely content within its post-Partition frontiers and has no unfulfilled territorial claims or desire for territorial aggrandizement. In publicly eschewing any desire or interest to expand beyond its present national boundaries, it evocatively brings out a concept of 'Indian exceptionalism' in its foreign policy. At its root lies the conviction that India stands uniquely on the world stage by virtue of its civilization, culture, diversity, and a long history of coping with events that would have broken up any other state. The historicity of this conviction can be seen from the following quotation by Abu Arryhan Mohammad ibn Ahmad al-Beruni (973–1048 CE), the eleventh-century Arab scholar on India, when he states, 'The Indians believe that there is no country but theirs, no nation like theirs, no king like theirs, no religion like theirs, no science like theirs.'[11]

This conviction, burnished after India's independence, by an overlay of international temper and respect for universal values imparted by Jawaharlal Nehru, and a tenor of high morality and righteousness deriving from Mahatma Gandhi, has informed the exercise of a foreign policy that has non-aggrandizement, non-aggression, and non-interference as its cornerstones. India has always sought recognition and special treatment on this basis. During the seven decades since independence, this theme has acquired many dimensions.

It has led India to emphasize its internationalism and pronounce on all international and global issues that have engaged the international community, because they resonated internally, and given the multifarious diversity of Indian society, obviated a unidimensional position. The reconciliatory nature of its national character saw India taking initiatives in international conflict resolution and Indian diplomats taking pride in their drafting prowess. For a country with hardly any real power to exercise in the international system, it adopted non-alignment as the best route to promote its diplomatic presence in the world.

'Indian officials believe they are representing not just a state but a civilization.'[12] They believe that in this incarnation India has something to offer to the rest of the world. Consequently, Indian leaders see their multi-ethnic, multicultural state well suited to the 21st century. As a result, India has often created animosities where none existed, for example, its relations with Southeast Asia in the early days were marred by an overemphasis on the shared cultural affinities. It also failed to recognize that others may not be imbued with a similar global mission or to understand the motivation of inimical forces that had a significant impact on India's security.

Strong support for a multipolar world has been the leitmotif of India's foreign policy, starting with its leadership of the

Non-Aligned Movement (NAM). The end of the Cold War meant that India's settled relationships, and worldview arising therefrom, underwent a cathartic change. It meant the loss of a major great power ally. If there were no blocs, non-alignment seemed redundant. Nationally, at the political level, the break-up of the Congress hegemony in India's electoral politics gave regional political parties a role in governance and the making of policies. At the economic level, the inability of India's 'socialistic pattern of society' to deliver prosperity provoked economic reform and liberalization; if the statist system was inadequate to meet the political aspirations of India's growing millions, then the federal constitution had to be given greater salience.

An early realization that India's size and diversity precluded any international military, nuclear, or financial umbrella from any major power engendered the trend towards resilience as an over-arching theme. At the same time, India's discomfort with a single superpower became manifest in the international developments of that decade. The nascent movement towards multipolarity in the 21st century, provoked by the rise of China, was a mixed blessing for India, not without its own discomfort. The view that the country is on track to join a putative multipolar trilateral international power structure with United States and China presents India with a Hobson's choice. The growing consciousness of India's recognition as an emerging global power and its active role in extra-UN groupings like the G-20,[13] BRICS,[14] and India, Brazil and South Africa (IBSA)[15] reinforces its conviction in favour of multipolarity.

It signifies India's intention to move towards a global role which could mean forsaking the sanctuary which non-alignment[16] has afforded so far, albeit through the way-station of describing it as 'strategic autonomy'. It has also allowed India to use multipolarity to advance its interests and ensure it is not enmeshed in international situations that could demand a more determinate response.

A natural corollary of this worldview has been the tendency to search for the 'middle ground' on any international issue as a guiding principle in a latter-day manifestation of Prince de Talleyrand's[17] dictum 'et surtout pas trop the zele'. Only when absolutely incumbent does India actually take a policy decision and, then too, generally strives to anchor it to a middle ground. Notwithstanding India's manifest attraction for reconciliatory resolution, it disguises the covert and unarticulated churn between two strands of the idea of India itself—the secular liberal that veers towards pragmatism and the majoritarian that favours realism. This dichotomy is the outcome of the partition of India based on religion. Nevertheless, its origins in the domain of foreign policy can be traced to an illustrious progenitor, the *Arthashastra* of Kautilya or Vishnugupta, who was also known as Chanakya.[18]

Interestingly, the question of 'recognition' of the newly created state of Israel in 1948 brought in the open the strong discord between the two views of an emerging India—Mahatma Gandhi and Jawaharlal Nehru's secular view, which gave equal respect to all religions and no privileges to Hinduism, and V.D. Savarkar's view of a Hindu nation and polity.[19] The Indian National Congress having rejected the idea of a Hindu state championed by the Hindu Mahasabha[20] could not bring itself to support a Jewish state. India's decision—to recognize Israel but have no diplomatic relations with it—reflected a middle ground resolution imposed by the interplay of strong sentiments by opposing ideologies. It also lay behind India's dissenting vote in UN Special Commission on Palestine[21] against the partitioning of Palestine, and India's proposal for a single state with autonomous regions for the Arabs and the Jews there.[22] India was firmly of the view that neither should the calamity of partition be visited on other peoples nor would the partition engender a viable and secure Palestine. Nehru almost exclusively articulated and shaped democracy and secularism as the bases of India's foreign policy. It eclipsed the theocratic basis championed by the majoritarian Hindu adherents led by V.D. Savarkar.[23]

The contending majoritarian and secular views within India's polity, to some extent, are reflected in the ideological and electoral platforms of India's two national level political formations, the Indian National Congress[24] and the BJP,[25] although they are not always adversarial on foreign policy issues. This contestation is to be viewed in broad terms as policy choices at a particular juncture and not in narrow religious or sectarian terms.

Yet the overt manifestation in India's foreign policy decisions of the shadow play of these forces may often seem anodyne in articulation. For instance, while the ideological successors of the majoritarian view were always in favour of opening diplomatic relations with Israel,[26] it was a Congress government led by P.V. Narasimha Rao that took the step in May 1992. This illustrates another feature of the contestation: votaries of the liberal strand have found opportune moments to impart a hard edge to foreign policy gaining strength from the majoritarian view. Some important foreign policy decisions in the last 70 years that illustrate this anomaly are the policies towards Israel, on nuclear weaponization, economic liberalization, and relations with the United States. This strategy has enabled India to respond in 'hard' terms to evolving situations warranted by the changing political and security environment and the shifting balance between the great powers.

Spanning the political spectrum, this contestation is both inter-party and intra-party. On foreign policy issues, difficult to handle domestically, the predilection to look for the middle ground is pervasive. Internally, this contestation is reflected on a number of issues, too many to recount. For example, while successive Indian governments have considered the possibility of having a uniform civil code,[27] in practice this contestation, as manifested in vote banks, has ensured that separate personal laws for Hindus, Muslims,[28] and Christians have prevailed. Nevertheless, the broad trend of Indian foreign policy decision-making remains liberal, non-aggressive, and open to dialogue on both regional and international issues.

At the same time, it is difficult to find a single enunciation of India's foreign policy which reflects consensus across the political spectrum. It has led observers to question whether India even has a strategic culture. The absence of an informed discussion on this subject either in parliament or in academia has supported such a contention. The closest one gets, apart from the reference to foreign policy in the Indian constitution, are the Five-Year Plan goals stated in each Plan document. Yet, even in that document, there is little mention of how India's foreign policy is expected to contribute to the goals leaving it with structural disabilities.

The end of the Cold War brought a realization that India's foreign policy is only one instrument in India's armoury of policy instruments to meet national goals and, in this sense, not something separate from the others. It has slowly transformed the tendency to separate 'foreign policy' from the country's domestic policy and to see it, in the idiom of the earlier century, as an end in itself. Increasingly, the idea that foreign policy and a nation's power are reciprocally related has taken hold. The movement of foreign policy issues to the public space during the US invasion of Iraq in 2003 fostered this transition. The public demonstrations then forced a decision through parliament on a government that would have preferred an open mandate. The exponential increase of transnational issues needing global solutions and greater involvement of civil society in national decisions, such as terrorism, climate change, pandemics, and natural and man-made disasters, has increased the salience of public diplomacy, both domestically and internationally.

In this context a significant target for public diplomacy is India's 'generation next' which accounts for about 65 per cent of India's population.[29] It is nationalistic but has no experience or memory of the partition or any of the defining moments of India's political history: the India–China War of 1962; India–Pakistan wars of 1948, 1965, or 1971; the Emergency in 1975–77; or the destruction of the Babri Masjid in 1992. An aspirational generation, it gives little heed to the strata in Indian society to which it belongs. The proliferation of electronic media, particularly online and television advertising, coupled with rapid growth in internet and cell phone penetration and increasing facility with social networking sites which makes them an ideal vehicle for dissemination of ideas and views.

Foreign policy issues have not only become news fodder for the common Indian but also witnessed a change in the composition of the makers and implementers of foreign policy, that is, those joining the Indian Foreign Service (IFS). In the early decades up to the 1990s, foreign policy—its making and practice—was a preserve of the few. It was axiomatic that India's multi-ethnic, multi-religious, multi-linguistic, and multicultural ethos would demand, when giving voice on international issues, a widening of

In its largest interpretation, India's basic national purpose is to create and enhance the capabilities of its people and, to this end, harness all available instruments of domestic and foreign policy. It embodies two constituent elements—the security and the prosperity of India's population. This book will take this definition of India's national purpose in assessing the character and outcome of India's diplomacy. The resilience and efficacy of India's diplomacy critically depends on the extent to which a coordinated view can emerge in response to rapid world developments.

These trends provide the reference point to look at the evolution of Indian diplomacy, particularly after 1990. If the narrative misses issues that may appear important, it will be for no other reason than they would only serve to reinforce the argument in the text.

The end of the Cold War forced India to revisit some of the long-accepted tenets of its foreign policy. This is the starting point of the narrative on Indian diplomacy. Five important changes characterize the world since the 1990s:

1. There is a continuing erosion of national sovereignty in a globalized, multipolar, and fractious world with increasing recourse to global governance and regulation to deal with international security, diplomatic, financial, monetary, development, and environment issues.

2. During the Cold War, thanks to the sanctuary afforded by non-alignment, India could wait before entering a conflict or siding with one bloc or the other in order to seize its best advantage. In the dire economic and political circumstances in which India found itself, this was its best foreign policy option. Despite its idealistic basis, India's 'non-aligned' stance thus contained a healthy dose of realpolitik. The end of the Cold War and globalization also saw India's relative political decline because the pitfalls of the high moral stance of earlier decades came home to roost.

3. The rethink of India's foreign policy continued to demonstrate a large degree of cognitive disability or an unwillingness to break the mould. While this position was buoyed after 1997 by India's consistently high rate of growth, it highlighted the need to 'find

a new organizing principle'. Brajesh Mishra, as national security adviser, stated this succinctly when he said that 'in the post-Nehru period non-alignment became a mantra just as Gandhiji's non-violent struggle had become "the moral path"; the fact that these policies were grounded in strict rationality and realpolitik were lost sight of. Escapism was often couched as being principled and I can safely state that neither Gandhi nor Nehru would have appreciated being made into icons to propagate dogma. There is a new India today that is ready to question these shibboleths and take decisions on the basis of national interest.'[30] India's initiatives to develop alliances and partnership with major international players have been one preferred path.

4. The growing number of nuclear weapon states and an equal number of aspirants have made nuclear war increasingly unlikely. It has engendered the realization that while nuclear weapons act as a deterrent, their use is a recipe for annihilation. India has two nuclear states in its neighbourhood, China and Pakistan, two other non-NPT (Nuclear Non-Proliferation Treaty) states Israel and North Korea, one potential aspirant, Iran, while others wait in the wing.

The world's population will reach 9.7 billion by 2050, with India being the largest at 1.70 billion. Providing secure and sustainable economic, political, and social development has to be the overarching goal of any Indian government's policy, domestic and foreign. What is India's place in the region and the world 30 years after the Cold War ended? There is a growing opinion that India is on track to become the third most powerful country by 2030, though far behind the United States and China. It will depend entirely on whether India's leadership can define a new organizing principle as the basis of India's foreign policy. India will need to harness the country's resources and market and provide unending opportunities for its people to maximize their talent and skills. Regardless of India's future trajectory, its choices and action will condition that of its neighbours and, thus, impact the prosperity and security of its own population and the nearly two billion in the neighbourhood.

In Chapter 1 we look at how the major foreign policy issues perennially in public debate stem from heritage issues of the end of British rule and India's partition, and equally inevitably, they relate to India's neighbours in South Asia, China, Myanmar, and the seas around India. Some of these issues are directly related to the fact of the partition itself. Others arise from real or imagined perceptions of 'Indian hegemony'. In most cases, these issues are marked by their intractability, the enmeshing of contiguous domestic interests, and the presence of the second-largest Muslim community in the world. In every way, these issues constitute 'the bread and butter' of Indian diplomacy.

In Chapter 2 the set of countries includes those with which India has had a conjoint relationship since the British era. Since independence, this sub-region, comprising the countries that give out on the Persian Gulf, are seen as part of India's extended neighbourhood. India's relationships with these countries are complex, given the intersection of strategic proximity, great power interests, energy, and religion. Important as they are to India, they represent a major challenge to its diplomatic posture.

Chapter 3 speaks about how India has had diplomatic relations before independence with all the major world powers barring Portugal, France, and the United Kingdom, countries that that colonized it. The period since then neatly breaks down into that during the Cold War and after the break-up of the erstwhile Soviet Union. India's foreign relations have grown in diversity and complexity after the 1990s and into the 21st century. The chapter will elaborate this development, attempting to highlight major trends and particular landmarks that have affected India. The response to India's rising stature vis-à-vis the five permanent members of the United Nations Security Council (P-5) and other Western powers such as Germany, Russia, Japan, and Australia, is the substance of this chapter.

Chapter 4 showcases how Jawaharlal Nehru's vision almost exclusively defined a role for India in the comity of nations built on its democratic, secular, and plural polity. It is only in recent years that experts are seeking to review whether some of Nehru's major decisions were in line with India's national interest or if there could have been another way.[31] At the same time, choices by India's leaders have always imposed themselves on India's policy and public pronouncements on international issues. In many ways, judgement in the public discourse on India's diplomacy is measured by how it has fared in the UN councils, in regional organizations to which India belongs, and on global issues which are trending towards systems of international regulation and surveillance. In the last 25 years, India's participation in international groupings—regional, inter-continental, and international—has hugely expanded beyond the UN system. This chapter will cover India's track record in the UN, particularly the Security Council, in regional security and economic organizations, and in groupings of emerging economies. Further, it will look at the country's stance on global issues such as international trade, nuclear proliferation, climate change, and international cooperation in combating non-state terror, pandemics and diseases, and natural disasters.

Chapter 5 attempts to look at the perspectives that impelled India's partners in groupings like BRICS, IBSA, and G4 to come together starting from different origins and trajectories. It speaks highly of Indian diplomacy to have been able to carve out areas of common interest following the Cold War that saw the US' emergence as the only superpower in a rapidly globalizing world. Each of India's partners in these 'purpose-built groupings' came with their own domestic imperatives, challenges, and opportunities that were vastly different from India's.

Chapter 6 looks at India's long-standing relations of civilization and culture with countries in the Arab and Islamic world; countries of Central, Southeast, and Northeast Asia; Africa, and South America. Yet the end of the Cold War and India's phenomenal growth trajectory changed the matrix of these relations and provoked new initiatives—diplomatic, political, economic, and people-to-people—which have redefined their character. In many cases, the changes have been path-breaking and mutually beneficial. Although the chapter has a very wide coverage, I have selected issues, cutting across regions, commonalities, and divergences of action and response.

Chapter 7 attempts to look at the structure that underlies the making and practice of Indian diplomacy, the IFS, which has been pronounced as being either good enough or inadequate in terms of its strength and specialization to meet the expanding goals of a country which encompasses one-fifth of humanity. A plethora of committees has recommended increases in the strength, greater attention to specialization, and newer ways of organization and evaluation. Only in the last five years has the consensus on boosting the strength been realized. The increasing complexity, in spread and depth, of issues that Indian diplomacy confronts has led to specialized tasks being assigned to specialists from outside the service or to other government ministries.

Yet another factor that has directly influenced the diplomatic structure is the phenomenal diversity and complexity in technology-based global information flows. It has increased the variety of tools available to the Indian diplomat, leading to the growing demand to deal with the practice of diplomacy that goes 'beyond the state'. The growing role of the Indian parliament and its impact on foreign policy is yet another issue that bears discussion. This chapter will look at the extant state of 'projection' issues that confront Indian diplomacy and consider how far it has been able to cope with them.

Chapter 8 tries to assess how Indian diplomacy has performed in the context of meeting the country's national goals. It discusses what changes seem necessary in response to fast-changing world developments.

Chapter 9 gives a view of how Prime Minister Modi has stamped himself as a 'foreign policy prime minister', much like Jawaharlal Nehru, though the difference in substance, content, and style is marked. So also is the complexity of the world order and the multiplicity of means of communication. What has succeeded and what has failed in Modi's intensive exercise of diplomacy with a remarkable record of travel and interaction? How much of it is ephemeral and what will cast a stamp on the future projection of India's diplomacy?

My aim is to give the reader a succinct, yet comprehensive, view of the major challenges that India's diplomacy faces, understand the limitations under which it has functioned, and draw lessons for the future.

Notes

1. Larry Diamond, 'Chinese Communism and the 70-year Itch', *The Atlantic* (13 October 2013), http://www.theatlantic.com/china/archive/2013/10/chinese-communism-and-the-70-year-itch/280960/.

2. 'Russian Revolution of 1917', *Encyclopaedia Britannica*, https://www.britannica.com/event/Russian-Revolution-of-1917.

3. Arun Swami, 'India's Elections a Harbinger of Sectarian Politics', *East Asia Forum* (26 March 2017), http://www.eastasiaforum.org/2017/03/26/india-elections-a-harbinger-of-sectarian-politics/?utm_source=subscribe2&utm_medium=email&utm_campaign=postnotify&utm_id=60825&utm_title=India+elections+a+harbinger+of+sectarian+politics.

4. Nilanjan Mukhopadhyay, 'BJP's Uttar Pradesh Win: Turning Point for Modi?' *Al Jazeera* (12 March 2017), http://www.aljazeera.com/indepth/opinion/2017/03/bjp-uttar-pradesh-win-turning-point-modi-170312142735789.html.

5. Jayant Jacob and Gulam Jeelani, 'Election Results: Why the Muslim Vote Didn't Count Much in PM Modi's UP Win', *Hindustan Times* (13 March 2017), http://www.hindustantimes.com/assembly-elections/myth-or-negation-why-muslim-vote-didn-t-count-much-in-pm-modi-s-up-win/story-cOF9sFDnI3IPv45AVE0p4M.html.

6. Nishant Shankar, 'BJP Shining in Muslim Stronghold Setback for Mayawati, Akhilesh', *Indian Express* (11 March 2017), http://indianexpress.com/elections/uttar-pradesh-assembly-elections-2017/up-elections-results-bjp-shinning-in-muslim-stronghold-a-big-jolt-to-maya-akhilesh-samajwadi-party-bsp-bhartiya-janata-party-uttar-pradesh/.

7. Tufail Ahmed, 'UP Elections 2017: Muslims Need to Embrace Development, Rise above Counterfeit Socialism', Firstpost (12 March 2017), http://www.firstpost.com/politics/up-election-results-2017-why-muslims-need-to-embrace-bjp-rise-above-counterfeit-secularism-3330368.html.

8. Rabindranath Tagore, a Bengali poet, novelist, educator, and Nobel Laureate for Literature (1913), https://allpoetry.com/Where-The-Mind-Is-Without-Fear.

9. C. Raja Mohan, 'Beyond Non-alignment', in Kanti P. Bajpai and Harsh V. Pant (eds), *India's Foreign Policy* (New Delhi: Oxford University Press, 2013).

10. While keeping in view the fundamental objectives of India's foreign policy listed in the text, India has adopted and pursued certain principles to realize these objectives. Some of these principles are given in Article 51 under the Directive Principles of State Policy in the Constitution of India. These principles are promotion of international peace and security, friendly relations with other countries,

respect for international law and international organizations like the UN, and finally the peaceful settlement of international disputes. The principles of India's foreign policy and its objectives are closely interlinked.

11. Al-beruni, a great philosopher, mathematician, and historian, was born at Khiva in 973 CE. He was two years younger than its ruler, Mahmud of Ghazni. He came to India in the war-train of Mahmud and lived in the country for many years. Attracted by Indian culture, he learnt Sanskrit and studied several books concerning Hindu philosophy and culture. He travelled far and wide and wrote a masterly account of India in his book *Tahqiq-i-Hind*, also known as *Kitabul Hind* (1017–31 CE). For additional information, see http://www-groups.dcs.st-and.ac.uk/~history/Biographies/Al-Biruni.html.

12. S.P. Cohen, *India: Emerging Power* (Washington, DC: Brookings Institution Press, 2001) cited by Priya Chacko in *Indian Foreign Policy: The Politics of Postcolonial Identity from 1947 to 2004* (London and New York: Routledge, 2012).

13. A group of finance ministers and central bank governors from 19 of the world's largest economies and the EU set up in 1999 to discuss key issues related to the global economy. The mandate of the G-20 is to promote growth and economic development across the globe. G-20 consists of the members of the G-7 (seven industrialized nations), 12 other nations (including China, India, Brazil, and Saudi Arabia), and rotating council presidency from the EU. The committee's inaugural meeting took place in Berlin in December 1999. For additional information, see https://en.wikipedia.org/wiki/G20_developing_nations.

14. BRICS is the acronym for the intercontinental group of five emerging economies: Brazil, Russia, India, China, and South Africa who have decided to come together to address common issues of development and growth. India was the Chair of the Eighth BRICS summit held in Panaji, Goa, in India from 15–18 October 2016. See also http://www.newindianexpress.com/nation/New-Delhi-to-Host-2016-BRICS-Summit/2015/07/10/article2912208.ece1.

15. The IBSA forum groups India, Brazil, and South Africa, three economically advanced developing countries which share common economic and political interests in a globalizing world, particularly South-South Cooperation. For additional information, see https://en.wikipedia.org/wiki/IBSA_Dialogue_Forum.

16. https://en.wikipedia.org/wiki/India_and_the_Non-Aligned_Movement.

17. The French statesman Charles Maurice de Talleyrand, Duc de Talleyrand-Périgord (1754–1838) for half a century had served every French regime except that of the Revolutionary 'Terror'. Charles Maurice de 'Talleyrand,' *Encyclopedia of World Biography* (2004). Encyclopedia.com. (29 April 2016), http://www.encyclopedia.com/doc/1G2-3404706279.html.

18. Chanakya (350–275 BCE) was a teacher, philosopher, economist, jurist, and royal advisor. He is traditionally identified as Kauṭilya, who authored the ancient Indian political treatise, the *Arthashastra*. He is considered the pioneer in the field of political science and economics in India, and his work is thought of as an important precursor to classical economics. Originally a teacher at the ancient university of Takshashila, Chanakya assisted the first Mauryan emperor Chandragupta in his rise to power. He is widely credited for having played an important role in the establishment of the Maurya Empire. See, Chanakya, *Arthashastra*, translated and edited by L.N. Rangarajan (Delhi: Penguin, 1992).

19. See Rajendra Abhyankar, *Evolution and Future of India Israel Relations* (Tel Aviv University, 2012), wttp://www.tau.ac.il/humanities/abraham/india-israel.pdf.

20. The Akhil Bharatiya Hindu Mahasabha (All-India Hindu Grand Assembly) is a Hindu nationalist political party formed to protect the rights of the Hindu community in British India, after the formation of the All India Muslim League in 1906 and the British India government's creation of separate Muslim electorates under the Morley-Minto reforms of 1909. The oldest Hindu nationalist political party, after Indian independence, it is seen as having an umbilical link with the BJP, currently holding power in the central government. See https://en.wikipedia.org/wiki/Akhil_Bharatiya_Hindu_Mahasabha.

21. The United Nations Special Committee on Palestine (UNSCOP) was created on 15 May 1947 in response to a United Kingdom government request that the General Assembly 'make recommendations under article 10 of the Charter, concerning the future government of Palestine'. The British government had also recommended the establishment of a special committee to prepare a report for the General Assembly. The General Assembly adopted the recommendation to set up the UNSCOP to investigate the cause of the conflict in Palestine and, if possible, devise a solution. UNSCOP was made up of representatives of 11 nations, including India. UNSCOP visited Palestine and gathered testimony from

Zionist organizations in Palestine and in the United States. The Arab Higher Committee boycotted the Commission, explaining that the Palestinian Arabs' natural rights were self-evident and could not continue to be subject to investigation, but rather deserved to be recognized on the basis of the principles of the United Nations Charter. The Report of the Committee dated 3 September 1947 supported the termination of the British mandate in Palestine. It contained a majority proposal for a Plan of Partition into two independent states (see Chapter 6) and a minority proposal for a Plan for one Federal union with Jerusalem as its capital (see Chapter 7). On 29 November 1947, the General Assembly adopted Resolution 181, based on the UNSCOP majority plan (with only slight modifications to the proposed recommendations). For additional information, see http://www.1948.org.uk/introduction/; UN Report of the United Nations Committee on Palestine (1948) https://unispal.un.org/DPA/DPR/unispal.nsf/0/07175DE9FA2DE563852568D3006E10F3.

22. Shamir Hasan, 'India's Palestine Policy', in Rajendra. M. Abhyankar (ed.), *India and West Asia: Defining a Role* (New Delhi: Academic Foundation, 2000).

23. See http://www.britannica.com/biography/Vinayak-Damodar-Savarkar.

24. Indian National Congress, http://inc.in/.

25. See http://www.bjp.org/.

26. Rajendra Abhyankar, 'The Evolution and Future of India-Israel Relations', Research Paper No. 6, The Hartog School of Government and Policy, Tel Aviv University (March 2012), http://www.tau.ac.il/humanities/abraham/india-israel.pdf.

27. Ashwin Upadhyaya, 'Why India Urgently Needs Uniform Civil Code', *Oneindia* (11 March 2016), http://www.oneindia.com/feature/why-india-urgently-needs-uniform-civil-code-2037892.html.

28. In declaring unconstitutional the 'triple talaq' for Muslim women and placing it in the context of Articles 14 and 21 of the Constitution a step has been taken towards bringing extant religious law in conformity with the constitution. http://www.aljazeera.com/news/2017/08/india-supreme-court-suspends-muslim-divorce-law-170822052829982.html.

29. Kishan S. Rana, 'India's Foreign Policy and the Youth of India', *Simply Decoded* (31 March 2014), http://www.simplydecoded.com/2014/03/31/indias-foreign-policy-youth-india/.

30. Quoted by Raja Mohan from Brajesh Mishra, 'Rising World Players in Asia: Implications for Regional and Global Security', Presentation at 36th Munich Conference on Security and Policy (4–5 February 2000).

31. Ramachandra Guha, 'An Indian Fall', *Prospect Magazine*, http://www.prospectmagazine.co.uk/features/jawaharlal-nehru-ramachandra-guha.

CHAPTER ONE

Inherited Challenges

*I*ndian diplomacy has been tested to the hilt, for different reasons and by different countries, and will continue to be tested in the times to come. The first set of countries to do so includes India's contiguous neighbours grouped under the South Asian Association for Regional Cooperation (SAARC). This is because these countries are able to develop countervailing equities, and secondly, because India fears being accused of acting like a hegemon. To some extent, the same considerations have applied to Myanmar, although contact with that country has seen a long hiatus since the beginning of military rule until the early 1990s.

While relations with the People's Republic of China (PRC) had a positive start following India's independence, India's high profile in international councils nurtured under Prime Minister Nehru turned out to be a red rag to the Chinese bull. Nevertheless, India steadfastly utilized its global access to supplant Taiwan with the PRC in the United Nations Security Council (UNSC). India has been stumped by China because of its size and burgeoning economic power which have added to its political and military muscle across the globe. China's power as a veto-wielding member of the UNSC has been its major strength not only in confronting India but also in using Pakistan to keep India mired in South Asia.

While the India–China Agreement for Maintaining Peace and Tranquillity on the Border (1993)[1] has tremendously expanded trade and technology exchanges between the two countries, it has not been an unalloyed blessing. Though India has gained much-needed (electronic) goods and machinery at highly competitive costs, competing Indian goods have been subjected to unrealistic prices, aggravating security concerns relating to other imports, and having a debilitating impact on domestic production.

At the same time, despite nearly 20 years of India–China talks,[2] on their nearly 2,000 kilometre-long border in the north, the Chinese have not shown any hurry to settle this long-pending issue. It has reinforced the view that China has more to gain by not settling the issue than by settling it. It keeps India occupied in a low-intensity manner, while keeping the threat of hostilities open, constraining India from effectively addressing China's enhance-ments in the Indian Ocean (IO). The countries in this group continue to pose a formidable challenge to India's diplomacy.

South Asia: An Overview

India's neighbours in SAARC[3] play a huge role in the country's inherited challenges. In most cases, these challenges are marked by their intractability and enmeshing of the domestic and inter-national dimensions. Inevitably, Indian public debate on major foreign policy issues also revolves around these concerns. An overview of the cross-cutting features of the SAARC sub-region will elucidate the common challenges to enhance regional coop-eration that these countries face.

The SAARC region accounts for one-fifth of humanity, but has some of the lowest standards of living and the highest rates of population growth. Despite decades of domestic and international resources devoted for poverty alleviation, a major breakthrough towards prosperity is yet to be achieved. The region's collective inability to promote joint developmental efforts is further exac-erbated by the high level of mutual distrust coloured by continu-ing tension between India and Pakistan. It has cast a malignant shadow on SAARC itself and led other SAARC countries to look beyond the region. Yet their geographical discontinuity and

fractious character has ensured that there is not much evidence of
their ganging up against India, nor has India's Muslim population
taken up cudgels for its co-religionists in the region.

Again, the SAARC region is one of the least well-connected
regional grouping in the world—whether by road, rail, air, sea,
and ether. This has been detrimental to meaningful implementation of regional schemes for poverty alleviation, human rights
reform, electoral congruity, and boosting of intra-SAARC trade
based on comparative advantage and mutual benefit.

India's total area far exceeds that of all SAARC members combined. India has land borders with six of eight states, totalling 14,000
kilometres and is the only state to border all states of South Asia,
except Afghanistan (if not for Pakistan-occupied Kashmir [PoK]).
Nepal and Bhutan are landlocked; Bangladesh and Maldives fear
sea-level rise, while India's coastline in the Indian Ocean region
is 7,000 kilometres. India accounts for 81 per cent of South Asia's
gross domestic product (GDP) and is four times larger than the
next largest country, Pakistan. Indian diplomacy towards SAARC
countries is thus a function of its overwhelming size and geographical and geopolitical domination of the subcontinent.

Within SAARC, India's relations with Pakistan stand on their
own since most outstanding issues trace their roots to partitioning
of undivided India. It sets a natural barrier to their resolution.
India's diplomacy vis-à-vis Pakistan is thus subject to the vicissitudes of political relations between the two countries and the
role that the great powers, particularly the United States, have
played since 1990. Its diplomacy has had to work within this
political and international context while being circumscribed by
Pakistan's nuclear deterrent. So far, India's policy has been based
on the premise that 'a failed state' in its neighbourhood will be
worse than the present state where the trappings of democracy are
regularly subverted by the Pakistan Army pursuing its line on the
indispensability of the 'India threat' to assure its permanence and
control. Thus, the Pakistan Army and Inter-Services Intelligence
(ISI)[4] remain in control of Pakistan's foreign policy towards India,
the United States, and Afghanistan.

For most other SAARC neighbours the defining features
have been historicity, contiguous borders, and a real or imagined

perception of Indian hegemony. In diplomatic terms the sky is the limit as far as building relations with these neighbours is concerned. However, to reach this point, India will have to follow a sustained and politically bipartisan policy, emphasizing its intention to assist these countries economically while keeping strictly within the parameters of sovereign equality.

Indian diplomacy towards its SAARC neighbours has seen different phases over the last 70 years. India's attitude and relations with its neighbours, other than Pakistan, have been greatly influenced by the fact that it is the successor state to the British Empire. At independence, India chose to conduct bilateral relations with these countries, carrying on with the tenor of British times. With the exception of Sri Lanka, never governed from Delhi, and of Nepal, never ruled by the British, there was undoubtedly a continuation of the spirit of 'empire' with the others.

The fact that India's independence preceded those of its neighbours also gave it a first-mover advantage in tailoring its bilateral relations with these countries. While India retained an 'imperialist' tenor to its relationships, it remains moot whether an alternate path could have been taken, based on sovereign equality and the common bond of anti-colonialism and economic development. It explains, to some extent, India's long-standing allergy to the interference of other countries in the affairs of the Indian subcontinent. This tendency was further enhanced after the Bandung Conference (1955)[5] which led to the doctrine of 'Panchsheel'[6] and NAM.[7]

Indian diplomacy leveraged a weak hand, both politically and militarily, by building a phalanx of recently liberated states into NAM that eventually encompassed two-thirds of the membership of the UN. By any reckoning, this was a remarkable performance for a recently liberated state that was fighting the ills of domestic poverty. It earned great dividends for India bilaterally in being able to garner aid, in kind and cash, to move its development forward and in being able to stamp its mark in the international councils of power and influence within and outside the UN.

At the same time, its success internationally encouraged India into adopting a profile in the South Asia region that emphasized its strengths and the presumption to lead these nations politically, economically, and culturally. It helped that other than Pakistan, all other neighbours became part of NAM, subscribing to its basic tenet of not being part of any military bloc and preserving an independence of judgement on international issues.

India's foreign policy came to articulate these values during the period 1947–62 but it failed to recognize that its neighbours, despite their like-minded response to international developments centring on the Cold War, were not always ready to accept India as their cultural, economic, or political leader. The marked absence of the needed sensitivity on India's part that, having finally got out of colonialism, its neighbours were loath to succumb to the leadership of yet another power, was significant. That this sensitivity was lacking in India's outreach to its neighbours was illustrated, in those years, by India's relations with the countries in Southeast Asia. It was one reason which delayed a close relationship with the Association of Southeast Asian Nations (ASEAN)[8] countries until the early 1990s.

Founded in 1961, NAM reached its lowest mark at the 17th Summit on 17–18 September 2016 at Isla Margarita in Venezuela. The presence of only a handful of leaders, out of 120 member states, demonstrated the changing dynamics in the group due to their varying economic condition and political interest in a splintered world.[9]

Strategic Views under Indian Prime Ministers

The period since independence has seen 15 prime ministers[10] from the Indian National Congress, the BJP, and the Janata Party. The Congress monopolized the post of the prime minister between 1947 and 1989 (except for a brief gap between 1977 and 1980), but since then until 2014, India has had multiparty coalitions. Every national level political party and some regional parties as well have been part of governance at the centre. This has developed a common understanding amongst all political parties of the cardinal points of India's foreign policy despite their ideological differences. It has, nevertheless, not been possible till today to enunciate India's foreign policy, its goals, and strategies in the form of a White Paper of the Indian parliament. Neither has any

Indian government explained its foreign policy through official White Papers and concept documents. As a result, there is lack of clarity about the principles and goals, and their changing content, that guide India's foreign policy. Neither is it linked with any national security strategy.

Jawaharlal Nehru, India's first prime minister, who also was the foreign minister during his own prime ministerial tenure, laid down a policy based on the former colonial tenet which saw India as the security provider in the sub-region. It implied two con-comitants: first, that India's smaller neighbours should approach India in case of a perceived threat, whether external or internal, and second, they should refrain from going to a country seen as inimical to India. Furthermore, while force was the last resort, intervention by other regional or great powers was seen ipso facto as a threat to Indian security.

This also meant that India would take an interest, short of interference, in the domestic political developments of the con-cerned neighbour. For example, the signing of friendship treaties with Nepal and Bhutan continued to be seen in the hegemonistic mould. With other neighbours too, underlying the policy was a mix of dominance and magnanimity. India's intervention on 'humanitarian grounds' was only considered necessary to defuse situations which could ultimately threaten Indian security.

During the prime ministership of Indira Gandhi (1966–77 and 1980–84), this policy received a boost on its interventionist logic. The 1971 Bangladesh War with Pakistan originated from a growing concern over the huge numbers of Bengali refugees from East Pakistan fleeing the atrocities of the Pakistan Army into India.[11] The United States refrained from entering this conflict, and there was no international action despite India's pleading. Similarly, the stamping out, with Indian military assistance, of the Janatha Vimukthi Peramuna (JVP) insurgency in Sri Lanka[12] in the same year and the raising of concern at the treatment of Tamils in north Sri Lanka occasioned yet another refugee influx into India in July 1983.[13] This justificatory trend was reinforced in 1987 by Prime Minister Rajiv Gandhi (1984–89) who sent Indian troops to Sri Lanka under the India–Sri Lanka Agreement of 1987[14] and in 1988 to oust a Sri Lanka terrorist group from Maldives.[15]

A more balanced view became incumbent only in 1990 with the end of the Cold War coupled with India's faltering economy and increasing security concerns in the neighbourhood. The withdrawal of the Indian Peace-Keeping Force (IPKF)[16] from Sri Lanka in 1990 by Prime Minister V.P. Singh (1989–90) signalled India's intention to treat internal developments in its neighbours at an arm's length. It was given greater structure by Prime Minister Inder Kumar Gujral (1997–98). The Gujral Doctrine[17] was based on extending non-reciprocal economic concessions and assistance to India's neighbours. The goal was to minimize their threat perceptions from India to enable the country to look beyond South Asia. Bangladesh and Nepal were the first to benefit through water-sharing agreements on the rivers Ganga (Farakka) and Kosi respectively. A similar concession on the river Teesta was filibustered in 2016 by West Bengal Chief Minister Mamata Bannerji.[18] This is a classic example of the need to factor in the interests of the contiguous states in the making of India's foreign policy.

The principle of non-reciprocal action towards its neighbours is now embedded in India's foreign policy. During the prime ministership of Atal Behari Vajpayee (1998–2004), a new dimension was added to this policy. The effort was to give bilateral relationships in SAARC a security component through agreements covering anti-terrorism, extradition, and legal assistance in criminal matters. There was also a concomitant increase in agreements covering military exercises and increasing military training opportunities in Indian defence institutions. India's fears have persisted that its smaller neighbours will develop linkages beyond the subregion and are increasingly factored in its policy.

During Manmohan Singh's prime ministership (2004–14) India was assailed by serious security challenges, including the terror attack in Mumbai on 26 November 2008 by Lashkar-e-Taiba (LeT), a Pakistan-based terror group, and the likely backlash from the United States' withdrawal from Afghanistan. India's foreign policy gave prominence to its own economic growth and to regional economic cooperation. It required that nothing would be allowed to interrupt India's domestic economic growth. This precluded any attempt to involve the country's armed forces in missions and operations in the neighbourhood. This policy remained in place for the decade of Congress rule.

A degree of testing the efficacy of Indian policy on long-standing intractable issues with its neighbours, particularly China, Pakistan, and Bangladesh, is visible since May 2014 with the assumption of office by Prime Minister Narendra Modi.

The progressive withdrawal from the precepts laid down by Jawaharlal Nehru has been particularly marked in the post–1990 period. Five reasons were responsible for this change.

First, the regional security landscape in South Asia has become more fraught due to five elements: (a) the United States' presence in Afghanistan after 9/11 and its dependence on Pakistan, (b) the fallout of the nuclear tests of 1998 by India and Pakistan and the latter's continued intensification of terror attacks across India despite sporadic attempts at peace, (c) the political changes in Nepal after the end of the monarchy and in the Maldives after the end of the dictatorial rule by Maumoon Abdul Gayoom, (d) the political dominance of President Rajapaksa in Sri Lanka, and (e) the increasing Chinese activity across the Line of Actual Control (LoAC).

Second, there has been a change in the Indian domestic political landscape with the waning of the Congress' predominance that brought in coalition governments at the centre and the states. It brought in new ways of dealing with the country's national problems. Third, the major economic and financial crisis at the beginning of the 1990s was the decisive moment for India's foreign policy. Bringing back economic solvency required a complete overhaul of India's foreign policy in order to support a more liberalized economic policy. This included opening up relations with Israel, stepping up relations with major groupings like the ASEAN, opening up vis-à-vis the United States and building new groupings of like-minded emerging economies such as Brazil, South Africa, China, and Russia. Fourth, the beginning of Pakistan-sponsored insurgency in Kashmir from 1889 affected India's regional image and raised the cost of retaliation. Fifth, while India continued to bulk large in policy formulation amongst its neighbours, its political salience lessened with greater involvement of both major powers and others with religious or economic interest.

It called for re-tailoring India's relations with the South Asian region in two significant ways: first, accede to the role of non-regional powers and entities while building up its own relations through regular consultations on regional developments, and second, an outreach to build bilateral relations with members of SAARC through trade, financial assistance, and political advice when warranted.

Role of Contiguous Indian States

Another aspect which has not yet become a marker in the making of India's foreign policy towards its neighbours[19] is the absence of a role for contiguous states of the Indian union in influencing and often determining the course of bilateral relations with the SAARC neighbours. This happens more by default than design. Allowing for their views in policy formulation could be useful in leveraging India's economic and cultural strength.

More often than not, the contiguous Indian states are fully capable of harnessing the economic, commercial, and cultural potential of the bilateral relationship with the SAARC neighbour far more effectively than when it remains within the exclusive domain of the central government. The extent to which the Indian government has allowed or acquiesced in the contiguous state government's role has had an important effect on the tenor and substance of India's relations with its neighbours.

Unfortunately, the transmission of ideas and people from the neighbouring country to the contiguous state have continued to be viewed as disruptive of national identity or governance. The influence of West Bengal on Bangladesh relations; Tamil Nadu on Sri Lanka; Bihar, and Uttar Pradesh on Nepal; Punjab, Rajasthan, and Gujarat on Pakistan; and Kerala, Andhra Pradesh, and Tamil Nadu on the Maldives need to be seen in this light. The need to co-opt these relationships to build mutually beneficial relations with SAARC neighbours remains an unfinished task of Indian diplomacy.

Pakistan

There have been times when India-Pakistan relations have witnessed periods of relative calm but never has there been a completely tension-free phase. The last six decades have been marked by four overt conflicts between the two countries and a continuing asymmetric war since 1989 by Pakistan-sponsored terrorist groups, not only in Jammu and Kashmir (J&K) but elsewhere in the country. Equally, regular attempts to carve out an area of manoeuvre for promoting mutual peace and security have yielded mixed results. From the Shimla Agreement (1972)[20,21] up to the present, bilateral efforts have led to the on-again-off-again promotion of a Composite Dialogue Process (CDP).[22] At the same time, people-to-people contact, particularly relations in culture, media, and non-governmental sectors, even though interrupted regularly after Pakistan-instigated terror attacks in India, have served to leaven the political and strategic tension between the two countries. India's effort to normalize bilateral relations suffers from both ideological and structural issues.

As a country with an unbroken tradition of secularism and democracy, India's diplomatic challenges arise from the fact of dealing with a theocratic polity that has alternated between military dictatorships and democratic elected governments. Further, the India–Pakistan dialogue to promote peace and security depends on the domestic developments in both the countries, the geopolitical situation in their neighbourhood, and their respective relations with United States and China.

Kashmir

At its independence on 15 August 1947, India was partitioned to create the independent state of Pakistan for the Muslims of British India. Although all princely states were legally required to accede to either India or Pakistan, the state of Kashmir signed the instrument of accession to India only on 26 October 1947.[23] It had the support of the largest political party in Kashmir. Despite an agreement by Hari Singh, the ruler of Kashmir, with the Government of Pakistan, through the Stand-Still Agreement,[24] Pakistan sent tribal invaders in October 1947 and regular troops in May 1948 to capture the state. The outcome left Pakistan occupying a third of the state that had legally, and irrevocably, acceded to India.

Pakistan ceding the Aksai Chin portion of occupied Kashmir to China adds further complexity. The area is now a vital link in the Chinese strategy to link Pakistan's Gwadar port, which they are building and will have a controlling interest, through Sinkiang to Ürümqi as a part of China's ambitious 'One Belt, One Road' (OBOR) project, also known as the Silk Road Economic Belt.[25]

The ensuing UN-ordered ceasefire led to the UN Commission on India–Pakistan (UNCIP) Resolution of 1948[26] that decreed that a referendum would be conducted in Kashmir to ascertain the wishes of the Kashmiri people *but only after* Pakistan had withdrawn from the occupied territory and Indian forces had restored law and order in the entire area. By not withdrawing from PoK until today, the question of a referendum has become a non sequitur. Regular elections to the J&K Legislative Assembly, the last in 2014, with a voting turnout of 65.23 per cent, have asserted the entrenchment of a vibrant democracy in the state.

For India, J&K, with its Muslim majority in the Srinagar valley is the touchstone of its secular polity while Pakistan regards it as the unfinished business of India's partition. Yet the original justification, based exclusively on religion, for a separate country was overturned with the creation of Bangladesh. While Pakistan's erstwhile eastern wing separated to become Bangladesh in 1971, India, at 161 million, has almost as many Muslims as Pakistan (174 million).

Wars

While the state of J&K is an integral part of the Indian union, Pakistan since 1948, has gone to war four times over Kashmir: the India–Pakistan War in Kashmir in 1948,[27] the border conflict in 1965,[28] the India–Pakistan War in 1971,[29] and finally, Pakistan Army's attempt to take and retain the high ground in Kargil in 1999.[30] All wars, except for 1971, maintained the status quo. While creating Bangladesh, the resulting Simla Agreement (1971)[31] between the two countries established the exclusivity of bilateral negotiations to settle their outstanding issues without recourse to the UN or third-party mediation.

Accordingly, the hitherto demarcated Ceasefire Line (CFL),[32] established in 1949, was transformed, after adjustments, into the Line of Control (LoC). According to India, the purpose of

UNMOGIP (United Nations Military Observer Group in India and Pakistan) to monitor the cease-fire line as identified in Karachi agreement of 1949 was no longer operative due to to the changed positions held by the two sides after the 1971 war.[33] Despite the prevalence of tensions from 1971 till 1989, the LoC remained largely trouble-free till the onset in 1989 of Pakistan-sponsored insurgency by Islamic groups.

The Lahore Declaration of 1999[34] which sought to revive the dialogue process was immediately overshadowed by the assumption of power by General (later President) Pervez Musharraf in a military coup in Pakistan. Its consequence was Pakistan's attempt in 1999 in Kargil to change the facts on the ground. It was settled by Indian military action, though it saw United States mediation between both sides to defuse the situation. It established the principle of maintaining the sanctity of the LoC in Kashmir but equally embedded the United States as an interlocutor.

Governance

Negotiations between India and Pakistan have remained hostage to the nature of Pakistan's governance and its desire to maintain 'parity' with India. As Pakistan governance has increasingly passed into the hands of the Pakistan Army, any attempt to conduct normal relations with India has withered. Furthermore, the increasing attacks by radical Islamic groups on the Pakistan state itself have called into question its political stability and held it hostage to talking peace with India. The aftermath of the dastardly terror attack on Mumbai on 26 November 2008 has amply demonstrated both the collusion and inability of the Pakistan government. A corollary has been that the principle of bilateral resolution in the Shimla Agreement, and the international community's acceptance of the same, which has been regularly sought to be jettisoned by Pakistan.

Pakistan's single-minded effort since its independence, often at great cost to itself, has been to continue to assert parity with India on the back of its ally-like relationship with the United States and all-weather friendship with China. A related consequence has been the disavowal by successive Pakistan governments of commitments on India-Pakistan issues accepted by their predecessors. It has been a damper on any enduring forward movement in building peace.

Country	Area (sq. km)	Population (in million) 2015	Border with India (km)	GDP USD (in billion) 2015 (nominal)	Per capita USD (ppp)
India	3,287,263	1,324.17	4,761	2,308.0	6,266
Pakistan	796,095	193.20	2,912	250.0	4,886
Bangladesh	143,998	162.95	4,053	205.3	3,581
Myanmar	676,578	54.59	1,463	90.93	1,400
Nepal	147,181	29.98	1,690	21.6	2,488
Sri Lanka	65,610	20.79	31	80.4	11,068
Bhutan	38,395	0.797		2.2	8,158
Maldives	298	0.427	450	30.0	14,980
Afghanistan	652,230	31.82		21.3	1,976

Source: Based on economic data sourced from the International Monetary Fund, current as of April 2015. https://en.wikipedia.org/wiki/South_Asian_Association_for_Regional_Cooperation, various sources.

Pakistan's aspiration to achieve parity with India, even though only between 15–20 per cent the size of India on any metric (see Table 1.1), was an important factor in its acquisition of nuclear weapons and missile technology. India's nuclear tests in May 1998[35] and Pakistan's copycat test immediately thereafter[36] significantly changed the matrix of their bilateral relationship.[37] While creating a situation of mutual deterrence it put a cap on the level of Indian retaliation to Pakistan's continuing asymmetric war.

The Role of the United States

The United States' 15-year-long war in Afghanistan has crucially hinged on Pakistan's cooperation in logistic and military terms.[38] This has given Pakistan the ability not only to project its own interests in the US through its proxies like the Taliban, but to continue to receive military and development assistance from that country. It pandered to the Pakistan Army's 'indispensability' to the US' Afghan war effort. It also played to Pakistan's ploy that only continuing financial subventions would enable it to fight the radical Islamic groups assiduously nurtured by its own intelligence agency, the ISI. Pakistan's circular reasoning defeats comparison or emulation. The internationally accepted epithet that Pakistan is the epicentre of world terrorism has a solid foundation.[39]

China

Pakistan's 'all-weather' friendship with China developed after the former's facilitation of the United States' opening to China[40] has stood the latter well. It is unlikely that China will assume the US' mantle as Pakistan's largest provider, although it has developed assets in Pakistan to keep India confined within South Asia. China's economic and military support to Pakistan to develop nuclear and missile weaponry, and military and naval hardware, has significantly boosted the capacity of Pakistan's armed forces. On its part, China has used the access to develop Gwadar port,[41] for oil and gas terminals and as a bunkering facility for People's Liberation Army Navy (PLAN). It became formally operational on 14 November 2016.[42]

Organization of Islamic Cooperation[43]

Pakistan, in terms of its size and population, is one of the largest countries in the Islamic world. Its predilection to play the 'Islamic card', almost at will, through the Organization of Islamic Cooperation (OIC), provides it verbal fuel, though of doubtful value, to secure the passage of anti-India resolutions on Kashmir and on the 'Muslim community' in India. Yet it remains an important strand in its diplomatic campaign against India. After the 9/11 attack on the New York World Trade Center (WTC), a corrective movement within the OIC led to the first OIC summit outside the region in Kuala Lumpur. Its goal was to strategize the portrayal of Islam as a benign and inclusive religion. The effort was filibustered then by the more radical OIC members and was never pursued again even in the face of the rise of the Islamic State in Iraq and Syria.

The idea was carried forward by Sudanese President Omar al-Bashir and articulated by his foreign minister at the 29th Conference Islamic Foreign Ministers at Khartoum in 2012.[44] It was a major defeat for Pakistan and required President Musharraf to threaten withdrawal from the organization. It was in the backwash of this sentiment that at its Jeddah officials' meeting in 2003, Qatar, speaking for itself, revived the idea that India be made a member of the organization. Although this suggestion was again filibustered as being without authority (read Saudi Arabia's concurrence), it was clearly an idea that resonated with many OIC members.

These developments, in the background of the WTC terror attack, led to the pervasive linking of Islam with terror. It gave rise to fear that financial resources of Islamic countries in Western banks could be sequestered in retaliation. It brought a realization that Islamic countries needed to diversify their investments geographically. India, with the world's second largest Muslim population, good relations with all other members of the OIC, and its economic success was the ideal alternative.

It transformed the optics of India's relations with the OIC members, particularly in the Gulf. What was considered by the Gulf countries as a one-sided came to be seen as mutually beneficial. Until then, the one-sided perception of the Gulf countries saw India and Indians, seeking these countries for jobs, crude oil, and for the spiritual sustenance of its large Muslim population. For the first time, the Gulf countries started looking at India as an emerging economic power with a recurring demand for oil. Its growing middle class provided opportunities for investments. It was in this context that the late Saudi King Abdullah bin Abdul-Aziz, while on a state visit to New Delhi on 26 January 2006 as the chief guest at the Republic Day, offered India 'observer status' in the OIC.

Ten years on, the Saudi proposal remains on the table without any likelihood of an Indian response. It goes back to India's decision that as a secular state it will not be a member of any religion-based organization and its past history with the OIC. At its founding conference in Rabat, at the behest of Saudi Arabia, Pakistan, Jordan, and Morocco, India was expelled after being invited to the inaugural session.

India's view is that if it has to exceptionally join the OIC it has to be as a founding member, and not an observer. Another serious obstacle is that India will be loath to accept all the anti-India resolutions passed by that organization over the decades of its existence.[45]

Despite this, Pakistan's salience in the OIC has not reduced. It is the only member with an 'Islamic Bomb' and with its A.Q. Khan Network still active, it becomes the source for other nuclear aspirants within the organization. Pakistan has garnered moral, material, and financial support from important Gulf countries, particularly Saudi Arabia, which has assumed the role of its default mentor, providing oil and financial subventions, religious and doctrinaire sustenance and an open exile for its ousted leaders. It has enabled Pakistan to ride periods of low relations with the US increasingly making their relationship transactional.

The multidimensional crisis in Syria since 2011 which has exposed the the family-run Saudi state's soft underbelly has sought to draw in Pakistan as its handmaiden. The unending nature of the sectarian war amongst the Islamic countries, particularly Syria and Yemen, owes much to the Saudi's active use of their oil wealth to shore up the family through military, political, and religious tactics.

Economics and Trade

Despite the vicissitudes of their political relations trade between India and Pakistan[46] has continued through these years, even though the latter has not reciprocally extended a most-favoured-nation (MFN) status,[47] or non-discriminatory treatment, to India. Neither does it provide transit facilities to Indian goods to Afghanistan. Under these circumstances, the bulk of bilateral trade of about USD 2.5 billion moves through Dubai.

Composite Dialogue Process

When inaugurated in 1998, the CDP encompassed the issues of peace and security, J&K, terrorism, drug trafficking, concerns regarding Sir Creek, Siachen, and the Wullar Barrage/Tulbul navigation project and, finally, the promotion of friendly exchanges in various fields.[48] It engendered a number of confidence-building measures (CBMs) many of which are still in existence. The CBMs include keeping respective diplomatic missions at normal strength at the level of ambassadors, regular contact between the military operations directorates of their armed forces, opening of road and rail links and border trade across the India–Pakistan international boundary and the LoC in Kashmir.

The CDP was reinforced by the revival of the ministerial level India–Pakistan Joint Commission[49] and 'back-channel diplomacy' by designated representatives that produced a blueprint for settling the Kashmir issue.[50] It was seen as the touchstone of India–Pakistan relations from 2004 until 2008 and required Pakistan to wind up its infrastructure of terrorism and desist from allowing its territory to be used against India.

The Pakistan-sponsored LeT's seaborne terrorist attack on Mumbai from 26 to 29 November 2008[51] signalled the end of the CDP. In that attack, over 164 innocent civilians were killed and 293 injured, including 28 foreign nationals.[52] Nine terrorists were also killed in the process. India's financial and commercial capital was brought to its knees. After initially denying it, Pakistan confirmed that the attack was indeed planned and had originated from its territory. India's exhortation that the perpetrators of this attack be tried met with minimal action. Both Hafiz Saeed, LeT head, and Zaki-ur-Rahman Lakhvi remain free despite purported legal action. While some CBMs were in force, the Manmohan Singh government, in its last months, also tried to revive the dialogue process but the attempt remained stillborn.

The Narendra Modi government also sought to revive the bilateral dialogue process by restarting the foreign secretary level talk in 2014. That attempt too did not go ahead due to a lack of minimal agreement on the parameters between the two countries.[53] There appears a 'now-you-see-it-now-you do not' quality about India's Pakistan policy under Prime Minister Modi. His inviting all SAARC heads of governments to attend his swearing-in ceremony was a novel initiative to highlight the new Indian government's intention to prioritize SAARC countries in its foreign policy. It seemed more tactic than strategy considering that soon after the Indian government called off India–Pakistan foreign secretary level talks after the Pakistan ambassador in Delhi, in keeping with earlier practice, met representatives of Kashmir-based separatist groups. The Indian government took the view that Pakistan can talk either to the Indian government or to the

Kashmir-based separatist groups. It reversed the position taken by the earlier Congress governments.

Quite against accepted diplomatic norms, dictated by the primacy of public expectations, that heads of government should only meet when the lower levels have a 'product' to show, Modi visited Prime Minister Nawaz Sharif on 25 December 2015[54] to personally wish him on his birthday. Considering there had been no visit in a decade by an Indian prime minister to Pakistan, this visit could have been better prepared. It reciprocated Nawaz Sharif's visit to Delhi at the time of the Modi swearing-in ceremony; yet the larger purpose in readying the two sides for more substantial engagement was never addressed. At the same time, the promise of substantial discussions provoked on 2 January 2016 the attack by Jaish-e-Mohammad (JeM), the Pakistan based terror group, on the Pathankot air force base,[55] the hub of India's air warfare, along the India-Pakistan border in Punjab.

Once again, in order to establish Pakistan's culpability, the government invited Pakistani investigators, which included the ISI, on a fact-finding visit to India's premier airbase. Despite public projection that it was India's attempt to be open in fixing culpability, the attempt came to nought. Yet it allowed the Pakistan Army and its intelligence access to the airbase. A reciprocal visit by Indian investigators was however not proposed by Pakistan. The Pakistan-sponsored terror attacks in Punjab had expanded the terror field to cover the entire India-Pakistan international border and not the LoC alone. While showing India as a soft target for punishment it has neither improved the prospects for a bilateral dialogue nor affected Pakistan's ability to hit India at will.

Opinion remains divided on the strategy to be adopted vis-à-vis Pakistan. One view suggests that despite terror attacks India cannot afford to disrupt its growth trajectory—a reason adduced by the Manmohan Singh government to avoid any retaliation to the Mumbai terror attack of 2008 and others that came after.[56] This important consideration is frequently articulated.[57] The back-channel attempt by both sides to move forward towards a peace process by freezing the LoC in Kashmir while 'making borders irrelevant' still remains on the table.[58] Its other elements include demilitarization and dividing J&K on both sides of the

LoC into seven autonomous regions to be 'jointly managed' by both India and Pakistan.

However 'at the heart of Modi's efforts is the desire to make terrorism the focus of India–Pakistan negotiations. This approach runs counter to India's policy since the 1990s, which was based on an understanding with Pakistan that a long-term composite dialogue between the countries would feature Kashmir and security (read terrorism) as the co-equal primary issues of discussion. Modi has signalled that India under him will only discuss terrorism and will refuse to talk about Kashmir.'[59] Further in his independence day speech on 15 August 2016 Modi asserted that 'If Pakistan continues to raise the issue of human rights violations in India–occupied Kashmir then India will do just the same in Pakistan's most sensitive province.'[60]

Outlook for the Future

India's relations with Pakistan will continue to remain vexed in the future until such time that the latter's civilian government can override the army's overarching political and economic power. It remains the single impediment to a successful outcome, given the army's vested interest in keeping tension alive and controlling the civil space. Pakistan's policy of gaining 'strategic depth' in Afghanistan and nurturing India-focused radical Islamic groups further exacerbates the situation. Yet the Pakistan Army fights the same groups at home. India has accepted the reality that oscillates between periods of dialogue and its absence. At the same time, the Indian government states that it remains open to a structured dialogue once the parameters and content are agreed.

The India-Pakistan situation has entered an increasingly volatile phase. In referring to the human rights abuses in Baluchistan and PoK, Prime Minister Modi in his Independence Day Address on 15 August 2016 added a new variable to the matrix. It raised the stakes in the war of words following Pakistan's terrorist forays in Punjab that included targeting Indian Army bases and terror attacks in Gurdaspur, Udhampur, the Pathankot airbase and Pampore. The reverberations of the severe attack on the Uri military base, killing 19 soldiers and wounding more, were felt across the country.

In response to growing public pressure for the government to retaliate,[61] India on 28 September 2016 carried out a cross-LOC attack against Pakistan terrorist-launching bases up to 2 kilometres across the LoC. Although Pakistan continued to maintain that there were no strikes, these were widely hailed in India.[62] The positive effect on public support for the Modi government appeared to augur well but left a question mark on whether it represented a change in policy.

India's hard-line stance on talks with Pakistan has seen a back-lash from Pakistan buoyed by its participation in the China-Pakistan Economic Corridor (CPEC) while it has become more difficult for Pakistan's civilian government under Nawaz Sharif to control the jihadi groups with their rising image within Pakistan's public.[63] Yet, with the next Indian general elections due in 2019 and people's perception of unfulfilled economic commitments, it is likely that a new dialogue initiative with Pakistan may be long in coming.

Internationally Isolating Pakistan

The public clamour after the terror strike on the Indian Army headquarters in Uri prompted the government to consider the means at its command to retaliate. High on the list is the attempt to isolate Pakistan internationally, especially since thinking through a military response also raises the question on whether its armed forces are capable of launching such a strike and following up on its repercussions.[64]

The diplomatic isolation of Pakistan is not a new strategy. India has now articulated it as a coordinated overall strategy to have Pakistan declared a terrorist state. It has major implications on the issue of sanctions by the P-5 and the world body. The success of an uninterrupted global strategy remains moot, given that the US is unlikely to take a hard position. At this point, with continuing US and Western preoccupation with Afghanistan, it appears difficult to believe that the UNSC can be brought around to declaring Pakistan a sponsor of international terror.

As part of this strategy, India, citing continuous cross-border terrorism by Pakistan, declined to attend the 19th SAARC Summit in Islamabad on 9–10 November 2016.[65] Four SAARC followed the Indian move. Yet this needs to be followed up by a sustained and calibrated strategy on isolating Pakistan. Much will depend on the extent India finds 'kinship in Washington's own priorities in the region: containment of China, the war in Afghanistan, and the broader war on terrorism.'[66]

Nevertheless, a long-term diplomatic isolation strategy should not deter India from preparing a viable hard strategy regardless of the time it takes.

Indus Water Treaty[67]

The question of reopening the 1960 Indus Water Treaty (IWT), negotiated under the aegis of the World Bank, is an option being explored. The treaty has held despite four wars between India and Pakistan and continuing cross-LoC terrorist strikes since 1989. As provided in the agreement, the two countries have taken recourse to the redress mechanisms in the IWT to avoid becoming an issue in their bilateral relations.

Under the treaty, Pakistan holds the right to the water of the three western rivers in the Indus basin (Indus, Jhelum, and Chenab) and the rights to the eastern rivers (Ravi, Beas, and Sutlej) belong to India. All the rivers coming down from the Himalayas pass through Kashmir, making their upper reaches part of the Indian-held part of the state. About 80 per cent of the water that flowed through these six rivers in the 1950s was allocated to Pakistan. However, India has certain non-consumptive use rights over the waters of the western rivers.

The latest dispute concerns the Kishanganga and Ratle hydro-power projects[68] on whether India can draw down the water in the reservoirs below the dead storage level in an event other than an unforeseen emergency; second, whether India's diversion of water for the run-of-the-river projects was a violation of the IWT. Four other technical questions on the design of the Indian projects are still unresolved. Pakistan decided to take the matter to The Hague-based International Court of Arbitration (ICA) after two days of talks in New Delhi on 14–15 July 2016 between IWT commissioners and officials of the two countries.

The Kishanganga Hydroelectric Plant is a USD 864-million dam that is part of a run-of-the-river hydroelectric scheme designed to divert water from the river Kishanganga to a power plant in the Jhelum basin. It is located 5 kilometres north of Bandipore in J&K. India will have an installed capacity of 330 MW. Construction on the project began in 2007 and is expected to be completed in 2016. Under the IWT, India is allowed only non-consumptive use of water from the three western rivers in the Indus basin—Indus, Jhelum, and Chenab.

The Kishanganga and Ratle projects are on the western rivers. They are run-of-the-river hydropower projects that do not hold back any water, though Pakistan's objection is about the height of the gates in the dams from which the water flows downstream. The three eastern rivers—Ravi, Beas, and Sutlej—are reserved for India's use. The World Bank has suspended its tribunal pending their experts' bilateral talks with both the countries.[69] In its detailed response to the World Bank's announcement pausing two separate processes to resolve the dispute between India and Pakistan over Kishenganga and Ratle projects, New Delhi expressed its readiness to bilaterally resolve its differences with Islamabad over the implementation of the Indus Waters Treaty. 'This was done to safeguard the treaty, since referring the matter simultaneously to the processes sought by each of the countries risked contradictory outcomes and worked against the spirit of goodwill and friendship that underpins the Treaty.'[70]

Whether the IWT can be opened to put non-military pressure on Pakistan remains moot even though India can claim that it is not getting a fair share of these waters given that the treaty dates back to over 55 years. The ensuing period has seen an increase in population and increasing dangers from the effects of climate change due to the upward movement of the snow line in the Himalayas. Since the Indus, and all of its tributaries, flow through India-held Kashmir the opportunity to create a pressure point exists. The success of this option, if indeed it is viable, will depend on India's thinking through Pakistan's military backlash in Kashmir and on the IBL, and second, on retaliation from China which is an upper-riparian state for the entire Indus water system. Yet the option exists and possibly the time for looking at it may have come.

Following its nuclear tests in May 1998 India's nuclear doctrine laid down the principle of 'no first use' (NFU) in order to assure the major powers that it was not India's intention to be the cause of a nuclear war originating in the Indian subcontinent. Pakistan, on its part, has made no such declaration and latest reports suggest that it has increased the number of nuclear weapons and has developed tactical nuclear weapons that are expected to restrict the damage from their use. China has stuck to its NFU policy, declared in 1964, even though it is not widely take as an immutable policy. Most other nuclear states do not follow this policy, and Russia in 2000 rescinded such a commitment made by the Soviet Union.

India's holding on to this commitment has enabled it to move further on developing its nuclear power assets starting with the US–India Agreement on Civil Nuclear Cooperation (2005). It has still to be accepted as a member of the restricted nuclear groupings that determine the international transmission of nuclear technology and its use. The somewhat vague reference to India's NFU commitment, in the BJP manifesto prior to the 2014 general election which brought Narendra Modi to office, had introduced a doubt about India retaining its commitment.[72] Does this keep the issue open and has the time come to review it? The evaluation relates to deciding on the extent to which nuclear cooperation with other NPT-ordained nuclear powers, none of whom has such a declaration, will suffer in case India rescinds its commitment. It will also have to evaluate whether the parity this will introduce vis-à-vis Pakistan will reduce its belligerency on the Kashmir issue.

The upshot of the foregoing is that despite having suffered relentless terror attacks, sponsored and carried out by Pakistan proxies, India has yet to develop viable hard power options to deter them. So long as this inertia continues, so will Pakistan's current strategy to wrest Kashmir. The cross-LoC attacks on 28 September 2016 signals the start of a new phase in India's military responses to Pakistan-sponsored terrorism. It shows India's readiness to cross the LoC, a principle held as sacrosanct since the Kargil war.

Nevertheless, much will hinge on the receptivity of the Kashmir population, progressively inured to India's policy and blandishments.[73] It requires a clear internal policy on Kashmir to bring the population back into the national mainstream while taking active steps to develop hard options.

Afghanistan[74]

Although the newest entrant to SAARC, Afghanistan has been part of India's political, military, and cultural space from the time of Emperor Ashoka (265–38 BCE). The legacy of the two countries' history goes back to at least 1000 CE when invaders from Afghanistan and Central Asia repeatedly came to India on campaigns of plunder, pillage, conquest, and conversion. During the colonial era, with Afghanistan becoming the pawn in the Great Game with Russia, undivided India provided cannon fodder for the Anglo–Afghan wars.

Afghanistan was always perceived as an Indian ally. India's independence and the 1948 India–Pakistan conflict in Kashmir meant the loss of a common border with Afghanistan, with the exception of a thin sliver of land, now part of PoK.

Brief History

From 1947 until the Soviet invasion of 1979, relations remained settled around a growing border trade. With Afghanistan joining NAM in 1961, the two countries developed a degree of political affinity on regional and international issues. India was the only South Asian nation to recognize the Soviet-backed Democratic Republic of Afghanistan. For an India increasingly dependent on Soviet military and diplomatic support after the Indo–Soviet Treaty of Peace and Friendship (1971), its backing on the Afghan issue was a way to recompense Moscow.

India's support to successive Afghan regimes continued after the withdrawal of Soviet forces in 1989 until the victory in 1992 of the Pakistan-backed, US-funded mujahideen. India–Afghan relations ended with the outbreak of another civil war (1996–98) against the mujahedeen factions. It brought to power Taliban, the Islamic militia nurtured by Pakistan through the ISI. The period of Taliban rule in Afghanistan (1996–2001), when the country became susceptible to the ISI's bidding, saw overt hostility to India and the beginning of cross-border terrorism in J&K by Pakistan-based Islamic groups.

India had no diplomatic relations with Afghanistan during this period and supported the Northern Alliance composed of Afghan Tajik and Uzbek groups opposed to the Taliban. India experienced first-hand Taliban hostility with the hijacking of Indian Airlines flight 814 to Kandahar in December 1999.

The presumed complicity in the attack on New York's WTC on 11 September 2001, of the Taliban, who harboured Osama bin Laden, led the US to militarily dislodge Afghanistan's Taliban regime.

Afghanistan presents a significant challenge to Indian diplomacy of preserving its interests while not adding another dimension to the relations with Pakistan. Afghanistan is, and will, remain part of India's strategic neighbourhood despite the absence of geographical contiguity. India has always been the recipient of the fallout from any change of regime in that country.

India's policy towards Afghanistan seeks friendly and non-exclusive relations with Kabul without denying access to its other neighbours. Its goals remain insulating India, particularly the Kashmir valley, from Islamic sectarianism sweeping much of the Middle East and its neighbours; supporting an inclusive government in Afghanistan that would reject the Taliban credo; continuing its economic presence in the country; and fostering Afghanistan's integration within the region and the global economy. India's strategy aims at preserving these interests through institutional leverage with other like-minded powers from the region and outside such as Iran, Russia, China, and the United States and maintaining an effective presence on the ground. India's Strategic Partnership Agreement (SPA) in 2011 with Afghanistan, when fully operational, is intended to support this policy.

The Aftermath of the US Occupation

Following the 9/11 attack, India fully supported the United States' 'global war on terror' that evoked worldwide scepticism and opposition.[75] For India, only after the 9/11 attack the United States finally accepted India's refrain of two decades regarding

Pakistan's complicity in nurturing terrorist groups. Nevertheless, the United States' continuing engagement in Afghanistan, where Pakistan is the kingpin, prevents its capacity to make good on the goals of the much touted 'global war on terror'.

The US' military presence allowed India to re-establish and protect its interests in Afghanistan, build strong people-to-people relations, and support the US presence. Yet while supporting American presence in Afghanistan, India had predicated the United States' departure on achieving political stability and security. As the United States became enmeshed in the Afghan situation, with 140,000 troops at its height, ensuring political stability became increasingly elusive. New Delhi had to acquiesce in the sudden US decision, due to domestic imperatives arising from President Obama's completion of his tenure, to drawdown by end-2014.

India's investment of USD 2 billion in infrastructure and humanitarian projects, of which nearly all have been delivered, has created for it immense goodwill while coincidentally raising Pakistan's hostility. Terror attacks by Pakistan-based groups on Indian projects, personnel, and Indian diplomatic missions have unleashed a proxy war between the two countries. Hence, the completion of its infrastructure projects in complete security remains India's immediate challenge. For the future, India's development assistance will remain an important plank on the assumption that the operationalization of the bilateral SPA provides the basis to carry out the projects in security and safety. India pledged an additional USD 1 billion in aid during President Ashraf Ghani's visit to New Delhi.[76]

India-Afghan Strategic Partnership

The SPA[77] signed during President Hamid Karzai's tenure gave India an important place in his worldview. India expects the SPA to serve as the basis for future cooperation. The agreement covers political and security dialogue, trade and economic exchanges, and people-to-people contact. India has concerns, which Afghanistan shares, regarding Pakistan's sponsorship of cross-border terrorism from within its borders.[78] From India's point of view, the SPA's strategic dimension provides the platform to consider denial of sanctuary and war-fighting material to Al-Qaeda and Taliban-affiliated terror groups.

Nevertheless, the agreement still needs to be operationalized, having suffered first from India's earlier reluctance to provide defence hardware to Afghanistan and, secondly, a cooling off by President Ashraf Ghani towards India after he assumed power in 2014. Distancing from India, Ghani's first visits were to China and Pakistan to pursue a 'bold' initiative to resolve the overarching issues with Pakistan.[79] The failure of these initiatives, in a large measure due to US pressure, has led to a warming of the bilateral relationship. India, for its part, has also agreed to supply military hardware to Afghanistan under the SPA.[80,81] During President Ghani's visit to India on 25 April 2015, both sides agreed to strengthen the SPA keeping in view the long-term needs of Afghanistan.[82] During the visit of Abdulla Abdulla, the chief executive of the Afghanistan government, to Delhi in February 2016, the bilateral relationship appeared to have been put on an even keel.[83] Yet, 'in the recent years, the pace of Indo–Afghan bilateral cooperation in the political, security, development, and cultural areas has continued to accelerate, on the basis of the Afghanistan-India strategic partnership agreement (SPA).'[84]

At the second meeting on 11 September 2017 of the India-Afghanistan Strategic Partnership Council in New Delhi India agreed to 'extend assistance for the Afghan National Defence and Security Forces to fight against terrorism, organized crime, trafficking of narcotics and money laundering. The Indian side reiterated its support for an Afghan-led and Afghan-owned peace and reconciliation process.'[85] India also agreed to undertake new development projects in Afghanistan.

'India and Afghanistan need to conduct a strategic review of their bilateral, regional and international partnerships to deal with the changing geo-political dynamics. Afghanistan, India, and the United States must operationalise their trilateral dialogue for a serious and well-coordinated strategy against terrorism. The future of Afghanistan and security for the world will depend on a holistic and sincere fight against terrorism both at the regional and the global level. India, in this context, will continue to hold a strategic place in Afghanistan's foreign policy in all areas of cooperation including domestic development and security.'[86]

While India's outreach towards the majority Pashtuns has multiplied manifold it will continue to retain its links to Afghan minorities such as the Tajiks, Uzbeks, and Hazaras whom it supported during the Taliban regime (1996–2001).

At the same time, the increasing profiles of India and China in Afghanistan have also meant increasing dissonance between the two countries.[87] They remain opposed on the inclusion of the Taliban in the governance of the country. The lines of divergence have become increasingly pronounced on the stabilization of Afghanistan with China and Pakistan on the one side and India and the United States on the other. Yet, the US' continuing reliance on Pakistan makes for a difficult equation.

Deterring Islamic Radicalism

Widening disorder and Islamic radicalism in Pakistan now engulf Afghanistan as well. The announcement of an Al-Qaeda branch in South Asia and the Islamic State of Iraq and the Levant's (ISIL) growing adherents in Pakistan threatens inroads into India. India sees a complex linkage between the various terrorist groups operating from Pakistan's Federally Administered Tribal Areas (FATA) and contiguous Afghan provinces of Kunar and Nuristan. Regardless of the entities they target, organizations like the LeT[88] and JeM[89] come together on an anti-India platform and have been responsible for terror attacks across the LoC in J&K and across the International Boundary Line (IBL), particularly Punjab.[90]

Through operationalizing the SPA and other levels of dialogue with the Afghan government, India's challenge remains the blocking of bases for training and running infiltration by these terror groups. In India's view, Afghan stability will depend on its emergence as an economically integrated state in South and Central Asia and the world. India's proactive steps to end Afghanistan's isolation include the Indian-built 218-kilometre road from Zaranj (Iran) to Delaram (Afghanistan) to connect Afghanistan to Iran's road network. It is also working on a trilateral project to connect

economic profile in Afghanistan is expected to grow as the country stabilizes.

India's struggle for independence against the British brought
the two peoples together, particularly by 'Frontier Gandhi', Khan
Abdul Ghaffar Khan, who sought to create a separate Pashtun
state, Pakhtoonistan, astride both sides of the Durand Line which
separates the two countries, through nonviolent struggle. While
this remains the Pashtun dream, it brought the two countries
closer, given their hostility to the new state of Pakistan. Until
1979, India's diplomatic outreach to Afghanistan was successful in
keeping successive Afghan governments friendly and supportive.
The United States' covert war against the Soviet occupation of
Afghanistan brought Pakistan and its ISI as a major player. The
conduit of funds, training, and weapons to the Afghan mujahedeen
through ISI established an enduring covert relationship between
Pakistan and Afghanistan.

Although this relationship was overshadowed once the Soviet
Union was forced out of Afghanistan, it acquired an even more
prolific, lethal, and global character after 9/11. This explains
India's failure in getting the United States to act against Pakistan
while continuing to fund it for support in its Afghanistan
operation. So long as the United States remains engaged in
Afghanistan there is no likelihood of its stopping Pakistan's
financial, military, and other support. This would remain true no
matter the extent to which India-US relations move forward.

The balancing of its relations between the two triangles—
Pakistan–India–Afghanistan and Pakistan–India–United States—
will remain the challenge for Indian diplomacy in the coming
years. The extent to which China's rise will embolden Pakistan
towards further brinkmanship in relations with India is yet
another matrix in the equation.

Bangladesh

Created in 1971 amidst violence and genocide, Bangladesh,[92]
erstwhile East Pakistan, among all of India's neighbours, has the
shortest history as a sovereign state in South Asia. It has complex

civilizational links with the Indian state of West Bengal and to India itself. These facts have determined its relationship with India and the nature of its national identity. The conflict between the 'spirit of 1947' and the 'spirit of 1971' has meant divisions in the country's national consciousness between a secular Bengali ethos with that of orthodox Islamic tendency. It has embedded in Bangladesh's policy paradigm the twin ideas of India's 'hegemonistic' intentions and a claim to 'lebensraum'[93] towards India's northeast region.

The euphoria in India and Bangladesh after the 1971 India–Pakistan War which led to the birth of the latter country soon evaporated with mutual recriminations, hostility, and a range of outstanding issues which have defied solution because of mutually competing interests, differing expectations, unfulfilled commitments, and bureaucratic neglect and inefficiency. The situation was exacerbated by continued delays in India's delivery of commitments and on finalizing the outstanding issues on land boundary, sharing of river water, economics, trade, and climate change.[94]

Consequently, the promise of a reinforcing natural partnership between them was belied in disputes on the border and water sharing, support to insurgency and terrorism, illegal migration, and trade and economic exchanges. Moving the relationship to an even keel remains the greatest challenge to India's diplomacy.

Political Relations

Bilateral relations have seen a period of warmth after Bangladesh Prime Minister Sheikh Hasina Wajed's visit to India in 2011. The reciprocal visits by Prime Ministers Manmohan Singh (2012) and Narendra Modi (2015)[95] have created the framework for a harmonious outcome. It is important to factor in the continuing power play between the two leading political personalities in Bangladesh—Sheikh Hasina[96] (leading the Awami League) and Begum Khaleda[97] (leading the Bangladesh National Party)—that has constrained Indian options and the possibility of mutually beneficial initiatives.

The continuing rivalry, for the best part of the last two decades, between the 'two Begums' has seen them alternate the leadership of the country. Their rivalry has repeatedly vitiated the political atmosphere, making relations with India the touchstone of 'independence' for both leaders vis-à-vis their domestic constituencies. A good number of mutually beneficial India-Bangladesh projects have foundered on the shoals of their bitter rivalry.

President Sheikh Hasina, as the daughter of Sheikh Mujib-ur-Rahman,[98] the founding president of Bangladesh, is portrayed as pro-Indian, given that she lived in self-exile in Delhi after Mujib's assassination.[99] She came back to lead the Awami League in 1981. Begum Khaleda Zia,[100] the wife of General Ziaur Rahman[101] and the head of the Bangladesh National Party (BNP), was the prime minister in 1991–96 and 2001–06. She has since been embroiled in controversy over charges of corruption levelled against her sons and for giving increasing latitude to Islamic-oriented political parties. Their continuing political struggle became important in the context of the effort to revert Bangladesh to a secular state when in March 2016 the Bangladesh Supreme Court summarily rejected the 20-year old petition.[102,103] Although 'secularism' is one of the four fundamental principles according to the country's original 1972 constitution, Ziaur Rahman removed it from the Constitution in 1977 and Islam was declared the state religion. In 2010, the Supreme Court restored secularism as one of the basic tenets of the Constitution, but Islam remained the state religion.

President Sheikh Hasina's visit from 7 to 10 April 2017 to New Delhi still did not resolve the Teesta River dispute, which in the end determined the success of the visit. It has given fodder to the BNP to criticize the three memorandums of understanding (MoUs) on defence cooperation. While two of them are between higher defence training institutions in the two countries, the third sets up a framework for defence cooperation which includes military supplies and technology transfers from India. A credit line of USD 500 million has been provided for this purpose. Although these are not defence agreements, these have been criticized by the BNP which was responsible for the country's heavy dependence on China. Even though a new line of credit of USD 4.5 billion was also extended the publicly perceived gains in Bangladesh have verged on the negative.[104]

Border Issues

Bangladesh shares a porous border of 4,351 kilometres along five eastern states of India—West Bengal (2,217), Assam (262), Meghalaya (443), Tripura (856), and Mizoram (318)—in addition to a riverine border (781) which again borders 25 Indian districts. Bangladesh is in effect 'India-locked' just as the Indian north-east region is 'Bangladesh-locked'. India considers the 'Siliguri corridor'—a narrow strip between its northern border and Bangladesh connecting India to its north-east region—as vulnerable. Equally, it fuels suspicion in Bangladesh that India could militarily carve out a corridor across the north-east in the event of a war with China.

The Land Boundary Agreement (LBA) between Bangladesh and India and related matters signed in 1974[105] left an undemarcated segment of 6.1 kilometres, with 111 and 5 enclaves respectively in India and Bangladesh. Their transfer to Bangladesh due to political compulsions was only approved in May 2015 by the Indian parliament. The LBA signed in June 2015[106] came into effect in July 2015. It involved the exchange of cadastral maps and granted the inhabitants of enclaves transferred to the other country the right to remain there. It has removed a major irritant in the bilateral relationship.

Similarly, the demarcation of the maritime boundary created an adversarial situation given that the exclusive economic zone (EEZ) bears on offshore reserves of natural gas in the Bay of Bengal. Bangladesh went, on 8 October 2009, for arbitration over the delimitation of maritime boundary under the United Nations Convention on Law of Sea (UNCLOS). The court, in The Hague, concluded its hearings on 18 December 2013. The arguments covered issues including the location of the land boundary terminus, delimitation of the territorial sea, EEZ, and the continental shelf within and beyond the 200 nautical miles. The award by the UN Permanent Court of Arbitration gave Bangladesh 19,467 square kilometres of the total disputed area of 25,602 square kilometres.[107] India has accepted the judgement.

Bangladesh's susceptibility to floods and droughts in the low-lying areas, particularly in the Ganga delta, regularly flares up water-sharing disputes. India and Bangladesh share 54 common rivers, and India's actions, real or imagined, as an upper riparian state have made water sharing a perennial problem. It engenders a strong level of mutual hostility and potential for future conflict. India's building of the Farakka Barrage in 1977[108] on the Ganga accepted the principle of equitable water sharing; yet it was only in 1996 that India, taking a non-legalistic view under the Gujral Doctrine, could put in place an agreement satisfactory to Bangladesh.

Bangladesh seeks similar resolution on five more rivers. India's desisting from building a dam on the river Tipaimukh has helped.[109] However, a veto by West Bengal to a proposed agreement on the Teesta[110] highlighted the need for India to bring in its contiguous states in resolving issues.

Chinese action as upper riparian state to harness the waters of the Himalayan rivers would eventually require a cooperative effort by India and Bangladesh as lower riparian states to safeguard adequate flows to these rivers. The Tibetan plateau is the source of 10 of Asia's major river systems, meandering to 11 countries; these include the Indus, Sutlej, Brahmaputra, Irrawaddy, Salween, and Mekong. About two billion people depend on these rivers from Afghanistan to the Ganga–Meghna–Brahmaputra basin in South Asia and, thence, to the Mekong in the Southeast Asia. The reason for China's intransigence on Tibet is clear—water. Tibet's vast store of water resources is key to sustaining China's northwest region, revitalizing its deserts and the Yellow river itself. China's need and the water requirements of the other lower riparian states sets up a contesting and conflicting situation often prompting analysts to say that 'China's thirst will leave others thirsty'.[111]

Similarly, the vulnerability of Bangladesh to sea-level rise could inundate a population of 70 million in the delta, leading to forced migration into India pursuing their idea of lebensraum and will equally require an India–Bangladesh understanding on jointly combating the effects of climate change.[112]

In keeping with extending non-reciprocal treatment, India has extended zero-duty to 50 import items from Bangladesh. Their trade turnover in 2014–15 was USD 6.9 billion in India's favour.

India's extending of USD 1 billion credit line in 2012 for infrastructure development and a further USD 2 billion in 2015 has somewhat corrected the sense of imbalance. The Indian corporate sector investment, amounting to USD 2.5 billion, has also contributed. Nevertheless, the pervasive view of India as the 'giant neighbour without the attributes of a good neighbour and hence to be treated with caution'[113] has failed to advance important economic projects and has made it difficult to hook the Bangladesh economy to the Indian one through a preferential trading arrangement. The visit of Prime Minister Modi to Dhaka in June 2015 appeared to have given a fillip to a further strengthening of bilateral trade and economic relations.[114]

Illegal Migration

The India-Bangladesh border has become a route for smuggling livestock, food items, medicines, and drugs from India to Bangladesh and illegal migration from Bangladesh into India. The issue of unfettered migration is politically sensitive in both countries. Primarily for economic reasons, the numbers are estimated between 20–25 million.[115] In India, a lack of political consensus has eluded a definite census, while Bangladesh has been reluctant in official discussions to acknowledge its existence. The building of a border fence and shoot-on-sight orders to the Indian Border Security Force (BSF) and sporadic attempts at deportation have only raised humanitarian concerns and led to skirmishes with Bangladesh border guards.

Given its continuing nature, it has raised resentment, particularly in the Indian north-east region, and concern at the spread of Bangladeshi migrants throughout the country. The lack of political will on both sides has left the issue unresolved and this remains a major irritant in bilateral relations.

The porous border and the assiduous cultivation of vote banks in Assam from Bangladeshi migrants have led Bangladesh to create equities against its giant neighbour. It includes safe havens to Indian insurgent groups from Tripura (National Liberation Front for Tripura), Assam (Liberation Front of Assam), and Nagaland (National Democratic Front for Bodoland). A transit route for Pakistani militants, a hub facilitating Pakistan's ISI network, terror links with Bangladeshi militant Harkat-ul-Jihad-al-Islami (HuJI) with an eye on committing terror acts and smuggling of fake currency and small arms have been other areas of concern for India.[116] The two countries have achieved a measure of resolution of these issues through political will.

'Bangladesh and India are at a historic juncture of diplomacy embedded in a rich matrix of history, religion, culture, language and kinship. While energy has witnessed new highs in an exponential expansion of bilateral cooperation, there are rich prospects for an India-driven proposal for a joint venture among BBIN (Bangladesh, Bhutan, India and Nepal) countries. the two countries see themselves converging around a sense of indispensability, not just as neighbours battling the scourge of terrorism, but as leading economic partners whose collective strengths can transform not just their own economies, but also that of the region and the world.'[117]

Nepal

Nepal's unique geographic, religious, and political features have carved for it both challenges and opportunities arising from the need to balance between its two huge neighbours, India and China, while preserving its sovereignty.

Any change in Nepal has a profound impact on India, arising from four factors: first, its geography which positions it as a buffer state;[118] second, its Hindu identity asserted during the country's monarchic period;[119] third, its open border which has influenced politics, economy, and society in both countries;[120] and fourth, an ingrained Nepali perception of India's dominating role.[121] In these lie the challenges that Indian diplomacy faces.

Nepal's border with India is 1,850 kilometres while that with China is 1,415 kilometres. The Chinese side is marked with uninhabited mountains—dotted with the world's highest peaks, including Mount Everest—and borders China's Tibet Autonomous Region (TAR). On the Indian side, it runs along the highly populous states of Uttar Pradesh and Bihar, the Gangetic basin and abuts the 'Chicken's Neck', a narrow strip of land between Nepal and Bangladesh which connects India with its north-east region. Thus, on both the sides, it abuts sensitive and conflict-prone areas within its giant neighbours.[122]

Nepal and India share a unique relationship[123] based on the commonality of religion, open borders, and deep-rooted contacts of kinship and culture between the people of the two countries, particularly in the contiguous Indian states of Uttarakhand, Uttar Pradesh, Bihar, West Bengal, and Sikkim. An estimated six million Nepalis live and work in India.

The long tradition of free movement of people across the border consolidated in the Treaty of Peace and Friendship of 1950 and the Revised Treaty of Trade between the Government of India and the Government of Nepal[124] gives Nepali nationals 'national treatment' in India in the matter of settlement, employment, and travel within India. It has helped to alleviate the disadvantages resulting from Nepal's land-locked situation. India is Nepal's largest trade partner, the largest source of foreign investment, and tourist arrivals. At the same time, periodic exhortation by Nepal for the revision of the treaty has become a barometer of the health of the bilateral relationship. An India–Nepal Eminent Persons Group has been meeting to consider changes and modifications to the treaty.[125]

The enmeshing of domestic politics, economics, and development in the two countries has left the Indian government with a narrowing range of options in the background of China's active steps to build its relations with Nepal through aid, trade, investment, and better connectivity through Tibet, across the Himalayan border.

The Earthquake in 2015[126]

An already poor infrastructure received a major jolt when Nepal suffered a massive earthquake on 25 April 2015, measuring

7.8 on the Richter scale, followed by aftershocks which lasted until 12 May 2015. It led to huge destruction of property and infrastructure, causing loss of 8,700 lives. The Nepal government has estimated that USD 6.1 billion will be required for the reconstruction and rehabilitation of the displaced and has called for massive international assistance. More than eight million people have been affected and one million are in need of food aid.

Even as the earthquake affected parts of the Indian states of Bihar, Uttar Pradesh, West Bengal, and Rajasthan, India was the first country to rush with relief to the stricken nation. Its Operation Maitri[127] included the positioning of military field hospitals and airborne assets for dropping food, relief materials, medicines, and evacuating the marooned and rehabilitating power and communication grids. India pledged USD 1 billion for Nepal's post-earthquake reconstruction programme.[128] The operation was an earnest effort by India in bringing bilateral relations to their fraternal level. Yet a timely and excellent all-round effort by the Indian Army, Air Force, and Disaster Relief Agency was almost set to naught by Indian press coverage[129] that detracted from the tragedy Nepal had suffered. It again brought up the barely subdued sentiment of hegemony to which India remains prone.

Political Developments in Nepal

A 10-year civil conflict between Maoist insurgents and the monarchic state ended in 2006 leading to a peace deal and a direct rule by the king. The violent sweeping aside of the decades-old monarchy and the rise of peoples' power embodied in a Marxist insurgency (1996–2006) saw the overthrow of entrenched internal interests and structures. The once Hindu kingdom was declared a federal, democratic, and socialist republic. An interim constitution was promulgated and peaceful elections were held. The Maoist combatants were demobilized with a commitment to integrate them within the Nepalese Army. The Maoist-oriented political party, United Communist Party of Nepal (Marxist)—UCPN (M)—assumed office, determined to write a new constitution, build closer relations with China, and seek renegotiation of the India-Nepal Treaty.

India had welcomed the historic Comprehensive Peace Agreement (2006)[130] towards political stabilization of Nepal through peaceful reconciliation and an inclusive democratic process. The comprehensive peace agreement comprises a cease-fire, including the management of arms and armies of both the national army and the Maoist group by the UN. It calls for political, economic, and social change in the country and adherence to humanitarian law and human rights principles, including through the establishment of a National Human Rights Commission, a Truth and Reconciliation Commission, and a National Peace and Rehabilitation Commission. The agreement calls for the election of a constituent assembly to end the transition period and calls on the UN to observe and assist the electoral process. The agreement also calls for the nationalization of all property belonging to the king and the queen. The first Constituent Assembly transformed itself into the Parliament after successfully promulgating the new Nepal's Constitution with an overwhelming two-thirds majority.[131]

Yet an era of divisive politics was ushered in, raising serious doubts on UCPN (M)'s democratic credentials. It also raised the issue of compatibility and military discipline in absorbing the Maoist cadres into the Nepalese Army that remains a major political force in the country.[132] Any attempt to cut its power could well lead to an assault on the democratic process itself. India has played a leading role in helping the Nepalese Army in its modernization through provision of training and military equipment. This stems from the fact that India has always had Nepali (Gurkha) soldiers in its army and provides pensions and healthcare to them after their retirement.

Nevertheless, a constitution was proclaimed amid violent protests by minority Madhesi groups, after seven years of painstaking deliberations, which set up a seven province federal structure.[133] The Madhesi (or Madhyadesi)[134] who live in the flat southern region of Nepal (the Terai plains) bordering India had felt that the new constitution marginalized them and were seeking changes to correct this sentiment. Their protests were accompanied by a blockade of fuel and essential goods coming regularly from India. The Nepal government believed that India had a hand in promoting the blockade since it was not consulted before the new constitution was approved in parliament.[135]

India-Nepal Treaty

The Treaty of Peace and Friendship (1951) which confirmed the open borders has yielded economic benefits to the people of both countries through opportunities for economic activity, employment, settlement, and ease of travel for pilgrimage and tourism. Yet it has also opened the door to illegal trafficking and smuggling and has allowed easy transit to miscreants, terrorists, and political exiles. Furthermore, resentment over a large number of Indian migrants' reciprocally acquiring Nepalese citizenship has also created negativities.[136]

India's imposition in 1989 of a 13-month long economic blockade of Nepal left an indelible impression on the country that it needs to diversify its dependencies by giving greater salience to China in its economy. That Nepal also has the largest trade deficit with India did not help.

During Prime Minister Modi's visit to Kathmandu in April 2015, India has agreed to renegotiate the treaty and has sought Nepalese proposals while refraining from airing its own suggestions.[137] As the two countries move forward on this matter, a holistic view of the gains and losses to either side will help to remove the animus that it generates. At the same, both sides will, each for its own reasons, consider China's interest in building deeper links with Nepal.

At the third meeting on 5 April 2017 of the Eminent Persons Group Nepal and India reached an understanding to revise the provisions deemed 'unequal' for a sovereign country in the 1950 Nepal-India Peace and Friendship Treaty. The EPG had preliminary discussions on the 1950 treaty, open border, border security, trade, and transit and water resources.[138]

Water Resources

India's interest in developing Nepal's huge hydropower potential for mutual benefit has been hamstrung by pervasive Nepalese sentiment of exploitation.[139] The success of hydroelectric projects on important Nepalese rivers like Kosi has not been able to moderate it. Rivers are Nepal's largest asset and their mutually beneficial utilization for the good of the peoples of both countries and the subregion has to remain a major goal of Indian policy.

Security and Borders

Mutual security concerns related to the open border have led to the setting up of mechanisms to address cross-border crime, human trafficking, and create a legal framework to meet these challenges. India and Nepal have agreed to update the treaty on extradition and sign an agreement on mutual legal assistance on criminal matters. It is expected that these will help in India's fight against Indian Maoist groups whose presence has been noted in 200 districts of the country.

Similarly, the long-pending disputes over the border areas of Kalapani and Sushta need early resolution.

Despite India having taken important steps to arrest the degrading of the bilateral relationship, it appears to be spiralling out of control. The need to build confidence, trust, and mutually beneficial economic cooperation between the two sovereign countries must remain the basis of the relationship. India has agreed to renegotiate the treaty of 1950 and to sign an agreement on water and power trade that will effectively utilize Nepal's hydroelectric potential. India's immediate and fulsome assistance during the Nepal earthquake of 2015 has been appreciated as also its extension USD 1 billion credit line for building Nepal's infrastructure. The requirement is for Nepal to renew itself after the devastating earthquake in conditions of political harmony and cooperation.

Sri Lanka

The island of Sri Lanka, or Ceylon as it was known during colonial times, or Taprobane even earlier, was coveted for its spices and its strategic location on the sea routes of the world. Over the centuries, Sri Lanka has mirrored the growing importance of the IO right into the 21st century. The shift of the international economy to Asia has meant new attention to the security of the sea-lanes of communication and trade centring on the IO. The IO is seen as an 'ocean of transit' between the Atlantic and the Pacific Oceans. With the rising salience of China in the Asia Pacific and the IO,[140] there is an increase in the naval, military, and commercial importance of Sri Lanka[141] as it straddles the IO.

A Brief History

Sri Lanka embodies the microcosm of both the challenges and opportunities inherent in India's relations with its neighbours. Relations between India and Sri Lanka are historically intertwined in a mix of mythology, culture, religion, migration, and language.

A mere 48 kilometres of sea, the Palk Strait,[142] stands between India and Sri Lanka and has been the scene of major events in the relations between the two countries. Sri Lanka is the home to the four important religions of the Indian subcontinent—Buddhism, Hinduism, Islam, and Christianity. All the communities on the island trace their origins to the Indian subcontinent. The majority Sinhala,[143] who are both Buddhists and Christians, trace their origins to the east coast of India. The visit in 2300 BC, of Mahinda and Sangamitta, son and daughter of Indian emperor Ashoka, to the Sinhala kingdom of Anuradhapura, is credited with bringing Buddhism to the island. It remains the majority religion in the country.

The Tamils, numbering a third of the island's population, come from the southern Indian state of Tamil Nadu.[144] While a majority follows the Hindu religion, others follow Christianity and Islam. Although the Lankan Tamils share the same language and religion (Hinduism), they are distinct from the Indian Tamils.[145] The latter were brought as indentured labour for the tea plantations in the central highlands by the British from the southern-most districts of India.

Relations of trade, conquest, and marriage between the Chola and Chera kingdoms in South India and Sri Lanka's Kandyan kingdom were a characteristic of the subregion since the 13th century before it became a part of the colonial project, first by the Portuguese, then the Dutch, and finally the British. The British ruled Sri Lanka directly from London and followed a similar trajectory as in India to plant the Westminster model of democracy.

Sri Lanka secured its independence in 1948, a year after India. In international relations, both countries opted to pursue non-alignment and avoided joining Western military pacts. The comprehensive development of their bilateral relations covers trade, services and investment, development cooperation, science and technology, culture, education, and security.

The last 60 years have seen a dramatic change in the perception of the IO from aspirations of making it a 'Zone of Peace' to viewing it as an 'an ocean of transit' between the Atlantic and the Pacific as the centre of economic gravity of the globalized economy shifts towards Asia. The IO is a major sea-lane connecting the Middle East, East Asia, and Africa with Europe and the Americas. Boasting of rich living and non-living resources, from marine life to oil and natural gas, IO is economically crucial to Africa, Asia, and Australasia, the three continents bordering it, and the world at large. The IO is a critical waterway for global trade and commerce.

It has meant an increasing presence of regional and great powerful navies, particularly China, equipped with sophisticated weaponry to combat piracy and safeguard the sea-lanes of communication. Their seeking to set up basing and bunkering facilities on IO island-states has heightened international rivalry. The growing Chinese profile in Sri Lanka has included the construction of port facilities at Hambantota,[146] in the east, of which the first phase was completed in 2014 at a cost of USD 361 million and the second estimated at USD 750 million and the port of Colombo.[147] China has also financed infrastructure road projects, particularly the highway from Colombo to the Bandaranaike International Airport.

India's Role in Sri Lankan Politics

India's engagement with Sri Lanka is a function, on the one hand, of the balance between Sri Lanka Tamil aspirations and India's security and on the other, between politics in the Indian state of Tamil Nadu and the broader India-Sri Lanka relationship. At any given moment, the state of the triangular relations between the governments of India and of Sri Lanka and the state government of Tamil Nadu determine the state of the bilateral relationship. In no other case with its neighbours does a contiguous Indian state have such a major impact.[148]

The earliest political issue was of Sri Lanka granting citizenship to the thousands of Tamil indentured labour from Tamil Nadu, or the 'Indian Tamils', taken by the British to work on the tea plantations in the central Sri Lanka highlands. These Tamils, and their natural increase, identified with India, and remained stateless for decades before the two countries agreed to grant them Sri Lankan citizenship. The Indian Tamil community's activism to work within the given political system, despite internal constitutional changes in Sri Lanka, was responsible for the eventual granting of Sri Lankan citizenship.

The Sri Lanka Tamil community came to the island during the same historical period as the Sinhala. During the colonial period the community flourished. After independence, it launched a political struggle to secure its rights within Sri Lanka's unitary constitution. The Sinhala Only Act of 1958 converted the country's political system into a majoritarian democracy, as did the constitutional change that brought in a presidential system of government in the 1980s. Both changes had a profound impact on the political, and later the militant, struggle of the Sri Lanka Tamils.

Although over a million Tamils live in Colombo, the provinces of Jaffna, Trincomalee, and Vavuniya have been the traditional homeland of the Tamils. The Sinhala Only Act made intercommunal strife a feature of the political landscape. The ethnic riots of July 1983 introduced a seminal change in the situation, first by equating anti-Tamil with anti-Indian, and secondly, by freeing the militant side of the Tamil political movement. The island-wide devastation by the anti-Tamil riots brought India into the picture as an intermediary to work out a package for the devolution of political power to the Tamils within a united Sri Lanka.

Over almost five years the Indian role transformed from the political to military with the signing of the India–Sri Lanka Agreement (ISLA) of 1987[149] which brought in the IPKF to disarm the Tamil militant groups, particularly the Liberation

Tigers of Tamil Eelam (LTTE), which had declared the goal of an independent Tamil state, Eelam. India's decision to send its army to disarm the LTTE was a result of its policy against two states on the island and the political backlash in Tamil Nadu following the stream of Tamil refugees fleeing atrocities by the Sri Lankan Army and the Sinhala community.

The failure of the Indian Army to disarm the LTTE vitiated Sri Lanka's political atmosphere with diverse interests baying for the withdrawal of the Indian Army. India was also unable to protect the gains from political devolution achieved through the 13th Amendment to the Sri Lanka Constitution, and the IPKF returned to India in March 1990. The military struggle between the two sides ran parallel to peace-making attempts by Western donors without leading to any lasting result until the Sri Lanka Army, strengthened by heavy equipment from Pakistan and China, ended the LTTE in May 2009. The period until 2009 saw India's withdrawal from an active role in peace-making with the LTTE.[150] At the same time, the ISLA, including its annexed letters, was not abrogated.[151] This could have relevance in the context of Sri Lanka ports being used in the future by interests inimical to India.

India has extended credit lines for the reconstruction of Jaffna after the destruction during the Eelam War IV in May 2009 when the Sri Lanka Army decimated the LTTE. The trauma of the war on the Sri Lanka Tamils continues to this day[152] while the question of political devolution to the Tamils is no longer seen as a negotiated outcome. India continues to retain its interest in the Sri Lanka Tamils securing their minority rights. The political change in the country in 2014 after the assumption of office by President Maithripala Sirisena has brought the two countries closer.[153]

Fishing Rights

The issue of fishing rights around the island of Katchatheevu in the Palk Strait, although resolved on paper, still remains a major irritant in the bilateral relationship. Historically, Tamil fishermen from Tamil Nadu and North Sri Lanka have been fishing in the prawn-rich waters around the island of Katchatheevu which lies in the narrow stretch of water between the two countries. At

independence, the island fell in Indian maritime waters, although
fishing was continued by both countries.

In 1975, India and Sri Lanka signed the Katchatheevu Agreement[154] that transferred the island to the latter while keeping it open for fishing by both sides. The arrest of fishermen and confiscation of their boats remain a perpetual issue between the two countries during the fishing season. Successive elected governments in the state of Tamil Nadu have never accepted the agreement signed during the state of Emergency in India (1975–77), due to the likely loss of vote bank of the Tamil fishing community in the state. The continued fishing by that community, with increasingly sophisticated fishing vessels, has meant regular arrest, detention, and destruction of fishing boats by the Sri Lanka Navy.

The issue became vitiated during the four Tamil Eelam wars between 1990 and 2009 between the Sri Lanka Army and the LTTE because of the use of this channel for the movement of Tamil militants, refugees, contraband, and arms and ammunition. The increasing use of more sophisticated fishing boats and nets by fishermen from both sides has made the problem intractable. The agreement remains a stick that the Tamil Nadu government uses to call for reopening the issue as a political ploy to leverage the interests of the Tamil party that holds the state government.

Trade and Economics

Their bilateral relationship has been close enough for India and Sri Lanka to enter into the Indo-Sri Lanka Free Trade Agreement (ISFTA), signed on 28 December 1998, which came into effect on 1 March 2000.[155] This has been the most successful of India's free trade agreements (FTAs). Bilateral trade turnover increased from USD 658 million in 2000 to USD 3.32 billion in end August 2015, accounting for 15 per cent of Sri Lanka's total trade. India is Sri Lanka's largest trading partner globally, while Sri Lanka is India's second largest trading partner in the SAARC. It is the number one source of supplies, accounting for 20 per cent of Sri Lanka's total imports, and the third largest export destination for Sri Lankan products absorbing 6 per cent of total exports. Among tourists, Indian visitors are the largest single group accounting for 27 per cent of total arrivals. India is among the top five foreign investors in Sri Lanka accounting for USD 2.6 billion of which USD 436 million was in grants.

The proposals for building on the success of the bilateral FTA by entering into a Closer Economic Cooperation agreement that would include trade, investment, and services has remained elusive. Sri Lanka's fear of completely tying its economy to India remains an important factor, preventing the scaling-up of the FTA.[156] Sri Lanka is now pursuing with India an agreement on trade and investment that will cover technology development.

Bhutan and the Maldives

The two countries at either end of India present an interesting contrast in the outcome of India's diplomacy. While both have near homogenous populations, there are major contrasts in geography, religion, culture, economics, and polity. They have the highest per capita income in SAARC, water resources, and tourism. The tenor of their relationship with India is the unifying feature. With the growing profiles of regional and international players to the north and in the IO, India's challenge is to retain its position as the 'default partner' for these countries.

Bhutan

Bhutan,[157] like its western neighbour Nepal, is a landlocked Himalayan kingdom with a population of 750,000, predominantly Buddhists, sandwiched between two large neighbours, India and China.[158] Following India's independence, a veneer of friendship and goodwill with Bhutan and its people was overlaid on the Treaty of Friendship and Cooperation (1949). Its small, largely Buddhist, homogenous population has long-standing links with places of pilgrimage in India. A great respect for the monarchy is a feature of the Bhutanese society that in its enlightened self-interest ushered in an elected democracy.

The 1949 Treaty, which was imperialistic in its mould, effectively placed Bhutan's foreign and defence relations in India's hands. It was renegotiated in 2007[159] to loosen these strings in the areas of foreign policy and defence. Crucially dependent on India, even for its defence, it has tread a very harmonious path to building a relationship of trust and partnership with India. The oft-imagined hegemonistic view of India has not been allowed to cloud the relationship, and India has responded in equal measure. An impression of equality has thereby been engendered between two very unequal entities.

Bhutan, for the present, appears to have decided to stick with India despite China's growing profile in Nepal and other SAARC countries. India remains Bhutan's largest provider of external aid. It has built a mutually beneficial paradigm for utilizing its water resources that India has been unable so far to repeat in Nepal. India is overwhelmingly Bhutan's largest trading partner, and zero-duty access to Bhutanese products has helped to bolster that country's external trade.

The security relationship between the two countries is based on Indian armed forces being placed on the Bhutan-China border and active cooperation to prevent terrorist groups from the region and insurgent groups from India's northeast region gaining a foothold in Bhutan.

Doklam Crisis[160]

The disputed territory is located at the Doka La pass, a trijunction where Bhutan borders the Indian state of Sikkim and the Tibet Autonomous Region of China. For India, Chinese encroachment in Doklam meant it would bring Chinese forces closer to its vulnerable 'Chicken's Neck'—the narrow Siliguri Corridor that connects India's northeast to the rest of the country. The Doklam military standoff which lasted between June and August 2017 between India and China tested the strength of the India Bhutan security relationship and Bhutan's own perception of China.

Although 'the Bhutanese government has so far not strayed from the Indian position and pursued a resolution to the border conflict independently of India', Bhutanese public sentiment did not favour the Bhutanese official position. 'The Indian government, too, probably realize[d] that it stretched the crisis out long enough to gain credibility, but not so long as to play into a possible Chinese strategy to drive a wedge between Bhutan and India.'[161]

The Indian government continued to emphasise a diplomatic resolution leaving little incentive for the Bhutanese government to do anything other than continue to incrementally increase its engagement with China, as it did before the crisis.

At the same time, India will have to be mindful that the crisis aroused public sentiment in Bhutan which will be need careful handling.

Maldives[162]

Since independence in 1966, the Maldives has presented a contrasting development in its bilateral relationship with India when compared to Bhutan.

The Republic of Maldives, close to a thousand kilometres southwest of the Indian coast, comprises a group of about 1,200 coral islands in the IO, 26 atolls in the Arabian Sea which do not measure more than 2.4 metres above the mean sea-level. The increasing strategic importance of the country in the IO has increased its international profile. The Maldives is 1,200 kilometres from the US naval base of Diego Garcia and is part of China's OBOR project.

It has been subject to the influence of radical Islamic groups, with a good number reportedly having joined the ISIL in Syria. 'Renowned for pristine beaches and crystal blue waters, the Maldives is rapidly gaining prominence as a haven for jihadist recruitment. Maldivian men—reportedly 200 of them—have been streaming to Iraq and Syria to join the ranks of the Islamic State (IS) militant group, the al-Qaeda-affiliated Jabhat al-Nusra organization, as well as other radical organizations. This is a large number considering the Indian Ocean archipelago of around 1,200 islands has a population of roughly 359,000 people (*Indian Express*, 15 April 2015). Not only does the Maldives thus have the world's largest number of jihadists per capita active in Iraq and Syria, but it also accounts for the biggest number of jihadists from any South Asian country fighting in these countries. Several jihadists have taken their wives and children to the Middle East battle zones with them (Haveeru Online, February 5, 2015; Maldives Independent, Sept 21, 2015 and Dhivehi Sitee, December 2, 2015).'[163] The small population of 390,000, almost entirely Sunni Muslims, inhabiting about 500 of these islands, the Maldives remains susceptible to Islamic radicalism from West Asia.

India and the Maldives developed close economic, political, and security relations in the long period of dictatorial rule by President Maumoon Abdul Gayoom (1978–2008). India-Maldives relations stepped up after the Indian Army's intervention in 1988 to defeat the Tamil terrorist group People's Liberation Organisation for Tamil Eelam's (PLOTE) attempt to take over Male, the country's capital. In a successful operation, the Indian armed forces secured the island and the country and returned back to India within 24 hours.

Thereafter, in a calibrated policy of assistance and support, India developed the Maldives' coastal navy, set up a helicopter station in Male, and increased military training slots in Indian defence institutions. This was coupled with assisting the Maldivian people by constructing and running the Indira Gandhi Hospital, the island's first full-scale medical facility; developing mangroves to protect the coral islands from erosion; and increasing scholarships in Indian educational institutions. The Maldives and India have agreements on maritime boundary, anti-terrorism, drug trafficking, disaster management, and coastal security.

The democratic changes in the Maldives, following a popular upsurge of the ousting of President Gayoom, continue to create a politically unstable situation. India supported the election of Ahmed Nasheed, the first democratically elected president (2008–12). It committed in 2009 a credit line of USD 100 million as development assistance. India chose to stay away from the internal political developments that saw Nasheed ousted by a group of religiously conservative parties. The appointment of Abdulla Yameen as president paved the way for an election that led to the victory of a political party supported by the exiled former president, Gayoom.

President Abdulla Yameen, Gayoom's half-brother, since taking office in 2013, has embarked on developing his relations with the neighbouring Muslim countries and China. The arrest of his opponents starting with former President Nasheed on charges of terrorism and later the heads of major opposition parties has revived the tendency towards absolutism. Former President Nasheed was granted asylum by United Kingdom and now operates from Colombo.

At the same time, Maldives' relationship with both China and Saudi Arabia has grown by leaps and bounds. China looks at the country as a link in the OBOR project and in its 'string of pearls' strategy and adjunct to its presence in Gwadar, Pakistan. The Saudis have always seen it as supporting Sunni Islam and and establishing its primacy, vis-à-vis Iran, in China's eyes.[164]

Meanwhile, continuing political turmoil has diverted attention from the Maldives greatest challenge—the rise of the sea level[165] due to global warming[166] which could wipe out a number of islands of the Maldivian archipelago. The Maldives leads the 'climate vulnerable' group of countries in the Climate Change Agreement (2015). It provides India a unique opportunity. India, with its geographical proximity, can become the default alternative in case global warming inundates the inhabited Maldives' islands. India needs to consider the possibility of working out such an understanding with the Maldives.

India–Maldives relations are in a trough from the high level attained in earlier years.[167] India's role as the 'default economic and security provider' for Maldives is threatened by the growing presence of China and Saudi Arabia. Nevertheless, India will remain Maldives closest neighbour in a position to provide assistance in any emergency as during the 2014 water crisis. India's effort to bring bilateral relations on an even keel are motivated by the need to keep radical Islam away from the mainland and ensure that the country does not become a cat's paw for interests inimical to India.

Treaty-Related Legacy

The next set of India's inherited challenges are countries with treaty relations with erstwhile British India or arising from being part of the British Empire. Apart from Sri Lanka, it includes China, Myanmar, the Gulf States, Iraq, Iran, and Yemen. This section will consider China and Myanmar which are both part of India's immediate neighbourhood.

China and India are two of the oldest civilizations in the world with a relationship going back centuries. The cultural contact between the two civilizations facilitated the spread of Buddhism to China and Southeast Asia.[168] During the 19th century, China's growing opium trade with the British triggered the First and Second Opium Wars. During World War II, India and China played a crucial role in halting Japan's progress. Their modern relationship began in 1950 when India was among the first countries to end formal ties with the Republic of China (Taiwan) and recognize the People's Republic of China (PRC) as the legitimate government. India championed the Chinese case for permanent membership in the UNSC and saw it to a successful result. Together India and China were instrumental in enunciating the five principles of peaceful coexistence in their bilateral agreement on Tibet that later became the founding mantra of NAM.[169] China and India are today the most populous and fastest growing economies in the world. The resultant growth in their relative international diplomatic and economic influence has introduced an element of rivalry in their bilateral relationship.

In 2012, China described Sino-Indian ties as 'the most important partnership in the twenty-first century'; yet a wide range of threats and perceptions, weighted more on the Indian side, has kept the relationship from stabilizing at any level, except possibly the economic and commercial, although even the latter is not immune from the effects of the former.[170]

Moreover, at the people-to-people level, sentiment in both countries is marked by ignorance and schizophrenia. A 2013 BBC World Service Poll stated that 36 per cent of Indians view China positively with 27 per cent expressing a negative view, whereas 23 per cent of Chinese people view India positively with 45 per cent expressing a negative view. Unlike its other neighbours in the Indian subcontinent, the Himalayas have kept the two countries apart through the centuries. The populations on both sides of the high mountain range have mixed infrequently and had to rely on historical records and those of travellers for a definition of the mores, thoughts, and attitudes of the other. This hiatus is reflected in the fact that there is still minimum information on, and contact

inherited challenges

at, the people-to-people level. The reason is not merely the tremendous difference in the languages spoken on either side of the Himalayas but goes down to a fear of the unknown. Surprisingly, neither country has done enough to bridge this gap.

A Brief History of Sino-Indian Interaction

The fact that both the countries were colonized by the British did not necessarily build a sympathetic bond between the two once freed from colonialism. Nevertheless, the two countries had even relations, until the 1950s, in a common desire neither to submit to another power again nor to fall within their spheres of influence. The Panchsheel Agreement, or the five principles of Peaceful Coexistence,[171] became their guiding paradigm for bilateral and international relations. These principles were respect for each other's territorial integrity and sovereignty, non-aggression, non-interference in each other's internal affairs, equality and shared benefit, and peaceful coexistence.

Jawaharlal Nehru believed that a détente between India and China could stabilize Asia and keep the superpowers at bay. Not only did India consistently vote for China in the UN but conceded sovereignty over Tibet which China had annexed in 1950. The period till the early 1960s was marked by an aura of bonhomie encapsulated in the slogan 'Hindi-Chini-bhai-bhai' (Indian and Chinese brothers), hailing Sino-Indian friendship. India's growing role as the leader of NAM in the third world, the escape of the Dalai Lama from Lhasa to India in 1959, and Chinese support to Naga and Mizo insurgencies in India's northeast region worsened bilateral relations. These further plummeted after the Chinese military intrusion in November 1962 into Aksai Chin in the Ladakh region in the western Himalayas and the then North-East Frontier Agency (NEFA), now Arunachal Pradesh, in the eastern sector.[172] Nehru's conviction that China would not indulge in military adventurism was over-optimistic, and India lost face internationally, denting Nehru's personal prestige too at the same time. Even more important, the Indian military adventure was a way to recapture power for Chairman Mao Zhe Dong who was at that time suffering a mild eclipse in his power.[173]

The ensuing break in diplomatic relations between the two countries was only restored in 1967 in spite of the hostilities in September 1967 at the Nathu La ridge and on 1 October 1967 at Cho La. Following the visit of Indian External Affairs Minister Atal Biehari Vajpayee to China in 1978 relations were fully restored in July 1979.[174] Yet it introduced a high level of mistrust of China into the practice of Indian diplomacy. Rajiv Gandhi's meeting with Chinese President Zhao Ziyang in October 1985 and his visit to Beijing in 1988 revived the relationship. A growing realization on both sides helped: that border and territorial issues should not hold back the vast economic potential between the two countries. The signing of the landmark agreement on Maintenance of Peace and Tranquillity along the LoAC[175] during the visit in September 1993 by Prime Minister Narasimha Rao brought about a degree of stability on the 4,000-kilometre-long border.

Border Talks

Nineteen rounds of talks have yet to produce a way forward.[176] Although on the eve of (former) President Pranab Mukherjee's visit to China in May 2016,[177] it had indicated that it is ready to accelerate border talks, in reality, the delay suits China. By lingering on settling the border issue, China keeps a powerful leverage in its hand in the context of India–Pakistan relations and India's goal to transcend South Asia in pursuit of its global ambition.

The intractability arises from the two sides adopting different sources for defining the border. India bases its position on the McMahon Line, demarcated through an agreement between the British government and the then independent state of Tibet. With its takeover of Tibet, China does not recognize any agreements of the erstwhile Tibetan government. China also states that it has exercised sovereignty beyond the McMahon Line. Presently, both the sides patrol the border based on their own maps creating a room for conflict. The decision for exchanging respective maps has yet to be implemented. Furthermore, settling the border issue will inevitably require mutual adjustments in the border for which neither appears politically ready.

The 1993 Agreement is based on the principle that the two countries will let other relations move forward without being clouded by the border issue. It has also enabled both the countries to stick to their formal positions in the border negotiations that have moved from the bureaucratic to the political level to give negotiations a political impulse. The appointment of special representatives in 2003, Agreement on Political Parameters and Guiding Principles (2005),[178] and the Working Mechanism for Consultation and Coordination on India-China Border Affairs (2012)[179] are intended to achieve this goal. Nevertheless, it has not prevented China from periodic forays across the LoAC or from asserting their claim to the state of Arunachal Pradesh. Aksai Chin remains in Chinese possession and recent developments make the area an important staging point in China's road and rail projects linked to the Pakistan port of Gwadar.

Defence and Counterterrorism

Aimed at building a level of trust, the two countries have developed greater bilateral military interaction with joint military exercises, high-level military exchanges, and joint naval exercises. An annual defence dialogue entered its seventh edition in 2015.[180] Former Defence Minister Manohar Parrikar's visit to Beijing in April 2016[181] was intended to boost the dialogue to ministerial level. It came in the background of India's 'in principle' agreement to the long-pending US proposal to finalize a logistic support agreement with the United States. Here again, periodic disruptions have been used by China to keep the relationship from stabilizing at any level, for example, the denial in 2010 of Chinese visa to an Indian general who belonged to the state of J&K.

Although India and China have exchanged information on counterterrorism action, China's continually delaying the UNSC classification of Masood Azhar, the mastermind behind the Pathankot airbase terror attack, as a terrorist demonstrates its resolve to keep the Pakistan factor in play.[182] China has continued to stone-wall even after the statement by the BRICS Summit at Xiamen, China on 4 September 2017 which in paragraph 48[183] expressed concern over the security situation in the region and the violence caused by the Taliban, ISIS, al-Qaeda and its affiliates including Eastern Turkistan Islamic Movement, Islamic Movement of Uzbekistan, the Haqqani network, Lashkar-e-Taiba, Jaish-e-Mohammad, Tehrik-i-Taliban Pakistan (TTP) and Hizb ut-Tahrir.

This was in contrast to a vague reference to terrorism in the 2016 BRICS Summit at Goa that had called on all nations to adopt a 'comprehensive approach in combating terrorism'.

At the Xiamen Summit, the BRICS leaders called for swift and effective implementation of relevant UN Security Council resolutions and the Financial Action Task Force (FATF) international standards worldwide. Also, in a move that could cause consternation in Pakistan, the BRICS declaration named Lashkar-e-Taiba besides the JeM for spreading violence. The inclusion of both the groups followed a tough stand against Pakistan enunciated by US President Donald Trump in his recent policy statement on Afghanistan and South Asia.[184]

Trade and Economic Relations

Since 1993, bilateral commercial and economic relations have seen a tremendous upsurge just as China's economic footprint in South Asia has expanded.[185] China is India's largest trading partner with a bilateral turnover of approximately USD 74 billion (2015–16).[186] The trade is heavily weighted in favour of China with Indian exports being USD 7.5 billion against imports from China of USD 52.26 billion during the same period (15 April 2015 to 30 January 2016). Not only is the huge imbalance a matter of concern for India but so is China's trade-dumping action in India. India has filed 177 anti-dumping cases in World Trade Organization (WTO) against China. China is India's largest supplier of power plant equipment and has a significant share of technology hardware imports. A Five-Year Development Programme for Economic and Trade Cooperation[187] signed in 2014 is expected to improve the situation.

The growing trade deficit against India has been accompanied by concerns regarding the high proportion of primary materials, like iron and manganese ores in the Indian export basket, and security-related issues on Chinese technology imports. Bilateral investments have grown steadily, and China committed USD 20 billion for infrastructure projects President Xi Jinping's visit to New Delhi in December 2014. Energy security has goaded both the countries to compete as well as work together on oil and gas projects in Sudan, Syria, Peru, and Columbia. Again, this has not prevented China from warning India off its offshore exploration with Vietnam in the South China Sea.

International Issues

Despite regular high-level exchanges and cooperation in defence and in the international arena, the bilateral political relationship remains shrouded in uncertainty. China's phenomenal rise, its aggressive postures in its neighbourhood and a close relationship with Pakistan combine to make for a Chinese strategy of 'periodic disruptions' in the bilateral relationship. The Doklam crisis which continued from June to August 2017 illustrates this strategy. The standoff between Indian and Chinese troops at Doklam plateau in Sikkim sector of the India-China border began in mid-June when India accused China of constructing a road in the disputed territory towards Doklam plateau. The Royal Bhutanese Army had also raised a similar objection. Doklam is a tri-junction between India, Bhutan and China. India had intervened in the issue, supporting Bhutan's stand and asking China to halt all of its construction work. China claimed they were constructing the road within their territory and had been demanding immediate pull-out of Indian troops from the disputed area. New Delhi had expressed concern over the road building, apprehending that it may allow Chinese troops to cut India's access to its northeastern states. Of the 3,488-km-long India-China border from Jammu and Kashmir to Arunachal Pradesh, a 220-km section falls in Sikkim. China also claims that Thimphu has no dispute with Beijing over Doklam.

'After 10 weeks, the latest chapter in the long-running China-India-Bhutan border dispute has come to an end. India and China agreed to remove their troops from a disputed region called the Doklam Plateau, claimed by both China and Bhutan. (The area is not claimed by India, but it is very close to the Indian border,

and of extreme strategic importance to New Delhi.) Although
the dust-up failed to attract much attention from the international community, it is nonetheless worthy of note, both for what
it says about a rising China's more forward-leaning approach to
its neighbors, and also for what it says about the Trump administration's strangely inattentive approach to an increasingly restive
Asia.'[188] Yet it has the possibility of bringing in the United States
to both defuse and mitigate the tension.[189]

India-China relations suffered with India's nuclear tests in
1998 with the UNSC passing a condemnatory resolution under
China's leadership of the Council. The United States' staunch
championing of its civil nuclear cooperation with India was yet
another strand of this issue. China continues to oppose India's
entry into the four nuclear technology denial regimes,[190] such
as the Nuclear Suppliers Group (NSG) by drawing parity with
Pakistan,[191] the Missile Technology Control Regime (MCTR)
on which Italy put a hold,[192] the Wassenaar Group,[193] and the
Australia Group.[194]

India has still not received unequivocal Chinese support
for its permanent membership of the UNSC. Both India and
Pakistan were accepted, after a decade, as full members of the
Shanghai Cooperation Organisation (SCO) in July 2015. Their
membership became operational at the SCO meeting in Astana,
Kazakhstan on 8–9 June 2017. The entry of both India and
Pakistan in a China-led organization of Central Asian countries,
primarily devoted to cooperation in terrorism, brings both gains
and concerns.[195]

At the same time, China and India have found ways to work
together in the Climate Change Negotiations (where they are part
of the BRICS), the G-20 economic grouping, and the BRICS
grouping where they have been prime movers in setting up the
BRICS Development Bank. China's international initiative, Asian
Infrastructure Investment Bank (AIIB) has India as a founder
member.

Indian diplomacy's greatest challenge vis-à-vis China arises
from its goal of attaining a benign image in South Asia and an
international role as the third largest emerging economic power.
China's strategy of 'periodic and sectoral disruption' of bilateral

relations aims at keeping the relationship unsettled while its 'all-weather friendship' with Pakistan aims at keeping India locked up in South Asia.

US' continued interest in Asia provides the framework within which India's policy towards China will play out. President Trump's forthcoming visit to Asia will be an indicator of US policy in the region. He will visit Japan, South Korea, China, Vietnam and the Philippines on a trip expected to be dominated by the North Korea nuclear threat. His visit will include attending two major summits, the Asia–Pacific Economic Cooperation forum in Vietnam and the Association of Southeast Asian Nations conclave in the Philippines.

President Trump and Prime Minister Narendra Modi met on the sidelines of the Asean summit in Manila.[196] It was their third encounter so far, following a day-long, substantive meeting accompanied by their respective delegations in June in Washington DC and an 'impromptu interaction' during the G-20 summit in Hamburg, Germany in July. For India the challenge will remain of deciding where India should position itself vis-à-vis its relations with the United States.

India's China policy has five dimensions. First, to manage periodic disruptions in sectoral improvements. Second, to counter China's use of its overwhelming economic and military superiority and UN permanent membership to create zones of tension in India's neighbourhood through cooperative action with United States, Japan, Vietnam, and Australia. Third, confronting the resources war in Africa, by India's own initiative recognizing that their aid focus is different. Fourth, managing the unresolved border issues while handling emerging tensions on water sharing of the Himalayan rivers and China's connectivity projects through Aksai Chin that it occupies. Fifth, responding positively to Chinese foreign investment inflow, excluding strategic sectors, and China's regional economic plans so long as they do not exclude India, like the OBOR, AIIB,[197] and the BRICS-founded New Development Bank (NDB).[198]

India's China strategy under Prime Minister Modi appears to have become more realistic as it acknowledges that fundamental differences in strength and outlook exist. According to C. Raja

Delhi now acknowledges the enduring contradic-
tions between the interests of the two countries at the bilateral,
regional, and global level, seeks to manage those responsibly,
refuses to limit its relationship with other countries by looking over its shoulder at Beijing, and rolls out the red carpet for
Chinese capital.'[199]

Myanmar

Myanmar, erstwhile Burma, and India have a historic relationship dating back to antiquity and the spread of Buddhism over
the region. Burma was a province of British India until 1937
after which it was governed directly from London. The linkage
between India and Burma continued with some memorable
events: the exile of the last Mughal emperor from India to
Rangoon, now Yangon, where he died; and of Thibaw, the last
Burmese king to Ratnagiri in Maharashtra, till he died. During
the Indian Independence struggle, important leaders such as
Mahatma Gandhi, Jawaharlal Nehru, Bal Gangadhar Tilak, and
Subhash Chandra Bose were sent to the cellular jail in Mandalay.
During World War II, the British Indian Army fought in the
Arakan operations against the Japanese Army.

Brief History

After Indian independence in 1947 and the Burmese in 1948,
the two countries shared warm relations, reflecting those between
Prime Ministers Nehru and U Nu respectively. India and Burma
signed a Friendship Treaty in 1951 and agreements on their land
boundary (1967) and maritime boundary (1986). A large resident
Indian community was involved in administration and trade. The
overthrow of the democratic government led to restricted relations between the two countries (1962–88) with concerns about
drug trafficking and support to Indian insurgent groups in Burma.
India's opposition to military rule, the jailing of Aung San Suu
Kyi, and the support to pro-democracy protest groups and the
Kachin National Army (KNA) further restrained any forward
movement.

Prime Minister Rajiv Gandhi's visit to Yangon in 1987 broke the impasse that was consolidated by the visits of Narasimha Rao in 1993 and Atal Behari Vajpayee in 2002. The national election in 2015 put Daw Aung San Suu Kyi's National League for Democracy in the government in an uneasy accommodation with the Army that still holds important portfolios and control.

India's 'Look East', policy inaugurated in the late 1990s, was based on a greater degree of Indian circumspection on internal developments in Myanmar and the launching of cross-border transport and communication projects to develop connectivity with Myanmar, not only with India's north-east but also to ASEAN. Since 2014, after the election of Narendra Modi, the focus of the 'Look East' policy has been enhanced to 'Act East' to demonstrate India's determination to build this link into ASEAN.

Rajiv Bhatia, a former Indian ambassador to Myanmar writes,

> The two countries have related to each other as neighbours, strangers, even adversaries at times, but mostly as friends and partners. Happily, neither has treated the other as irrelevant to its national interests. In this fundamental perception lies the hope that, drawing right lessons from history, they will strive to strengthen recent trends and transform friendly relations into a more effective and expanding partnership. This hope is stronger today, with Myanmar embarking on the path of reform and re-calibrating its foreign relations, and India according a higher priority to relations with Myanmar in the light of changing regional equations.[200]

Myanmar, since its political opening starting 2011, has been wooed not only by its ASEAN partners but also by the United States as part of its pivot to Asia. It will remain a major conduit in China's strategic and economic projection into Asia. It fulfills the same role as Pakistan in China's India strategy. The long-standing relations of kinship, language, and religion between the people of western Myanmar and those of the Indian states of Arunachal, Nagaland, Manipur, and Mizoram add complexity to the relationship. The tenor and intensity of India–Myanmar relations must then be viewed through the India–China–Myanmar triangle within which both competition and cooperation are possible.

Recent political changes in both the countries have once again put the focus on their bilateral relations. Prime Minister Modi's visit to Myanmar in September 2017 was this third since taking office. His earlier visits being in November 2014 and for the India–ASEAN Summit (2015). His current visit was both bilateral and for attending the East Asia Summit at Nay Pyi Taw. The visit was aimed at strengthening existing cooperation in areas of security and counter-terrorism, trade and investment, infrastructure and energy, and culture.[201] It was marked by the international outcry on the violence by the Burmese Army against the Muslim Rohingyas in the western Rakhine state.

The violence which has led to flight of nearly 250,000 Rohingyas to Bangladesh has provoked international condemnation and marred Aung San Sui Kyi's image. 40,000 Rohingyas are also reportedly staying in India. Modi supported Suu Kyi's statement, attributing the violence of the last few weeks to extremists. 'We share your concerns about the extremist violence in the Rakhine state and especially the violence against the security forces and how innocent lives have been affected and killed.'[202] India extended assistance to develop infrastructure in Rakhine state as a solution to the violence.

India's challenge in Myanmar remains to ensure minimum disruption in its growing cooperation with the Myanmar government on projects for connectivity, oil and gas, and security cooperation while keeping in tune with the potential political changes in the country.

'Look East' to 'Act East'

Myanmar with a 1,600-kilometre border with India's north-east region could become a bridge to activate India's 'Act East' policy to boost its growing relationship with ASEAN. Much will depend on the way India can provide viable ways for a democratizing Myanmar to combat Chinese influence.

The need to open links with the Myanmar regime became imperative not only due to China's growing influence in the country. It was equally important to build a level of trust to eliminate north-east insurgent groups receiving safe haven and Chinese-made weaponry. Even more, it was realized that Myanmar had mineral resources and oil and gas that would be needed by the fast-growing Indian economy. The Myanmar–India Friendship Highway across the Manipur border and the ASEAN is now planned for completion by 2020 after the reconstruction of bridges on the route, and Myanmar to India's north-east through the Kaladan multimodal transport project which has been inordinately delayed due to flawed feasibility studies.[203]

The 'Act East' policy[204] was consolidated by bilateral high-level visits, Indian credit lines to promote infrastructure development, and investments by the Indian corporate sector in oil and gas prospection and exploration. India's timely and prompt response when Cyclone Nargis hit Myanmar in 2008 did much to build bilateral trust. Relief assistance was delivered over land and by Indian naval ships. India was the first country accepted by the government for such assistance.

Counter-Insurgency

Although politically Myanmar is on its way towards a democratic system, which will give equal space and voice to its warring groups in the north of the country, a military consolidation of the Myanmar Army and its international borders is a work in progress. While it has kept the country's northern regions under the control of the Kachin and the Shan from being dominated by either the central government or China, they have nevertheless provided a tool for promoting insurgent movements in India's north-east region.

There have been media reports followed by comments and analyses by experts of the existence of Chinese military bases in Myanmar. Two cases have stood out, namely the Great Coco Island SIGINT collection station in the Andaman Sea and a naval base on Hainggyi Island in the Irrawaddy delta. These stories have gained further credence through the 'String of Pearls' theory of Chinese-built ports in Pakistan, Sri Lanka, Bangladesh, Myanmar, Thailand, Cambodia, and the South China Sea. While India's chief of naval staff has ruled out the existence of Chinese bases in Myanmar, Chinese fishing boats have been apprehended near the Andaman Islands with depth sounding equipment. India needs to cooperate with Myanmar to ensure the security of the Bay of Bengal. India can work with Myanmar to develop more mature development plans, especially for developing natural resources benefitting the Kachin and other ethnic groups in Myanmar. There are concerns of arms and drugs trafficking from Myanmar to Northeast India. 'There is potential for strategic military cooperation, which enables the Myanmar government to provide stability to its ethnic majority regions like the Shan state which in turn secures India's own north-east region'.[205]

The two governments were able to reach an understanding on military-to-military cooperation in the context of eliminating drug trafficking and insurgent group bases inside Myanmar. Largely due to the understanding reached between the two governments, Indian Air Force strikes were possible inside Myanmar against camps of National Socialist Council of Nagaland (NSCN-Khaplang faction) and the Manipur-based Kanglei Yawol Kanna Lup (KYKL) in retaliation for the killing of 18 Indian Army soldiers in Manipur.[206] While this was the first time that India launched a cross-border air raid into Myanmar, a lack of political coordination on the Indian side in handling the public perception of the action was clearly visible. If India expects to repeat such action not only would it require working with Myanmar's forces but also the better handling of its political and public relations fallout. It must also be underlined that this action was undertaken with the acquiescence of the Myanmar government.

Regional Cooperation

Aside from ASEAN, India and Myanmar work together in two subregional organizations—the Bay of Bengal Initiative for Multi-Sector Technical and Economic Cooperation (BIMSTEC)[207] and the Mekong–Ganga Cooperation (MCG).[208]

BIMSTEC (1997) brings together Bangladesh, India, Myanmar, Sri Lanka, Thailand, Bhutan, and Nepal for cooperation spanning across South and Southeast Asia. It is an adjunct to India's partnership with ASEAN and an alternative, towards its east, to SAARC. Although India bulks large, the absence of Pakistan makes it possible for the organization to avoid inertia coming from deep-seated differences. It held its fourth summit in Goa,

India 2016.[209] The next Summit is expected to be held in 2017 in Kathmandu, Nepal.

MCG was founded in 2000, bringing together India and five ASEAN riparian states of the river Mekong—Cambodia, Lao People's Democratic Republic, Myanmar, Thailand, and Vietnam—to promote cooperation in tourism, culture, education, and transportation. Its six meetings so far have shown that it too suffers from lack of manpower and funds in promoting schemes of cooperation beyond what is envisaged in SAARC and ASEAN. India bulks large in this organization too.

There is a need to evaluate areas in which these intra-subregional organizations can provide additional benefits while increasing the effectiveness and delivery of regional organizations such as SAARC and ASEAN.[210]

❧

This chapter has demonstrated that the Indian diplomacy has continued to be tested constantly by all its neighbours, large and small. It has two interesting elements, first, the nature of the issue varies not only with the country, and second, it depends on the changing parameters of their relationships with the rest of the world.

All the countries in South Asia as also Myanmar are still developing while only China and India, in the sub-region, have the possibility of assisting their development process. Yet the intermeshing religion, ethnicity and traditions places limits on mutually harmonious development of the region. At the same time, it places parameters on building regional structures on security and cooperation.

The challenge which India faces in its neighbourhood will only grow and continue to test the resilience of its diplomatic practice.

Notes

1. See http://www.claudearpi.net/maintenance/uploaded_pics/ Agrreements_on_the_Border.pdf.

2. Stephen Westcott, 'The On-going Saga of China-India Border Talks', *The Diplomat*, http://thediplomat.com/2016/05/the-ongoing-saga-of-the-china-india-border-talks.

3. SAARC, an organization of South Asian nations, founded in 1985, is dedicated to economic, technological, social, and cultural development, emphasizing collective self-reliance. Its seven founding members are Bangladesh, Bhutan, India, The Maldives, Nepal, Pakistan, and Sri Lanka. Afghanistan joined the organization in 2007. Meetings of heads of state are usually scheduled annually; meetings of foreign secretaries are held twice annually. The headquarters are in Kathmandu, Nepal. The 11 stated areas of cooperation are agriculture; education, culture, and sports; health, population, and child welfare; environment and meteorology; rural development (including the SAARC Youth Volunteers Program); tourism; transport; science and technology; communications; women in development; and the prevention of drug trafficking and drug abuse. The charter stipulates that decisions are to be unanimous and that 'bilateral and contentious issues' are to be avoided. The 18th SAARC Summit in 2014 was held in Khatmandu. The 19th summit scheduled to be held in Islamabad, Pakistan on 15–16 November 2016 was indefinitely postponed. Following the rising diplomatic tensions after the Pakistan-sponsored Uri terrorist attack, India announced its boycott of the summit. Later, Bangladesh, Afghanistan and Bhutan also pulled out of the summit.

4. https://en.wikipedia.org/wiki/Inter-Services_Intelligence.

5. The first large-scale Asian-African or Afro-Asian Conference—also known as the Bandung Conference (Indonesian: Konferensi Asia-Afrika)—was a meeting of Asian and African states, most of which were newly independent, which took place on 18–24 April 1955 in Bandung, Indonesia. In all there were 29 countries, representing more than half the world's population, which sent delegates. http://www.britannica.com/event/Bandung-Conference.

6. The Five Principles of Peaceful Coexistence between independent nations were enshrined as the founding credo of the non-aligned countries. https://en.wikipedia.org/wiki/Five_Principles_of_Peaceful_Coexistence.

7. NAM was founded in Belgrade in 1961 and was largely conceived by India's first prime minister, Jawaharlal Nehru; Indonesia's first president, Sukarno; Egypt's second president, Gamal Abdel Nasser; Ghana's first president Kwame Nkrumah; and Yugoslavia's president, Josip Broz Tito. All five leaders were prominent advocates

of a middle course for states in the developing world between the Western and Eastern Blocs in the Cold War. The phrase itself was first used to represent the doctrine by Indian Diplomat V.K. Krishna Menon in 1953 at the UN. The 17th NAM Summit was held on September 17–18 at Margarita Island, Venezuela in 2016. It was the first time that a sitting Indian prime minister did not attend the summit. India was represented by Vice President M.H. Ansari, See https://en.wikipedia.org/wiki/Non-Aligned_Movement.

8. http://www.asean.org/asean/asean-structure/asean-summit/.

9. Al Jazeera, 'Venezuela: Non-Aligned Summit Fizzles for Madura', *Venezuela* (18 September 2016), http://www.aljazeera.com/news/2016/09/venezuela-aligned-summit-fissles-maduro-160917212039058.html.

10. List of Prime Ministers of India, https://en.wikipedia.org/wiki/List_of_Prime_Ministers_of_India.

11. Gary J. Bass, *The Blood Telegram: Nixon, Kissinger, and a Forgotten Genocide* (New York: Alfred A. Knopf, 2013), p. 499. See book review by Dexter Filkins, *The New York Times*, http://www.nytimes.com/2013/09/29/books/review/the-blood-telegram-by-gary-j-bass.html.

12. JVP Insurrection https://en.wikipedia.org/wiki/1971_.

13. Frances Harrison, 'Riots That Led to a War', BBC, http://newsvote.bbc.co.uk/mpapps/pagetools/print/news.bbc.co.uk/2/hi/south_asia/3090111.stm.

14. 'Indo-Sri Lanka Agreement to Establish Peace and Normalcy in Sri Lanka', http://www.satp.org/satporgtp/countries/shrilanka/document/papers/indo_srilanks_agreement.htm. See alsohttp://newsvote.bbc.co.uk/mpapps/pagetools/print/news.bbc.co.uk/2/hi/south_asia/3090111.stm.

15. https://en.wikipedia.org/wiki/1988_Maldives_coup_d%27%C3%A9t.

16. 'Indian Peace-Keeping Force', https://en.wikipedia.org/wiki/Indian_Peace_Keeping_Force.

17. The Gujral Doctrine emphasized on the importance of unilateral accommodation for friendly and warm relations with India's neighbours. Former Prime Minister I.K. Gujral propounded the doctrine when he was the union minister of external affairs in 1996–97 in the H.D. Deve Gowda government. See B.G. Verghese, 'Give Gujral Doctrine a Chance', http://www.rediff.com/news/oct/30diplo1.htm.

18. 'Modi Sings Mamata's Tune on Teesta Issue: Was Bangladesh the Ice-Breaker They Needed?', Firstpost, http://www.firstpost.com/

politics/modi-sings-mamatas-tunes-on-teesta-issue-was-bangla-desh-the-ice-breaker-they-needed-2283612.html.

19. P.S. Suryanarayana, 'Federalism and Foreign Policy: Regional Inputs in India's Neighbourhood Strategy,' *IPCS*, New Delhi (31 January 2014), http://www.ipcs.org/article/india/ipcs-debate-federalism-and-foreign-policy-regional-inputs-in-indias-4283.html.

20. 'The Simla Agreement 1972', http://mea.gov.in/in-focus-article. htm?19005/Simla+Agreement+July+2+1972.

21. See also http://www.news18.com/news/india/indo-pak-shimla-agreement-40-years-later-485305.html.

22. Sumona Dasgupta, 'Kashmir and the India-Pakistan Composite Dialogue Process', RSIS Working Paper, No. 291 (21 May 2015), https://www.rsis.edu.sg/wp-content/uploads/2015/05/WP291.pdf

23. 'Instrument of Accession of Kashmir to the Republic of India, 26 October 1947', http://www.jammu-kashmir.com/documents/ instrument_of_accession.html. See also, 'Letter from Hari Singh, the Ruler of Kashmir to Lord Mountbatten, Viceroy of India', http://www.jammu-kashmir.com/documents/instrument_of_ accession.html.

24. Standstill Agreement between India and Pakistan on 12 August 1947. Identical telegrams were sent by the prime minister of Kashmir to the dominions of India and Pakistan on 12 August 1947. The text is as follows: 'Jammu and Kashmir Government would welcome Standstill Agreements with India (Pakistan) on all matters on which these exist at present moment with outgoing British India Government. It is suggested that existing arrangements should continue pending settlement of details.' Reply from Government of Pakistan sent on August I5 1947: 'Your telegram of the 12th. The Government of Pakistan agree to have a Standstill Agreement and Kashmir for the continuance of the existing arrangements pending settlement of details and formal execution.' Reply from Government of India,: 'Government of India would be glad if you or some other Minister duly authorised in this behalf could fly to Delhi for nego-tiating Standstill Agreement between Kashmir Government and India dominion. Early action desirable to maintain intact existing agreements and administrative arrangements.' The representative of Kashmir did not visit Delhi and no Standstill Agreement was con-cluded between the state and the dominion of India.

25. The Chinese Overseas Ports Holding Company Ltd (COPHCL), a Chinese state-owned enterprise, officially took control of the strategically important port at Gwadar in Pakistan. The Chinese

firm officially signed a 40-year lease for over 2,000 acres of land in Gwadar, marking a milestone in the implementation phase of the China–Pakistan Economic Corridor (CPEC), a major bilateral initiative to build transportation and other infrastructure along the length of Pakistan, connecting the country's Arabian Sea coast with the Himalayan border with China. CPEC was unveiled during Chinese President Xi Jinping's April 2015 state visit to Pakistan, where Gwadar was high on the agenda. Ankit Pande, 'Chinese State Firm Takes Control of Strategically Vital Gwadar Port', *The Diplomat* (13 November 2015), http://thediplomat. com/2015/11/chinese-state-firm-takes-control-of-strategically-vital-gwadar-port/.

26. Resolution adopted by the United Nations Commission for India and Pakistan on 13 August 1948. Document No. 1100, Para 75, dated (9 November 1948), https://www.mtholyoke.edu/acad/intrel/uncom1.htm.

27. See http://news.bbc.co.uk/hi/english/static/in_depth/south_asia/2002/india_pakistan/timeline/1947_48.stm.

28. See https://history.state.gov/milestones/1961-1968/india–pakistan-war

29. 'India-Pakistan War of 1971', https://en.wikipedia.org/wiki/Indo-Pakistani_War_of_1971.

30. 'The Kargil War, May 1999', http://www.globalsecurity.org/military/world/war/kargil-99.htm.

31. 'The Kargil War, May 1999'.

32. http://www.un.org/en/peacekeeping/missions/unmogip/background.shtml.

33. Simla Agreement, https://en.wikipedia.org/wiki/Simla_Agreement

34. 'The Lahore Declaration, February 1999', http://mea.gov.in/in-focus-article.htm?18997/Lahore+Declaration+February+1999.

35. 'List of Indian Nuclear Tests', https://en.wikipedia.org/wiki/List_of_nuclear_weapons_tests_of_India.

36. 'Pakistan's Nuclear Tests', http://www.nti.org/learn/countries/pakistan/nuclear/.

37. Akhilesh Pillalamaari, 'Pakistan's Nuclear Weapons Programme: Five Things You need to Know', National Interest, 21 April 2015, http://nationalinterest.org/feature/pakistans-nuclear-weapons-program-5-things-you-need-know-12687?page=show.

38. C. Christine Fair and Sumit Ganguly, 'An Unworthy Ally, Time for Washington to Cut Pakistan Loose', *Foreign Affairs* (September–October 2015), https://www.foreignaffairs.com/articles/pakistan/2015-08-18/unworthy-ally.

39. Farid Zakaria, 'Pakistan Is Epicentre of Islamic Terrorism', http://edition.cnn.com/2010/OPINION/05/05/zakaria.pakistan.terror/.

40. David Ignatius, 'Nixon's Great Decision on China, 40 Years Later', *The New York Times* (12 February 2012), https://www.washingtonpost.com/opinions/nixons-great-decision-on-china-40-years-later/2012/02/10/gIQAtFh34Q_story.htm.

41. *The Maritime Executive*, 'China's Gwadar Port Nears Completion' (14 April 2016), http://www.maritime-executive.com/article/chinas-gwadar-port-nears-completion.

42. Gwadar port, Pakistan, https://en.wikipedia.org/wiki/Gwadar_Port.

43. 'Organization of Islamic Cooperation, Jeddah', http://www.oicun.org/2/23/#.

44. In the OIC Foreign Ministers Conference, Khartoum 2012, the suggestion to invite India to join the OIC was filibustered by Pakistan President Musharraf, http://www.tribuneindia.com/2003/20030527/world.htm#1.

45. Rajendra Abhyankar, 'India and the OIC: To Join or Not to Join', *Gateway House* (23 January 2013), http://www.gatewayhouse.in/india-and-the-oic-to-join-or-not-to-join/.

46. Nisha Taneja and Samridhi Bimal, 'Will Pakistan Finally Open up Its Trade to India?', *East Asia Forum* (13 August 2015), http://www.eastasiaforum.org/2015/08/13/will-pakistan-finally-open-up-its-trade-to-india/.

47. 'Pakistan Has Still Not Granted Most Favoured Nation Status to India: Nirmala Sitharaman', *Economic Times* (9 December 2015), http://articles.economictimes.indiatimes.com/2015-12-09/news/68899827_1_favoured-nation-status-pakistan-way-mfn-status.

48. Sajad Pader, 'The Composite Dialogue between India and Pakistan: Structure, Process and Agency', Working Paper, South Asia Institute, Department of Political Science, Heidelberg University, No. 65, February 2012, http://archiv.ub.uni-heidelberg.de/volltextserver/13143/1/Heidelberg_Papers_65_Padder.pdf.

49. Ministry of External Affairs, 'Joint Statement Issued by India and Pakistan during Visit of External Affairs Minister to Pakistan' (8 September 2012).

50. Devirupa Mitra, 'Former Indian, Pakistani Envoys Spar-Talk-at Mother of All Track IIs', *The Wire* (30 April 2016), http://thewire.in/2016/04/30/former-indian-pakistani-envoys-urge-continued-dialogue-32777/.

51. 'Mumbai Massacre: Background Information', *Secrets of the Dead*, http://thewire.in/2016/04/30/former-indian-pakistani-envoys-urge-continued-dialogue-32777. Also see, 'Mumbai Attacks', https://en.wikipedia.org/wiki/2008_Mumbai_attacks.

52. '2008 Mumbai Attacks', *Wikipedia*, https://en.wikipedia.org/wiki/2008_Mumbai_attacks.

53. Sabah Ishtiaq, 'India–Pakistan: A Dialogue or Failed Diplomacy', Observer Research Foundation, New Delhi, 2 May 2016.

54. 'PM Modi Lands in Lahore on a Surprise Visit, Meets Pak PM Nawaz Sharif', *The Indian Express* (25 December 2015), http://indianexpress.com/article/india/india-news-india/pm-modi-lands-in-lahore-on-a-surprise-visit-meets-pak-pm-nawaz-sharif/.

55. Navjeevan Gopal and Kamaldeep Singh Brar, 'Terror Attacks Pathankot Air Force Base, India–Pakistan Thaw', *The Indian Express* (3 January 2016), http://indianexpress.com/article/india/india-news-india/terror-attacks-pathankot-airbase-india-pakistan-thaw/.

56. Satyabrata Pal, 'The Pathankot Attack Must Not Be Allowed to Derail the India–Pakistan Dialogue', *The Wire* (10 January 2016), http://thewire.in/2016/01/10/the-pathankot-attack-must-not-be-allowed-to-derail-the-india-pakistan-dialogue-18974/.

57. 'Former Diplomats Pitch for Continuation of Indo-Pak Dialogue', *Outlook* (29 April 2016), http://www.outlookindia.com/newswire/story/former-diplomats-pitch-for-continuation-in-indo-pak-dialogue/938483.

58. G. Parthasarathy and Radha Kumar, 'Frameworks for a Kashmir Settlement', *Delhi Policy Group*, 2006.

59. Kanti Bajpai, 'Narendra Modi's Pakistan and China Policy: Assertive Bilateral Diplomacy, Active Coalition Diplomacy', *International Affairs*, 93:1(2017): 69–91, p. 73.

60. Saad Khan, 'India-Pakistan Relations: A Paradigm Shift', *The Diplomat*, 17 August 2016, http://thediplomat.com/2016/08/india-pakistan-relations-a-paradigm-shift/.

61. Sreemoy Talukdar, 'Uri Terror Attack: Modi's Biggest Headache Isn't Pakistan, but an Enraged Indian Public', Firstpost (21 September 2016), http://www.firstpost.com/world/uri-terror-attack-modis-biggest-headache-isnt-pakistan-but-an-enraged-indian-public-3013078.html.

62. Ian Marlow, Unni Krishnan, and Faseeh Mangi, 'India Says It Hit Pakistan Terror Camps after Attack on Army', *Bloomberg News* (29 September 2016), http://www.bloomberg.com/news/articles/

2016-09-29/india-attacked-pakistan-terror-camps-says-no-more-ops-planned.

71

inherited challenges

63. Touqir Hussein, 'Are India-Pakistan Relations Doomed?' *The Diplomat*, 6 April 2017, http://thediplomat.com/2017/04/are-india-pakistan-relations-doomed/.

64. Manoj Joshi, 'Uri Attack: There Are No Military Options That Will Give India the Outcome It Wants', Observer Research Foundation, New Delhi, 19 September 2016, http://www.orfonline.org/research/uri-kashmir-terrorism/.

65. NDTV, 'Pakistan Postpones Islamabad SAARC Summit after Members Pull Out', http://www.ndtv.com/world-news/pakistan-postpones-saarc-summit-in-islamabad-after-member-nations-pull-out-1468640.

66. Hussein, 'Are India-Pakistan Relations Doomed?'

67. Mervyn Piesse, 'The Indus Treaty Revisited: India-Pakistan Water Sharing', *Future Directions International* (29 October 2015), http://www.futuredirections.org.au/publication/the-indus-treaty-revisited-india-pakistan-water-sharing/.

68. 'Indus Water Dispute Going to Arbitration Again', *The Third Pole* (18 July 2016), https://www.thethirdpole.net/2016/07/18/indus-water-dispute-going-to-arbitrators-again/.

69. Zofeen Ibrahim and Joydeep Gupta, 'India Resists World Bank Move to Resolve Indus Water Treaty Dispute', *Dawn* (6 January 2017), https://www.dawn.com/news/1306778.

70. 'The World Bank: The Indus Waters Treaty 1960 and the World Bank', 1 August 2017, http://www.worldbank.org/en/region/sar/brief/fact-sheet-the-indus-waters-treaty-1960-and-the-world-bank.

71. No first use (NFU) refers to a pledge or a policy by a nuclear power not to use nuclear weapons as a means of warfare unless first attacked by an adversary using nuclear weapons. Earlier, the concept had also been applied to chemical and biological warfare. China declared its NFU policy in 1964 and has since maintained this policy. India articulated its policy of NFU of nuclear weapons in 2003. The North Atlantic Treaty Organization (NATO) has repeatedly rejected calls for adopting NFU policy, arguing that preemptive nuclear strike is a key option in order to have a credible deterrent that could compensate for the overwhelming conventional weapon superiority enjoyed by the Soviet Army in the Eurasian land mass. In 1993, Russia dropped a pledge given by the former Soviet Union not to use nuclear weapons first. In 2000, a Russian military doctrine stated that Russia reserves the right

to use nuclear weapons 'in response to a large-scale conventional aggression'. This is because the balance of forces was reversed. NATO now enjoys a clear superiority in conventional weapons. https://en.wikipedia.org/wiki/No_first_use.

72. Ankit Panda, 'No, India Won't Abandon Its No First-Use Nuclear Doctrine', *The Diplomat* (14 April 2014), http://thediplomat. com/2014/04/no-india-wont-abandon-its-no-first-use-nuclear-doctrine/.

73. 'Vendors, Transporters Defy Separatist Call, Come Out on Streets', *NDTV* (2 October 2016), http://www.ndtv.com/india-news/vendors-transporters-defy-separatists-call-come-out-on-streets-1469153.

74. Rajendra M. Abhyankar, 'Afghanistan After the 2014 US Drawdown; The Transformation of India's Policy', *Asian Survey*, 55(2): 371–97.

75. The War on Terror, also known as the Global War on Terrorism, refers to the international military campaign that started after the 9/11 attacks on the United States. US President George W. Bush first used the term 'War on Terror' on 20 September 2001. The Bush administration and the Western media have since used the term to argue for a global military, political, legal, and conceptual struggle against both organizations designated as terrorists and regimes accused of supporting them. It was originally used with a particular focus on countries associated with Islamic terrorism organizations including the Al-Qaeda and like-minded organizations. In 2013, President Barack Obama announced that the United States was no longer pursuing a War on Terror, as the military focus should be on specific enemies rather than a tactic. He stated, 'We must define our effort not as a boundless "Global War on Terror", but rather as a series of persistent, targeted efforts to dismantle specific networks of violent extremists that threaten America.' https://en.wikipedia.org/wiki/War_on_Terror.

It has never had world-wide acceptance and is seen at best seen as a device by Western powers to give their targeted actions against countries or persons who do not accept their positions and at worst a cover for continuing US, UK, and Western attacks on their political opponents in the world. See Global Policy Forum, https://www.globalpolicy.org/war-on-terrorism.html.

76. Ankit Panda, 'India Pledges $1 Billion in Assistance to Afghanistan', *The Diplomat* (15 September 2016), http://thediplomat.com/2016/09/india-pledges-1-billion-in-assistance-to-afghanistan/.

77. 'India–Afghanistan Strategic Partnership Agreement', http:// president.gov.af/Content/Media/Documents/StrategicPartnership Agreement-AfgandIndia25Sept2011English51020111647 3222553325325.pdf,http://eoi.gov.in/kabul/?0354?000.

78. Praveen Swami, 'Why PM Modi's Kabul Visit Matters', *The Indian Express* (22 December 2015), http://indianexpress.com/article/ explained/why-pm-narendra-modis-kabul-visit-matters/.

79. Suhasini Haider, 'India Rebuffs Afghanistan on Strategic Meet', *The Hindu* (29 August 2015), http://www.thehindu.com/news/national/ india-rebuffs-afghanistan-on-strategic-meet/article7592059.ece.

80. Ankit Pande, 'A Turning Point in Afghanistan–India Relations?' *The Diplomat* (24 November 2015), http://thediplomat.com/2015/11/ why-afghanistan-and-india-are-about-to-transform-their-relationship/.

81. 'Joint Statement between India and Afghanistan', Ministry of External Affairs, Government of India (December 2015), http:// www.mea.gov.in/bilateraldocuments.htm? dtl/26247/Joint+State ment+between+India+and+Afghanistan+December+25+2015.

82. 'Joint Statement during Visit of President of the Islamic Republic of Afghanistan to India' (28 April 2015), http://mea.gov.in/bilateral-documents.htm?dtl/25137/Joint+Statement+during+the+State+ Visit+of+President+of+Islamic+Republic+of+Afghanistan+to+In dia+April+28+2015.

83. 'Indo-Afghan Relations', Embassy of India, Kabul, http://eoi.gov. in/kabul/?0354?000.

84. M. Ashraf Haidari, 'Afghanistan Celebrates India's Post-Independence Achievements', *The Diplomat*, 18 August 2016, http://thediplomat.com/2016/08/afghanistan-celebrates-indias-post-independence-achievements/.

85. Sowba, 'India-Afghanistan Second Strategic Partnership Council Meeting, 2017', *Cloud Affairs*, 12 September 2017, https://www. affairscloud.com/india-afghanistan-second-strategic-partnership-council-meeting-2017/.

86. Shaida Abdali, 'Strengthening India-Afghanistan Strategic Relations in an Unceratain World', Brookings India Centre, 25 April 2017, https://www.brookings.edu/events/india-afghanistan-and-connec-tivity-in-south-asia-address-by-h-e-shaida-abdali-ambassador-of-afghanistan-to-india/.

87. Baisali Mohanti, 'India-China Rivalry Could Have Deadly Consequences for Afghanistan', *The Diplomat* (9 March 2017),

http://thediplomat.com/2017/03/china-india-rivalry-could-have-deadly-consequences-for-afghanistan/.

88. Lashkar-e-Taiba, http://web.stanford.edu/group/mappingmilitants/cgi-bin/groups/view/79.

89. Jaish-e-Muhammad, http://web.stanford.edu/group/mapping-militants/cgi-bin/groups/view/95. See also 'Interpol Issues Red Corner Notice against Jaish-e-Mohammad Chief Masood Azar', *Dawn* (18 May 2016), http://www.dawn.com/news/1259121.

90. '2016 Attack by Jaish-e-Muhammad on the Indian Air Force Base at Pathankot' (3 January 2016), https://en.wikipedia.org/wiki/2016_Pathankot_attack. Prior to this there had been an attack by the same organization in Gurdaspur, Punjab, on 27 July 2015. https://en.wikipedia.org/wiki/2015_Gurdaspur_attack.

91. Ankit Panda, 'India, Iran, Afghanistan Finalize Chabahar Port Agreement', *The Diplomat* (18 April 2016), https://en.wikipedia.org/wiki/2015_Gurdaspur_attack.

92. 'The Bangladesh Liberation War', https://en.wikipedia.org/wiki/Bangladesh_Liberation_War.

93. 'Lebensraum' or the territory that a state or nation believes is needed for its natural development,or 'living space', https://en.wikipedia.org/wiki/Lebensraum.

94. Smruti S. Pattanaik, 'Four Decades of India-Bangladesh Relations, Historical Imperatives and Future Directions', Institute for Defence Studies and Analyses, New Delhi (2012), http://www.idsa.in/system/files/book/book_indbang.pdf.

95. 'A Fresh Beginning to India-Bangladesh Relationship', Indian Council for World Affairs, New Delhi (19 August 2015), http://www.icwa.in/pdfs/VP/2014/BangladeshvisitofPMVP19082015.pdf.

96. 'Bangladesh-India Relations', https://en.wikipedia.org/wiki/Bangladesh%E2%80%93India_relations.

97. Syed Zain al-Mahmood, 'Bitter Political Rivalry Plunges Bangladesh into Chaos', *The Wall Street Journal* (22 February 2015), http://www.wsj.com/articles/bitter-political-rivalry-plunges-bangladesh-into-chaos-1424652921.

98. 'Sheikh Mujibur Rahman', https://en.wikipedia.org/wiki/Sheikh_Mujibur_Rahman.

99. 'Sheikh Hasina', https://en.wikipedia.org/wiki/Sheikh_Hasina.

100. 'Begum Khaleda Zia', https://en.wikipedia.org/wiki/Khaleda_Zia.

101. 'Ziaur Rahman', https://en.wikipedia.org/wiki/Ziaur_Rahman.

102. Jennifer Newton, 'Bangladesh Considering Abandoning Islam as Its Official Religion Following Wake of Extremist Attacks', *Mailonline* (2 March 2016), http://www.dailymail.co.uk/news/article-3473136/Bangladesh-considering-abandoning-Islam-official-religion-following-wake-extremist-attacks.html.

103. Maher Sattar and Ellen Barry, 'In 2 Minutes, Bangladesh Rejects 28-Year-Old Challenge to Islam's Role', *New York Times* (28 March 2016), https://www.nytimes.com/2016/03/29/world/asia/bangladesh-court-islam-state-religion.html.

104. Prakaash Nanda, 'Sheikh Hasina in India: Bangladesh PM Should Return Home with Her Head Held High, Notwithstanding the BNP Threat', Firstpost (11 April 2017), http://www.firstpost.com/world/sheikh-hasina-in-india-bangladesh-pm-should-return-home-with-her-head-high-notwithstanding-the-bnp-threat-3377952.html.

105. 'India–Bangladesh Land Boundary Agreement 1974', Ministry of External Affairs, Government of India, https://www.mea.gov.in/Uploads/PublicationDocs/24529_LBA_MEA_Booklet_final.pdf.

106. 'Presidential Assent to Land Boundary Agreement Ahead of PM Modi's Visit to Dhaka', *Economic Times* (1 June 2015), http://economictimes.indiatimes.com/news/politics-and-nation/presidential-assent-to-land-boundary-agreement-ahead-of-narendra-modis-visit-to-dhaka/articleshow/47503293.cms.

107. Haroon Habib, 'Bangladesh Wins Maritime Dispute with India', *The Hindu* (9 July 2014), http://www.thehindu.com/news/national/bangladesh-wins-maritime-dispute-with-india/article6191797.ece

108. 'Sharing the Water of the Ganges', https://en.wikipedia.org/wiki/Sharing_the_water_of_the_Ganges.

109. 'Tipaimukh Dam: What Is the Current Position?', *Hydropolitiks Academy* (1 February 2015), http://www.hidropolitikakademi.org/en/tipaimukh-dam-what-is-the-current-position.html.

110. Roomana Hukil, 'India–Bangladesh Relations: Significance of the Teesta Water-Sharing Agreement', IPCS, New Delhi (23 April 2014), http://www.ipcs.org/article/india/india-bangladesh-relations-significance-of-the-teesta-water-sharing-agreement-4403.html.

111. Uttam Kumar Sinha, 'Examining China's Hydrobehaviour', Institute for Defence Studies and Analyses, New Delhi (6 May 2011), http://www.idsa.in/event/ExaminingChinasHydrobehaviour.

112. 'Ganges-Brahmaputra Delta, Bangladesh', *Union of Concerned Scientists*, http://www.climatehotmap.org/global-warming-locations/ganges-brahmaputra-delta-bangladesh.html.

113. Jayanth Jacob, 'Five Things to Know about India-Bangladesh Ties: From Trade to Security', *Hindustan Times* (6 June 2015), http://www.hindustantimes.com/india/5-things-to-know-about-india-bangladesh-ties-from-trade-to-security/story-qgVND0m AQ4S1DpmYpzd5lJ.html.

114. 'Joint Declaration between Bangladesh and India During Visit of Prime Minister of India to Bangladesh-Notun Projonno-Nayi Disha', Ministry of External Affairs, Government of India (7 June 2015), http://www.mea.gov.in/bilateral/documents.htm?dtl/25346/Joint_Declaration_between_Bangladesh_and_India_during_Visit_of_Prime_Minister_of_India_to_Bangladesh_quot_N.

115. 'Illegal Migration to India', https://en.wikipedia.org/wiki/Illegal_immigration_to_India.

116. Bharti Jain, 'India Proposes Anti-Terror Pact with Bangladesh', *The Times of India* (20 February 2016), http://timesofindia.indiatimes.com/india/India-proposes-anti-terror-pact-with-Bangladesh/articleshow/46307043.cms.

117. Pankaj Patel, 'The Time is Right for India and Bangladesh', *The Hindu Business Line*, http://www.thehindubusinessline.com/opinion/sheikh-hasina-visit-and-india-bangladesh-trade/article9616091.ece.

118. Biswas Baral, 'India's Self-Defeating Paranoia over China in Nepal', *The Diplomat* (14 May 2016), http://thediplomat.com/2016/05/indias-self-defeating-paranoia-over-china-in-nepal/.

119. Prashant Jha, 'Nepali Secularism Has Pronounced Hindu Tilt', *Hindustan Times* (16 September 2015), http://www.hindustantimes.com/analysis/nepali-secularism-has-pronounced-hindu-tilt/story-W4C6pf4mDCK7eJsYvnGfOL.html.

120. Pushpita Das, 'Need to Effectively Manage the India-Nepal Border', Institute for Defence Studies and Analyses, New Delhi (19 September 2013), http://www.idsa.in/idsacomments/ManagetheIndiaNepalBorder_pdas_190913.

121. Madhvi Bhasin, 'India's Role in South Asia-Perceived Hegemony or Reluctant Leadership', *Indian Foreign Affairs Journal*, 2008, globalindiafoundation.org, http://www.globalindiafoundation.org/MadhaviBhasin.pdf.

122. Shastri Ramachandran, 'India Bristles as China Woos Nepal', *DNA* (30 March 2016), http://www.dnaindia.com/analysis/column-india-bristles-as-china-woos-nepal-2195550.

123. 'Indo-Nepal Treaty of Peace and Friendship', https://en.wikipedia.org/wiki/1950_Indo-Nepal_Treaty_of_Peace_and_Friendship.

124. 'Revised Treaty of Trade between the Government of India and Government of Nepal', Ministry of Commerce, Government of India (October 2009), http://commerce.nic.in/trade/nepal.pdf.

125. Lekhanath Pandey, 'Nepal Ready to Keep 1950 Treaty Title Intact', *The Himalayan*, Nepal (19 March 2017).

126. 'April 2015 Nepal Earthquake', *Wikipedia.org*, https://en.wikipedia. org/wiki/April_2015_Nepal_earthquake.

127. Ravi Pandalai, 'India's Humanitarian Assistance and Disaster Relief Effort in Nepal', Institute of Defence Studies and Analyses (15 May 2015), http://www.idsa.in/idsacomments/ IndiasHumanitarianAssistanceandDisasterRelief_spandalai_180515.

128. 'India Pledges USD 1 Billion Aid for Nepal's Reconstruction Programme', *The Indian Express* (25 June 2015),http://indianex-press.com/article/india/india-others/india-pledges-usd-1-billion-aid-for-nepals-reconstruction-programme/.

129. Utpal Parashar, 'Nepal Earthquake: Indian Media Faces Complaints against "Insensitivity"', *Hindustan Times* (4 May 2015), http:// www.hindustantimes.com/world/nepal-earthquake-indian-media-faces-complaints-about-insensitivity/story-uiDOy FUnKcxnwRdwFun9GL.html.

130. 'Comprehensive Peace Agreement Held between Government of Nepal and Communist Party of Nepal (Maoist)', http://www. brookings.edu/fp/projects/idp/Nepal_PeaceAgreement.pdf.

131. THT Online, 'Constituent Assembly transforms into Parliament after Promulgation of Nepal's Constitution', The Himalayan, September 20, 2015, https://thehimalayantimes.com/kath-mandu/constituent-assembly-dissolves-after-promulgation-of-nepals-constitution/.

132. Nihar Nayak, 'Imperative of PLA Integration into Nepalese Army', Institute of Defence Studies and Analyses, New Delhi, June 13, 2008, http://www.idsa.in/idsastrategiccomments/ ImperativeofPLAIntegrationintotheNepalArmy_NNayak_130608.

133. 'Nepal Adopts Historic Constitution amid Protests', Firstpost (21 September 2015), http://www.firstpost.com/world/nepal-adopts-historic-constitution-amid-protests-2440108.html.

134. Hari Bansh Jha, 'Nepal's New Constitution: An Analysis from the Madhesi Perspective', Institute of Defence Studies and Analyses, New Delhi (24 September 2015), http://www.idsa.in/idsacom-ments/NepalsNewConstitution_hbjha_240915.

135. '2015 Nepal Blockade', https://en.wikipedia.org/wiki/2015_ Nepal_blockade.

136. Rajeev Kumar, 'China–Nepal "All Weather Friendship": Should India be Wary?' *Indian Defence Review* (10 April 2016), http://www.indiandefencereview.com/spotlights/china-nepal-all-weather-friendship-should-india-be-wary/.

137. Yubaraja Ghirme, '2014 and Beyond: India-Nepal Agree to Refresh 1950 Treaty', *The Indian Express* (5 August 2015), http://indianexpress.com/article/world/neighbours/india-nepal-agree-to-review-adjust-update-1950-treaty/.

138. AM Republica, 'Nepal-India EPG Meet Agrees to Scrap Unequal Provisions in 1950 Treaty', My Republica, l6 April 2017 published on 1 October 2017, http://www.myrepublica.com/news/17717/.

139. Rajeev Ranjan Chaturvedy and David M. Malone, 'Hydro-Diplomacy: A Neglected Opportunity for Nepal and India', *The Hindu* (27 June 2011), http://www.thehindu.com/opinion/op-ed/hydrodiplomacy-a-neglected-opportunity-for-nepal-and-india/article2139749.ece.

140. R. Hariharan, 'The Angularities of India, China and Sri Lanka Ties', *The Citizen Daily* (26 May 2016), http://www.thecitizen.in/index.php/OldNewsPage/?Id=136.

141. P.K. Balachandran, 'Sri Lanka on Way to Becoming Indian Ocean Naval Hub', *The Indian Express* (19 January 2016), http://www.newindianexpress.com/world/Sri-Lanka-on-Way-to-Becoming-Indian-Ocean-Naval-Hub/2016/01/19/article3234701.ece.

142. 'Adam's Bridge', https://en.wikipedia.org/wiki/Adam%27s_Bridge.

143. 'Sinhalese people', https://en.wikipedia.org/wiki/Sinhalese_people.

144. 'Sri Lanka Tamils', https://en.wikipedia.org/wiki/Sri_Lankan_Tamils.

145. 'Indian Tamils of Sri Lanka', https://en.wikipedia.org/wiki/Indian_Tamils_of_Sri_Lanka.

146. 'Hambantota Project Talks with China Should be Speeded Up: China', *Economic Times* (8 April 2016), http://articles.economictimes.indiatimes.com/2016-04-08/news/72161495_1_hambantota-port-colombo-port-city-project-maithripala-sirisena.

147. 'China, Sri Lanka to Redefine Colombo Port City Project', *The Hindu* (10 April 2016), http://www.thehindu.com/news/international/china-and-sri-lanka-decide-to-make-port-city-into-a-financial-hub-as-part-of-20-year-plan/article8455509.ece.

148. Rajendra Abhyankar, 'India-Sri-Lanka Relations: Future Imperfect', in Shrikant Paranjpe and Rajendra Abhyankar (eds), *India and Sri Lanka: Future Imperfect* (New Delhi: G.B. Books, 2014), pp. 13–45.

149. 'Indo-Sri Lanka Agreement to Establish Peace and Normalcy in Sri Lanka' (29 July 1987), http://www.satp.org/satporgtp/countries/shrilanka/document/papers/indo_srilanks_agreement.htm.

150. R. Hariharan, 'Looking Back at the Indo-Sri Lanka Accord', *The Hindu* (29 July 2010), http://www.thehindu.com/opinion/lead/looking-back-at-the-indosri-lanka-accord/article538650.ece.

151. Dilip Bobb, 'Running out of Time, Delhi Talks Focus on a New Treaty', *Indian Today* (29 February 1988), http://indiatoday.intoday.in/story/sri-lanka-wants-long-term-friendship-treaty-with-india-to-salvage-prestige-at-home/1/328996.html.

152. Frances Harrison, *Still Counting the Dead, Survivors of Sri Lanka's Hidden War* (London: Portobello Books, 2012).

153. Muhammad Akbar Notezai, 'Interview: Patrick Mendis: A Discussion of Sri Lanka's Foreign Policy under President Maithripala Sirisena', *The Diplomat* (30 April 2016), http://thediplomat.com/2016/04/interview-patrick-mendis/.

154. V. Suryanarayana, 'India, Sri Lanka and the Kachchatheevu Crisis', IPCS, New Delhi (6 May 2013), http://www.ipcs.org/article/india/india-sri-lanka-and-the-kachchatheevu-crisis-a-fact-sheet-3917.html.

155. 'Indo-Sri Lanka Free Trade Agreement (ISFTA), Sri Lanka Export Development Board (EDB)', April 2014, http://www.srilanka-business.com/pdf/indosrilankaedbfinal.pdf.

156. T. Ramachandran, 'No to CEPA but Nod for Economic and Technology Collaboration with India: Ranil', *The Hindu* (9 December 2015), http://www.thehindu.com/news/international/sri-lanka-will-never-sign-cepa-with-india-pm-wickremesinghe/article7966271.ece.

157. 'Bhutan Country Profile', *BBC* (11 October 2015), http://www.bbc.com/news/world-south-asia-12480707.

158. Smruti S. Pattanaik, 'Modi's Maiden Foreign Visit: Consolidating Bharat for Bhutan Relations', Institute for Defence Studies and Analyses, New Delhi (18 June 2014), http://www.idsa.in/idsa-comments/ModisBhutanVisit_sspattanaik_180614.

159. 'India-Bhutan Friendship Treaty, 2007', http://carnegieendowment.org/newsletters/SAP/pdf/march07/india_bhutan_treaty.pdf

160. Akhilesh Pillalamarri and Aswin Subanthore, 'What Do the Bhutanese People Think About Doklam?', *The Diplomat*, 14 August 2017, http://thediplomat.com/2017/08/what-do-the-bhutanese-people-think-about-doklam/.

161. Pillalamarri and Subanthore, 'What Do the Bhutanese People Think About Doklam?'.

162. CIA, The World Factbook, The Maldives, https://www.cia.gov/library/publications/the-world-factbook/geos/mv.html.

163. Sudha Ramachandran, 'The Maldives: Losing a Tourist Paradise to Terrorism', The Jamestown Foundation, Terrorism Monitor: 14(2) (22 January 2016), https://jamestown.org/program/the-maldives-losing-a-tourist-paradise-to-terrorism/.

164. James Dorsey, 'Why Saudi Arabia, China and Islamic State are courting the Maldives', This Week in Asia, 12 March 2017, http://www.scmp.com/week-asia/geopolitics/article/2077913/why-saudi-arabia-china-and-islamic-state-are-courting-maldives.

165. Damian Carrington, 'The Maldives Is an Extreme Test Case for Climate Change Action', The Guardian, 26 September 2013, http://www.theguardian.com/environment/damian-carrington-blog/2013/sep/26/maldives-test-case-climate-change-action.

166. Damian Carrington, 'The Maldives, a Fledgling Democracy at the Vanguard of Climate Change', Grist (26 September 2013), http://grist.org/climate-energy/the-maldives-a-fledgling-democracy-at-the-vanguard-of-climate-change/.

167. K. Deepalakshmi, 'India Maldives Relations at a Glance', The Hindu (20 April 2016), http://www.thehindu.com/specials/indiamaldives-relations-at-a-glance/article8460835.ece.

168. P. Stobdan, 'Asia's Buddhist Connectivity and India's Role', Institute of Defence Studies and Analyses, New Delhi (19 February 2016), http://www.idsa.in/issuebrief/asias-buddhist-connectivity-and-indias-role_pstobdan_190216.

169. 'Pranab Mukherjee Recalls Indian support to China's UN membership', NDTV (26 May 2016), http://www.ndtv.com/india-news/pranab-mukherjee-recalls-indian-support-to-chinas-un-membership-1412538.

170. Prashant Kumar Singh's review of book by Tien-sze Fang, Asymmetrical Threat Perception in India-China Relations (Oxford University Press, 2014) in Journal of Defence Studies, 9(41): 145–50, http://www.idsa.in/system/files/jds/jds_9_4_2015_tienszeFangChina.pdf.

171. 'Doctrine of Panchsheel as the Core Principles of Nonalignment', Ministry of External Affairs, New Delhi, www.mea.gov.in/Uploads/PublicationDocs/191_panchsheel.pdf.

172. 'Events Leading up to the Sino-Indian War 1959–62', https://en.wikipedia.org/wiki/Events_leading_to_the_Sino-Indian_War.

173. Claude Arpi, 'Why Mao Attacked India in 1962', *Indian Defence Review* (31 May 2016), http://www.indiandefencereview.com/spotlights/maos-return-to-power-passed-through-india/.

174. 'China-India Relations', https://en.wikipedia.org/wiki/China%E2%80%93India_relations.

175. 'Agreement between the Government of the Peoples' Republic of China and the Government of the Republic of India on the Maintenance of Peace and Tranquillity along the Line of Actual Control in the China-India Border Areas', 7 September 1993, http://in.chineseembassy.org/eng/ssygd/zygx/xy/t80697.htm.

176. 'India, China Hold New Round of Talks to Resolve Border Dispute', *The Indian Express* (20 April 2016), http://indianexpress.com/article/india/india-news-india/india-china-hold-new-round-of-talks-to-resolve-border-dispute/.

177. 'Ready to "Accelerate" Talks with India to Resolve Border Dispute: China', *The Economic Times* (23 May 2016), http://economictimes.indiatimes.com/news/defence/ready-to-accelerate-talks-with-india-to-resolve-border-dispute-china/articleshow/52400885.cms.

178. 'Agreement between the Government of the Republic of India and the Government of the People's Republic of China on the Political Parameters and Guiding Principles for Settlement of the India-China Boundary Question', Ministry of External Affairs, Government of India (11 April 2005), http://www.mea.gov.in/bilateral-documents.htm?dtl/6534/Agreement+between+the+Government+of+the+Republic+of+India+and+the+Government+of+the+Peoples+Republic+of+China+on+the+Political+Parameters+and+Guiding+Principles+for+the+Settlement+of+the+IndiaChina+Boundary+Question#.

179. 'India-China Agreement on the Establishment of a Working Mechanism for Consultation and Coordination on India-China Border Affairs', Ministry of External Affairs, Government of India (17 January 2012), http://mea.gov.in/bilateral-documents.htm?dtl/17963/IndiaChina+Agreement+on+the+Establishment+of+a+Working+Mechanism+for+Consultation+and+Coordination+on+IndiaChina+Border+Affairs#.

180. 'India China Hold Talks to Boost Defence Ties', *The Tribune* (9 April 2015), http://www.tribuneindia.com/news/nation/india-china-hold-talks-to-boost-defence-ties/64799.html.

181. Atul Aneja, 'Parrikar's Arrival Signals Acceleration in India China Security Dialogue', *The Hindu* (18 April 2016), http://www.

thehindu.com/news/national/parrikars-arrival-signals-accelera-tion-in-indiachina-security-dialogue/article8486575.ece.

182. Sutirto Parthanobis, 'Doval Raises Masood Azhar with China during Talks on Terror, Border', *Hindustan Times* (21 April 2016), http://www.hindustantimes.com/india/doval-raises-masood-azhar-with-china-during-talks-on-terror-border/story-IMXM3UDNMCYpt8N4BJSFyI.html.

183. Express Web Desk, 'BRICS Summit 2017: Full Text of BRICS Leaders Declaration at Xiamen, China', 4 September 2017, http://indianexpress.com/article/india/brics-summit-2017-full-text-of-declaration-signed-at-xiamen-china-russia-brazil-south-africa-brazil-4828219/.

184. PTI, 'China Avoids Masood Azhar Ban After BRICS Declaration Names His Terror Group', 4 September 2017, https://www.ndtv.com/india-news/china-avoids-masood-azhar-ban-after-brics-declaration-names-his-terror-group-1745931.

185. Ashlyn Anderson and Alyssa Ayres, 'Economics of Influence: China and India in South Asia', Council on Foreign Relations, Washington, DC (7 August 2015), http://www.cfr.org/econom-ics/economics-influence-china-india-south-asia/p36862.

186. 'China-India Economic and Trade Relations', Embassy of India, Beijing, http://www.indianembassy.org.cn/DynamicContent.aspx?MenuId=97&SubMenuId=0.

187. ET Bureau, 'China President Xi's India Visit: Five Year Trade and Economic Development Plan Signed', *Economic Times*, 19 September 2014, http://economictimes.indiatimes.com/news/politics-and-nation/china-president-xis-india-visit-five-year-trade-and-economic-development-plan-signed/articleshow/42846651.cms.

188. Thomas E. Kellog, 'The China-India Border Standoff: What does Beijing Want?', *The Chicago Tribune*, 1 September 2017, http://www.chicagotribune.com/news/sns-wp-china-india-comment-3c5af5c4-8f4a-11e7-84c0-02cc069f2c37-20170901-story.html.

189. Daniel S. Markey, 'Armed Confrontation between China and India', Council on Foreign Relations, Washington, DC (27 November 2015), http://www.cfr.org/china/armed-confrontation-between-china-india/p37228.

190. Gulshan Luthra, 'India Fails to Get MCTR Membership but Earns Wide Support', *Business Standard* (12 October 2015), http://www.business-standard.com/article/news-ians/india-s-fails-to-get-mtcr-membership-but-wins-wide-support-115101200544_1.html.

191. Varghese K. George and Atul Aneja, 'US Backs but China Opposes India's NSG Bid', *The Hindu* (15 May 2016), http://www.thehindu.com/news/national/us-backs-but-china-opposes-indias-nsg-bid/article8601776.ece.

192. Tom Kington and Vivek Raghuvanshi, 'Italy Blocks Indian Application to MTCR', *Defence News* (17 October 2015), http://www.defensenews.com/story/defense/policy-budget/warfare/2015/10/17/italy-blocks-indian-application-mtcr-uav-missile-technology-control-regime/74019832/.

193. Wassenaar Arrangement (The Wassenaar Arrangement on Export Controls for Conventional Weapons and Dual Use Goods and Technologies) on which the United States supports India's entry. https://en.wikipedia.org/wiki/Wassenaar_Arrangement.

194. The Australia Group is an informal group of countries (now joined by the European Commission) established in 1985 (after the use of chemical weapons by Iraq in 1984) to help member countries to identify those exports which need to be controlled so as not to contribute to the spread of chemical and biological weapons. President Obama, during his visit to India in November 2010, agreed to support India's entry to the group. https://en.wikipedia.org/wiki/Australia_Group.

195. Farzana Sheikh, 'India and Pakistan Bring Risks to Shanghai Cooperation Organization', *Chatham House*, London (10 July 2015), https://www.chathamhouse.org/expert/comment/india-and-pakistan-bring-risks-shanghai-cooperation-organization.

196. Yashwant Raj, 'Trump to Skip India in Asia Tour, but could Meet Modi' Hindustan Times, 29 September 2017, http://www.hindustantimes.com/world-news/trump-to-skip-india-in-asia-tour-but-could-meet-modi/story-cueDBOjDlvWb0ddemKoa1J.html.

197. Rachel Middleton, 'World Bank's Rival Asian Infrastructure Bank Launched by China with 100 Billion Capital', *The International Business Times* (18 January 2016), http://www.ibtimes.co.uk/world-banks-rival-asian-infrastructure-investment-bank-launched-by-china-100b-capital-1538463.

198. James T. Areddy, 'Brics Development Bank Pins Hope on China's Bond Sale', *The Wall Street Journal* (10 March 2016), http://www.wsj.com/articles/brics-development-bank-pins-hope-on-china-bond-sale-1457613691.

199. C. Raja Mohan, 'Delhi Seems Ready to Compete with Beijing Where It Must and Cooperate Where It Can', *The Indian Express*

(16 April 2016), http://indianexpress.com/article/opinion/columns/india-china-dialogue-towards-new-realism-2755457/.

200. Rajiv Bhatia, 'India-Myanmar Relations: A Critical Review', *Voice of India*, 9 August 2012, http://voiceof.india.com/india-myanmar-relations-chat-with-ambassador-rajiv-bhatia/india-myanmar-relations-a-critical-review.

201. K. Yhome, 'The Importance of Modi's Visit to Myanmar', *India Writes*, 1 October 2017, http://www.indiawrites.org/the-importance-of-modis-visit-to-myanmar/.

202. Huizhong Wu, 'Indian Prime Minister Blames Rohingya Violence on Extremists', CNN, 7 September 2017, http://www.cnn.com/2017/09/06/asia/modi–india-myanmar-rohingya/index.html.

203. Sudha Ramachandran, 'The Trouble with India's Projects in Myanmar', *The Diplomat* (21 September 2016), https://thediplomat.com/2016/09/the-trouble-with-indias-projects-in-myanmar/.

204. Ramachandran, 'The Trouble with India's Projects in Myanmar'.

205. Namrata Goswami, 'China at Your Doorstep: Looking East from India's Northeast', Institute for Defence Studies and Analyses, New Delhi (18 March 2014), http://www.idsa.in/issuebrief/Chinaatyourdoorstep_ngoswami_180314.

206. Wasbir Hussain, 'What India's "Hot Pursuit" Strategy Is and Is Not', *The Wire* (11 June 2015), http://thewire.in/2015/06/11/what-indias-hot-pursuit-strategy-is-and-is-not-3690/.

207. https://en.wikipedia.org/wiki/Bay_of_Bengal_Initiative_for_Multi-Sectoral_Technical_and_Economic_Cooperation.

208. P.K. Bhattacharya, 'BIMSTEC Shows Way to Regional Cooperation', *The New Indian Express* (27 June 2015), http://www.newindian-express.com/world/BIMSTEC-Shows-the-Way-to-Regional-Cooperation/2015/06/27/article2889146.ece.

209. Bay of Bengal Initiative for Multi-Sectoral Technical and Economic Cooperation, https://en.wikipedia.org/wiki/Bay_of_Bengal_Initiative_for_Multi-Sectoral_Technical_and_Economic_Cooperation#BIMSTEC_Summits.

210. Arendt Michael, 'The Story of Four Lost Groupings', *Business Line* (9 May 2015), http://www.thehindubusinessline.com/opinion/story-of-four-lost-regional-groupings/article6975236.ece.

CHAPTER TWO

Conjoint Legacy

*I*ndia's continuous and historic relationship with its extended neighbourhood, comprising Iran, Iraq, Yemen, and the GCC (Gulf Cooperation Council) countries, during the British period has today flourished through political exchanges, trade and investments, tourism and pilgrimage, and people-to-people contact.[1] Over seven million Indians live and work in this region, mainly in the GCC countries, sending back remittances annually of USD 68.91 billion (figure in 2015).[2] They are India's closest sources of crude oil and a major destination for its exports. The annual Haj pilgrimage sees about 200,000 Indian Muslims going to Mecca, Medina, and other Shia pilgrimage sites in Iraq, Iran, and Syria. India also cooperates with these countries on defence and security, counterterrorism, and intelligence exchange.

Minister of State for External Affairs M.J. Akbar's visit to Iraq, Syria, and Lebanon from 21–23 August 2016[3] aimed at resuscitating India's relations with the Arab and Muslim world.[4] The idea was to strengthen economic relations with the countries of the region, assure access to oil, and assess the costs and benefits of enhanced relations with Iraq and Syria presently beset with sectarian conflict. The visit complemented that of Prime Minister Modi's to Saudi Arabia and Iran—arch-rivals for strategic hegemony in the region—and to United Arab Emirates (UAE) and Qatar to explore options for expanding Indian footprint in the region.

The two visits also balance Modi's visit, in July 2017, to Israel.[5–7] Given the large size of the Iranian market and its importance in facilitating India's access to Afghanistan and Central Asia, Indian policy aims, particularly, at deepening its interdependence with Iran. This will also underpin India's relations with Iraq and Syria. Indian economic and strategic relations with Iraq have declined since the US–led invasion of 2003, while relations with Syria have been politically close. Since Iraq and Yemen are, for the greater part, embroiled in wars and sectarian strife, investments and trade in the oil and gas sector still remain the significant highlights in those countries. While India's relations with Saudi Arabia and Iran are equally important, India will have to manage the triangular balance of its relations between them.

The first historically recorded maritime trade route in the world was, in fact, between the Indus valley civilization and the civilization of Dilmun, which was located on the island of Bahrain and the adjacent shore of Saudi Arabia. By 2000 BCE, Dilmun acquired a monopoly on trade between the Indian subcontinent and the civilizations of Mesopotamia. Records and historical artefacts demonstrate that traders from Dilmun stayed for extended periods in South Asia and vice versa. They traded in cotton and spices that were not available at home. Eventually, Arab traders from Yemen and Oman dominated the trade between India and the Arabian Peninsula. In Roman times, Yemen was the conduit for some highly valued types of incense, both natively sourced and traded from India. At the same time, Oman was dominating the IO trade between India, the Middle East, and East Africa. By the end of the 1st millennium CE, trade between India and Arabia became the economic backbone of the Arabian Peninsula.

Interestingly, most goods flowed from India toward Arabia. The latter had little to export to India except the currency used to purchase spices, cloth, and other goods. One exception to this rule, however, was the pearl industry, which was the most important export of the Gulf region until the discovery of oil. Pearl diving was a way of life in places like Basra, Abu Dhabi, Dubai, and Qatar. The Basra pearls were highly coveted in India.

Relations between the Gulf region and India grew even stronger during the British Raj, when they acquired a strategic–military component in addition to an economic one. By the mid-19th century, the British had come to dominate the subcontinent. British influence and control over Arab territory mostly flowed because of the British need to protect sea lanes. The British established a protectorate over Abu Dhabi in 1820 and conquered Aden in 1839, administered as a province of British India. Later on, protectorates were established over Oman, Qatar, Kuwait, Bahrain, Dubai, and the other states that would make up the UAE. British affairs in Gulf Arab states were all administered by British officials in India and were garrisoned mostly by Indian soldiers under British command.

The relationship between India and the Gulf states began to reverse after Indian independence and upon the discovery of oil. The balance of trade, with crude oil exports bulking large, began to shift more in favour of the Gulf kingdoms. Yet independent India could not tie the Gulf kingdoms economically in the way the British had done. The Gulf countries used the Indian rupee as currency, which, at India's independence, was pegged to the British pound. In 1959, India introduced the Gulf rupee, a separate currency, for the Gulf region. At the devaluation in 1966 of the Indian rupee, the Gulf states introduced their own currencies, Oman being the last to do so in 1970.

Despite India's inward economic turn after independence, India had important relations with the Gulf region. By the 21st century, India was exporting more to the Gulf region than the EU. For example, in the '2012–13 financial year, India exported $51 billion to the GCC, mostly food, garments, jewellery and petrochemicals', according to the *Financial Times*.[8] About 15 per cent of India's exports go to the Gulf. India was also Dubai's largest trade partner until 2013 when China surpassed it.

Relations with the GCC transformed after 2000 owing to India's economic success following its economic liberalization process. Previously perceived as a source of professional manpower and a market for their crude oil, India is now seen as an equal economic partner. Two-way investment collaborations in a wide range of industry and real estate has become the norm.

With political and economic changes in the region the position and importance of the IO has also changed and enhanced the demands on India's role in that region. Will the religious, political, and economic catharsis the region is undergoing change India's equities and prospects there?

The Chhatrapati Shivaji Maharaj Vastu Sangrahalaya (formerly the Prince of Wales Museum), Mumbai, holds archaeological artefacts from Iraq[9] which were acquired when Iraq was administered by the British colonial government from Mumbai (formerly Bombay). This was the case with all the countries which give out on the Persian Gulf, except Iran. If not for the waters, all these countries would have been India's contiguous neighbours. The British Indian Amy had fought in theatres of war across the region, from the countries of the lower Gulf all the way up to Turkey. Between Turkey and India, there was no overarching power with a continental reach.

Iraq

A Brief History[10]

Links between India and Mesopotamia go back to 1800 BCE and have encompassed trade, commerce, literature, and religion.[11] During the colonial period, Iraq was administered from Mumbai. India established diplomatic relations with Iraq immediately on its independence in 1947 when it was still under the British. The Treaty of Friendship (1952) between the two countries set the tenor of their relations. Although part of the US-sponsored Central Treaty Organization (CENTO)[12], commonly known as the 'Baghdad Pact', Iraq joined NAM[13] on the assumption of power by the Arab Ba'ath Socialist Party (ABSP)[14] in 1958. The ABSP continued in power till Saddam Hussein was ousted in 2003, while its remnants provided the nucleus for the ISIL.[15]

With Iraq, India successfully harnessed its pre-colonial contact to build a strong relationship, particularly after the ABSP took power in 1963, centred in the early years on the supply of crude oil.[16] The fact that the Baa'th Movement strictly distinguished between authority of the state and religious authority made it more acceptable to the secular ethos of the Indian state. Iraq and India remained close allies, following their respective independence from the British, based on the historic contact between their peoples.

The relationship received much ballast in the post-independence period first with the indispensability of Iraqi oil, followed by Iraq's adoption of non-alignment in external policy. In the 1980s, Iraq's need of Indian technical, managerial, and teaching professionals, military training and Indian skilled, semi-skilled, and unskilled labour for the country's economic development became a vital point of contact and a reason for mutually beneficially bilateral relations. All this meant continued Iraqi political support to India in international forums, including the Islamic Conference Organization. India's bilateral relationship was marked by Iraq's consistent political support on the Kashmir issue during the Saddam Hussein years (1968–2003)[17] and economic cooperation based on Iraq's position as one of India's two largest suppliers of crude oil.

Politics[18]

Iraq's continuous embroilment, for the four decades after 1980, in wars meant continued political support but a scaling down of economic relations, including, crucially, the supply of oil. Saddam Hussein's recurrent obsession with possessing the Nuclear Bomb saw its attempt to build a reactor being demolished by Israeli military aircraft.[19] Saddam Hussein's megalomania led the country into the Iraq–Iran War which lasted almost for a decade (1980–88), the invasion of Kuwait, and its reversal by the UN-mandated Gulf War I (1990–91) followed by the UN sanctions, the Oil-for-Food programme (1996), and the US invasion and subsequent occupation (2003–11) based on a spurious case of possession of weapons of mass destruction.

Never in recent memory was any country subjected for so long to continuous external wars either by its own leadership or by outside powers. Among Iraqi families, there is not one left which has not lost a member in the wars. Moreover, most of the population up to the age of 40 would have only seen war, terror, and civil strife.

The United States' invasion of Iraq, which ousted Saddam Hussein and the Ba'athist regime, and the ensuing sectarian conflict and insurgency, influenced bilateral relations between India and Iraq. Lacking a UN Security Council mandate under Chapter VII of the Charter, India opposed the invasion. The events surrounding India's position brought about a major change in the way foreign policy decisions were seen by Indians. This was the first time a foreign policy issue was decided on the Indian streets and against the government's preferred option. Thanks to a vociferous public opposition in major cities, the United States' request to the Indian government for a provision of 15,000-strong combatant troops for northern Iraq did not secure the Indian parliament's approval.[20] The making of Indian foreign policy, for the first time, had descended to the Indian streets.

Bilateral relations remained at a low key even though India kept its diplomatic representation open. During this period, India stayed out of taking a position on developments in Iraq. A semblance of normality was achieved from 2005 when the first elected government took office under Nouri al-Maliki, although under continuing US occupation. There was no respite in religiously motivated violence against the Sunnis during his two terms, with alleged complicity of government forces and Shia militia. The US withdrawal, at the end of 2011, a signal for the restoration of Iraqi sovereignty, only ended up fuelling sentiments in favour of autonomy by diverse groups, including the Kurds, and the continued alienation of the minority Sunnis who formed the core of the ISIL.

Oil

Until the Iraq–Iran War began in 1980, Iraq provided 50 per cent of India's crude oil requirement. Gulf War I in 1991, which reversed Saddam Hussein's invasion of Kuwait, was yet again a cause for disruption of Iraqi oil supplies. The destruction of its oil facilities meant that supply from Iraq was minimal until after Gulf War II in 2003 and the US occupation. It also led to a review of exploration blocs granted to India by Saddam Hussein. In its quest for energy security, India has pursued the restoration of these contracts. India's corporate sector oil majors who had taken exploration contracts in Iraqi Kurdistan had to sell them due to the continuing uncertainty on ownership and revenue-sharing between the central Iraqi government and the regional government of Iraqi Kurdistan. Nevertheless, with its increasing oil production and

falling oil prices during 2017 India's oil imports from Iraq and
Iran have been leap-frogging each other. Nevertheless, Saudi
Arabia remains the largest supplier[21] although the scenario is
likely to change with oil prices expected to rise strongly in early
2018.[22] India sources a major portion of its crude oil requirements
from the Gulf region that includes Iran, Saudi Arabia, Kuwait, and
Qatar, all of whom are involved in the unrest in the region stemming from the long-running Syrian civil war.[23]

Project and Manpower Exports

Saddam Hussein's zeal to build Iraq in the late 1970s led to India,
for the first time, realizing its potential in manpower exports
and in civil, mechanical, and electrical infrastructure projects. In
1980, when the Iraq–Iran War started, Indian companies had a
contract value of USD 3 billion and 22,000 skilled and unskilled
manpower in Iraq. In addition, there were Indian doctors, engi-
neers, and teachers working with the Iraqi government. India also
provided military training to the Iraqi Army and Air Force both
in situ and in Indian institutions. The experience gained in Iraq
was leveraged in later years into a major foreign exchange earner.

The eight-year-long Iraq–Iran War disrupted oil supplies from
both countries and led to an India-led NAM initiative to broker
peace. The end of the war became possible when the two bel-
ligerents had nothing left to achieve. Iran eventually regained all
its territories lost to Iraq and access to the Shatt al-Arab. Iraq was
forced to withdraw as the long war had become untenable both
from the point of view of resources and funds, as the country saw
a downslide from the economic boom of the 1980s. While the
United States was supportive of Iraq in order to curb Iran, eventually, with the growing strength of the latter, a 'dual containment'
policy was put into place.

India's Repatriation Policy Changes

For India, it catalysed a policy challenge relating to the repatriation of Indian nationals from abroad, particularly in the Middle
East. Hitherto government policy had decreed that no one would
be repatriated at government cost, not distinguishing between

Indians long settled abroad and nationals who worked there. The repatriation in October 1980, at government cost, of over 10,000 Indian from Iraq was the first time that the Indian government assumed financial responsibility for bringing its people home.[24]

This precedent was subsequently used in crises in Sri Lanka (1983), Lebanon (2006), and Libya (2011). With the continuing instability in the region, repatriation of Indian nationals has now become a national policy. The economic success of Indians abroad has also led to a conscious policy catering to persons of Indian origin (PIOs) and non-resident Indians (NRIs).[25] A corollary of this interest has been the active role that the Indian government has taken to rescue Indians kidnapped by radical Islamic groups in the region. The inter-mixing of insurgencies by radical Islamic groups throughout the region, particularly in Iraq, Yemen, and Syria, has meant that freeing Indians abducted while working on Indian projects has become an important part of the country's outreach.

India's relationship with Iraq changed with the disappearance of secular ethos in Arab political thought.[26] Future governments in Iraq will be based on Islam which alone gives political power to Iraq's Shia majority. The need to establish a democratic structure that gives rights to the Sunni and other religious minorities remains a challenge. A halfway house seems to have been reached, a la Lebanon, with a confessional distribution of the posts of president, prime minister, and speaker of the house. Yet until the minority Sunnis, who ruled during Saddam's time, secure their political rights the system's future will remain uncertain.

For India, the challenge is to find a via media to deal with an Iraqi government with its religious orientation and imbued with optics different from the professed secular government of Saddam Hussein. In renewing its relationship with Iraq, India still needs to delineate the elements that will strike a balance of advantage for both sides.

Iran[27]

Prime Minister Narendra Modi's visit to Iran was an opportunity to craft a strategic relationship with the country and to enhance

India's influence in West Asia.[28] The centrepiece of the trip was the basket of agreements on the development of the Chabahar Port and onward connectivity with Afghanistan. The set of interlinked outcomes following the contract for the development and operation for 10 years of two terminals and five berths included the extension of credit lines of USD 500 million for the port and of Rs 30,000 million for importing steel rails. MoUs were also signed on the provision of services by Indian Railways, including financing to the tune of USD 1.6 billion, for the Chabahar–Zahedan railway line that is also part of the trilateral agreement between India, Iran, and Afghanistan on a transit and trade corridor.

At the same time, Iran has made it clear that it will not be averse to the linking, by road and rail, of the Chinese-controlled and constructed Gwadar port in Pakistan. India–Pakistan rivalry in the region is at the heart of apprehensions that their opposing interests could deny both Chabahar and Gwadar ports the potential to become the fulcrum of development in Central Asia and the region. The membership of the Shanghai Cooperation Organisation (SCO) by India and Pakistan and Iran's likely entry opens the possibility of that organization becoming the catalyst of reducing conflicting interests and promoting all round growth.[29] Much will depend on India's being able to construct the port on time and develop the road/rail network connection through Afghanistan. While Tehran has kept negotiations going on the giant Farzad B gas field exclusively for Indian investment it still appears to look for other international bidders.[30]

A Brief History

India's ties with Iran are historic, encompassing trade, culture, language, and literature. During the colonial period, the protection of its dominion in Iraq and the goal of winning Iran's oil-rich provinces were major markers. India opened diplomatic relations with Iran in 1950, although the former's adherence to NAM and proximity to the USSR and the latter's US-backed regime of the Shah of Iran made the relationship distant. India was one of the first countries to recognize the government after the Islamic revolution of 1979 led by Imam Khomeini.

Iran–India relations developed on a broader basis in the 1990s[31] owing to the importance of Iran's geographic location spanning across South, Central, and West Asia. For India, relations with Iran thereafter attained strategic significance on four counts: for its energy security, for access to pursue its interests in Central Asia, owing to its status as a major Muslim country, and for its potential to influence events in Afghanistan, Pakistan, and the Gulf. India's conduct of successful relations with Iran has imposed the need to balance these relations within the three strategic triangles whose third axes are Saudi Arabia, Israel, and the United States, respectively.[32]

This has particularly been in evidence after the US invasions of Afghanistan (2001) and Iraq (2003), UN and US sanctions on Iran's nuclear programme, and Israel's belligerent stand on the issue. India and Iran both opposed the Taliban rule in Afghanistan and supported the Northern Alliance during 1996–2001. Yet they have differed on the issue of the continued presence of the United States in Afghanistan.

Iran's centrality to Pakistan, Afghanistan, and Iraq has given it crucial leverage in current developments in all three regions. India has strived with some difficulty to maintain bilateral relations on an even keel, playing up the convergence of their views. The increasing differences between Iran and Saudi Arabia remain a concern for India.

Nuclear Issue

India expected Iran, as signatory of the NPT, to clarify its nuclear programme and opposed it in the International Atomic Energy Agency (IAEA) meetings in 2010. India was acutely conscious that Iran's acquiring nuclear weapons capability would put further pressure on an already fraught situation in the neighbourhood. Nevertheless, India observed UN sanctions and went some distance in meeting US sanctions at a significant cost to its energy security. It supported the talks between the UN P-5+1 and Iran to resolve the issue. The Joint Comprehensive Plan of Action reached in July 2015[33] between the P-5+1, mainly the United States and Iran, which came into force on 16 January 2016 puts a cap on Iran's nuclear weapons development for 15 years and places strict limits on its nuclear enrichment activity. In return, Iran's financial resources, which had been sequestered in US and European banks, have been freed and it is now able to build its exports of crude oil. It has empowered Iran to take a more active role supporting the governments in Syria and Iraq. Iran has indicated its readiness to work with the US in both countries against ISIL. President Trump's decision on continuing with the Iran Nuclear Deal (JCPOA[34]) still remains open. Until now, even the Trump administration has had to concede, however grudgingly, that Iran has abided by the JCPOA's requirements. Not renewing the certification for JCPOA will deny IAEA nuclear inspectors' access and, more importantly once again spur development by Iran of its nuclear weapons.[35,36]

Oil and Natural Gas

Iran provided about 50 per cent of India's crude oil requirements before the Iraq–Iran War (1980). The supply was disrupted after the imposition of UN and US sanctions on the country. Iran in 2016–17 was the second largest oil supplier when India imported 542,400 bpd from Iran, compared to 225,522 bpd a year earlier. Average oil volumes supplied by Iran over this period were the highest on record. However, in 2017–18 India has decided to reduce its oil offtake from Iran due to delay in finalization of the Farzand B gas field in India's favour.[37] India is an important supplier of petroleum products to Iran and has a major interest in oil and gas exploration and prospection contracts in the country.

Indian trade and industry have made important strides with Iran and bilateral annual trade turnover in 2015 was USD 15 billion.

Transit to Central Asia

In the context of continuing denial of transit facilities by Pakistan, Iran has become India's gateway to Central Asia and Afghanistan. It has invested in the construction of a road from Zaranj to Delaram in Afghanistan to link the Iranian road network with that of Afghanistan. The north-south railway corridor also provides a transit for Indian exports to Russia and the Central Asian republics. The India–Iran collaboration on the development of Chabahar in the Persian Gulf will be a major entry point for Indian goods. At the same time, India needs to speed up the port development that suffers when compared to Gwadar, being developed by China on Pakistan's Makran coast. The strategic significance of the two ports is inescapable.[38]

The rise of ISIL apart, its disintegration of the region has empowered Iran by driving Iraq, Syria, and Russia closer to it.

> The prognosis seems inevitable: Iranian hegemony in Iraq and Syria, as well as its political influence in Lebanon, Gaza, and Bahrain. If India desires any influence in the region, it must prepare to navigate these tricky geopolitical shoals. Even as India maintains its equities with the Gulf countries and Israel, it will have to forge a more strategic relationship with Iran.[39]

According to Gopalaswami and Handjani, 'The "civilizational relationship" has a long way to go before facts on the ground can meet the ambition of politicians in both Tehran and New Delhi. Political will and economic incentives exist on both sides to elevate the relationship from a mere trading partnership to a strategic partnership'.[40]

Yemen[41]

Yemen is a replication of the unending civil war in Syria both in terms the intensity of violence affecting its diverse population and in the role of regional and international powers embedded on different sides of the conflict. The sectarian war which has pitted Iran and Saudi Arabia has destroyed the fabric of the country.[42] The escalating armed conflict since 2015 has created 'a complex humanitarian emergency, killing more than 10,000 Yemenis and displacing over 3.1 million people of a total population of 27 million. As of May 2017, over 17 million people are facing crisis or emergency levels of food insecurity as a result of the conflict.'[43]

> The war in Yemen is defined by four major conflicts over political control between the national, regional, and international forces: 1) the national conflict between the Houthis and the Hadi government; 2) the regional fight between Saudi Arabia and its

are taking advantage of the conflict to entrench themselves in local
communities across Yemen; and 4) the sectarian and tribal divides
that are affecting local power dynamics.[44]

None of the cease fires negotiated so far have held longer than
48 hours, including that by the US in November 2016. Under
President Trump 'the U.S. has backed Saudi Arabia's crusade to
re-install Sunni general Abd-Rabbu Mansour Hadi in power.
The Saudis say they cannot abide a Yemen controlled by Houthis,
adherents of the Zayd sect of Shia Islam, who rose up to stake their
claim in a government that had excluded them from power'.[45]

The road to recovery for Yemen is a long one, but it must start
with a cessation of hostilities to begin to heal the devastating
human cost of this war. Putting Yemen's future first by providing
better healthcare and working to regain the Yemeni brainpower
that fled the country should be the number one priority of its
political elite before the damage becomes irreparable.

With the process of ending hostilities stalled because of the
unwillingness of all warring parties to engage in a peace deal,
the country is at risk of falling into an abyss. Yemen has been
on the UN 'List of Least Developed Countries' ever since 1971,
when the list was first compiled. Prolonging this devastating war
threatens to keep Yemen in that position for a long time to come.

History[46]

Like Iraq, during the British colonial rule, Aden was also
administered from Bombay Mumbai during 1839–1939. India
recognized the Yemen Arab Republic (1962) and the People's
Democratic Republic of Yemen (1967) when the country was
ideologically divided during the Cold War. On the conclusion of
the civil war and the merger of North and South Yemen, India
recognized the Yemen Arab Republic (1994). India's long relationship with the country led to a multi-denominational Indian
community settling there for well over a century. The unique
people-to-people contact also led to communities of Yemeni
origin settling down for generations in Hyderabad and other
cities in the Deccan.

India has had long-standing relations with Yemen[47] and it is recorded that Netaji Subhash visited Aden in 1919 and Mahatma Gandhi in 1931 on his way to the Round Table Conference in London.[48] India–Yemen relations, since their independence, have been supportive and marked by a regular diplomatic exchanges. Yemen has consistently supported India in international forums. Bilateral merchandise trade volume although only USD 2.5 billion, includes imports of crude oil and gas.

The sectarian conflict between the Houthi (Zaidi Shia) and the Saudi-led coalition is the third theatre of war in the primarily religious sectarian war raging across West Asia, along with Mosul in north Iraq and Aleppo in northeast Syria. Interestingly, the United States, which had earlier backed the Houthi, has switched support to the Saudi-led Sunni coalition that is determined to ensure that Sana'a does not come under Shia control.

India's intention has been to preserve its equities in the region without getting involved either militarily or at an ideological level. The Saudi military intervention in 2015 in Yemen to quell the Houthi rebellion forced India to launch an overseas naval operation—christened 'Rahat'[49]—to evacuate 4,640 Indian and 964 foreign nationals from the strife-torn country.

The war in Yemen is essentially local in nature. Apart from the sectarian Sunni–Shia dimension, it is also tribal, and has much to do with the governance of the country. The entry of Saudi Arabia has enhanced the religious–political dimension of the hostilities. The United States' contradictory policy supports Saudi Arabia is on the opposite side of the Yemeni regional sectarian conflict, the Iraqi Army (mostly Shia) in Mosul in Iraq against ISIL, and in Aleppo, Syria the militant Sunni groups ranged against Assad.

The Gulf and the Arabian Peninsula are part of the extended neighbourhood of India. Any turmoil there would affect India in multiple ways, because of its oil imports, the presence of a large Indian workforce in these countries, and its effect on the Indian Muslim community. India's role, at this stage, must rest on securing the fullest information on the events there through intelligence exchanges with Saudi Arabia and Yemen, keeping an equidistant profile, and meeting the requirements of the Indian population still in the region, including evacuation when necessary.

The Gulf is going through a major catharsis which threatens the balance within the Gulf Cooperation Council. The fall-out from the long-running Syrian civil war has enmeshed the major Gulf powers. Saudi Arabia, Qatar, and the UAE have backed the Islamic groups battling to remove President Bashar Assad and were involved in financing the Islamic State (ISIL) in its early successes. The blow-back from the involvement on these countries has unsettled the environment making for underlying instability in the region.

It has been further compounded by Saudi Arabia's so far failed attempt to deny the Shia Houtis participation in the governance of Yemen even though it has succeeded getting US military support for its military campaign. Its 'anti-terrorism' alliance set up in 2015 called Islamic Military Alliance to Fight Terrorism (IMFAT) of 34 mainly Muslim Sunni countries through which it conducts the war in Yemen.[51] It is 'Sunni' in its make-up excluding Iran, Iraq, and Syria even though they are opposed to the ISIS.[52]

Secondly, the on-going crisis within GCC has had two effects. First, the UAE–Saudi-led alliance against Qatar which could have far-reaching implications for GCC's cohesion.[53] While all three countries were instrumental in supporting and even funding the ISIS in Syria, the goal now is to put Qatar in the doc given its maverick policy bent. Yet that country has played a mediatory role between the US and Taliban and its access to the more radical Islamic regimes has been useful. It also hosts a US air base. All of this has brought in the Trump administration to mediate in the fracas.

To quote James M. Dorsey, in a larger context,

> it could also determine the ability of small states to chart their own course in the shadow of a regional behemoth whether that is Saudi Arabia in the Middle East or China in Asia. It also has parallels with efforts by peoples like the Catalans in Spain, the Kurds in Iraq or Ambazonians in Cameroon to secede and form independent small states of their own that is likely to mushroom with Kurds in Syria and others likely to put forward similar demands.[54]

Second, the rapid changes in international relations have provoked hitherto unimaginable contacts in the Middle East. The opening of contacts, albeit unofficial, between Saudi Arabia and Israel in pursuit of common goals on Iran and to eliminate ISIS and the Assad regime could signal a very different pursuit of the issue of Palestine and Arab peace.[55]

These internecine conflicts between the Gulf countries have been playing out in the background of the on-going tension between Saudi Arabia and Iran which while sectarian at its roots increasingly manifests itself in the two countries being ranged on opposing sides in the on-going wars in Syria and Yemen. In Syria Iran supports the Assad regime together with Russia and the Hezbollah while in Yemen it supports the Shia Houtis seeking power in that country. Saudi Arabia supports most militant radical groups against Assad while in Yemen it stands by the Sunni government of Abdul Mansur Hadi. Their overall tension reflects on the UAE's relations with Iran and on Shia unrest in Bahrain.

India's Policy

India has been able to maintain an equidistant policy on the on-going tension and conflict in the Gulf keeping in view its long-term and crucial interests with every GCC member and Iran. For India, its relations with the GCC will become even more important in the decades to come as it rise in the global economic hierarchy increases its political interests. It will require increased security cooperation with each of the GCC members. First, the strategic dimension of its energy security given that India annually imports 75 per cent of its oil and 55 per cent of its natural gas requirements from the Gulf, particularly Saudi Arabia, Iran, the UAE, and Qatar. The continuing instability in the Gulf could pose a threat to energy supplies. Second, India's large expatriate population estimated at 7 million working in the GCC remit approximately USD 40 billion annually. Their security and working conditions dictate a policy which is non-partisan and with an access to all the sides of the on-going conflicts.[56] Third, India's policy based on equidistant and staying away from taking positions on the political and religious aspects of the on-going instability in the region serves it well in the context of growing multi-polarity of international actors in the region.[57] Fourth, India's aspirations to increase its profile in the Indian Ocean through the Indian Ocean Rim Organisation (IORA) to counteract the increasingly moribund nature of activities under SAARC provide yet another justification for the basis of India's current priorities with the GCC.

India's Link West policy directed towards the Gulf is 'strongly forged and deeply anchored'.[58] Collectively the GCC is India's largest trade partner, of which the UAE is the largest. Yet Indo-Gulf trade is heavily weighed against India with its exports being half of its import bill, of which petroleum and its products takes the lion's share. Although in August 2004 GCC and India signed a Framework Agreement on Economic Cooperation covering trade in goods and services and investment, lack of political consensus on both sides has delayed its finalization and no time limit has been set. It is unlikely that in the present unstable situation in the region this is likely to happen soon. Besides there are seemingly unbridgeable issues on both sides on trade and intellectual property which make an early resolution difficult.[59]

Brief History

The GCC[60] comprises six sovereign sheikhdoms of the Persian Gulf—Bahrain, Kuwait, Oman, Qatar, Saudi Arabia, and the UAE—with all of whom India has historic and societal ties. Before India achieved independence, all these countries, except for Saudi Arabia, were administered from Bombay. With Saudi Arabia, the earliest contact was made by the Indian Muslim community for the annual Haj pilgrimage to Mecca and Medina and to other sites like Najaf and Karbala in Iraq.

Trade and commerce were the drivers of a relationship that saw Arab merchants coming to the Kerala coast and Indian traders settling in Dubai, Oman, and Bahrain. The earliest Indian presence in Oman is recorded in 1781. Following the independence and partition of India and Pakistan, a tilt in favour of the latter was inevitable despite ties to both countries through of religion, family, and trade.

The member countries of the GCC are some of the major migration corridors from India. About seven million Indian migrants work in this region.[61] Migration to the GCC countries started in the 1930s with the discovery of oil in the Gulf, which became more prominent during the early years (1970–73) of the oil boom.

Economics, Trade, and Energy

The rich reserves of crude oil and gas have made the Gulf countries India's closest and major source, accounting in 2014–15 for 50 per cent of annual oil and gas requirements. Their growing oil revenues jump-started these economies into the modern world, creating a demand for a professional, skilled, and semi-skilled work force. India is one of the largest suppliers of such labour, and remittances from the GCC account for 4 per cent of India's GDP, over USD 40 billion annually. India's phenomenal economic growth has created opportunities for two-way investments in the petrochemicals, pharmaceuticals, real estate, and the education sectors. The synergy between GCC's financial resources and Indian skills, manpower, and technology has made GCC India's largest trading partner.

The GCC–India Framework Cooperation Agreement (2004) is expected to finalize an FTA to put their trade cooperation on a firmer basis. The last round of talks was held in New York between Indian External Affairs Minister Sushma Swaraj and her GCC counterparts when she called for the early finalization of the GCC–India FTA and operationalizing the GCC–India Framework Agreement.[62] The consolidation within the GCC itself, in line with the WTO requirements, and reservations from Indian trade and industry have slowed down the trade negotiations.

Politics and Security

The GCC founding summit stated that the Gulf states would meet regional threats 'jointly and independently of foreign interference' laying laid down strategic guidelines:

- The security of the Gulf is the responsibility of its people.
- Member states shall strive to keep the region free from international tensions and conflicts.

- Member states reject all military interference in the region by foreign powers, and especially by the superpowers.
- Member states shall reject foreign military bases.
- Member states shall not join any international bloc.

Given that all six states remain dependent on foreign military bases and personnel, weapons systems, training, and advice, these GCC principles are at best a declaration of intent. Bahrain and Oman both have US bases on their territory, while Saudi Arabia has multiple military facilities that have been 'overbuilt' to accommodate US military intervention in the region. Six subsequent summits and scores of meetings of military experts, chiefs of staff, and ministers of defence have demonstrated the illusory nature of these principles.

The rapid increase in their economic exchanges has spurred political, strategic, and security cooperation between India and the GCC. The success of their economic relationship has, to some extent, blunted India's concern with the GCC members' traditional proximity to Pakistan. During the late Saudi King Abdullah bin Abdulaziz's visit to New Delhi on 26 January 2006, he offered India 'observer status' in the OIC which started the process in earnest. It complemented the greater understanding after 9/11 between the two countries on intelligence sharing, counterterrorism, mutual legal assistance in criminal matters, money laundering, extradition, and deportation. The deportation to India of the accused in terrorist acts from the UAE and Saudi Arabia are important examples.

In consequence, India has pursued strategic and defence cooperation with each of the GCC members, especially the UAE, Oman, and Qatar, including naval exercises and military training.

The GCC and the Strategic Gulf

Regional developments have emboldened the GCC to adopt an increasingly strategic role in the context of the sectarian conflict raging in Syria, Iraq, and Yemen. Iran's active pursuit of its nuclear ambitions and the growing US and Chinese profiles in the Gulf has complicated the security matrix of the region. The US' Fifth Fleet is based in Bahrain while Chinese naval ships have been increasingly visiting Gulf ports since their participation in international anti-piracy operation off the Somali coast. Since 60 per cent of the world's oil flows through the Straits of Hormuz and the Bab el-Mandeb, the two choke points in the Gulf, the security of these sea lanes of communication has become crucial, particularly for India and China.

With the United States reaching self-sufficiency in oil, a question has risen vis-à-vis its role as the security provider in the Gulf. It will also depend on whether President Donald Trump will continue to shift the US military focus from the Gulf to the Asia-Pacific. In the light of the current US administration's view on the Iran Ånuclear agreement, it is moot whether the former could enter into an agreement with the latter on managing the Gulf.

India remains acutely conscious of China's developing port facilities at Gwadar in Pakistan, Hambantota in Sri Lanka, and Sittwe in Myanmar in the IO region.[63] Its OBOR project would further enhance its significance. India's challenge remains in securing oil supply and ensuring that the Gulf region does not become a source of religious strife or a battle-field for regional and great power rivalry. In either case India will be affected directly.

Saudi Arabia[64]

Saudi Arabia is the acknowledged leader of the Gulf countries, in terms of its religious status as the guardian of the two holy sites of Mecca and Medina and also of its oil wealth, close relations with the United States, and its population, which is half of the total Arab population in the Gulf.

During Prime Minister Modi's visit to Saudi Arabia on 3 April 2016,[65] King Salman bin Abdulaziz Al Saud bestowed on him the King Abdulaziz Order of Merit medal, the kingdom's highest honour that was given to any Indian leader for the first time. This was only the fourth visit ever by an Indian prime minister to the kingdom. It was possibly to note a degree of equidistance in Saudi Arabia's relations with Pakistan and India. It could suggest that a perceived hardliner on the religious matrix has a better chance of reaching agreements with the Saudis, who practise and propagate Wahhabism, a hardline interpretation of the Sunna.[66]

Just days before the visit, the United States and Saudi Arabia jointly announced sanctions against four individuals and three organizations in Pakistan involved in financing terrorist organizations, including the Al-Qaeda, the Taliban, and the LeT. The joint announcement was unprecedented.[67] Four years ago, the kingdom deported a senior LeT official to India who had been involved in the 2008 LeT attack on Mumbai, backed by Pakistani intelligence. Modi also met Crown Prince Mohammed bin Nayef who is minister of interior and the kingdom's top counterterrorism official.

Economics has played an important role in the Saudi–India relationship. About 3 million Indians work in Saudi Arabia, almost half of the 7.3 million Indians present in the Gulf states. Bilateral trade in 2015 was almost USD 40 billion, and India imports a fifth of its oil from the kingdom. Modi met senior Aramco officials to discuss more energy and investment opportunities.

The seeming tilt in Saudi Arabia's relations during the visit has also been attributed to Pakistan's rebuffing Saudi request for troops to assist them in their military operations in Yemen.[68] However, this is in the realm of conjecture as Pakistan remains an important beneficiary of Saudi financial and oil assistance and a safety valve for Pakistan's leaders. It is unlikely that Saudi Arabia will tone down its relations with Pakistan, the only Muslim member of the nuclear club. At the same time, ahead of Modi's visit, Saudi Foreign Minister Adel al-Jubeir insisted that Saudi Arabia's 'relations with Pakistan do not come at the expense of [its] relations with India'. This in itself is a remarkable statement.

Since 2000, Saudi Arabia's ties with India have truly become two-dimensional. They have grown significantly over the last two decades based on their burgeoning energy ties and the Indian diaspora in the Saudi kingdom. At a time when Riyadh has been losing its market share with other countries such as China and the United States, it has emerged as the top supplier of crude oil to India, supplanting Iraq.[69] Saudi Arabia's investment in Indian industry has been minimal, with oil prices ruling around USD 40 a barrel. There is information that the extended Saudi Arabian economy is pulling out its investments abroad. Even for India, Saudi Arabia is not a major investment destination, unlike the UAE.

Nevertheless, India and Saudi Arabia have vowed to boost investments and trade substantially. Prime Minister Narendra Modi invited cash-rich Saudi firms to invest in infrastructure and in joint ventures for oil exploration. A joint statement issued after the talks between Modi and Saudi King Salman bin Abdulaziz said that both countries agreed to forge a deeper partnership in the energy sector focusing on investment and joint ventures in petrochemical complex. Of the five agreements, the most important was the Investment Promotion Cooperation between Invest India and the Saudi Arabian General Investment Authority (SAGIA).[70]

India and Saudi Arabia have found synergies they can exploit based on the supply of crude oil to India and as alternate investment destinations for Saudi funds. If the US pivots to the Asia-Pacific or demands that Saudi Arabia pay for its security cover, the Saudis may well be tempted to diversify their strategic assets.

It is a time when Saudi Arabia is evaluating its relationships with the single goal of perpetuating the existing monarchical family system in the face of threats, both external (arising from the possible scaling down of the US presence in the Gulf), and internal (due to contradictory pressures from groups like ISIL and those wanting moderation and democracy). At the same time, the salience of the Palestinian issue in the entire Arab discourse has been eclipsed by events that threaten the security of all countries in the Persian Gulf. In this context, the Saudis have shown rare alacrity in opening relations with Israel, a seeming anathema so far.[71] It is thus not beyond conception that the country would intensify relations with India.

Saudi Arabia's diplomacy uses both the GCC and the OIC based in Jeddah as instruments of its foreign policy. In the 1990s, under Pakistan's tutelage, it used the OIC for repeated resolutions on Kashmir and on the state of Indian Muslims.

It was after 2001 that Saudi Arabia started looking at India differently. That was when the bilateral relationship acquired a mutually beneficial character—the fact that India could be the largest destination of Saudi oil and an alternative venue for its investments. India, for its part, realized that Saudi Arabia was a destination for its industry and professionals. With the spread of its linkages across the Arab and Islamic world, Saudi Arabia was a valued interlocutor for a country with the second largest Muslim population in the world. Their intelligence and security cooperation after 9/11 was boosted by enabling agreements. The deportation in 2012 of Sayed Zabiuddin, also known as Abu Jundal, a key suspect in November 2008 Mumbai attacks, signalled a sea change in Saudi Arabia's counterterror priorities.[72]

As India's capabilities grow, it might do more in terms of providing maritime security, intelligence sharing, evacuating expatriates when necessary, and contributing to UN peacekeeping operations. It could also potentially do more for capacity building within these countries with the support of the host governments. However, India will likely remain wary of picking sides or getting involved in non–UN–sanctioned military interventions in the region unless its interests are directly affected.[73]

UAE: Renewing Old Ties[74]

Sheikh Mohamad bin Zayed al Nahayan, Crown Prince of Abu Dhabi's visit as Chief Guest for Republic Day 2017, his second since the earlier one in February 2016, was an affirmation of the tremendous increase in the high level bilateral direction of the relationship between the two countries.[75] It was a fit recompense for the landmark visit, after 34 years, on 16–17 August 2015 by Prime Minister Narendra Modi.

During the Modi visit, in a break from protocol Crown Prince Sheikh Mohammed bin Zayed Al Nahyan, along with his five brothers, was also present to receive Modi. The aim of the visit was to increase bilateral cooperation in energy and trade and market India as an attractive business destination. The elevation of the relationship to a comprehensive strategic partnership epitomized the growing contact between the two countries over decades. The subsequent visits in quick succession not only broadened the horizon of bilateral contact between the two countries but pledged USD 75 billion for setting up a UAE–India Infrastructure Investment Fund to support investment in railways, ports, roads, airports, and industrial corridors and parks. The UAE is a major investor in India with investments amounting to USD 5 billion (2016). Among the other new areas taken up for bilateral action are an MOU on cooperation in cyber space and cyber crime and the setting up of an India–UAE policy planning Strategic Dialogue which held its first meeting on 20 January 2017.

Strategic Partnership

The strategic partnership is expected to lead to a regular strategic dialogue between the two countries. It was opportune given the unstable state in the Gulf and West Asia coupled with the rise of Islamic radicalization and misuse of religion by groups and countries for inciting hatred, perpetrating and justifying terrorism. The joint commitment by the two sides opposing terrorism in all forms and manifestations, wherever committed and by whomever, was a positive sign which will build further on their security cooperation. It was significant that the two sides called for adoption by in the UN of India's proposed Comprehensive Convention on International Terrorism (CCIT) and working together to prevent funds reaching terrorist groups, drug trafficking, and extradition. The establishment of a dialogue between their national security advisors (NSAs) and National Security Councils will also help to keep these issues under regular review.

The two sides will cooperate to strengthen maritime security, including maritime transport and coastal surveillance systems, in the Persian Gulf and the Indian Ocean vital for their security and prosperity. It will include strengthening of defence relations—including regular exercises and training of naval, air, land, and special forces—and coastal defence and joint manufacture under the 'Make in India' programme.

Trade, Energy, and Investment[76]

The UAE imports goods worth USD 30.3 billion (2015) from India, which is 11.5 per cent of India's total exports, comprising gems (USD 12.6 billion), clothing, aircraft, machinery, and electronic equipment. India imports goods worth USD 20.3 billion, or 5.2 per cent of Indian global imports, mainly crude oil and gems. A good portion of Indian exports are re-exported within the Gulf countries and Iran, and Pakistan.

On energy cooperation, the UAE's ADNOC has partnered with the Indian Strategic Petroleum Reserve Ltd in filling the tanks in Mangalore, of three locations, in Phase I holding 5.33 MMT of oil which will meet 10.5 days of India's requirement.[77] The two countries will also cooperate in peaceful uses of nuclear energy, including in areas like safety, health, agriculture, and science and technology.

A Growing Relationship

The growing relationship between the UAE and India has been fuelled by the realization that India's policy of non-interference in UAE's internal affairs and the reliability of Indians in running their prosperous economy are reinforced by India's attraction as an investment destination. Almost 1.5 million Indian nationals, mostly non-Muslims, live in the UAE far larger than the local population. The predominance of non-Muslim Indian diaspora in the Gulf countries is a sign marking the confidence that their social structure and mores will remain immune.

The slow fraying of ties between the UAE and Pakistan, its traditional ally, following the latter's refusal to back the Saudi-led air strikes in Yemen, may have also played a role. Pakistan's decision had then evoked trenchant criticism from the UAE's foreign minister and an equally sharp retort from Islamabad. The growing distrust between the UAE and Pakistan also dates to the use of a private airstrip belonging to Crown Prince Sheikh Mohammed bin Zayed by the United States for drone attacks in Pakistan.

Thus, in reference to the Kashmir dispute, the two sides called on nations to 'fully respect and sincerely implement their commitments to resolve disputes bilaterally and peacefully, without resorting to violence and terrorism'. A position far different from that of the OIC.

Qatar[78]

Prime Minister Narendra Modi's visit on 4–5 June 2016 was also aimed at rejuvenating the bilateral relationship, given Qatar's important role as an investor in the Indian market and as a major supplier of crude oil and natural gas. It was in response to the visit in March 2015 to India of the Emir of Qatar H.H Sheikh Tamim Bin Hamad al Thani.

India–Qatar cooperation in diverse sectors has been steadily growing in an excellent framework provided by historically close ties and regular and substantive engagement, including at the highest levels of the two governments. The large, diverse, accomplished, and highly regarded Indian community is making an important contribution to Qatar's progress and in nurturing the bonds of deep-rooted friendship and multifaceted cooperation between the two countries.

In Qatar, like in Saudi Arabia, energy issues featured prominently on the agenda. In 2015, India imported 65 per cent of its liquefied natural gas (LNG) from Qatar, making the state its largest provider. Qatar will remain an important partner for India. Likewise, for Qatar, India, as one of Asia's largest LNG importers, is an important energy market. In line with his tendency to pitch India as a destination for foreign investment, Modi, during his visit, outlined opportunities in the country for Qatari business leaders. He pushed for expanded business ties between the two countries. He also addressed an audience of Indian expatriates in Qatar.

The two countries signed a range of agreements, including memorandums on tourism, financial cooperation, infrastructure investment, cultural cooperation, and health care cooperation. According to an MoU signed during the visit, Qatar will invest in India's National Investment and Infrastructure Fund. Moreover, Modi and his Qatari counterpart discussed broader strategic issues facing the region.

Oil and Gas

The total trade turnover between India and Qatar was USD 15.67 billion in 2014–15, bulking heavily in favour of the latter. India imports petroleum products such as ethylene and propylene, ammonia, and urea. Qatar was the first country where India invested in *in-situ* production of urea and has an interest in crude oil and gas–based projects.

A large number of Indian companies are undertaking the implementation of many major projects in Qatar in infrastructure, information technology, energy, construction, and water and electricity fields. There are 26 companies which are 100 per cent owned by Indians working in Qatar in various fields such as infrastructure, contracting, information technology, gold trade, and food items trade. Nearly 6,500 Qatari–Indian companies in joint venture partnerships are working practically in all fields in the country.

Many Indian companies such as L&T, Dodsal, Punj Lloyd, Shapoorji Pallonji, Voltas, Tata motors, Simplex, TCS, Wipro, Tech Mahindra, Aptech, and NIIT have set up offices in Qatar and have secured major contracts/business. The large Indian community in Qatar includes Indian professionals who constitute an important component. Air India, Jet Airways, and Qatar Airways operate direct flights between India and Qatar.

Indian information technology (IT) companies in Qatar have executed some very prestigious projects in the country. They are doing businesses in the areas of consultancy, SAP, enterprise applications integration, logistics management, and security services, etc. NIIT and Aptech are successfully running their IT training institutes in Qatar.

Three Indian banks—State Bank of India (SBI), Canara Bank, and Syndicate Bank—have their presence in Qatar and manage substantial remittances to India through their exchange houses. A number of exchange houses involving Indian banks, channelize remittances to India, whose value was estimated in 2015 at nearly USD 4.2 billion. Doha Bank, one of the leading Qatari banks, which started operations from January 2015 has a brokerage firm in India (Doha Brokerage) with 41 per cent stake while 59 per cent is by local brokers of Kochi. The largest Qatari bank, the Qatar National Bank, started operations in Mumbai in 2013.

In July 2013, the Qatar Investment Authority (QIA) decided to invest USD 300 million in a special purpose vehicle formed by developer RMZ Corp to buy and build leased office assets, mainly in South India. Baring Private Equity has a 21 per cent stake in the vehicle which it bought in 2012 for Rs 500 crore. Reports indicate that some private Qatari investors have also invested in

conjoint legacy

real estate in India, including in hotels and other properties that are not in the public domain. Qatar's sovereign Wealth Fund—the Qatar Investment Authority (QIA)—is the main Qatari investor in India. Qatar Foundation Endowment picked up 5 per cent stakes in Bharti Airtel with an investment of USD 1.26 billion in July 2013. The QIA also invested USD 150 in India's e-commerce major Flipkart and acquired an additional stake of USD 100 million in December 2015.

Investments by Indian companies in Qatar include a USD 100 million joint venture to be set up in Mesaieed Industrial Area between Qatar Industrial Manufacturing Company (QIMC) and KLJ Organic Limited to manufacture chlorinated paraffin wax and caustic soda, hydrochloric acid, calcium chloride, and sodium hypochlorite as byproducts and co-products.

Foreign Policy

With a foreign policy often perceived as maverick Qatar is currently embroiled in a squabble with Saudi Arabia and the UAE both of the latter having cut off diplomatic and other contact, given thirteen conditions for the restoration of relations which include closure of the Al Jazeera network and ceasing support of radical Islamic groups in Syria, Egypt and Iraq and close relations with Iran.[79] Qatar has stood firm on its positions and has rallied Turkey and Iran on its side. Qatar has become reliant on Turkey and Iran for food imports since the embargo was imposed on 5 June and insists with its huge wealth it can survive the embargo for an indefinite period. Given that it shares a gas field Qatar will find it impossible to cut its relations with Iran. Turkey has equally opposed Saudi exhortations on closing down its contacts with Qatar.

While Qatar refused to buckle under the stringent conditions, both Saudi Arabia and the UAE have come under international criticism on grounds that they are themselves equally to blame in the funding of radical Islamic groups particularly in Syria as well as strong regulations against journalists and free speech. While Kuwait took the lead in trying to mediate between the two sides the stand taken by US Secretary of State Tillerson against Saudi and UAE position has toned down the rhetoric and war drums and moved towards a peaceful resolution.[80] The US president said he was confident a diplomatic dispute between Qatar and its Arab neighbors could be 'solved pretty quickly'. Qatar's emir, in turn, said he believed Trump's 'interference will help a lot'.[81]

Qatar has frequently taken the role of a 'change factor' in international affairs not only in West Asia and the Gulf but also vis-à-vis the advanced nations. In pursuit of its role, Qatar offered Doha as the venue for talks between the Afghan government and the Taliban;[82] like Saudi Arabia and Turkey, it supports militant Islamic groups opposing Bashar al-Assad in Syria;[83] and its activist policy has been remarkable in supporting the entrenched governments in the misnamed 'Arab Spring'.[84] It supported Egyptian President Mohamed Mursi after his election, clearly taking a side eventually overthrown by the army at the behest of the Egyptian people. Qatar continues to have its chips in the ongoing sectarian conflict in the Arab and Islamic world.

An important instrument of its projection is Al Jazeera—a television channel, which has Arabic and English services, is entirely funded by the Qatari state. The channel has often been responsible for creating tension and bad blood between Arab and other countries. India was for long wary of giving permission to Al Jazeera to operate in India lest it become a tool in the hands of those wanting to disturb communal peace in the country.[85]

India has excellent relations with Qatar, and it has ensured that it stays away from the complications of Qatar's foreign policy and its current tension with Saudi Arabia and UAE.

Oman[86]

The Sultanate of Oman is a strategic partner of India in the Gulf and an important interlocutor at the Gulf Cooperation Council (AGCC), Arab League, and Indian Ocean Rim Association (IORA) fora. Oman also accords a high priority to its ties with India. The two countries across the Arabian Sea are linked by geography, history, and culture and enjoy warm and cordial relations, which are attributed to historical maritime trade linkages, intimacy of the royal family with India, and the seminal role played by the Indian expatriate community in building of Oman, which is acknowledged by Omani Government.

Sushma Swaraj, minister of External Affairs and Overseas Indian Affairs, visited Oman in 17–18 February 2015, reciprocating the visit of Yusuf bin Allawi, the Omani minister responsible for foreign affairs who had visited Delhi soon after the Modi government took office. Since then Minister of State for External Affairs M J Akbar visited Oman to attend the 5th India-Arab Partnership Conference, 14–15 December 2016. Minister Responsible for Foreign Affairs Yousuf bin Alawi bin Abdullah, visited India on 2–3 April 2017.

Oman and India's contact goes back to the 17th century, which was based on trade both with the Gulf and east African countries where the Indian trading community from Gujarat had a prominent role. Omanis also developed ties of friendship and family in India and are seen by the other Gulf Arabs as being closest to India. Even considering the Arabs from the Gulf who have had long-standing relations with India, the Omanis are a case apart when it comes to relations with India.

Some important bilateral agreements between the two countries are the MoUs on Combating Crime, Cooperation in Agriculture, Civil Aviation, Avoidance of Double Taxation, Bilateral Investment Promotion and Protection, Treaty of Extradition, on Manpower, on Joint Investment Fund, and Agreement on Legal and Judicial Cooperation in Criminal Matters.

Trade and Investment

Bilateral trade between the two countries reached USD 4.18 billion, and mutual investment is roughly USD 7.5 billion. Oman's top exports to India are urea, LNG, polypropylene, lubricating oil, dates, and chromite ore. The Oman India Joint Investment Fund (OIJIF), a private equity fund backed by the State General Reserve Fund (SGRF), Oman's sovereign wealth fund, and India's largest lender SBI, has recently approved a second tranche of USD 300 million to develop infrastructure projects to build joint ventures in technology, agriculture, marine, telecom, power, petrochemicals, water treatment, and logistics. These investments by the SGRF will contribute to the 'Make in India' initiative to create a manufacturing hub in India.

In the face of the ongoing turmoil in the upper Gulf, Oman is investing in its strategic partnership with India to diversify Muscat's web of international allies. The main drivers for the deepening ties are the presence of 700,000 Indian expatriates and India's interest in securing access to hydrocarbon-rich and stable countries within close geographic proximity. Falling oil prices have forced Oman to decrease their oil dependence and grow other sectors such as agriculture, shipping, manufacturing, mining, transport, tourism, and logistics in accordance with its five-year plan (2016–20) to reduce the sultanate's economic dependence on oil by 50 per cent in line with its long-term Vision 2020 to develop human capital. In this regard, India is seen as an ideal partner.

The Energy Triangle: Middle East to India Deepwater Pipeline (MEIDP)

Intense talks have gone on between Oman, India, and Iran on construction of underwater pipelines to supply India with gas from Iran, establishing an Indo–Middle Eastern energy triangle. Iran and Oman signed a USD 60 billion contract in 2013 for gas supply to the sultanate for 25 years via a pipeline connecting Iran's Hormozgan province with Oman's Sohar. The MEIDP is a planned 805-mile pipeline that brings India into the fold. MEIDP will export 31.5 million standard cu mt gas per day from Iran's Chabahar Port, transiting the Gulf of Oman to Oman's Ras al-Jafan, before traveling across the Arabian Sea to Gujarat, bypassing Pakistani waters.[87] South Asia Gas Enterprises (Sage), the undertaker of the USD 4 billion pipeline project are awaiting the Indian government's approval to the non-binding framework agreement.

MEIDP is proposed to pass over land in the Sultanate to give revenue in the form of transit fees. Sage Advisory Board Chairman TNR Rao told Oman Tribune that they were waiting for the Indian government, which was trying to settle other deals with Iran, to 'make up its mind' and go ahead with a non-binding framework agreement. The other deals under negotiation include development rights for Iran's Farzad B gas field, which has 20tcf of extractable reserves, and agreements for the management and development of Chabahar Port. India feels its consortium of state-owned firms led by ONGC Videsh, which discovered Farzad B, should be allowed to develop the field. Buyers of gas in the USD 4 billion pipeline project include state-owned firms Indian Oil Corporation, Gas Authority of India Ltd and Gujarat State Petroleum Corporation, while the potential suppliers include Oman's Ministry of Oil and Gas and National Iranian Gas Exports Company.[88]

Transit

New Delhi's International North-South Transit Corridor (INSTC) project is expected to counter China's OBOR initiative. It will be 'a multi-modal transportation route linking India Ocean and Persian Gulf to the Caspian Sea via Iran, and onward to northern Europe via St. Petersburg in Russia'. It could improve India's access to the Middle Eastern, the Caucasian, Central Asian, and European markets with the India-financed Chabahar port in Iran serving as the route's outlet to the Indian Ocean. As New Delhi gets increasingly invested in the Arabian Gulf and the region's security landscape, India's geopolitical rivalries with China and Pakistan are likely to intensify in Oman and other GCC states, possibly leading Oman to play a balancing role.

Strategic Partnership

During the visit of Indian Defence Minister Manohar Parrikar in May 2016 India and Oman signed a series of pacts aimed at enhancing bilateral defence ties. According to these pacts, India will provide weapons to Oman. New Delhi is also interested in setting up defence production facilities in the sultanate. Simultaneously, Oman has agreed to purchase Indian small arms systems, built and sold by India's state-run Ordinance Factory Board. Strategic cooperation between the two countries has become essential for safeguarding the waterways, with Oman proving to be exceptionally reliable in supporting operations with ships and aircraft within the region. India clearly sees itself as a stakeholder in Oman's security and cohesion.

India and Oman have boosted defence cooperation and collaborated on crime prevention and maritime issues ever since the 1970s, when Oman became the first country to establish defence ties with India. In 1996, Oman was the first GCC member to sign an MoU with India on combating transnational crime and terrorism. In 2008, New Delhi and Muscat formed a 'strategic partnership', institutionalizing biennial naval and air exercises. Oman is the only country with which India has exercises in army, navy, and air force.

Oman seeks to strengthen its security in the southern part of its territory, amid fears of Salafist–jihadist groups from Yemen, such as the Al-Qaeda and ISIS spilling over into Dhofar, while ensuring the flow of trade across the Omani-Yemeni border. To continue pursuing this balancing act, Oman is looking both at its closest western allies—the United States, the United Kingdom, and Germany chiefly—and in the East like India and China.

This security dimension is especially important for Oman given the uncertainties on the succession issue in the state. Observers have warned of militant Islamist extremism in neighbouring Yemen striking Oman amid a period of instability in the post-Qaboos era. By deepening its ties with India, Omanis are giving yet another powerful player in the global economy higher stakes in the sultanate's continued stability and prosperity. India's improving ties with Iran have implications for its relations with Saudi Arabia and other Arab Gulf states. A closer relationship with Oman, known for a neutral, flexible, and pragmatic foreign policy, could help India navigate the sensitive geopolitical fault lines in the region.

Oman has been equally keen to expand its relations with China, its top export partner, and has an interest in China's OBOR project. Sino-Omani bilateral trade reached USD 23 billion in 2013. In addition to the economic potential of joining China's OBOR, defence ties with Beijing have been on the rise since China's decision to participate in anti-piracy efforts in the Gulf of Aden, with Chinese ships making regular port calls at the Omani port of Salalah.

Moreover, Djibouti located at the southern entrance to the Red Sea, is a tiny, barren country, with a population less than one million. Yet since the turn of the century, it has become a base for various European, Asian, and American forces, who have all camped in the region for one reason or another.[89] With a French base in existence for some time, it now has military bases from the US, Japan, Italy with both Saudi Arabia and Iran considering similar deployment to prosecute the war in Yemen. Oman has had a long-standing naval and maritime history with the ports on Africa's eastern coast.

The triangle of unending tension that China, India, and Pakistan represent is as much a challenge for Oman as the United States, Iran, and the GCC triangle. Just as Oman has successfully designed a neutral and independent stance between Iran and Saudi Arabia, a similar level of indispensable neutrality can be expected from Oman at an intra-regional level.

Bahrain[90]

India's bilateral trade and commercial exchanges with Bahrain is about 5,000 years old, dating to the Indus Valley civilization. It traces its origins to the Dilmun civilization in Bahrain. Ancient Bahraini traders had flourishing trade exchange of Bahraini pearls and spices with India. Bahrain is the smallest country in the Gulf by area (712 square kilometres) and population (1.2 million).

India and Bahrain enjoy excellent bilateral relations characterized by cordial political, economic, and cultural contacts. Minister for External Affairs Sushma Swaraj visited Bahrain on 23 January 2016 for the first ministerial meeting of the India–Arab League Cooperation Forum, holding 'wide-ranging' discussions with Bahrain's Foreign Minister Khalid bin Ahmed Al Khalifa.[91] Like other Gulf sheikhdoms Bahrain is also facing a 'crunch' due the continuing low crude oil prices and has sought to diversify its economy. India has invited Bahrain to participate in India's flagship 'Make in India' programme.

Bahrain has been a favourite destination for Indian nationals. Out of 350,000 Indian nationals working in Bahrain, as many as 220,000 are from the state of Kerala. Indians are preferred over other expatriates from the subcontinent because of the trust factor, strong work ethics, and the 'apolitical' orientation of Indian expatriates.

Bahrain hosts the headquarters of the US Fifth Fleet and its role in Gulf security is crucial.[92] With a population of 46–60 per cent adhering to Shia Islam, and its physical proximity to Saudi Arabia and Iran, inevitably a GCC military force mustered by Saudi Arabia put down the democracy protests in 2011 ruthlessly. The pervasive fear that Iran across the Hormuz Straits could use the Shia Bahraini population to create sectarian disturbances was an important reason.[93] Bahrain's value as a 'safety valve' for the Saudi royalty and population, with a short causeway of 18 kilometres, cannot be underestimated. Any change in the monarchy in Bahrain would immediately affect Saudi Arabia.

Bahrain has been an important watching post for the movement of Pakistan-based terrorists. Home Minister Rajnath Singh visited Bahrain on 23 October 2016 to raise the issue of Pakistan-sponsored terrorism in India.[94]

India has maintained excellent relations with Bahrain whose royal family has owned property in Mumbai since before Independence.

Kuwait[95]

The relationship between India and Kuwait goes back into history. The Indian rupee was legal tender in Kuwait till 1961, and Kuwaiti princes still own properties in Mumbai. Kuwait hosts a large expatriate Indian population and provides 10–12 per cent of India's oil imports while India is among the largest trade partners of Kuwait.

Kuwait played a major role in India's evacuation of its expatriate populations during the Iraq–Iran War (1980–88) when 10,000 Indians in Iraq were airlifted between 10 and 20 October 1988, majority from Kuwait. During the traumatic Iraqi invasion of Kuwait which led to the first Gulf War (1991) India had provided all help to the beleaguered Kuwaiti population. The 1990 airlift of Indians from Kuwait was carried out from 13 August 1990 to 20 October 1990 after the Iraqi invasion of Kuwait. Air India helped evacuate 175,000 people by civil airliners. The operation was carried out before the Persian Gulf War in 1990 to evacuate

Indian expatriates from Kuwait.[96] During the Second Gulf War as well India was ready to put similar procedures in operation through Kuwait. It will, like Jordan, will always have value as a staging post for repatriation of beleaguered Indian expatriates in the region.

The bilateral relationship is based on oil, trade, and Kuwaiti investments in Indian industries.[97] After Saudi Arabia (24 per cent), Kuwait is the second largest Arabian Gulf supplier of oil to India. Investments in India are over USD 3.5 billion, of which USD 3 billion is by Kuwait Investment Authority (KIA). In December 2015, KIA announced an investment of USD 300 million in GMR Infrastructure Ltd. Earlier, in October 2015, KIA made a substantial investment in the Interglobe Aviation's (Indigo Airlines) initial public offer (IPO). In 2013, KIA had made an investment of USD 5.37 million in the Power Grid Corporation of India Ltd. Other significant Kuwaiti economic presence in India includes investments by Alghanim Group of Kuwait, the KAPICO group, National Aviation Services, Agility Logistics, Hasibat Holding Co, KGA Group, KCIC, KIPCO, Global Investment House, and Kuwait Finance House, etc. India–related funds launched in Kuwait include India Fund (October 2005), Tijari India Fund (December 2006), India Equity Fund (January 2007), Kuwait Indian Holding Company, India Private Equity Fund, Third Real Estate Islamic Fund (May 2007), and Mayur Hedge Fund (August 2008).

Wrapping-Up

India's relations with the GCC countries move on two tracks and two levels—bilateral and regional. In bilateral relations with each GCC member India has strived to look at mutually productive avenues without interfering in either their domestic or in the intra-GCC rifts and conflicts. At the regional level India's goal has been to actively state its concerns while ensuring that they do not come in the way of the bilateral relationship. Neither has it accepted edicts by religiously oriented organizations of Arab and Islamic countries. Thus while India has regular meetings with the GCC and the Arab League, it has none with the OIC. India's relations since 2000 with the GCC have become two-way, wide-ranging and mutually beneficial. Rather than being seen as providers of jobs and remittances for Indians, and religious succour for its Muslim community, the relationship is anchored in the Indian market for oil and gas and the Indian economy as an investment destination.

The countries in the Gulf are equally deeply affected by the ongoing sectarian conflict in Syria, Iraq, and Yemen. Some are also participants, providing weapons and funding or troops to Sunni Islamic groups opposed to the Syrian regime. India's primary concerns at the ongoing developments include first, the movement of the radical Islamic groups to Afghanistan and Pakistan and the flow of their ideology to the Islamic community in India and, second, the safety of the large Indian diaspora in the region. Thus, intelligence exchange and strong cooperative counterterror action are the top priorities in India's dialogue with these states.

Indian Ocean[98,99]

The historic first-ever IORA Summit held on 7 March 2016 in Jakarta was an event that was on the cards for a long time. The leaders of the 21-nation grouping emphasized their shared objective to develop the potential of the blue economy through broader cooperation. The role of the major key players—India, Indonesia, South Africa, and Australia—will be crucial in realizing the goals of the organization.[100] With its 2017 summit, IORA looks poised to raise its profile as a deliberative forum in the region. The first-ever leaders' summit has infused the two-decade-old forum with purpose. The question now is whether its 21 member states will be able to sustain momentum.[101]

The Indian Ocean is the third largest body of water in the world after the Pacific and Atlantic oceans, and occupies 20 per cent of the world's ocean surface. It is nearly 10,000 kilometres wide at the southern tips of Africa and Australia. Its area is 68.556 million square kilometres, about 5.5 times the size of the United States. Forty-seven countries have it on their shores.[102]

It is a major sea lane connecting the Middle East, East Asia, and Africa and is a critical international waterway for global trade and commerce including half of the world's container cargo and two-thirds of its oil shipments. It accounts for 40 per cent of the world's offshore oil production apart from beach sands heavy in minerals.

The ocean features four critically important access waterways facilitating international maritime trade—the Suez Canal in Egypt, Bab-el-Mandeb (between Djibouti and Yemen), Straits of Hormuz (between Iran and Oman), and Straits of Malacca (between Indonesia and Malaysia). These 'chokepoints' or narrow channels are critical to the world oil trade as huge amounts of oil pass through them.[103]

'Whoever controls the Indian Ocean dominates Asia. This ocean is the key to the seven seas in the twenty-first century [and] the destiny of the world will be decided in these waters.'[104] It was remarkable that US Admiral Alfred Thayer Mahan (1660–1783) predicted this long before the world realized the import of his statement.

Despite its significant strategic position as a major trade route and a home to a large part of the world's population, the Indian Ocean was neglected for a long time. The sudden rise of India and China as global economic powers has significantly increased their energy needs and their dependence on the Gulf oil supplies. Consequently, their energy security interests give these two Asian players direct stakes in the security and stability of the peripheral region O, in particular, the safety of transit lanes from the Arabian Gulf towards the east coast of the Arabian Sea and the Bay of Bengal which surrounds India's long coastal area. This has positioned India and China as major contenders for the share of the ocean's dominion.[105]

IORA

The growing importance of the IO as an ocean of transit has meant a new fillip to the Indian Ocean Rim Association (IORA),[106] although established in 1997, agreed on a new charter in 2010 and adopted its current name in 2013.

It brings together the countries of three continents having different sizes, economic strengths, and a wide diversity of languages and cultures. Its 21 members include Australia, Bangladesh, Comoros, India, Indonesia, Iran, Kenya, Madagascar, Malaysia,

Mauritius, Mozambique, Oman, Seychelles, Singapore, Somalia, South Africa, Sri Lanka, Tanzania, Thailand, the UAE, and Yemen. The IORA countries, as a group, are not major players in the world economy due to a lower level of 'maritimization' by these countries. The United States and the European powers, followed by China, still hold a predominant role in the transit and security in, and of, the Indian ocean region. IORA's six 'Dialogue Partners' are namely, China, Egypt, France, Germany, Japan, and the UK, with two observers namely, Indian Ocean Research Group (IORG) and Indian Ocean Tourism Organisation (IOTO).

The IO region, including the waters and the countries that give out on it, comprises a vast reservoir of resources to exploit and a large untapped market. However, its features have the potential to create tensions and future conflict:[107]

1. Only 28 maritime borders, out of a possible 65, have been formally delimited, complicating territorial disputes.
2. The security of the major chokepoints like the Suez Canal, Bab el-Mandab, Hormuz, Malacca/Singapore, Sunda, and Lombok Straits are a matter of concern.
3. There is a serious problem of piracy, smuggling, and maritime terrorism in this region.
4. Possible contestation in the exploitation of resources—marine, biological, mineral, and energy—which are unequally distributed and not all littoral states have the required technology and resources can become stress points.
5. Military use of the waters, especially the international straits, for naval manoeuvres and transport of nuclear weapons can pose a threat to the security of nearby countries.
6. Issues of transit, security and communications for the land-locked states in the hinterland could create conflict.
7. There exists a threat to marine environment quality and resources and coral reefs from the negative effects of shipping and tourism.
8. There are growing concerns regarding the effects of sea-level rise due to climate change affecting the islands and major deltaic littoral states.

The above issues need to be taken up by the IORA, which covers two billion of the global population whereby it has to create a platform for trade, socio-economic, and cultural cooperation in the IORA. It has identified six priority areas, all of which are relevant to India's outreach in the IO: maritime safety and security, trade and investment facilitation, fisheries management, disaster-risk management, academic science, technology cooperation, and tourism and cultural exchanges.

Since the resources embedded in the IO are crucial to the growth and development of not only the littoral states but all the users of the ocean, IORA needs to promote a global regime for a harmonious exploitation of maritime resources while confronting terrorism, piracy, transport and the deployment of nuclear weapons. It is a far cry from the earlier Indian stance, and of the other non-aligned countries, of the Indian Ocean as a 'zone of peace'.

India's role as an emerging power makes it a crucial stakeholder in the security and prosperity of the Indian Ocean region. India's interests in IORA overlap with all its members in other regional and international forums that could be turned to its advantage. India's exposure in the IO has political, military, and economic dimensions. India will need to secure access to the needed technology in order to be able to exploit the ocean's resources for its development. Politically, India needs to leverage the common goal of the IORA countries to promote the development and security of their peoples. Militarily, India has to expand its naval reach in the India ocean region by intensifying its naval exchanges, including exercises with the navies of Australia, Indonesia, Iran, Malaysia, Singapore, South Africa, Sri Lanka, Thailand, and the UAE to include maritime surveillance, interdiction of piracy and terrorist groups, and escort tasks for shipment of raw materials and sensitive products.

India should also aim that its initiatives in the IORA will equally enhance its reach through the other cross-cutting entities of which they are members.

Notes

1. India's relations with Israel are dealt with in a later chapter.
2. 'Remittances to India', https://en.wikipedia.org/wiki/Remittances _to_India.

3. Ministry of External Affairs, Government of India, 'Official Visit of Minister of State for External Affairs M.J. Akbar to Iraq', 12 August 2016, http://www.mea.gov.in/press-releases.htm?dtl/27330/Offici al+visit+of+Minister+of+State+for+External+Affairs+MJ+Akbar +to+Iraq+August+2123+2016.

4. Ministry of External Affairs, Government of India, 'M.J. Akbar to Visit Lebanon, Syria, Iraq' (12 August 2016), http://www.mjakbar. org/2016/08/12/m-j-akbar-to-visit-lebanon-syria-iraq/.

5. JPost.com Staff, 'Modi Ends Historic Three Day Visit to Israel' Jerusalem Post, 6 July 2017, http://www.jpost.com/Israel-News/ Modis-Visit/LIVE-Indian-PM-Modi-arrives-in-Israel-for- historic-visit-498728.

6. Hindu Net Desk, 'Narendra Modi's Israel Visit, Top Quotes', *The Hindu* (6 July 2017), http://www.thehindu.com/news/ international/narendra-modis-israel-visit-top-quotes/article 19224537.ece.

7. Suhasini Haider, 'Modi Bids "Shalom" after Business End of Trip' *The Hindu* (6 July 2017), http://www.thehindu.com/news/national/ pm-bids-shalom-after-business-end-of-his-trip/article19225725.ece.

8. Quoted in Akilesh Pillalamarri, 'India and the Gulf States Share a Long History', *The Diplomat* (10 June 2016), https://thediplomat. com/2016/06/india-and-the-gulf-states-share-a-long-history/.

9. Ursula Sims-Williams, 'Nineveh', *Bombay and Histories of Indian Archaeology*, Ancient India and Iran Trust (23 October 2016), http://www.indiran.org/nineveh-in-bombay-and-histories-of- indian-archaeology/.

10. 'India-Iraq Relations', https://en.wikipedia.org/wiki/India%E2% 80%93Iraq_relations.

11. Jane McIntosh, 'The First Civilizations in Contact: Mesopotamia and Indus', *Civilizations in Contact*, Faculty of Asian and Middle Eastern Affairs, Cambridge University, http://www.cic.ames.cam. ac.uk/pages/mcintosh.html.

12. CENTO, originally known as the Baghdad Pact or the Middle East Treaty Organization (METO), was formed in 1955 by Iran, Iraq, Pakistan, Turkey, and the United Kingdom. It was dissolved in 1979. Central Treaty Organization, http://www.britannica.com/topic/ Central-Treaty-Organization.

13. 'History of Evolution of the Non-Aligned Movement', Ministry of External Affairs, Government of India (22 August 2012), http:// mea.gov.in/in-focus-article.htm?20349/History+and+Evolution+ of+NonAligned+Movement.

14. Jason Langley, 'Politics and Religion in Iraq and Syria: What Is the Ba'ath Party?' http://www.globalresearch.ca/the-baath-party-as-the-west-doesnt-want-you-to-know-it/5319120.

15. Mustafa Habib, Nawaz Shamdin, and Cathrin Schaer, 'Analysis: Iraq's Ba'ath Party: Where Are They Now?' *Middle East Eye* (13 February 2015), http://www.middleeasteye.net/in-depth/features/analysis-iraqs-baath-party-where-are-they-now-1079222336.

16. Rajendra Abhyankar, 'Iraq and the Begums of Oudh', *Stuff Happens: An Anecdotal Insight into Indian Diplomacy* (New Delhi: Har Anand Publications Pvt. Ltd, 2013), pp. 259–62.

17. Rajendra Abhyankar, 'A Conversation with Saddam Hussein Baghdad, 6 July 2002', *Stuff Happens: An Anecdotal Insight into Indian Diplomacy* (New Delhi: Har Anand Publications Pvt. Ltd, 2013), pp. 157–66.

18. Ministry of External Affairs, Government of India, 'India-Iraq Relations' (April 2015), https://www.mea.gov.in/Portal/ForeignRelation/Iraq_2015_07_02.pdf.

19. Rajendra Abhyankar, 'The Destruction on Osirak 7 June 1981: The Recurrent Obsession with the Bomb', *Stuff Happens: An Anecdotal Insight into Indian Diplomacy* (New Delhi: Har Anand Publications Pvt. Ltd, 2013), pp. 263–69.

20. Rajendra Abhyankar, 'Talabani, Barzani and the Kurds, 25 June 2003', *Stuff Happens: An Anecdotal Insight into Indian Diplomacy* (New Delhi: Har Anand Publications Pvt. Ltd, 2013), pp. 167–82.

21. Nidhi Verma, 'Iran Leapfrogs Iraq as India's No. 2 Oil Supplier in February: Trade Data', Reuters.com, 13 March 2017, http://www.reuters.com/article/us-india-iran/iran-leapfrogs-iraq-as-indias-no-2-oil-supplier-in-february-trade-data-idUSKBN16K0OA.

22. Talmiz Ahmed, 'Gulf Stability and the Oil Supply Scenario', *The Hindu*, 23 May 2016, http://www.thehindu.com/opinion/lead/gulf-stability-and-the-oil-supply-scenario/article6605374.ece.

23. Elizabeth Roche, 'M.J. Akbar to Visit Lebanon, Syria and Iraq', *Live Mint* (August 2016), http://www.livemint.com/Politics/26z7fvgFasC55XRUxiYl3I/MJ-Akbar-to-visit-Lebanon-Syria-Iraq.html.

24. Rajendra Abhyankar, *Stuff Happens: An Anecdotal Insight into Indian Diplomacy* (New Delhi: Har Anand Publications Pvt. Ltd, 2013), p. 212.

25. The subject of Indian diaspora has been covered in a later chapter.

26. Ajaz Ashraf, 'Iraq and India: A Forgotten Love Story', Firstpost (21 June 2014), http://www.firstpost.com/world/iraq-and-india-a-forgotten-love-story-1581885.html.

27. Kabir Taneja, 'The Reality of India-Iran Ties', *The Diplomat* (11 July 2016), http://thediplomat.com/2016/07/the-reality-of-india-iran-ties/.

28. Srinath Raghavan, 'The Takeaway from Iran', *The Hindu* (26 May 2016), http://www.thehindu.com/opinion/lead/modis-visit-to-iran-the-takeaway-from-tehran/article8646427.ece.

29. Manish Vaid, 'Chabahar and Gwadar: Antagonism Denying Potential Synergies', STS, Science and Technology Security Forum, 1 July 2017, http://stsfor.org/content/chabahar-and-gwadar-antagonism-denying-potential-synergies.

30. Bilal Abdi, 'Iran and India Further Talks on Oil and Gas Cooperation, Farzad B Gas Field', ET Energy World, 19 May 2017, http://energy.economictimes.indiatimes.com/news/oil-and-gas/-iran-and-india-further-talks-on-oil-and-gas-cooperation-farzad-b-gas-field/58744419. 'Farzad B gas field was discovered by OVL in the Farsi block about 10 years ago. The project has so far cost the OVL-led consortium, which also includes Oil India Ltd and Indian Oil Corp (IOC), over USD 80 million. Iran was initially unhappy with the USD 10 billion plan submitted by OVL for development of the 12.5 trillion cubic feet reserves in Farzad-B field and an accompanying plant to liquefy the gas for transportation in ships. The field in the Farsi block has an in-place gas reserve of 21.7 tcf, of which 12.5 tcf are recoverable.'

31. Vinay Kaura, 'India and Iran: Challenges and Opportunities', *The Diplomat* (11 September 2015), http://thediplomat.com/2015/09/india-iran-relations-challenges-and-opportunity/.

32. The three strategic triangles are: India-Iran-US; India-Iran-Israel; India-Iran-Saudi Arabia.

33. https://www.scribd.com/doc/271540618/Iran-Deal-Text.

34. 'The Joint Comprehensive Plan of Action (JCPOA) known commonly as the Iran deal or Iran nuclear deal, is an international agreement on the nuclear program of Iran reached in Vienna on 14 July 2015 between Iran, the P5+1 (the five permanent members of the United Nations Security Council—China, France, Russia, United Kingdom, United States—plus Germany),[a] and the European Union. The parties finalized the Joint Plan of Action in April 2015 agreed on an Iran nuclear deal framework for the final agreement and in July 2015, Iran and the P5+1 agreed on the plan. Under the agreement, Iran agreed to eliminate its stockpile of medium-enriched uranium, cut its stockpile of low-enriched uranium by 98%, and reduce by about two-thirds the number of its gas

centrifuges for 13 years. For the next 15 years, Iran will only enrich uranium up to 3.67%. Iran also agreed not to build any new heavy-water facilities for the same period of time. Uranium-enrichment activities will be limited to a single facility using first-generation centrifuges for 10 years. Other facilities will be converted to avoid proliferation risks. To monitor and verify Iran's compliance with the agreement, the International Atomic Energy Agency (IAEA) will have regular access to all Iranian nuclear facilities. The agreement provides that in return for verifiably abiding by its commitments, Iran will receive relief from U.S., European Union, and United Nations Security Council nuclear-related economic sanctions.' Joint Comprehensive Plan of Action', https://en.wikipedia.org/wiki/Joint_Comprehensive_Plan_of_Action.

35. Jeffrey Lewis, 'Trump's Next Self-Inflicted Crisis is a Nuclear Iran', *Foreign Policy* (30 August 2017), http://foreignpolicy.com/2017/08/30/trumps-next-self-inflicted-crisis-is-a-nuclear-iran/.

36. Ted Galen Carpenter, 'Abandoning the Iran Deal is Just One Example of Irrational US Diplomacy', *The National Interest*, 11 October 2017, http://nationalinterest.org/feature/abandoning-the-iran-deal-just-one-example-irrational-us-22680?page=show.

37. Reuters, 'Unhappy with Tehran India to Cut Imports of Iranian Oil', *Business Today*, 1 April 2017, http://www.businesstoday.in/current/economy-politics/tehran-india-to-cut-iranian-oil-purchases-gas-field-imports-of-iranian/story/249158.html.

38. Golnar Motevalli and Iain Marlow, 'India Slow to Develop Chabahar Port as China Races Ahead at Rival Hub', *The Economic Times* (5 October 2016), http://economictimes.indiatimes.com/industry/transportation/shipping-/-transport/india-slow-to-develop-chabahar-port-as-china-races-ahead-at-rival-hub/articleshow/54693856.cms.

39. Srinath Raghavan, 'India Slow to Develop Chabahar Port as China Races Ahead at Rival Hub', *The Economic Times* (5 October 2016), http://economictimes.indiatimes.com/industry/transportation/shipping-/-transport/india-slow-to-develop-chabahar-port-as-china-races-ahead-at-rival-hub/articleshow/54693856.cms.

40. Bharat Gopalaswami and Amir Handjani, 'Can India and Iran Turn the Page?' *The National Interest*, 14 January 2017, http://nationalinterest.org/feature/can-iran-india-turn-the-page-19057?page=2.

41. Ministry of External Affairs, Government of India India-Yemen Relations (December 2014), http://www.mea.gov.in/Portal/ForeignRelation/Yemen_December_2014_eng.pdf.

42. Amal Nasser, 'Is Yemen Falling into an Abyss?' *National Yemen* (22 November 2016), http://nationalyemen.com/2016/11/29/is-yemen-falling-into-an-abyss/.

43. Shoqi Maktary and Katie Smith, 'Pathways for Peace and Stability in Yemen, Search for Common Ground, 2017', https://www.sfcg. org/wp-content/uploads/2017/06/Pathways-for-Peace-Stability-in-Yemen.pdf.

44. Maktary and Smith, 'Pathways for Peace and Stability in Yemen, Search for Common Ground, 2017'.

45. Michael Brendan Dougherty, 'Trump's Yemen Policy is Immoral and Counterproductive', *National Review*, 13 July 2017, http://www.nationalreview.com/article/449471/trump-yemen-policy-immoral-counterproductive.

46. Embassy of India, Sana'a India-Yemen Relations (December 2016), http://eoisanaa.org/bilateral-relations/.

47. Shoaib Daniyal, 'Mercenaries and Merchants: A Short History of the Strong Ties between India and Yemen', Scroll.in, 10 April 2015.

48. Ibrahim Huri, 'Yemen-India Bilateral Relations: A Story of Historic Integration, Cooperation and Synergy', Research Gate, April 2016, https://www.researchgate.net/publication/307167676_Yemen_-_India_Bilateral_Relations_A_Story_of_Historic_Integration_Cooperation_and_Synergy.

49. Editorial, 'Just in Time', *The Hindu* (7 April 2015), http://www.thehindu.com/opinion/editorial/yemen-crisis-operation-rahat-rescues-indians/article7074434.ece.

50. Ministry of External Affairs, Government of India, 'Gulf Cooperation Council', February 2003, https://www.mea.gov.in/Portal/Foreign Relation/Gulf_Cooperation_Council_MEA_Website.pdf.

51. Desk, 'Saudi Arabia Forms Muslim "Anti-terrorism" Coalition', Al Jazeera (15 December 2015), http://www.aljazeera.com/news/2015/12/saudi-arabia-forms-muslim-anti-terrorism-coalition-151215035914865.html.

52. Naveed Ahmed, 'Pakistan and Saudi-led Anti-terrror Coalition: Regional Implications for Appointment of Gen. Raheel', Al-Jazeera (17 May 2017), http://studies.aljazeera.net/en/reports/2017/05/pakistan-saudi-led-anti-terror-coalitionregional-implications-appointment-gen-raheel-170517100721721.html.

53. Lewis Sanders IV, 'What is the Qatar Crisis?' *DW* (21 July 2017), http://www.dw.com/en/what-is-the-qatar-crisis/a-39795408.

54. James M. Dorsey, 'Battling for Independence: Small States Stake Their Claims', MWC News (5 October 2017), http://mwcnews. net/focus/analysis/68514-battling-for-independence.html.

55. John R. Bradley, 'Unlikely Allies: Israel and the Saudis', *The Spectator* (24 June 2017), https://www.spectator.co.uk/2017/06/unlikely-allies-israel-and-the-saudis/.

56. Stanly Johny, 'India's Balancing Act in the Gulf', Middle East Institute, 9 May 2017, http://www.mei.edu/content/map/indias-balancing-act-gulf.

57. Kadira Pethiyagoda, 'India GCC Relations: Delhi's Strategic Opportunity', Brookings Doha Center Paper No. 18, February 2017, https://www.brookings.edu/wp-content/uploads/2017/02/india_gcc_relations.pdf.

58. John Calabrese, '"Linking West" in "Unsettled Times": India–GCC Trade Relations', Middle East Institute, 11 April 2017, http://www.mei.edu/content/map/linking-west-unsettled-times-india-gcc-economic-and-trade-relations.

59. John Calabrese, '"Linking West" in "Unsettled Times"'.

60. 'The Gulf Cooperation Council GCC', *Global Security*, http://www.globalsecurity.org/military/world/gulf/gcc.htm.

61. Naresh Kumar, 'Recent Trend and Pattern of Indian Emigration to Gulf Countries: A Diaspora Perspective', 2014, http://paa2014. princeton.edu/papers/141653.

62. *Emirates 24/7*, 'FTA to Boost India's Links with UAE and GCC', 9 February 2016, http://www.emirates247.com/business/economy-finance/fta-to-boost-india-s-links-with-uae-and-gcc-2016-02-09-1.620406.

63. Benjamin David Baker, 'Where Is the "String of Pearls" in 2015?' *The Diplomat* (5 October 2015), http://thediplomat.com/2015/10/where-is-the-string-of-pearls-in-2015/.

64. 'India–Saudi Arabia Relations', https://en.wikipedia.org/wiki/India%E2%80%93Saudi_Arabia_relations.

65. Royal Embassy of Saudi Arabia, Washington DC, 'Saudi–Indian Joint Communique', 3 April 2016, https://www.saudiembassy.net/statements/saudi-indian-joint-communiqu%C3%A9.

66. Bruce Reidel, 'Saudi Arabia Tilts towards India', *AlMonitor* (6 April 2016), http://www.al-monitor.com/pulse/originals/2016/04/saudi-arabia-tilt-india-pakistan-salman-iran.html.

67. Chidananda Rajghatta, 'US, Saudi Arabia Join Hands to Sanction Pakistani Entities Ahead of PM Narendra Modi's Visit to Riyahd', *Economic Times* (1 April 2016), http://economictimes.

indiatimes.com/news/us-saudi-arabia-join-hands-to-sanction-pakistani-entities-ahead-of-pm-narendra-modis-visit-to-riyadh/articleshow/51649372.cms.

68. Mateen Haider, 'Pakistan will not Send Ground Troops as Part of Saudi-led Military Alliance: Aziz, *Dawn* (16 January 2016), https://www.dawn.com/news/1232480.

69. Harsh V. Pant, 'Why India and Saudi Arabia Continue to Grow Closer', *The Diplomat* (13 April 2016), http://thediplomat.com/2016/04/why-india-and-saudi-arabia-continue-to-grow-closer/.

70. Issac James Manayath, 'The Future of India-Saudi Arabia Relations', *The Diplomat* (30 April 2016), http://thediplomat.com/2016/04/the-future-of-india-saudi-arabia-relations/.

71. Akiva Eldar, 'What Saudi Arabia Can Offer Israel', *AlMonitor* (28 July 2016), http://www.al-monitor.com/pulse/originals/2016/07/saudi-arabia-egypt-visit-jerusalem-arab-peace-initiative.html.

72. FP Editors, 'Abu Jundal Arrest: US Squeeze on Pak, Saudi Nets Gain for India', Firstpost (26 June 2012), http://www.firstpost.com/world/abu-jindal-arrest-us-squeeze-on-pak-saudis-nets-big-gain-for-india-356987.html.

73. Tanvi Madan, 'Why Is India's Modi Visiting Saudi Arabia?' *Brookings* (1 April 2016), https://www.brookings.edu/blog/markaz/2016/04/01/why-is-indias-modi-visiting-saudi-arabia/.

74. 'India–United Arab Emirates Relations', https://en.wikipedia.org/wiki/India%E2%80%93United_Arab_Emirates_relations.

75. Wam, 'UAE, India Issue Joint Statement at End of Mohamad bin Zayed's Visit to India', Emirates247.com (26 January 2017), http://www.emirates247.com/news/emirates/uae-india-issue-joint-statement-at-the-end-of-mohamed-bin-zayed-s-visit-to-india-2017-01-26-1.647104.

76. 'UAE-India Relations', Embassy of India in United Arab Emirates, http://www.uaeembassy-newdelhi.com/uae-indiarelations_economic&trade.asp.

77. Press Information Bureau, 'Phase I of Strategic Petroleum Reserve (SPR) Programme at Three Locations has Capacity of 5.33 MMT' Government of India, Ministry of Petroleum and Natural Gas, 8 February 2017, http://pib.nic.in/newsite/PrintRelease.aspx?relid=158237.

78. Embassy of India, Doha, 'India-Qatar Relations', June 2016, http://indianembassyqatar.gov.in/pages/bilateralrelations.php.

79. Patrick Wintour, 'Qatar Given 10 Days to Meet 13 Sweeping Demands by Saudi Arabia', *The Guardian* (23 June 2017),

https://www.theguardian.com/world/2017/jun/23/close-al-jazeera-saudi-arabia-issues-qatar-with-13-demands-to-end-blockade.

80. Doug Bandow, 'Economic War against Qatar Backfires on Saudi Arabia and United Arab Emirates', HuffPost (31 July 2017), https://www.huffingtonpost.com/entry/economic-war-against-qatar-backfires-on-saudi-arabia_us_597ee4aae4b0c69ef7052971.

81. Editors, 'Trump Stopped Saudi Arabia, UAE from Invading Qatar, Report Says', *Daily Sabah* (20 September 2017), https://www.dailysabah.com/mideast/2017/09/20/trump-stopped-saudi-arabia-uae-from-invading-qatar-report-says.

82. Reuters, 18 October 2016, 'Some Taliban Officials Say Secret Peace Talks Held in Qatar', http://www.reuters.com/article/us-afghani-stan-taliban-peacetalks-idUSKCN12I0O2.

83. Jonathan Spyer, 'Qatar's Rise and America's Tortured Middle East Policy', *The Tower Magazine* (August 2014), http://www.thetower.org/article/qatars-rise-and-americas-tortured-middle-east-policy/.

84. Kristian Coates Ulrichsen, 'Qatar and the Arab Spring: Policy Drivers and Regional Complications', Carnegie Endowment for International Peace, 24 September 2014, http://carnegieendow-ment.org/2014/09/24/qatar-and-arab-spring-policy-drivers-and-regional-implications-pub-56723.

85. Rishi Iyengar, 'India Ban Al-Jazeera for 5 Days for Showing Incorrect Maps of Kashmir', *Time* (23 April 2015), http://time.com/3832585/india-al-jazeera-suspended-kashmir-dispute-maps/.

86. Embassy of India, Muscat, Oman, 'Oman-India Bilateral Relations', 9 December 2016, http://www.indemb-oman.org/inner.aspx?type=Menu&id=26.

87. Giorgio Cafiero and Cinzia Miotto, 'Oman Diversifying Allies with Closer India Ties', Middle East Institute, 1 October 2016, http://www.mei.edu/content/article/oman-diversifies-allies-closer-india-ties.

88. Jeta Pillai, 'A Step Forward in the ME Pipeline', *Oman Tribune* (5 July 2017), http://omantribune.com/details/42911/.

89. Abdul Latif Dahir, 'How a Tiny African Country Became the World's Key Military Base', *Quartz Africa* (28 August 2017), https://qz.com/1056257/how-a-tiny-african-country-became-the-worlds-key-military-base/.

90. Ministry of External Affairs, Government of India, 'Bahrain-India Relations', August 2014, https://www.mea.gov.in/Portal/ForeignRelation/Bahrain_2015_08_18.pdf.

91. 'India and Bahrain to Strengthen Ties in Trade, Counter-terrorism', *The Hindu* (24 January 2016), http://www.thehindu.com/news/

India-Bahrain-to-strengthen-ties-in-trade-counter-terror/article14017624.ece.

92. Abd al-Hadi Khalaf, 'The Elusive Quest for Gulf Security', *Middle East Research and Information Project*, http://www.merip.org/mer/mer148/elusive-quest-gulf-security?ip_login_no_cache=d122ef1 3e1ee438bab6d98c8c8d527c4.

93. Ethan Bronner and Michael Slackman, 'Saudi Troops Enter Bahrain to Help Put Down Unrest', *The New York Times* (14 March 2011), http://www.nytimes.com/2011/03/15/world/middleeast/15bahrain.html.

94. 'Rajnath Singh Leaves for Bahrain to Raise Pakistan Sponsored Terror in India', *The Indian Express* (23 October 2016), http://indianexpress.com/article/india/india-news-india/rajnath-singh-leaves-for-bahrain-to-raise-pakistan-sponsored-terror-in-india/.

95. 'Kuwait-India Relations', https://en.wikipedia.org/wiki/India%E2%80%93Kuwait_relations.

96. '1990 Airlift of Indians from Kuwait', https://en.wikipedia.org/wiki/1990_airlift_of_Indians_from_Kuwait.

97. Ministry of External Affairs, Government of India, 'India–Kuwait Relations', January 2016, https://www.mea.gov.in/Portal/ForeignRelation/Kuwait_13_01_2016.pdf.

98. Philomene Verlaan, Joseph R. Morgan, and Vctor Filipovich, 'Indian Ocean', *Encyclopedia*, 20 January 2016, https://www.britannica.com/place/Indian-Ocean/Trade-and-transportation.

99. Indian Ocean Rim Association, http://www.iora.net/support-staff.aspx.

100. Rajiv Bhatia, 'Back Indian Ocean Rim Pact to Promote the Blue Economy', *The Asian Age* (15 March 2017), http://www.asianage.com/india/all-india/150317/back-indian-ocean-rim-pact-to-promote-the-blue-economy.html.

101. Ankit Panda, 'Indian Ocean Rim Association Concludes its First-Ever Leaders' Summit', *The Diplomat* (8 March 2017), https://thediplomat.com/2017/03/indian-ocean-rim-association-concludes-first-ever-leaders-summit/.

102. Nadesan Satyendra, 'International Relations in an Emerging Multilateral World', *Tamilnation.org*, http://www.tamilnation.co/intframe/indian_ocean/.

103. Satyendra, 'International Relations in an Emerging Multilateral World'.

104. Cdr. P.K. Ghosh, US Rear Admiral Thayer Mahan quoted in 'Maritime Security Challenges in South Asia and the Indian

Ocean', Institute of Defence Studies and Analyses, 18 January 2004, http://tamilnation.co/intframe/indian_ocean/pk_ghosh.

105. Theodor Karasik, 'Why All Eyes Should be on the Indian Ocean', *English al-Arabiya*, http://english.alarabiya.net/en/views/news/world/2014/01/09/Why-all-eyes-should-be-on-the-Indian-Ocean.html.

106. Ministry of External Affairs, Government of India, http://mea.gov.in/in-focus-article.htm?20707/Indian+Ocean+Rim+Association+for+Regional+Cooperation+IORARC.

107. Dennis Rumley and Sanjay Chaturvedi, *Geopolitical Orientations, Regionalism, and Security in the Indian Ocean* (New York: Routledge, 2015 [2004]).

CHAPTER
THREE

Expanding Dimensions

*O*ver the last 70 years India's relations with advanced countries, particularly those with political, military, and economic
power, can be seen as a barometer of its own progress in achieving
great power status in the world. India has always believed that it
has been at the forefront of human civilization from the Indus
Valley settlements dating back to 2500 BCE. It has also believed
that greatness has always been its destiny. This underlying belief
has been at the root of its continual search for great power status
within the international system. The trajectory of India's relations
with the P-5 in the UNSC brings out the level of success it has
had in achieving its chosen goal.

A degree of parallelism is evident in the way India was seen in
pre-colonial period and now. Following the assumption in 1858
of direct rule over India by Britain, India[1] became the jewel in
the British crown, coveted by all European powers. Though it
ceased to become a battleground for contesting European powers
after 1858, it did initiate a level of cultural, religious, and scientific
exchanges with them. The implementation of the famous dispatch
in 1884 by Sir Charles Wood, prescribing the teaching of English
and European learning to Indians instituted a university system
that was responsible for the regular flow of knowledge and scholars to Great Britain and Europe.

During World War I, when over a million Indians fought as part of the British Indian Army, not much political contact was possible between European scholars and leaders of the Indian independence movement. The inter-War years saw the introduction of elected representation in India through the Morley-Minto Reforms (1919), the first step towards the eventual independence, and partition, of India.

Indian independence in August 1947 saw a slow flowering of its bilateral relations with the permanent European members of the UNSC, although British influence on events affecting India remained unparalleled. In those initial years, India's major concerns were securing economic aid through the Aid India Consortium and keeping the issue of Kashmir under constant watch in the UNSC to avoid unforeseen developments. By then it had become clear that Pakistan was unlikely to withdraw from the occupied portion of Kashmir as required by the 1948 Resolution of the UN Commission on India and Pakistan that would have set in train other provisions of that resolution.[2] Nevertheless, the possibility of a UNSC-mandated international mediation was always open, especially since India believed that the directly involved UNSC members, particularly the United Kingdom (UK), were working towards the transfer, in some form, of Kashmir to Pakistan.

The Aid India Consortium, which annually decided aid allocations for India, was crucial for starting the development process in a country left impoverished after long years of colonial rule. The Indian government started its Five-Year Development Plan in 1951, and full-scale development planning was introduced in the Second Five-Year Plan (1956–61) under the strong leadership of Jawaharlal Nehru and the economist. P.C. Mahalanobis. At the initial stage of the Second Five-Year Plan, foreign aid to India played a minor role in providing financial resources for economic development. However, from 1958 onwards, under the 'crisis' of foreign exchange and balance of payments, a new scheme of multinational foreign aid was formed under the leadership of the World Bank known as the International Bank for Reconstruction and Development (IBRD).

The Aid India Consortium[3] lasted throughout the Cold War, decolonization in Asia, and the residual influence of the United Kingdom and the sterling area in the 1950s and 1960s. The Indian government, under Nehru, played a key role in the negotiations of the Consortium. Up to the mid-1960s, the Aid India Consortium usually offered around USD 1 billion annually to India as economic aid, in which the US capital share was around 42 per cent while the World Bank and its affiliate, the International Development Association (IDA, established in 1960) occupied the second position with around 20–25 per cent. This was in addition to the US PL (Public Law) 480 wheat shipments to India, particularly from 1967 to 1974. The presence of this multilateral framework for aid to India was crucial to the acceleration of the country's economic development when it came to overcoming food crisis. This was one of the early successful tests of Indian diplomacy in moving towards the national goals of food self-sufficiency and economic development.

India's bilateral relations with the permanent members of the UNSC—Britain, United States, Soviet Union, France, and China—followed a trajectory that in the early years was still constrained by Cold War dynamics and India's steadfast non-aligned posture. In staying away from military pacts, India did not endear itself to the United States, although the Soviet Union took the opportunity to build itself up as the 'natural ally' of NAM. In the background of unremitting positions adopted by NAM and the Group of 77 (G-77) developing countries, to secure 1 per cent GDP of developed countries for annual aid flows to developing countries, their level of contact was both intense and fractious. The Second Development Decade—the 1970s—and the marathon conferences in United Nations Conference on Trade and Development (UNCTAD) became the raison d'être for the growing solidarity within the group of developing countries, whether members of NAM or G-77, and that of these groups with the Soviet Union.

For India, this period of heady international economic activism was marked by political imperatives arising from the partition of the subcontinent in 1947, which led to a continuing political and military contest to assert itself. The partition of Pakistan—west and east—from the rest of India immediately unleashed military action in Kashmir, keeping Indian leaders in thrall of British power in the UNSC. Until the 1971 India–Pakistan War, India faced the contest in a particularly virulent manner given matching military strengths and an even-handed UNSC stance. It not only laid the future trend of India–Pakistan contestation over Kashmir—both on the ground and in the UN—but stymied India's attempts to politically and economically assert itself.

From 1947 to 1972, India and Pakistan fought three limited military actions, of which the last resulted in the creation of an independent Bangladesh from the erstwhile East Pakistan. It conclusively demonstrated that religion alone was not sufficient in consolidating the people of a country and debunked the 'two-nation theory' promoted to create Pakistan. In terms of both military strategy on the ground in Bangladesh and diplomatic strategy in the UNSC, India's coordinated action was highly successful.

Nevertheless, Pakistan has continued its military forays into Kashmir beginning in 1989 with the infiltration by armed groups across the LoC in J&K that culminated in May–June 1999 in the attempt to capture Indian territory in Kargil (at a height of 32,000 feet), in the Drass sector of Kashmir. The Indian Air Force reacted with an imaginative use of air power. There was an overt US mediation too to preserve the sanctity of the LoC. During the last decade of the 20th century, there were 49 separate attacks by Pakistani terrorist groups across India. It included major cities (Bengaluru 2003, Mumbai 2008, and Delhi 2011), railways (Samjhauta Express 2007 and Chennai 2014), other infrastructure (Guwahati 2009, Pune 2010, 2012, and Srinagar 2013), and army camps and bases (Pathankot 2016) which have gone on to prove the prolific nature of the asymmetric warfare waged against India.

The end of the Cold War and the disintegration of the Soviet Union was a major blow to India and resulted in the loss of the country's biggest ally. Even more, the end of the power blocs removed the raison d'être for continuing with NAM, while the failure of a statist economic system dictated a more open economic system and a foreign policy that would promote Indian economic interests. As there were no blocs now, non-alignment became redundant, and it became even more imperative to build relations with the only super power. As if this was not enough, India found itself with minimal financial reserves, forcing it to sell gold to the World Bank to meet the economy's financial requirements.

The realization that there was no alternative to a complete overhaul of the country's policies led in 1991 to an economic reform policy aimed at changing the economic policy in favour of liberalization in tandem with a foreign policy which would build relations with the United States and other major Western countries. The success of the economic reform policy was quick, and from 1997 onwards, India was achieving an annual GDP growth of over 8 per cent per annum and over. The easier availability of financial resources permitted investments in infrastructure, improving prospects of foreign investment and collaborations. This development was not without its political upside with all major Western powers making a beeline for an India increasingly viewed as a major market and investment destination.

These broad trends in India's growth in the first decades of the era of liberalization will provide the backdrop for the assessment of India's relations with the five permanent members of the UNSC. With each of them India has had a wide range of bilateral relations which, over the years, has been inching towards a more equal partnership.

The United Kingdom

Of the European countries, India has had the longest relationship with the United Kingdom. British presence in India started in 1612 with the arrival of the East India Company for trading purposes. As its trading operations in India grew, the Company developed the attributes of a state. Since the Company had been incorporated with a charter from the British sovereign, it benefited from complete government support. In the hundred-odd years that it ruled over India, it had transformed into a military force to protect its interests on land and sea and created new ones through subordinations, alliances, and conquests.

The revolt of 1857 against the Company's rule was India's first war of independence,[4] when different parts of the country came together against the British rule. From 1858 until 1947, the country was under direct rule of Britain. The ups and downs in India's freedom struggle, particularly after 1900 until independence, when the country was partitioned, raised doubts on the future of relations between the two countries.

India's relations with the United Kingdom after gaining independence fall into in to four periods: 1947–65, when a high degree of uncertainty and suspicion marked the relationship; 1965–91, when the Cold War determined the tenor of their relationship; 1990–2016, which was marked by India's economic opening while the United Kingdom had resigned itself to being a middle power; and after 2016, when Britain's exit from the EU opens new opportunities for India to harness its relationship with a country that is a permanent member of the UNSC.

In the period from 1947 to 1965, India's choice of non-alignment as its foreign policy option determined the bilateral relationship, as also its strong support of decolonization round the world. The UK was seen by other Western powers as the country that could best deal with India. The Kashmir issue starts as much with India and Pakistan as it does with the UK. Pakistan's invasion in 1947–48 of the princely state with irregular and armed forces, despite an agreement to the contrary, left an open sore.

While facing the prospect of its waning power and influence and early withdrawal from Asia, the UK, had, as a member of Southeast Asia Treaty Organization (SEATO)[5] and CENTO[6], taken a relatively partial position on the issue of Kashmir. Yet India had to rely on its British connection for its international outreach, and the preferential tariff regime known as the Imperial Preferences, later Commonwealth Preferences, which covered 60 per cent of India's exports. It was through Jawaharlal Nehru's insistence that India became a member of the British Commonwealth.

The UK continued its aid to India regardless of its divergent foreign policy choices that had pitted India against it during the Suez crisis. During, and after the 1962 Chinese aggression, in northeast India, Britain provided armaments and ammunition to the Indian Army. India remained in thrall of the UK until 1965, when it shut down supply of weapons and armaments to both countries during the India–Pakistan War over Kashmir, grinding the conflict to a halt. The UK's impartial attitude during that war finally brought down the scales from Indian eyes. The peace agreement, the Tashkent Accord 1965, between India and Pakistan, brokered by the Soviet Union in Tashkent, froze the matter without suggesting any solution.

The Cold War saw India and the UK dealing with each other as much as was possible, even though both had divergent views on international developments. Furthermore, with the UK joining the European Economic Community (EEC)[7] in 1972, India faced the end of the Commonwealth trade preference regime.[8] India successfully negotiated a new trade regime with the EEC, finally severing a long-standing bond with the UK. The UK's inability to provide India any relief on trade was symptomatic of its emerging status as a middle power trying to enter a grouping that had much going for it. This was in direct contrast with France, which secured 'association agreements' with all its former colonies from the EEC. India had to develop its relations with the EEC without much help from the UK. Its success in developing a new basis for relations with the EEC, and later the European Union, was a major achievement of India's diplomacy.

The United Kingdom's decision in 1968 to run down its military presence in the Indian Ocean meant the withdrawal of British forces from Aden and the East. India then was wedded to the concept of the Indian Ocean as a 'Zone of Peace' which would ban nuclear weapons and keep out major powers in the IOR.[9] The island of Diego Garcia, in the Chagos archipelago, was handed over to the United States, marking the passing of British influence in the IOR. The 1971 Indo-Soviet Treaty of Friendship and Cooperation[10] was yet another area of disagreement between the two countries. India's support to Soviet presence in Afghanistan after 1979, was payback for the treaty that supported India during the India–Pakistan War of 1972. Nevertheless, the UK continued its defence assistance to India while tying it to the purchase of British defence material. In fact, from 1964 to 1977, India was the largest purchaser of British arms.

India's economic reform process and the end of the Cold War made for the possibility of renewed closer relations between the two countries. At the same time, though India accounted for 14 per cent of total world imports, the UK accounted only for 3.1 per cent of India's exports and 1.5 per cent of India's imports.[11] A more encouraging development was in the area of mutual bilateral investment. The purchase of Corus and Jaguar made the Tata group the largest private sector employer in the UK.

The India–UK strategic partnership agreement received a renewed boost during the visit of Prime Minister Theresa May in November 2016 to New Delhi. It focused on issues of counterterrorism, cooperation in civil nuclear energy, high technology trade, and space cooperation. It also aimed at promoting educational and research cooperation, a long-standing feature of the bilateral relationship. The UK would continue overseas aid to India and assured its support for India's permanent membership in the UNSC. The prospects for defence cooperation were, however, limited considering that India had moved away from procuring British equipment.[12]

Britain still imports a quarter of India's exports to the EU. In FY 2016, out of total exports of USD 35.35 billion to the EU, exports to the UK were USD 9.35 billion. The picture on FDI is even better. FDI inflow into India during 2000–16 was USD 23.1 billion. The UK is the largest investor in India while India invests more in UK than in the rest of the EU put together. It is the third largest source of FDI to the UK. A good deal of this investment came in because of the importance of London's financial market and, from India's point of view, its centrality for business with the EU.

The bilateral relationship has become highly unequal with the size of the Indian diaspora in the UK, which stands between 1.5 and 2 million, all of whom are heavily involved in the British economy. They have also increased their political activism within the British political system across the spectrum.

As the UK's process of exit from the EU moves ahead, no doubt it would simultaneously look at finding a new basis for its relationship with India.[13] This time around, in contrast with 1972, India and the UK will approach the issue with mutual interest. For India, Britain's UNSC membership is a major factor whereas for the latter a vibrant and growing economic relationship with India will continue its importance in the global economy.

One referendum, one election and 12 wobbly months later, Britain's negotiations to leave the European Union at last began on 19 June 2017. The United Kingdom's exit from the EU is to take effect in 2019. It has opened an opportunity for India to step up its bilateral relationship. The two countries have already initiated discussions on the possibility of an India–UK FTA. The Commonwealth has estimated that the trade agreement could boost post-Brexit UK exports to India from USD 5.2 billion to USD 7.8 billion.[15]

Though London remains a major financial centre for India's investors, its exit from the EU could impel India to shift base to other financial EU hubs like Frankfurt or Paris. In negotiations for a new trade and investment agreement, India and the UK would both have reasons to look for ways to protect these advantages.

India and the EU

The India–EEC relationship started with a focus on tariff preferences under the EEC's Generalized Preferences Scheme (GSP) that eventually more than made up for the loss of the British imperial tariff preferences. It boosted bilateral trade after India's economic opening in 1990. A progressive widening of the agreement to include trade, investment, and services followed closely on India's growing significance in the world economy, leading eventually to closer political relations. With the transition of the EEC in 2000 into the EU, the bilateral relationship too transformed and acquired a different political dimension. In 2004, recognizing India's status as an emerging economic power.

India and the EU entered into a strategic partnership[16] agreement. It governs India's bilateral relations with the entity even though India maintains close economic and political relations with each member of the EU individually.

The EU invited India in 2004 to become a 'strategic partner' (SP)—one of six then that included the US, Canada, Japan, Russia, and China—in recognition of its burgeoning domestic market.[17] It has ten other strategic partnerships with individual countries and five others which are regional: Africa and African Union,

Middle East, Latin America and Caribbean, UN and NATO. The EU still struggles with the goal and expected outcomes from these partnerships.

In the case of India the EU recognized India's prowess in IT and scientific research; the development of nuclear power; the extensive exploration of Antarctica; the advances in astronomy and astrophysics and innovative disciplines such as informatics, plant genetics; and the exploration of the seabed, ocean floor, and outer space to harness its inherent strengths.[18]

A note of caution is needed here. When one compares with the EU's other strategic partners it is clear that with India it was based on potential and not ground realities. India has still to convert that promise into reality. In the recent past the SP has suffered because of EU's action to wrongly leverage a bilateral issue between India and Italy to delay the bilateral Summit.[19] Yet the ageing population in Europe and its sluggish economic growth makes India an attractive partner, a prolific market, a destination for investment, and a source of highly trained professionals with a growing indigenous infrastructure for research and development.

The relationship between India and the EU continues to suffer due to two factors: first, the fact that India has had long-standing and substantial relations with all major EU countries and second, despite decades of presence in India the EU has not been able to overcome its trade-related focus. These two reasons have kept the EU from developing a dynamic relationship illustrated by the long delay in the finalization of the India–EU FTA.

The existence of close relations between India and each of the major European powers has meant that the EU has essentially had no catalytic role in the political dimension of its relationship with India. On the contrary, the EU's focus on contentious issues such as human rights, child labour, and death penalty abolition have riled India without securing any substantial advantages or results. In fact, the EU's stances on social issues have provided an 'out' to the major European powers in their dealings with India. They do not need to raise these disruptive issues in their bilateral discussions and yet get a free ride when the EU raises them. In a negative sense, it has reinforced Indian perception of the EU as primarily a trade body.[20]

The relationship has stagnated since 2009 because of the global economic downturn and the inability of the two sides to finalize the bilateral 'free trade plus agreement' since 2005.[21] The proposed India–EU FTA, officially known as the broad-based trade and investment agreement, has been stuck for the past few years due to a disagreement between the two sides over contentious issues such as the lowering of import duties on automobiles and alcohol by India and the recognition of India by the EU as a 'data-secure' country. India also wants FTA+ agreement to include a new EU-wide single bilateral investment treaty to replace the existing bilateral treaties. It is also not keen on extending the existing treaties with individual EU member countries after they lapse.[22]

After a gap of four years, the 13th EU–India Summit was held in Brussels on 31 March 2016 when Prime Minister Narendra Modi was visiting the country.[23] It reiterated the interest of both sides to move the relationship forward. Yet there was no assurance that bilateral relations will not be allowed to interrupt India–EU relations. The inability to agree on a way forward to finalize the bilateral trade agreement remains a major hurdle.[24] The 14th India EU Summit was held in New Delhi from 5–7 October 2017 in which the two sides agreed to increase their efforts to counter terror given major terrorist attacks both in India and EU in the last year. They also agreed to give a fresh impetus to the stalled negotiations on an EU–India Broad-based Trade and Investment Agreement (BTIA) where hurdles on intellectual property and duty cuts on EU exports of automobiles and spirits still continue.[25]

The United States

President Trump and Narendra Modi in their first meeting on 27 June 2017 reiterated that relationship was important to both sides.[26] It was a good beginning for a relationship which had been on the radar of every US president since Bill Clinton. At the same time, India has been made keenly aware that there will remain uncertainty on US policy bilaterally, regionally, and globally. It stems from the fact that Trump is 'transactional' and not 'strategic' in his approach.[27]

Already from his pronouncement since the Modi meeting we have seen discordant notes from Trump on climate change and Pakistan. On climate change Trump has changed US policy away from the Agreement leaving India to state that it remains committed. On Pakistan, Trump after stating that he called Pakistan to account for continuing to support terrorism in spite of getting vast US financial subventions seemed to change his tune after the rescue after five years of a US family for which Pakistan has taken full credit![28]

'Starting to develop a much better relationship with Pakistan and its leaders. I want to thank them for their cooperation on many fronts', Trump said in a tweet, triggering speculation on whether this meant a U-turn on his recently announced Afghan policy in which he had warned Pakistan to end support to terrorist organizations. Similar unpredictability can be seen on his statements asking India to use its trade surplus to correct the balance and exhorting India to increase its profile in Afghanistan. Above all was the statement of wanting to mediate to de-escalate tensions between India and Pakistan.[29]

Earlier US presidents have continued to exhort bilateral talks between the two sides and expectedly Trump's statement received a strong rebuttal from Indian authorities. The future direction and content of the US–India relations in the Trump presidency remains open. Yet it remains certain that so long as the US remains in Afghanistan it will not be able to change its relations with, and dependence on Pakistan. The increase of US troop deployment in Afghanistan under Trump is an indicator.[30]

President Barak Obama had called the US–India relationship as the 'defining relationship of the 21st century'[31] which put the seal on a bipartisan development that has made remarkable strides since 2000. It was a year in which all the variables in the relationship that had so far inhibited it came together. It was the success of Indian diplomacy, which took advantage of this constellation of trends responsible for the transformation of the bilateral relationship.[32] Indian diplomacy will now have to work through the initial uncertainties of Trump's India policy till the situation becomes clearer.

Since 1991 the Indian economy in a sustained run had shown an annual growth of 8–9 per cent on the back of its economic reform programme. India came to be recognized as an 'emerging global power', largely due to the heightened interest by both the US and the EU. The US' interest in India became a catalyst for a renewed forward-looking interest as much by the Gulf countries as the members of ASEAN. It became evident that good relations with the US would help to realize India's long-standing promise of being counted among the global powers. The country's nuclear tests in May 1998 were instrumental in unlocking the doors to a more intensive bilateral relationship, although it started with wide-ranging US sanctions on India. The removal of the sanctions by President Bush in 2001 improved interactions between the two countries.[33]

In the United States itself, the growing status of the nearly three million-strong Indian American community came to be seen, by both sides, as an asset in the bilateral relationship. The income level of the Indian American community was 25 per cent higher than the US national average, and their education level was higher. Seventy per cent had completed a university degree and, more importantly, Indian IT professionals were working wonders in making Internet more versatile and user friendly. In California's Silicon Valley—the sanctum sanctorum of the knowledge economy—an Indian IT professional was at a premium. According to the Asian-American Physicians of Indian Origin (AAPIO)[34] 5 per cent of all doctors in the US and 20 per cent of medical graduates employed in the US are of Indian-origin.[35] The Asian American Hotel Owners Association (AAOHA)[36] owns almost 1 in every 2 hotels in the US. Since 2004 it has a Political Action Committee to reach out to the political levels in the country. The widespread presence and influence of the Indian American community has been marked by increase in their political activism through the Political Action Committees (PAC) and India Caucuses in both the US House of Representatives[37] and the Senate.[38]

There remain equal imperatives for the United States in moving towards a closer relationship with India. As the only super power in the world, the United States became aware that even more than earlier, it needed to build disparate alliances to influence, if not dominate, world developments. The rise of China—economic, military, and political—made it necessary to develop its own equities in an increasingly fractured and fractious globalized world where making war or peace was becoming regional and beyond the UNSC's competencies. The shifting of the world's centre of military and economic gravity to China and the Asia-Pacific had created equal reason for the US to build up India's global political, economic, and military status.

President Bill Clinton's landmark visit to India in the millennium year harnessed these externalities for an enduring leap in the bilateral relationship. Even more, the visit to India in 2006 by President George W. Bush finally made the relationship bipartisan. Yet reservations have remained on both sides. On the Indian side, despite an understanding of the reasons, the hyphenation of the US' relationship with India and Pakistan did not fade. In India's view, the United States continues to pander to a state responsible for unrelenting terror not only in India but also across the world. On the US side, there was a belief that 'India wants to be treated like an ally of the United States without actually being an ally of the United States'[39] which was representative of the US' inability to move beyond the non-proliferation paradigm and treat India as part of the solution rather than its cause.

In the ensuing decade, India has carved out and widened the levels and intensity with which the two countries have come together to build synergies, in conception and action, while maintaining 'strategic autonomy' in decision-making.[40] Since 2000, like-minded bipartisan leaderships in the United States and India have facilitated tremendous strides in building intensive contacts in defence, science and technology, trade and investment, and people-to-people contacts.

Nevertheless, the forward movement from 2000 onwards was, to a large extent, due to the US' realization that China's rise was neither going to be peaceful nor conflict-free. The key elements of the US' 'pivot to Asia' policy launched by President Obama in 2012 were 'strengthening bilateral security alliances; deepening our working relationships with emerging powers, including with China; engaging with regional multilateral institutions; expanding trade and investment; forging a broad-based military presence; and advancing democracy and human rights.'[41]

While the reactions to the pivot strategy were mixed, particularly in the Middle East, it was evident that this was part of a China containment strategy. A logical corollary of this strategy was the United States' statement to assist India in its quest for global power.[42] Whether the pivot strategy survives, even under a different name, is not yet clear. President Trump's visit to Saudi Arabia, even though sale of armaments was high on the list, has created a new movement in US–Saudi relationship. The US support to the Saudi multinational anti-terrorism force (IMFAT) is an indication of a partisan approach of US foreign policy.[43]

The turnaround achieved by the Indian political establishment to afford the United States a level playing field is a major diplomatic success of the last two decades. Nevertheless, at the psychological level, there remain blocs that will prevent India from becoming an unmitigated ally of the United States. This despite the fact that according to a Pew Research Centre poll,[44] that India had one of the highest rankings for President Obama. In 2015, when President Obama visited India and Prime Minister Narendra Modi visited the United States, America's favourable image in India jumped to 70 per cent.

History

The historic synergy between the two countries[45] comes from their strong belief in freedom, equality, and human rights and ensured a bond between the two countries long before India's independence. An evocative marker of this shared commitment was the formation of the Hindustan Ghadar Party in 1913 in San Francisco with the goal of fighting for a United States of India. The Ghadar movement became a rallying point for Indian migrants to the United States, most of whom had come to California as farmers. While the movement flourished, it came up against resistance from the British, Canadian, and US governments that set to naught all of the Ghadar organization's plans to materially help the Indian independence movement. The incident of the ship *Komagata Maru*[46] illustrates British–Canadian intelligence cooperation. On the ship's arrival back in Kolkata (formerly Calcutta) from Vancouver, the Indian immigrant freedom fighters were arrested and hanged. The *Komagata Maru* episode influenced the course of the Ghadar movement, a heroic yet tragic episode in India's freedom struggle. Canadian Premier Justin Trudeau apologized on 17 May 2017, over a century later, for the tragedy in the House of Commons stating, 'No words can erase the pain and suffering they experienced.'[47]

Nevertheless, the exchange between the United States and India at the level of ideas continued with important leaders of the independence movement, such as Lala Lajpat Rai who founded the India Home Rule League in New York. Swami Vivekananda and Rabindranath Tagore visited the United States to speak about that struggle to American audiences. President Franklin Delano Roosevelt pronounced himself in favour of Indian independence even before World War II and his careful goading of the British in the background of the nascent Cold War was one more step towards that goal. However, post-1947 India had no visible domestic profile in the United States and the latter had no immediate pressing strategic, economic, or cultural links that demanded their involvement in the Indian subcontinent.[48]

Despite their historical experience of British colonialism and common adherence to an open democratic society based on non-discrimination and equal opportunity, ambient circumstances were never propitious to create circumstances in which India's relationship with the United States could soar. Following World War II, the United States remained the only economic and military power, of global dimensions, to systemically challenge the Soviet Union and its statist empire, planting an ethic which required a country to belong to one or the other camp. It led the United States and the Soviet Union to actively seek commitments from the large number of newly liberated countries.

India, emerging out of colonialism, was hard put to build a viable political and economic system that could accord with its world view that gave a prime place to peace and non-aggression between states. It left India with very little choice but to plough its own furrow, which it did with remarkable success through NAM in a fast de-colonizing world. NAM, led by India, Egypt, Yugoslavia, Ghana, and Nigeria, gave a possible alternative to recently liberated countries in keeping away from the Western and Eastern power blocs. At the height of the Cold War, NAM accounted for over a 100 member states[49] and even more if one took its economic counterpart, the UNCTAD G-77.[50]

The differences in their world view and the military and economic contrast between India and the United States was too great to be overcome. Even more significant has been an ingrained view of the United States in the Indian psyche which saw it as the antithesis of the egalitarian, peaceful, democratic, and socialist society that India set out to build. India's refusing to fall in line with the Cold War dynamics and its commitment to non-alignment inevitably put it into the dissident camp as far as Washington was concerned. As a result, despite synergies from similar political systems and ideals, until the 1990s the two countries were like a railway track with the two rails never intersecting!

The growing allergy to US policies during the Cold War resonated in the attitudes and official stances adopted by the Indian government. It was not until 1990, and the end of the Cold War, that India actively took steps to build its relationship with the United States. This stemmed from its own helplessness and the economic bankruptcy thrust on it by its economic policies. It required India not only to make political overtures to the United States but also to take steps to minimize, if not work to remove, the negative perception against that country in India's bureaucracy. Even more, there was a clear understanding that India's goal of becoming a great power could best succeed through opportunities available in the United States.

Between 1947 and 1992, six US presidents visited India, with Dwight Eisenhower as the first, in 1959. From then 1978, when Jimmy Carter stepped on Indian soil, the visits did not amount to much, with no effort on either side to create institutional mechanisms to allow regular, uninterrupted contact between the two governments. The United States could not get over its perception that despite the assertion of non-alignment, India was in the

Soviet camp. The US effort during these years was in the nature of a holding operation to ensure that India did not fully side with the East bloc.

As a result, the United States continued to regularly provide financial aid and, till 1978, wheat under the PL 480 dispensation. In the first decade of India's Independence (1947–59), the US, through the Aid India Consortium, provided USD 1.7 billion in gifts, including USD 931 million in food.[51] The Soviet Union provided about half as much, largely by setting up steel mills. In 1961, the US pledged USD 1.0 billion in development loans, in addition to USD 1.3 billion of free food. During 1974–84, when India's Green Revolution made the country self-sufficient in foodgrains, India lived a 'ship-to-mouth' existence, given the dependence of India's rationing system on the PL 480 wheat imports. Yet this import was susceptible to political vagaries and led to cut-offs when India criticized US military action in Laos, Cambodia, and Vietnam. The success of India's Green Revolution nevertheless was due to the discovery of short-grain wheat variety by US agronomist Dr Norman Borlaug who became an icon of the revolution.

United States also provided India its first experimental nuclear reactor, Apsara, and the heavy water to start India's nuclear energy generation. India's peaceful nuclear explosion (PNE) in 1974 set back this development and led to the imposition of US sanctions on trade in dual use and sensitive nuclear technologies which were lifted only in 2012 when the tenor and depth of the relationship changed.

Some other developments during these relative fallow years (1947–90) have had significant influence on the subsequent trajectory of the bilateral relationship. The 1962 Chinese aggression on the border with Arunachal Pradesh at Tawang in Northeast India was deeply unsettling to India and Nehru's policy of non-alignment and 'brotherhood' with China (as seen in the popular slogan of 'Hindi–Chini bhai–bhai'). It dealt a mortal blow to the principles India had propagated since its emergence as an independent nation. It equally dealt a blow to Nehru's prestige and health and became the cause for his demise. In the face of this attack on India, the United States responded to Nehru's appeal by flying in USD 80 million of military hardware. Still, the possibility of a military alliance remained a distant dream and the two countries remained ideologically far apart.

For the same reason, the India–Pakistan War of 1971 brought out the deep-seated animosities stemming from the views and priorities of the Nixon administration. Despite relentless violence against the Bengali people by the Pakistan Army in East Pakistan, the Nixon administration turned refused to take any action to protect its opening to China being facilitated by the Pakistan regime of General Yahya Khan. With war clouds gathering, India signed the 30-year Indo-Soviet Treaty of 1971 to get the weaponry needed and sought Soviet support in the UNSC. It laid the basis for a long-standing relationship between the two countries, which survived even after the Cold War. India's success in that war led to its decision to carry out the nuclear test in 1974 that imposed far-reaching US sanctions on dual-use and sensitive technologies.

The quick-start to the India-US relationship, in the early years, hinged on its defence component—the supply of equipment and the US intervention on the military dimension of the India–Pakistan relationship. Soon after the opening of the Indian economy and the recast of its foreign policy in 1991, two events need a mention: the Kicklighter proposals,[52] which proved the beginning of a bilateral, defence cooperation, and the visit in May 1990 to New Delhi of Deputy National Security Adviser Robert Gates in what was billed as an attempt to ward off a (nuclear) war with Pakistan.[53] The Indian version of the Gates visit is, however, different stating that the Gates mission had neither defused an ongoing crisis nor helped avert an undefined future crisis. According to Indian officials close to the developments, Gates did not even raise the nuclear issue.[54] Yet the Gates mission did establish the precedent of the United States sending a special envoy to defuse future India–Pakistan crises.

The US interest stemmed initially from the fact that Pakistan was a member of US-led military pacts in the 1950s and was later critical in the US policy of keeping the peace with the latter's involvement with Afghanistan from 1980 onwards. The US funding and provision of arms to the mujahideen, through Pakistan's ISI, to fight Soviet occupation of Afghanistan, started a transactional relationship with Pakistan that became the norm during the decade-long US occupation of that country. This relationship has inured the United States to considerations related to the building of a balanced relationship with India, making for a lingering element of distrust and tone-deafness on both the sides. Nevertheless, since the early 1990s, the India–US relationship has moved forward across multiple fronts resembling that between two allies even though their respective strategic visions have not harmonized.

India Civil Nuclear Agreement, 2006

A horrendous and related development in 1984 eventually had a profound effect on the US civil nuclear agreement of 2006. The leakage of methyl isocyanate (MIC) gas from a plant of Union Carbide India Limited in the Indian city of Bhopal[55] on 3 December 1984 affected 500,000 persons and killed over 3,500 persons in the city. The American plant owner, Union Carbide, paid a meagre compensation of USD 490 million for a massive tragedy which saw long-term health consequences. The impact of this tragedy was reflected on the effect of US–India civil nuclear agreement (2006) in promoting setting up in India of US-origin nuclear power plants. The Civil Liability for Nuclear Damage Act, 2010[56,57] passed by the Indian Parliament in fixing of responsibility lays down high limits to the amount of compensation by the seller of the plant. It is one of the finest legislative endeavours in the recent times. The exercise was significant because nuclear energy and the consequences of pursuing such an energy form were debated extensively in the Parliament for the first time. The result was a liability law that had an exceptional domestic political acceptability, but in many ways appeared to defy conventional international practice. An Indian nuclear insurance Pool has been set up to cover the suppliers' risk.[58]

The United States offered India full civil nuclear cooperation after New Delhi agreed to first separate its civilian and military nuclear facilities and open its civilian reactors to inspections by the IAEA. The biggest stumbling blocks were the liability clauses in a 2010 Indian legislation[59] that have acted to prevent several countries, including the United States, from selling nuclear reactors to India. Indian law makes a supplier, and not the operator, directly liable in case of a nuclear accident, while other national laws around the world make an operator primarily liable. If India were to follow global norms, the entire liability in case of an accident would fall upon the Nuclear Power Corporation of India, a government-owned company that operates all the nuclear power plants in the country. To get over the Indian parliament's strict nuclear liability law an India Nuclear Insurance Pool was instituted to facilitate negotiations between the operator and the supplier for the right of recourse by providing a source of funds through a market-based mechanism to compensate third parties for nuclear damage. 'It would enable the suppliers to seek insurance to cover the risk of invocation of recourse against them', according to a note of the Indian Ministry of External Affairs.[60]

'The Most Dangerous Place in the World?'[61]

President Bill Clinton characterized the Indian subcontinent in these terms during his visit to India in March 2000. Instead of stultifying it, this speech increased US interest in India. However, as far as the United States was concerned, the threat of nuclear war between India and Pakistan had not abated. Instead, it had gone into a higher matrix with the production of tactical nuclear weapons by Pakistan.[62]

Nevertheless, the Clinton visit, followed by that of Prime Minister Atal Behari Vajpayee to Washington in September 2000, led to the setting up of a prolific institutional structure for bilateral interaction over a wide front of issues. The India–US agreement on Civil Nuclear Cooperation of 2006, which became law in October 2008, was the crowning piece of a wide range of bilateral agreements. It helped mitigate the opposition India faced as a non-NPT nuclear weapon state and served as an earnest intention of the United States promoting India as a global player. After President Bush's visit to India in 2005, President Obama visited the country twice—in 2010 and 2015—which conveyed India's rise as 'accepted, supported, and validated' by the United States.[63]

India's five successive nuclear tests on 11 May 1998, although inviting sanctions from the US and other P-5 members, nevertheless unlocked the door to a surge in the bilateral relationship. In the words of Devin Hagerty, these nuclear tests 'destroyed the illusion that New Delhi could somehow be coaxed out of pursuing the ultimate currency of great power status. Once the illusion evaporated, the US and India could begin to relate to one another on a more realistic footing'.[64] It led for the first time, under President George W. Bush, to the 'de-hyphenation' of US policy towards India and Pakistan. The fact that Islamabad continued to support terrorism in Kashmir, its patronage of Taliban in Afghanistan, and the leaking of its nuclear and missile technology made it easier for the US administration to delink its relations between the two countries. India's support to the War on Terror after the 9/11 attacks gave it a greater fillip.

The 10-year Next Steps in Strategic Partnership (NSSP)[65] signed between President Bush and Prime Minister Atal Behari Vajpayee in 2004 established the basis for ever-widening cooperation in military matters, including regular military, air, and sea exercises. The United States and India agreed to expand cooperation in three specific areas—civilian nuclear activities, civilian space programmes, and high-technology trade. In addition, they agreed to expand their dialogue on missile defence. Cooperation in these areas was expected to deepen the ties of commerce and friendship between the two nations and increase stability in Asia and beyond.

This cooperation was accompanied, for the first time, with large-scale purchases of US defence equipment. The United States, in 2016, became the largest supplier of defence armaments and equipment to India.[66] Since 2007, India had bought approximately USD 13 billion worth of defence-wares, including the Super Hercules aircraft, the Apache attack and Chinook heavy-lift helicopters, P-81 patrol aircraft for the Navy, 145 ultra-light howitzers for the Army and has proposed F/A Super Hornet and F-16 aircraft production lines under the 'Make in India' programme.[67] The strategic convergence established after 2000 also enabled India to buy American nuclear fuel and technologies while retaining its nuclear weapons.

More important have been the agreements for defence cooperation signed between the two countries whose far-reaching content has raised concerns in some quarters. On 31 August 2016, India signed the Logistics Exchange Memorandum of Agreement (LEMOA) that was proposed by the United States in 2003. The two countries operationalised the agreement on October 14, 2017[68] introducing a significant departure from India's policy of not entering into a military agreement with any major power. It will allow the two countries' militaries to work closely and use each other's bases for repair and replenishment of supplies.

The LEMOA, which sets a precedent for other future military pacts between the two countries, is a version of the standard US Logistics Support Agreement (LSA) tailored for India which 'establishes basic terms, conditions, and procedures for reciprocal provision of logistic support, supplies, and services between the armed forces of India and the United States'. The increased Indian role in the IOR led to the government's decision to enter into this agreement. China's increasingly aggressive posture, both in South Asia and Southeast Asia, was equally responsible.[69] Although the United States had submitted drafts of three foundational agreements, India chose to proceed only on the logistics agreement (LEMOA), deferring the Communications and Information Security Memorandum of Agreement (CISMOA) and the Basic Exchange and Cooperation Agreement for Geospatial Information and Services Cooperation (BECA).

The announcement of the pact drew a sharp criticism at home from the Congress which called it a fundamental departure from India's time-tested policy of strategic military neutrality even though the agreement had been signed under the Congress. The Communist Party of India (CPI) and CP-Marxist (CPI-M) said the government had opined that it would give unfettered access to Indian military bases. The fact that it evoked strong political reactions from the opposition parties appeared to indicate that despite growing closeness between the two countries a high degree of negativity of perception still survives.[70] The government had to defend its action by stating that no obligation had been created on either side nor did it mean grant of base facilities to the Americans.[71]

The only similar case of an Indian agreement with a major power was the Indo-Soviet Treaty of Peace, Friendship, and Cooperation in August 1971 just ahead of the 1971 War. However, even that agreement was strategic in nature, with little cooperation at the level of the two militaries. The LEMOA, in contrast, allows Indian and American militaries to operate closely by using each other's bases for logistics support. Delhi's insistence on India–specific changes led to a change in content and in the name of the agreement. Proposed Indian changes are related to concerns of unfettered access and setting up of US military bases on Indian soil.

The provision of military logistics to United States has been a contentious issue in the past. During the First Gulf War, Prime Minister Chandra Shekhar's government came under fire, especially from the Rajiv Gandhi-led Congress, for allowing refuelling facilities for American aircraft on Indian soil. The question of military support to the United States also came up in 2003 during the Vajpayee administration when American forces invaded Iraq to overthrow President Saddam Hussein. Many ministers and officials of that government were keen on accepting the US proposal to send an Indian military division for the Second Gulf War but Prime Minister Vajpayee decided against it. Since then, India has only allowed its forces to operate abroad under the UN flag.

The overall India–United States relationship has reached a level where it creates a structure that builds a partnership which would increase India's salience in the world. Whether this happens in practice will depend more on India than on the United States, first, because it will require India to bring political will to bear on this issue and second, it will call for certain adaptations to its foreign policy. Finally, India will also have to deal with the reaction from China and Pakistan to this major change in India's policy orientation. The tilt towards the United States that has emerged after Pokhran II appears to have progressively become irreversible. In accepting Indian contentions on the structuring of bilateral agreements on nuclear and defence issues, the United States has also come to accept the concept of 'Indian exceptionalism'.

At the same time, certain issues have inhibited the bilateral partnership. On the United States' side, the most important factor is its near-permanent interest in catering to Pakistan given its continued need to keep the line open with Afghanistan and to keep an eye on Pakistan's nuclear arsenal. As a result, 'total de-hyphenation of US policy towards India and Pakistan remains a chimera'.[72] Similarly, with respect to China, despite aggressive postures both in Asia and in the South China Sea, it is unlikely that the United States will precipitate matters given the heavy linking of its economy to that of China. Under these circumstances, India will continue to have to deal with both these countries on its own.

China will continue its latter-day version of the Great Game with India by putting pressure on India's regional position. This is achieved through its port constructions at Hambantota (Sri Lanka), Gwadar (Baluchistan), and Sittwe (Burma); its pressure on India's joint oil drilling platform with Vietnam in the South China Sea; the growing road networks from Gwadar through Aksai Chin to Sinkiang and through Nepal and its continued military action on the LoAC in Arunachal Pradesh. Furthermore, the China–Pakistan axis makes the India-Pakistan LoC vulnerable with Pakistan continuing its terrorist activity extending into Punjab, Rajasthan, and Gujarat. At the same time, China can be expected to continue its high level of trade with India, further inhibiting any belligerent posture. At a time when the Indian economy needs a renewed boost, it would be counter-productive to take measures against China.

Though stalling Indian growth rate could prove a constraint in furthering India–US ties, endemic reasons on the Indian side are equally responsible for a drift in the relationship. India has so far been unable to develop a strategic consciousness to facilitate strong relations with the United States. India's inability to create linkages across issues, for example using US bids for fighter aircraft from Boeing and Lockheed Martin as leverage for securing India's other bilateral interests. Similarly, the possibility of looking for a trade-off between Indian defence purchases and accommodation on India's interests vis-à-vis Pakistan. Neither has India been able to bring a change in the US position despite increased activity by Pakistan-based terror groups across the international border.

The effect has been a level of mutual tone-deafness between the two partners that has stymied further movement in bilateral relations. In line with earlier Republican presidents, India expects a new momentum in the bilateral relationship once the Trump administration's policy towards South Asia and India and Pakistan clarifies. Nevertheless, India is aware that, unlike the Bush administration, US hyphenation between India and Pakistan will continue.

Russia

The changing of the world's geopolitical and strategic configuration for well over the last six decades has continued to provide a raison d'être for close relations between India and Russia. Surprisingly, during the Soviet period and after the Cold War ended, the cardinal points of the relationship have remained constant. Their common belief in a multipolar world and Russia's importance as a constant supplier of military hardware and sophisticated systems has been the basis for an enduring relationship. It is only since 2000 that the relationship has faced strains given India's growing closeness to the United States, particularly in defence imports, with Russia's countermoves to seek closer relations with Pakistan.

History

Soon after independence and the unveiling of non-alignment as its preferred foreign policy, Jawaharlal Nehru considered the Soviet Union as a counterweight to the West. Its state-led industrialization provided a template for India's socialistic pattern of society. Yet on the Soviet side, India was seen as an effete polity tied to the United Kingdom, its former colonial ruler.

It was with the visit of Nikita Khrushchev, first secretary of the Communist Party, and Prime Minister Nikolai Bulganin to India in 1955 that the Soviet view of India changed. For the Soviet Union India was well placed to create a break in the western Cold War linkages, much as three decades later, the United States under President Reagan tried to do the same, using India as the cat's paw. Nevertheless, given Nehru's view of the Soviet Union and Pakistan's membership in SEATO and CENTO, the breakthrough served India well.

In this sense, Indo–Soviet Union relations were shaped by practical considerations and not ideology. On the latter score, Soviet leaders had given up the possibility of Indian communist parties ever gaining political power at the centre. The only time that the CPI had any political power in the central governance of the country was in 1996 as part of the United Front government under H.D. Deve Gowda and Inder Kumar Gujral. However, by then it was too late.

Soviet leaders nevertheless tried to cultivate Pakistan in the 1960s with the Soviet Union moving equidistant between India and Pakistan, particularly during the mediation in Tashkent after the 1965 India–Pakistan War. An important reason for the Soviets to do this was India's decision to buy US and UK weaponry after the disastrous 1962 War with China. The same reason appears to have motivated Russia in 2016 to once again look at Pakistan for the sale of its defence equipment.[73] The India–Soviet Union Treaty of Peace and Friendship signed in 1971 made that country a major source of defence and heavy industrial equipment. It secured India a staunch supporter in the UNSC. It was the single most important factor in India's military success in the India–Pakistan War in 1971 that created Bangladesh.

Despite a degree of uncertainty during the prime minister-ship of Morarji Desai, the USSR remained India's principal source of military hardware, including transfer of military technology and licensed production of defence weaponry. It also provided technology and aid for the construction of the Bhilai and Rourkela steel plants, Ranchi Heavy Electricals plant, Bharat Heavy Electricals Limited, and the Indian Drugs and Pharmaceuticals Ltd.

The rupee trade instituted between India and the Soviet Union was responsible for bringing a good deal of industrial and defence equipment that India could not afford to buy from Western suppliers in free foreign exchange. In any case, Western sanctions on India also meant that much of this technology was barred to India. The Soviet Union was able to build solid influence in the country which helped in getting Indian (and often non-aligned) support on issues of its concern. The Soviet Union became India's leading trade partner during the 1980s and 1990s.

Cold War and After

The Soviet Union's implosion in 1990 surprised India, possibly more than others, causing an immediate reassessment of its policy across the globe. India lost its major supporter in the UNSC and a primary source of defence equipment and heavy plant and machinery. It weakened India's security in a world that was learning to cope with the United States in its new role as the only super-power. With Russia evaluating its options in a world with a single super power, India's salience, in its eyes, reduced.

The early years after the creation of Russia were marked by dissonance arising from a seeming difference in their world view. It was coupled with the outstanding rupee debt and uncertainty on the supply and quality of Russian defence equipment because of the dispersal of its manufacturing facilities within its successor states. Further, the likelihood of a rapprochement between Russia and China, eventually formalized in 1997, seemed anathema to India which would mean a compact between its main ally and its primary adversary.

Uncertainty and a low level of relationship marked the ensuing years until 2000 when neither could India get away from procuring Russian defence equipment nor could Russia avoid finding a via media to deal with the rupee debt. This was further complicated by recurring complaints regarding the deteriorating quality of Russian equipment due to the absence of adequate Russian control on the production units in the independent Central Asian Republics (CAR). The fall in overall demand for Russian equipment from these countries also made for a fall in quality and long delays in delivery. A case in point was the Indian order for the refurbished nuclear submarine *INS Vikramaditya*,[74] earlier *Admiral Goroshkov*, which after delays and cost-over-runs eventually cost USD 3 billion. Similarly, the Russian-made Kilo-class submarine *INS Sindhurakshak*, soon after its refurbishment, was lost after an explosion on 14 August 2013.

The situation stabilized in 2000 when Vladimir Putin became the president. The Russian perception that the West was out to undermine Russian influence in its political preserve of the South Caucasus, Central Asia, and Ukraine was heightened by the 'colour revolutions' in Georgia and Ukraine. The need to preserve a buffer between the EU and itself became the motivation for Russian belligerence.

The US invasion of Iraq (with whom Russia continued its close relations from the Soviet era), and the US bombing of Libya following a UNSC resolution (decision that Russia maintained exceeded US authority), cemented a Russian foreign policy which once again stood in contra-position to the United States and other Western powers. It reintroduced an element of multi-polarity despite there being only one super power. The UNSC's inability on peace-building in Syria was largely due to Russia and China opposing a biased orientation to the conflict at the behest of the Western powers that supported the Islamic groups fighting the Assad regime.

The Russian position on the US presence in Afghanistan fostered a positive tenor in India–Russia relations. Although India's estrangement from the United States was a thing of the past, its conviction that Russia would remain supportive and an important source of military hardware remained the bedrock of the relationship. The closing down of the rupee trade system and the use of hard currency in bilateral trade and defence transactions were not necessarily bad. It gave India the option to buy from other sources and be exacting with Russian suppliers.

Furthermore, Russia continues to be India's largest supplier of nuclear reactors despite the civil nuclear energy agreement with the United States. Apart from the Kudankulam nuclear power plant of which Units 5 & 6 were agreed to be taken up during Modi's visit to Russia in June 2017,[75] Russia is in line to build 18 reactors across India, apart from supplying nuclear fuel and technical assistance.

Although bilateral political relations have reverted to an even keel, the same cannot be said of bilateral trade turnover between the two countries. India's trade with Russia amounts to only USD 3.9 billion annually when compared with US 35 billion with

China and USD 100 billion with the United States. Similarly, during 2008–13, total FDI from Russia was USD 100 billion. Russia, with its massive reserves of crude oil and gas and with a moribund industry has effectively become a petro-state. As the fourth largest consumer and importer of oil, the complementarity between India and Russia is manifest. It is in this area, apart from defence wares, that India's relations with Russia will grow in the future.

The India–Russia Strategic Partnership,[76] signed in 2000, is based on mutual confidence that bilateral relations will not become hostage to disruptions like those that India faced with strategic partners such as Australia and United States after the nuclear tests in 1998. A common view against external interference in internal conflicts, an opposition to humanitarian intervention, and a preference for a pluralistic world order also inform the partnership. India's defence agreement with Tajikistan, which involved the construction in 2007 of an airfield at Aini or Gissar,[77] also involves close coordination with Russia that controls the civil aviation space over Tajikistan. The military base in Tajikistan gives India the reach not only to Pakistan's airfields but also in all of Central Asia. The airbase has been the first, and so far the only, instance of India developing a foreign military base. However, it is far from being operational as there are no fighter jets operating there. New Delhi had shown an interest to deploy a complement of helicopters and fighter jets, but Russian concern has kept the plans in abeyance. During his visit to New Delhi in December 2016, Tajik President Emomali Rahmon agreed to respond to any Indian request for the upgrading of the Ayni airbase.[78]

Nevertheless, there are worrying signals from Russia in the face of India's growing strategic ties with the United States.[79] Russia has made overtures to Pakistan,[80] and the two have started joint military exercises. The possibility of an axis between Russia, China, and Pakistan is now real. India will have to tread carefully given the fact that it is unlikely to get much joy from the United States on two of its perennial concerns—Pakistan and China.

The successful management of the transformation of the Soviet Union into Russia and the harnessing of commonalities with Russia to keep relations on an even keel is an important achievement of Indian diplomacy. The consistency of policy was necessary for stability and common purpose which Indian policy demonstrated during the decade of Manmohan Singh's prime ministership.[81] Yet the present flux in international relationships presents a major test for Indian diplomacy.

Shared Trust, New Horizons

Prime Minister's Modi's interaction with President Putin on 2 June 2017, his second state visit, on the margins the St. Petersburg International Forum (SPIEF) appeared to suggest that India–Russia relations were not only greatly diversified but moving along a 'very productive' path.[82] The visit appeared to reiterate bilateral reliability even though Moscow has softened its stand towards Pakistan-based Taliban and is consulting with China and Pakistan on the future of Afghanistan. Russian joint military exercises with Pakistan appear to be aimed at boosting sales of armaments to that country. Interestingly, at the same time, a Russian–Indian military exercise was launched at a military shooting range in Russia's Far East, involving 250 troops from each side. Russia's open support to the China–Pakistan Economic Corridor are other indications of Russia carving out a new furrow as India–US relationship intensifies.

Nevertheless, the Modi visit served to reiterate bilateral reliability in their relationship and was marked by a new momentum which included five significant agreements.[83] Modi and Putin also used the occasion for their 18th Bilateral Summit. The two sides reiterated their opposition to terrorism in all its forms and called for early conclusion of the UN Comprehensive Convention on International Terrorism (CCIT) and called for a multi-polar global order. Bilaterally, they agreed on creating an 'energy bridge' between the two countries and approved units 5&6 of the Kudankulam power plant. Russia also agreed to assist in coastal shipping and joint manufacturing and co-development of defence products. India agreed to the Russian S-400 air defence system. In the moving international scenario the visit was could mark a cross-road with their bilateral interaction being marked by synergies amidst a greater attention to other bilateral relationships.

Modi's earlier bilateral visit to Moscow on 24 December 2015 was for the 16th bilateral summit[84] helped to rejuvenate the relationship with the signing of 16 agreements involving six new nuclear reactors and the joint manufacture of Kamov-226 military attack helicopters under the 'Make in India' programme. With the participation of business leaders from both sides, an elevated target of bilateral trade worth USD 30 billion by 2030 was adopted. Above all, the summit appeared to have cleared the air between the two leaders and reiterated that India sees Russia as a steadfast ally.

On the side lines of the SCO Summit at Tashkent on 25 June 2016,[85] Modi and Putin reiterated their intention to step up bilateral relations, particularly in civil nuclear cooperation, where Russia will build 20 nuclear reactors by 2030, and in hydrocarbons where Oil and Natural Gas Corporation (ONGC) will receive space cooperation, assistance in the processing of diamonds, and new opportunities. There is an increasing congruence of views on global issues, particularly terrorism, Islamic space and Russia's actions in Syria. Russia remains supportive of India's candidature for the UNSC.

While it has been assured that it will not suffer in spite of India's closer ties with the United States, Russia is equally assured that it will remain a major supplier of defenceware to India even though it would have to compete with US weapons. It is unlikely that India or Russia will allow their bilateral relationship to wither regardless of how close the former gets to the United States. The issues of US relations with Pakistan and China will always militate against India's clean break with Russia. For the same reason, it is equally unlikely that the United States will forsake its relationship with Pakistan, howsoever transactional it becomes.

France

Neither India's relatively brief colonial past with France nor the difficulty of language stood in the way of France and India developing robust bilateral relations after independence. India's full-fledged dynamic relations with France, as indeed with all other EU member states, has continued in addition to the India–EU track.

It recognizes the historicity of the relationship and the potential of taking the relationship further than what would be possible on the EU track alone.

Modi's visit to France on 3–4 June 2017 was his third in as many years. In 2015, France was the first European country that Modi visited as prime minister. Last year, he was in Paris to attend the UN climate change conference. And this time, it was perhaps necessitated by his desire to meet the newly elected French president Emmanuel Macron so that the ever-improving bilateral ties under his predecessors, including Francoise Hollande, remained on track.[86] Relations between India and France have seen an upswing with bilateral trade increasing from Euro 5.13 billion in 2006 to Euro 8.5 billion in 2015. France is the 9th largest investor with nearly 1000 French companies based there.

India has found in France a reliable interlocutor which led to the former's first strategic partnership in 1998. French relationship with India moves along three main sectors: nuclear, space, and defence. This is apart from regular interaction on softer areas like culture and education. France supplied fuel for the Tarapur nuclear plant after India was subjected to sanctions after its 1974 test. It signed a civil nuclear agreement with India even before US senate approval for its agreement. It is to construct six nuclear reactors (EPR) in India. India has also taken advantage of the EU track as in the case of its participation in the International Thermo-Nuclear Energy Reactor[87] project at Cadarache in France.

On space technology France was India's earliest partners with French launches of Indian satellites INSAT and GSAT. After India acquiring its own launch capacity, EADS Astrium and Antrix have been regularly collaborating in this sector. While France–India defence collaboration goes back to the 1960s and 1970s the setting up in 1998 of a Higher Committee on Defence Cooperation has been instrumental in starting joint naval and air exercises. Largely due to a higher dependability factor India is procuring the Raffaele fighter aircraft from France in addition to contracts for 6 scorpene submarines, upgrading the MIG2000's and 490 MICA missile systems.

France has supported India's interests in the EU even though they differed in the Doha Round on the issue of agricultural subsidies. Their relationship has not been spectacular but has worked at bringing about synergies while keeping space for the differences between the two countries.

France's importance stems not only from its UN permanent membership but also its readiness to transfer to India high technology, including nuclear and space technology, and defence material. French interest in Indian culture and philosophy is another important strand that has strengthened the relationship. After the spate of terror attacks in Paris, cooperation in counterterrorism has become one more element in the bilateral relationship.

History

The French withdrawal from India in 1954, following popular protests, from its small colonial settlements or *comptoirs* on the eastern seaboard, at Puducherry (formerly Pondicherry) in Tamil Nadu state and Chandannagar (formerly Chandernagore) in West Bengal, was in stark contrast with Goa where the Portuguese had to face Indian military action. The transfer of the colonies was formalized in 1962.[88]

Historically, India and France have had differences stemming from India's non-alignment that surfaced during the 1956 Suez Canal crisis and, later the French wars in Indo-China–Vietnam, Laos, and Cambodia that ended the French colonial presence.

In 1962, France, under President Charles De Gaulle condemned the Chinese aggression on India, keeping its defence relationship with India intact. The French helicopter Alouette began to be manufactured in India in 1962 under license and has been a mainstay of the Indian Air Force. The sale of the French-built Mirage-2000 fighter aircraft to the Indian Air Force was yet another mainstay in India's armoury. Nevertheless, prior to 1990, a number of French companies found it difficult to do business in India and had to pull out. Since the 1990s, French interest in selling defence material to India has become the driver of the bilateral relationship and currently focuses on the sale of the multi-role Rafale fighter aircraft for the Indian Air Force. The Indian government and Dassault, the makers of Rafale, signed the agreement for the sale of 36 Rafale multi-role fighter aircraft at a cost of USD 7.87 billion in September 2016. The first aircraft will be received in 2019.[89]

The French instinct for timing in seizing the initiative to promote their bilateral interests has been much in evidence in the bilateral relationship. It was remarkable that France was the first to enter into a civil nuclear agreement even as the US, which had done the running on this issue, had to still receive Senate authorization. Similarly, President Jacques Chirac proposed a visit to Delhi in February 1976 at the height of the Emergency (1975–77). He was the first Western leader to visit India after the Emergency was declared. His Commerce Minister Raymond Barre was sent to 'prepare it'.[90,91] The economic motivation was very strong, with the French looking to sell six fertilizer plants and a heavy vehicle plant to India.

The period before 1990 saw the holding of back-to-back reciprocal festivals in India and France. While they did not significantly enhance the bilateral relationship, they nevertheless kept the relationship on a high note. The real change in the relationship however came about, as with the United States, with India's nuclear tests in 1998. As a permanent UNSC member, France too condemned the tests but, unlike the United States, did not impose sanctions. Indeed, it became the occasion for setting up a 'strategic partnership' between the two countries. Once again, President Jacques Chirac visited New Delhi while US sanctions were in force. India was invited to the G-8 Conference in June 2003 at Evian les Bains.[92]

1990 and After

During the ensuing decades, a regular exchange of presidential and prime ministerial visits from both sides despite changes of governments in both countries attest to the stability and maturity of the bilateral relationship. There were 25 rounds of dialogue at the NSA level. During the last presidential visit by President Hollande (23–26 January 2016),[93] who was the chief guest for India's 67th Republic Day, a follow-up on the Climate Accord and the sale of defence material were high on the agenda. The high point of the visit was the agreement on India's purchase of 36 French multi-role fighter Raffaele in flyaway condition, although the decision on whether to manufacture the aircraft on Indian soil is still pending.[94],[95] India's ratification of the Climate Change Accord on 2 October 2016 was equally a boost for France and for President Hollande.[96]

The bilateral relationship received a boost by the visit, and the countries agreed to cooperate in a number of areas, including the launch of satellites for climate change research, nuclear issues connected with the French nuclear energy plant at Jaitapur, the possibility of contracting additional nuclear plants, the consolidation of Indo–French-sponsored Global Solar Alliance, and counterterrorism initiatives. The two sides also upgraded their strategic partnership by expanding the scope of its content. French companies are expected to invest up to USD 10 billion in the next five years in India's industry through the 'Make in India' programme.

The relations between India and France have demonstrated a level of maturity that eschews comments on internal developments in India, confirms that only bilateral talks will lead to a solution to the intractable Kashmir issue, and focuses on high-technology trade in defence, nuclear, and non-defence sectors. By leveraging the long-standing cultural contact between the two countries, it has kept away from a relationship which is merely transactional.

G-4[97]

India, Germany, Japan, and Brazil formed the Group of Four (G-4) primarily to project jointly their eligibility to become permanent members of the UNSC.[98] Although the G-4 was formed over a decade ago, when the clamour for expanding the UNSC membership had peaked, it did not take on a life outside the issue itself. For India, which revived the grouping in 2015, the reasons were evident. Quite apart from activating a grouping with the three most eligible countries, it provides yet another level of contact with them to intensify close relations and provide the wherewithal to spur its industrialization plans. The needs of India's sustainable growth have given the group a new life based on a mutuality of interest with Germany which is a leader in sustainable advanced manufacturing, with Japan which can provide a renewed thrust to India's economic growth, and with Brazil, an emerging economy with which India is also associated in the BRICS grouping.

Germany[99]

Visiting Berlin on 30 May 2017 Prime Minister Modi said that 'pace of development of our relations is fast, direction positive and destination clear. Germany will always find India as powerful, prepared and capable partner'.[100] Modi and Merkel were focused on the scourge of terrorism which had seen incidents in Germany, France, UK, and Sweden. Following the meeting of the bilateral India–Germany Intergovernmental Consultations 12 MoU/greements were signed on cyber policy, development initiatives, sustainable urban development, continued development of cluster managers and skill development, railway security and promoting vocational training.

The most evocative sign of the success of Indian diplomacy was the unequivocal support that Germany provided to India when it carried out on 4 October 2016 surgical strikes across the LoC on the terrorist launch pads in Pakistan-held Kashmir.[101] It showed the extent to which the bilateral relationship has travelled when Germany (then Federal Republic of Germany or FRG) was critical of India for intervening in the 1971 Bangladesh Liberation War. Germany also rejected India's 1998 nuclear tests with Chancellor Helmut Kohl saying, 'this was the wrong decision for them to take, that we do not accept that decision, and that we do not see any reason that would justify such a decision and that we are deeply concerned about the positive effect that this decision might have in a region that is already marked by tensions.[102]

It is symptomatic of the changed international environment, especially after the Cold War, and the expanding level of common interest that the two countries share. After two decades of soul-searching, Indo-German relations have found a momentum that focuses on the rising fields of cooperation in science and technology, non-renewable energy, climate change, defence, counterterrorism, and building participative global governance to meet the challenges facing the world.

Yet during German Chancellor Angela Merkel's visit to New Delhi in October 2015, the two sides recognized that there was a long way to go. The press reports on the visit make this evident. Germanpress report[103] loquently captured the prevailing mood on the visit with its editorial titled, 'A First Step in the Right Direction—No More, No Less'.[104] *The Indian Express* in an editorial titled 'She Came and Went' pondered over the modest nature of agreements announced during the visit and placed the onus on India to raise its attractiveness as a partner through concrete socio-economic progress and improvements in bilateral relations in India's immediate neighbourhood.[105] *The Hindu* termed the visit as a *dosis realitaet* (reality check) for Merkel and Modi.[106] The headline 'Indo-German Partnership for the 21st century'[107] conveys the expectations of both countries: Germany, which considers itself a civilian power, while India continues to be guided by the principle of 'strategic autonomy' on global issues.

Germany's concept of civilian power has considerable relevance for India. It means that unlike a great power, Germany uses multilateral institutions and economic cooperation to achieve its foreign policy goals and avoids the use of military force, except in limited circumstances and in a multilateral context. It thus 'helps to "civilize" international relations by strengthening international norms.'[108] India and Germany, approaching their common ideas from either end, have as their foreign policy goals non-aggrandizement, eschewing the use of force, maintaining the sovereignty of other countries, and supporting a multilateral international power structure. As India moves into the ranks of the global economic powers it could well adopt the categorization of a 'civilian power' instead of non-alignment as it will perfectly incorporate what the country aspires for in the 21st century.

History

The common thread of partition runs through the relations between India and Germany. While India recognized the FRG, it stayed away from the German Democratic Republic (GDR) which it saw as a puppet regime. It was also occasioned by the fact that buoyed by the aid from the Marshall Plan, FRG became a member of the Aid India Consortium and a major aid donor. New Delhi learnt to balance its principles and realities in the context of conflicting intra-German interests. It was only in 1972 after Willy Brandt rescinded the Hallstein Doctrine[109] that in line with its non-aligned standing, India recognized the GDR. It went well with India's non-aligned policy with the FRG, a member of NATO, while the GDR was part of the Warsaw Pact.

It also signalled the waning of German interest in India—a period of 'benign neglect'[110]—in the context of its preoccupation with the enhancing of its position within Europe and its relations with the United States. A degree of indifference and reduction in aid flows resulted, although the GDR played a role in India's economic development. The FRG did not support India during the Chinese aggression in 1962 and backed Pakistan in 1971 because of the Indo-Soviet Treaty and its closer relations with the GDR. India's nuclear test of 1974 further increased the distance from the FRG.

Chancellor Helmut Schmidt followed a policy of benign neglect with a waning of affinity and the growing stress on building relations with China. The importance of cultivating a transatlantic relationship also distanced India from the German optics. It was seen in the fall of nearly 50 per cent in Official Development Assistance between 1971 and 1972.

The mutual political alienation between India and the FRG was only corrected during the visit of Prime Minister Rajiv Gandhi in 1988, when India launched an active German policy. Yet it failed to find support from Germany. The end of the Cold War, the fall of the Berlin Wall and the unification of the two Germanys rekindled the country's interest in India. An active German policy saw an emphasis on trade and culture, and science and technology. Economic reforms and broader shared interests have been the drivers of India's German policy since the later 1980s.

Future

Germany is India's largest trading partner in Europe and the second most important partner in terms of technological collaborations.[111] The economic relationship has expanded significantly over the years. Bilateral trade during 2015 was valued at €17.33 billion while in 2016 it was €17.46 billion.[112] Indo-German cooperation in trade and technology is one of the most dynamic facets of the bilateral partnership. The finance minister leads the Joint Commission on Industrial and Economic Cooperation from the Indian side and the economics minister from the German side. In addition, there are several Joint Working Groups in the fields of agriculture, automobile, infrastructure, coal, tourism, standardization, vocational education, etc. The Indo-German Energy Forum focuses on renewable energy, alternative fuels, energy efficient technologies, and the power sector.

The Indo-German Environment Forum focuses on water supply and sanitation, waste management, energy efficiency, and the Clean Development Mechanism (CDM) proposed in the Kyoto Protocol. Following the coming into force in October 2016 of the Paris Climate Change Agreement, Germany's climate-friendly industrial technologies and innovations to curb carbon dioxide emissions could see a major growth in bilateral cooperation. Apart from traditional sectors, knowledge driven sectors hold a good potential for collaboration in the fields of IT, Information Technology Enabled Services (ITES), biotechnology, auto components, renewable energy, green technology, advanced manufacturing, urban mobility and development, and the entertainment industry. There are several important trade fairs held in Germany in which Indian companies regularly participate to promote their products and technology.

Since 2000, Germany is the eighth largest foreign direct investor in India. German FDI inflows during April 2000–March 2017 were placed at USD 9.7 billion. The major German investments in India are in the sectors of transportation, electrical equipment, metallurgical industries, services sectors, chemicals, construction activity, trading and automobiles.[113] There are more than 1,600 Indo-German collaborations and over 600 Indo-German joint ventures in operation. India and Germany have a long tradition of academic and cultural exchanges. German scholarly tradition has played a key role in introducing Indian art, culture, literature, and philosophy to Europe and the wider world. The India-German Defence Agreement (2006) has helped not only to bring in sophisticated systems but the India–Germany High Defence Committee, at its annual meetings, has boosted military training and defence technology transfers as well as promoted joint defence production, counterterrorism, in addition to joint naval exercises in 2008.

India and Germany now share a forward-looking partnership based on mutual interest in multilateralism, global governance, conflict prevention, UN peacekeeping, non-proliferation, and Internet governance. India's international standing was boosted after the Heiligendamm Process (2007) which aimed to intensify cooperation between the G-8 and emerging economies.[114] After 2009, the exchanges between the two countries have been regular and at highest levels after India along with other G-20 members gave USD 10 billion to the International Monetary Fund (IMF) for shoring the European economies. Germany has supported the India–EU FTA despite continuing reservations on some of India's concerns.

Indian diplomacy was always keen on furthering ties with Germany, both before and after the Cold War. Its recognition of GDR a few months before FRG itself did so under Chancellor Willy Brandt's policy of 'Ostpolitik' acknowledged FRG's sensitivities while keeping a balance in its relationship with the two Germanys. Similarly, at the fall of the Berlin Wall India supported the reunification once it was obvious that this was the wish of the German people. Since then, the steady upward movement in bilateral relationship is based on shared global concerns and in keeping with their mutual predilection to act only when it can be useful. India needs to realize that today's Germany, with its belief in the concept of a 'civilian power', is an ideal paradigm for a country transitioning from non-alignment into a global power which will perforce be required to assume global responsibilities.

Japan[115]

Japanese Prime Minister Shinzo Abe on his fourth visit on 13 September 2017 to Ahmedabad, Prime Minister Modi's home state,[116] reiterated the close relations between the two countries since

2015. This is the fourth Annual Summit between Prime Minister Modi and Prime Minister Abe. 'The two leaders will review the recent progress in the multifaceted cooperation between India and Japan under the framework of their "Special Strategic and Global Partnership" and will set its future direction,' Prime Minister Modi's website stated. Modi also said that, 'India truly values the relationship with Japan and we look forward to further boosting our bilateral ties in a wide range of sectors.'[117]

During the visit, Abe and Modi agreed to deepen defence ties and push for more cooperation with Australia and the United States, as they seek to counter growing Chinese influence across Asia. Abe's visit comes less than three weeks after New Delhi and Beijing agreed to end the longest and most serious military confrontation along their shared and contested border in decades. In fact, Japan had come out in full support for India in its protracted military standoff with China at Doklam, near the Sikkim–Tibet–Bhutan tri-junction, saying no country should use unilateral forces to change the status quo on the ground.[118] India and Japan said deepening security links was paramount. This included collaboration on research into unmanned ground vehicles and robotics and the possibility of joint field exercises between their armies. There was also 'renewed momentum' for cooperation with the United States and Australia.

It was returned the visit on 11–12 November 2016[119] to Japan by Narendra Modi when the two countries signed the landmark civil nuclear cooperation agreement.[120] Apart from signing the bilateral civil nuclear cooperation agreement, a rare exception made for India, Japan also signed the agreement to establish bullet trains in India. The project for the first between Ahmedabad and Mumbai was launched during Prime Minister Abe's visit to Ahmedabad in 2017.

Japan has de-hyphenated its India–Pakistan relations, considering India as an important strategic player in Asia with visits of Japanese defence and foreign ministers to India. The presence of Prime Minister Abe as the chief guest at the Republic Day 2015 was another sign of the growing warmth and bipartisanship in the bilateral relationship. The foreign minister-level Eighth Strategic Dialogue was held in New Delhi on 17 January 2015. A new momentum was given to bilateral relations during Prime Minister Abe's visit to Delhi in September 2014.[121] The two sides laid out a Vision 2025 document that contains the way their strategic and global partnership will benefit the Asia–Pacific in the years to come.[122] It lays emphasis on cooperation in defence and technology transfer and security cooperation.[123]

History

India and Japan have a connection that goes back to two millennia, based on cultural and religious ties, particularly the spread of Buddhism. The university in Nalanda in Eastern India had Japanese scholars in order to build 'a sense of Asian consciousness of which Japan was an integral part'.[124] It was only after its victory in the Russo-Japanese War (1904–5) that Japan entered the political consciousness of the leaders of India's struggle for independence. The Japanese victory over a major European empire split the Indian National Congress Party between those in favour of a constitutional path and those, led by Subhash Chandra Bose, who favoured Japan's example in wresting independence by the use of military force. Japan became the symbol of Asian resurgence over predatory Western powers that had colonized them. It became a source of inspiration to Indian nationalists until the Japanese aggression against China in the 1930s.

During World War II, Japan, with its victories in the East, was highly inspirational for Indian nationalists, and especially so to Bose.[125] The Indian National Army (INA), with assistance from the Japanese Army, became an alternative option to secure independence from the British. In its drive through Burma and Northeast India, the Japanese Army captured the islands of Andaman and Nicobar, which were transferred to Bose. The INA soldiers fought alongside the Japanese in its conquest of Southeast Asia. The ultimate defeat of Japan in Arakan in Burma meant the end of the INA as well. Bose's death in an air crash in Taipei on 18 August 1945 ended the saga of the INA. His ashes have been preserved at the Renkōji Temple in Tokyo, since 18 September 1945. The small, well-preserved temple established in 1594 belongs to the Nichiren sect of Buddhism that believes that human salvation lies only in the Lotus Suta.

The Japanese invasion of China disappointed India, because it saw China as a fellow victim of colonialism. At the same time, India believed that peace and stability in Asia could only be assured with Japan in an important role. Judge Radha Binod Pal, in a dissenting judgement at the War Reparations Commission set up after WW II, opined against a harsh punishment to Japanese Class 'A' war criminals. One of them, Nobusuke Kishi, became the prime minister later, as did his grandson, Shintaro Abe. Justice Pal's act is still remembered and acknowledged by successive Japanese governments.

India remained officially in a 'state of war' with Japan until 1952, when it signed a separate peace treaty waiving all claims of reparations. India had declined to sign the San Francisco Peace Treaty in 1951, as it did not want to be part of a multilateral framework for security in Asia that excluded China and the Soviet Union and withheld the granting full sovereignty to Japan, forcing it to accept military bases on its soil. These went against India's non-aligned policy. This is another fact that remains a marker in the annals of India-Japan relations.

However, after the Chinese annexation of Tibet, India favoured a stronger Japan to keep China in check. The first treaty signed by Japan, after the end of US occupation in 1952, was with India. The treaty signalled Japan's return to Asian affairs and was helpful in its negotiations with Indonesia, Burma, and the Philippines.

India not only invited Japan to the first Asian Games in 1951 but also to the Bandung Conference in 1955[126] that set up the blueprint for NAM. Japan eventually became a part of the Western alliance in the Pacific that equally signalled a distance from India until the end of the Cold War. Cold War politics meant that the relationship lost steam with Japan which was seen as an American surrogate in Asia.

During the India–China War in 1962, Japan remained neutral in anticipation of economic gains from its relationship with China. The socialist economy in India was also seen as distant from Japan's economic preferences taking Japan towards intensifying its relationship with Southeast Asia. Once again, during

Indo-Soviet Treaty of 1971 widened the divide even further. It
was further exacerbated by India's nuclear test of 1974.

Policy of 'Look East'

Following the visit of Prime Minister Narasimha Rao to Tokyo in
1992, India inaugurated its 'Look East' policy, which was focused
on building close relations with ASEAN, Japan, and South Korea.
The Look East Policy, after a decade, has transformed into the
Act East policy to denote India's continued interest in growing
its bonds—economic and political—with ASEAN and East Asia.

The strengthening of the India-US relationship after President
Clinton's visit in 2000 provided a boost for moving the India-
Japan relationship forward. Paradoxically, India's nuclear tests in
1998 became the eventual trigger for the intensification of the
relationship with Japan, as indeed with other advanced countries.
Although Japan followed with even stronger sanctions than the
United States, eventually it too withdrew these following the US'
example. Japan supported the US–India civil nuclear agreement
although the Fukushima nuclear plant disaster (2011) had delayed
Japan's signing a similar one. Nevertheless, major Japanese turbine
manufacturers like Toshiba and Hitachi remain interested in the
Indian nuclear power market.

During the visit to Tokyo of Prime Minister Manmohan
Singh in December 2006 the two countries decided to boost
their relationship by declaring the establishment of a strategic and
global partnership.[127] It involves closer political and diplomatic
coordination on bilateral, regional, multilateral, and global issues;
comprehensive economic engagement; stronger defence relations;
greater technological cooperation as well as working towards a
quantum increase in cultural ties, educational linkages, and people-
to-people contacts. It is expected to harness the vast potential
of bilateral relations, drawing upon complementarities and each
other's intrinsic strengths and work together to address regional
and global challenges.

India and Japan now have regular 2+2 Dialogue (including the
foreign and defence secretaries). Since 2013, it has been further

strengthened by a trilateral dialogue between India, Japan, and the United States that gains importance in the background of rising Chinese equities in the Pacific and Indian oceans.

Economic Relations

In 2015–16, India–Japan trade reached USD 14.51 billion, showing a decrease of 6.47 per cent over 2014–15, when the total bilateral trade was USD 15.51 billion. India's export to Japan for 2015–16 was USD 4.66 billion whereas India's imports from Japan during 2015–16 was USD 9.85 billion.[128] Japan is also a major investor in India. The amount of Japan's cumulative investment in India from April 2000 to March 2016 has been USD 20.966 billion, which is nearly 7 per cent of India's overall FDI during this period. Japanese FDI into India has mainly been in automobile, electrical equipment, telecommunications, chemical, and pharmaceutical sectors.

Soon after independence India became a leading supplier of iron ore and cotton to Japan. Japan, as a member of the Aid India Consortium, granted yen loans for India's development. The end of the Cold War marked a major thrust in the bilateral relationship. In response to India's dire economic straits in 1991, apart from the Bank of England, the Bank of Japan extended USD 195 million as a loan with Indian gold as collateral. Japan also assumed a powerful position in the World Bank, the IMF, and the Asian Development Bank (ADB). The Suzuki-Maruti joint venture for manufacturing a small car became a runaway success in making an automobile which became available to the Indian masses. Its success story was instrumental in bringing to India all the major automobile manufacturers in the world.

Japan identified India's resurgent economy as Asia's new economic frontier and the pull of the Indian market became overwhelming, especially after South Korea's economic inroads. India is the single largest recipient of Japanese Official Development Assistance (ODA) since 2003.[129] India signed a Closer Economic Partnership Agreement[130] with Japan in June 2011. Currently, Japanese investment drives major industrial–infrastructure projects, for example, the Delhi–Mumbai and Chennai–Bengaluru industrial corridors.

Defence cooperation between the two countries was spurred by the Indian Navy's action in rescuing the Japanese ship *Alondra Rainbow* when it was subjected to an act of piracy in the Malacca Straits. Indian and Japanese Navies have conducted joint exercises in the IOR which since 2014 have become trilateral, including the United States as well. Japan is likely to supply US2 amphibian aircraft to the Indian Air Force and could eventually become a supplier of nuclear turbines and other high technology goods to India.

The Future

The India-Japan relationship can contribute to a balance of power in Asia as the United States' continues increased focus on Asia. Together with the iconic agreement on civil nuclear cooperation they have also strengthened their 'Special Strategic and Global Partnership' by enlarging the scope of their economic cooperation and exploring co-development and co-production in the defence sector. Far from drawing any new battle-lines in the Indo-Pacific region, the latest India–Japan annual summit has reinforced the contours of the existing diplomatic landscape and sent out an implicitly reassuring message to China.[131]

Brazil

The relationship between Brazil and India is more appropriately viewed on a systemic basis rather than at a strictly bilateral level. As acknowledged emerging powers, they have more to gain by working together in a multilateral setting that remains in a state of flux with a single super power and a diffusion of power to regional levels.

The remarkable initiatives taken by the two powers are a testimony to the efficacy of their diplomatic outreach to further their common goals. In particular, four separate, yet congruous, organizations have resulted from their efforts to assert themselves in the world:

- **G-4**, which groups the two emerging powers, Brazil and India, and two who have become major economic powers after their defeat in World War II, Germany and Japan. The group's motivation to seek permanent seats in an expanded UNSC gives it a status quo character in the sense of working within the existing international system. The G4 plans envisage a Council with a total membership of 25, including six new permanent members (Brazil, Japan, Germany, India, and two African countries) and an additional three elected seats.[132] In this context, this grouping caters to the extant international situation in which a permanent seat is seen as the currency of international power.[133]

- At the 70th General Assembly (2016), the consensual adoption of Decision 70/559 by the UN General Assembly to continue to use the text presented by the President of the 69th General Assembly in his letter dated 31 July 2015 as the basis for negotiations within the IGN process in the General Assembly. The G4 countries welcomed the expressions of flexibility made by numerous delegations during the past IGN session which resulted in the identification of areas of convergence in Member States' positions on all issues related to the five clusters as identified by GA resolution 62/557 Security Council reform. It was seen as a first step forward. This was taken a step further to work towards early intergovernmental negotiations (IGN) in the UNGA during the G4 meeting in New York on 20 September 2017.[134]

- There are still other groups within the UN membership which remain opposed to a partial expansion of the UNGA.[135] The United for Consensus (UfC) calls for a 25-member Council, which would be achieved by adding 'no permanent members to the Council, but would rather create new permanent seats in each region, leaving it to the members of each regional group to decide which Member States should sit in those seats, and for how long'. The Ezulwini Consensus represents the Africa bloc and proposes two permanent seats and two additional elected seats for Africa. Under the proposal, the permanent members would be granted 'all the prerogatives and privileges of permanent membership including the right to veto'.[136]

- This small grouping has taken on a new dynamism marked by considerable increase in the economic exchanges between all four countries, particularly between India and Japan and India and Germany.[137]

- **BRICS**,[138] a group comprising Brazil, China, India, Russia, and South Africa, started as an acronym but has introduced a major difference in the global financial economy with its membership of the group of G-20 countries. The five countries taken together cover 40 percent of the world's population and more than 25 per cent of the world's GDP. Their share of world GDP increased from 11 per cent in 1990 to 30 per cent in 2014. They divided themselves between China and India, which took advantage of globalization to integrate themselves into global supply chains, and Brazil, Russia and South Africa, whose primary products and natural resources benefited from globalization. Yet they remain plagued by endemic corruption and are threatened by the fall in commodity prices while growth rate in China and India remains risk-prone.[139]

- BRICS has enabled both India and Brazil to take initiatives jointly that would be difficult singly. The setting up of the BRICS Bank,[140] which is poised to give loans up to USD 30 billion, is an attempt to set up an international institution in contraposition to the World Bank wherein China has contributed the maximum seed capital. The grant of equal voting rights to all founders makes it different from the World Bank.

- More importantly, each BRICS member has been able to attain its own objectives through the BRICS grouping. While for Russia the organization has political significance in pulling it out of international isolation, for South Africa it reinforces the perception of the country as a leader in the African continent. For Brazil, BRICS gives it a global exposure which MERCOSUR[141] has failed to, while for India it marginally mitigates its growing closeness to the United States and brings it closer to Russia through this forum. It also creates another forum for an interaction with China.

- The 9th Summit of BRICS was held in Xiamen, China on 3–5 September 2017 soon after the shadow of the 73-day long India-China standoff at Doklam had been diplomatically resolved. It was also the first time that China accepted the specific inclusion of Pakistan-based terror groups, among others, Like Lashkar-e-Taiba (LeT), Jaish-e-Mohammad (JeM), and the Haqqani Network. They also expressed concern at the violence by ISIS and the terrorist movements in Uzbekistan. India and China demonstrated maturity at the Summit although OBOR and the China–Pakistan Economic Corridor which passes through occupied Kashmir still remain irritants in the bilateral relationship.[142] It is not clear whether China will agree to the UN now adding these terrorist groups to its list, neither is China likely to support expanding the UNSC, especially, with three of the five permanent members in decline—France, Russia, and United Kingdom.

G20,[143] which has since 2008 brought together the United States and other G7 members with giants such as China, India, and Russia, represents two-thirds of the world population, three-quarters of world trade and about 80 per cent of economic output. The other members are Argentina, Australia, Brazil, Britain, Canada, France, Germany, Indonesia, Italy, Japan, Mexico, Saudi Arabia, South Africa, South Korea, Turkey, and the European Union.[144] BRICS focused on the reform of the international financial institutions, World Bank and the IMF, has seen the power of its emerging economies grow. This was particularly evident after these countries provided USD 1 trillion for an emergency assistance during the financial crisis of 2008–09.

• The 12th BRICS Summit on July 7–8 2017 in Hamburg was marked by the first meeting between Presidents Trump and Putin and British Prime Minister May taking on President Trump on the climate change agreement. It also focussed attention on developing technology to deter 'lone wolf' terrorists.[145] Once again, the BRICS forum validates and strengthens the role of the emerging economies through this small set of countries that have assumed importance in global financial and development governance. Their current differences arise over issues ranging from global trade to measures to battle climate change.

IBSA[146] Established in June 2003, IBSA is a coordinating mechanism among three, multi-ethnic, multicultural and emerging democracies, which aim to foster an international architecture which allows them to participate as equal partners on global issues.[147] IBSA also expects to extend its expertise to cooperation and partnership with less developed countries. It represents three major democracies in South America, Africa, and Asia, across three continents and two oceans, working to develop cross-continental synergies based on their common strengths. In their regular meetings they have aimed a wide agenda on the softer issues of development and inclusive growth. They represent centres of dynamism in an otherwise stagnant economic scenario. The 8th IBSA Forum Trilateral Ministerial Commission met in Durban, South Africa, on 17 October 2–17 and decided that the next IBSA Summit in India will be held in 2018.[148] Their impact on systemic transformation is too early to judge. In the future, either others that incorporate these three countries will overtake the organization or it could continue to take a path free from the pressure of China or other super powers. Their attempt to mediate in the Syrian crisis was an example of a nuanced approach.

These four organizations have created a new paradigm for cross-continental cooperation between emerging economies and could eventually impart a degree of dynamism to the international order. It could help to give a new impetus to finding solutions to global issues like climate change, pandemics, trade, energy security, and resources scarcity. Yet this became possible, primarily thanks to high-level initiatives by leaderships in India and Brazil.

History: Brazil–India

Prime Minister Modi visited Brazil on 5–6 July 2014 for the BRICS summit which served to discuss bilateral relations. He has subsequently met Brazilian President Temer on the margins of the BRICS Summit in Xiamen, China.[149] During the last BRICS Summit in Goa in October 2016, Modi and Temer held a similar bilateral meeting.[150] The political upheavals in Brazil have prevented another Modi visit to Brazil.

Although direct diplomatic relations between Brazil and India were established in 1948, it was not until the first trade agreement was signed in 1963 that the relationship got any momentum. The visit in 1954 of President S. Radhakrishnan to Brazil was the first high-level visit to that country.

Although there had been a long-range contact between Brazil and Goa, due to the common Portuguese connection, in effect relations remained low soon after India's use of force on 19 November 1961 to evict the Portuguese from their colony.[151]

Brazil criticized India for the use of force to free Goa, and it remained a point of contention in bilateral relations. Portugal propped up organizations in Brazil to liberate Goa like the Movement of Resistance of Goans (MORG) that had a minuscule membership. Nevertheless, Brazil looked after the interests of

Portugal, after it broke diplomatic relations, following the Indian military intervention. Even though Portugal was a NATO member, none of the other members, especially the United States, came to Portugal's aid. The visit to Goa in 1965 by a Portuguese parliamentary delegation helped to establish in the Portuguese mind that the people were happy with the transition. Indira Gandhi visited Portugal in 1968. Yet the remnants of the animosity remained after Goa liberation and India's non-alignment ensured that relations between Brazil and India did not progress.

Portugal acceded to the EEC on 1 January 1986. Brazil's Economic Cooperation Agreement with India was the motivation to the normalizing of relations with India. The visit of President Henrique Cardoso in 1996 led to agreements in trade, scientific, and cultural cooperation. It was followed by the visit in 1992 of Prime Minister P.V. Narasimha Rao to Rio de Janeiro for the Earth Summit that brought the problem of global warming to the international platform. The visit in 2003 of External Affairs Minister Yashwant Sinha to Brazil led to the setting up of the Bilateral Joint Commission to push the growth of bilateral relations between the two countries.

In the new decade, there was a much more frequent interactions between the two countries, both bilaterally and internationally. There was a realization that their relationship could enhance their standing in the councils of global power. President Luiz Inácio Lula da Silva visited India in 2004 while President Dilma Rouseff visited in March 2012. Prime Minister Manmohan Singh reciprocated the visits in 2006, April 2010, and 2012. Thus, the momentum for bilateral visits came in the 2000s from initiatives taken at the highest level.

Bilateral trade between India and Brazil has been steadily increasing with investments by either country into the other. In 2015, Indian exports were USD 7.90 billion while imports amounted to USD 3.62 billion.[152] Brazilian FDI in India went into automobiles, IT, energy, and biofuels. Indian FDI concentrated on IT, pharmaceuticals, energy, and agribusiness.

In many ways, the India-Brazil relationship has a futurist character that depends on the way the major world powers accept these rising powers in the managing of the world. With the shifting of the economic impulse to the Asia–Pacific, much will depend on how these rising powers will be able to seize the initiative.

The G-4 grouping, working as it does within the existing world system, remains the best chance for these four countries to attain their goal of UNSC permanent membership. The fact that they have been leveraging the grouping for promoting common economic agenda speaks highly of the peaks that Indian diplomacy has attained.

Notes

1. The Government of India Act 1858 was an Act of the Parliament of the United Kingdom (21 and 22 Vict. c. 106) passed on 2 August 1858. Its provisions called for the liquidation of the British East India Company (which had been ruling British India under the auspices of the Parliament) and the transference of its functions to the British Crown. Due to the resignation of Lord Palmerston, the then prime minister, a revised Bill was passed on 2 August 1858. This Act provided that India was to be governed directly and in the name of the Crown. https://en.wikipedia.org/wiki/Government_of_India_Act_1858.

2. United Nations, 'Resolution Adopted by the United Nations Commission for India and Pakistan on 13 August 1948', https://www.mtholyoke.edu/acad/intrel/uncom1.htm.

3. Shigeru Akita, 'The Aid India Consortium, the World Bank and the International Order of Asia 1958–68', *Asian Review of History,* 2(2): 217–48, https://sovereignties.files.wordpress.com/2014/10/aid-india-consortium-akita.pdf.

4. New World Encyclopedia, 'First War of Indian Independence', http://www.newworldencyclopedia.org/entry/First_War_of_Indian_Independence.

5. South East Asia Treaty Organisation (1954–77), https://en.wikipedia.org/wiki/Southeast_Asia_Treaty_Organization.

6. Central Treaty Organisation (1955–79), https://www.britannica.com/topic/Central-Treaty-Organization.

7. 'European Economic Community', https://en.wikipedia.org/wiki/European_Economic_Community.

8. Commonwealth trade preferences, https://en.wikipedia.org/wiki/Commonwealth_free_trade.

9. Abhijit Singh, 'Indian Ocean Zone of Peace: Reality vs Illusion', *The Diplomat* (7 January 2015), https://thediplomat.com/2015/01/the-indian-ocean-zone-of-peace-reality-vs-illusion/.

10. 'The Indo-Soviet Treaty of Friendship and Cooperation', https://en.wikipedia.org/wiki/Indo-Soviet_Treaty_of_Friendship_and_Cooperation.

11. Rajat Pandit, 'India Remains World's Largest Arms Importer with 14% Total Share', *The Times of India* (22 February 2016), http://timesofindia.indiatimes.com/india/India-remains-worlds-largest-arms-importer-with-14-of-total-share/articleshow/51095168.cms.

12. Government of the UK, 'Prime Minister Theresa May and Prime Minister Naredra Modi Set Out a Bold Vision for the India–UK Strategic Partnership', Joint Statement between the Governments of UK and India, 7 November 2016, https://www.gov.uk/government/news/joint-statement-between-the-governments-of-the-uk-and-india.

13. 'UK Starts Trade Talks for Post-Brexit Deal with India', *The Hindu* (9 July 2016), http://www.thehindu.com/business/Economy/uk-starts-trade-talks-for-postbrexit-deal-with-india/article8824943.ece.

14. Editors, 'Britain and the European Union: Let the Brussels Games Begin', *The Economist* (22 June 2017), https://www.economist.com/news/britain/21723836-almost-year-after-referendum-vote-brexit-negotiations-last-begin-let.

15. The Commonwealth, 'UK India Bilateral Trade Deal to Boost UK Exports by 2.6 Billion', http://thecommonwealth.org/media/press-release/uk-india-bilateral-trade-deal-boost-uks-exports-26-billion.

16. European Parliament, DG for External Relations, Evaluation of the EU-India Strategic Partnership and the Potential for its Revitalization, AFET, 2015, http://www.europarl.europa.eu/RegData/etudes/STUD/2015/534987/EXPO_STU(2015)534987_EN.pdf.

17. Library Briefing, 'EU Strategic Partnerships with Third Countries', European Union, 26 September 2012, http://www.europarl.europa.eu/RegData/bibliotheque/briefing/2012/120354/LDM_BRI(2012)120354_REV1_EN.pdf.

18. On a personal note, the wheel had turned a full circle. During my first posting in 1972 to Brussels, India had struggled hard to find a viable relationship within the EEC as it was then after Britain accession left India bereft of the Imperial trade preferences. India's initial

attempts to work out an association agreement, like with former European colonies in Africa, were rebuffed. India was told that it, along with other South Asian countries, was 'non-associable'. India, to protect its bilateral trade, successfully worked out an alternative EEC–India bilateral trade agreement. That was 1972. In 2004, when I was the Indian ambassador, the EU (formerly the EEC) invited India to become a 'strategic partner'. Nothing could compare with the satisfaction I felt then. It had taken three decades. India had finally arrived. Now we have seen the departure of the United Kingdom from the EU, although it remains a UNSC permanent member.

19. TNN, 'Italian Marines Row Hits PM Modi's EU Plan', *Times of India* (15 March 2015), https://timesofindia.indiatimes.com/india/Italian-Marines-row-hits-PM-Narendra-Modis-EU-plan/articleshow/46569875.cms.

20. Rajendra M. Abhyankar, 'India and the European Union: A Partnership for All Reasons', *India Quarterly*, 65(4), http://iqq.sagepub.com/content/65/4/393.abstract.

21. PISM, 'EU-India Strategic Partnership Needs a Reality Check', *Polish Institute of International Affairs*, 35(137), https://www.pism.pl/files/?id_plik=20783.

22. Amiti Sen, 'India, EU Free Trade Pact Talks Stumble as Bilateral Investment Treaties Are Set to Lapse', *The Hindu Business Line* (6 December 2016), http://www.thehindubusinessline.com/economy/india-eu-free-trade-pact-talks-stumble-as-bilateral-investment-treaties-are-set-to-lapse/article9413994.ece.

23. European Commission, 'EU-India Summit: A New Momentum for the EU-India Strategic Relationship', *Press Release* (30 March 2016), http://europa.eu/rapid/press-release_IP-16-1142_en.htm.

24. Ankit Panda, 'Where Do European Union-India Relations Stand', *The Diplomat* (31 March 2016), http://thediplomat.com/2016/03/where-do-european-union-india-relations-stand/.

25. FR Staff, 'India-EU Summit 2017: India-EU Agree to Combat Terror, Talk on Free Trade; Three Key Pacts Inked', Firstpost (6 October 2017), http://www.firstpost.com/india/india-eu-summit-2017-three-key-pacts-inked-two-sides-agree-to-strengthen-trade-and-security-ties-4116323.html.

26. Steve George, 'Trump and Modi Affirm India-US Relations with a Hug', CNN Politics (27 June 2017), http://www.cnn.com/2017/06/27/politics/modi-trump-india-us/index.html.

27. Tanvi Madan, 'When Modi Meets Trump: Where do US-India Relations Stand', Brookings Institution, 23 June 2017, https://www.brookings.edu/blog/order-from-chaos/2017/06/23/when-modi-meets-trump-where-do-u-s-india-relations-stand/.

28. Elizabeth Roche, 'Has Trump Softened Stance on Pakistan after Hostages' Rescue?' Livemint (16 October 2017), http://www.livemint.com/Politics/bH79Cpg4Vky97zkxtKrErJ/Has-Donald-Trump-softened-stance-on-Pakistan-after-hostages.html.

29. Akshay Mishra, 'Trump may Become a Mediator between Indo-Pak Process: Nikki Haley, *India Today* (4 April 2017), http://indiatoday.intoday.in/story/donald-trump-nikki-haley-donald-trump-india-pak-peace-process-us/1/919985.html.

30. Steven Mufson, 'Trump's Afghanistan Troop Increase Adds to $ 1 Trillion in War Costs', *The Washington Post* (23 August 2017), https://www.washingtonpost.com/news/wonk/wp/2017/08/23/trump-decision-to-bolster-u-s-forces-in-afghanistan-will-add-to-the-trillions-of-dollars-of-war-costs/?utm_term=.cebf6680da0e.

31. Editors, 'Obama: India_US Relationship to be a "Defining Partnership" for the 21st Century', CNN Politics (24 November 2009), http://politicalticker.blogs.cnn.com/2009/11/24/obama-india-u-s-relations-to-be-a-defining-partnership-for-the-21st-century/.

32. Yashwant Raj, 'Barak Obama Leaves Office: Highs and Lows in India-US Ties during His Tenure', *Hindustan Times* (17 January 2017), http://www.hindustantimes.com/world-news/barack-leaves-office-highs-and-lows-in-india-us-ties-during-his-tenure/story-LSEjyLnWvWb0WbDFWXaj0L.html.

33. Jean Perlez, 'US Ready to End Sanction on India to Build Alliance' New York Times (29 August 2001), http://www.nytimes.com/2001/08/27/world/us-ready-to-end-sanctions-on-india-to-build-alliance.html.

34. American Association of Physicians of Indian Origin, http://aapio.org/AboutUs/History.html.

35. 'American Association of Physicians of Indian Origin', https://en.wikipedia.org/wiki/American_Association_of_Physicians_of_Indian_Origin#Doctors_of_Indian_ Origin.

36. AAHOA, 'Asian American Hotel Owners Association', http://www.aahoa.com/advocacy.

37. Yashwant Raj, 'Tulsi Gabbard Elected Co-chair of Congressional India Caucus', *Hindustan Times* (16 March 2017), http://www.hindustantimes.com/world-news/tulsi-gabbard-elected-co-chair-of-congressional-india-caucus/story-lbGR00KJy3dqPShf1hCA6J.html.

38. Mark R. Warner, 'Senate India Caucus', Washington, 25 March 2015, https://www.warner.senate.gov/public/index.cfm/senate-india-caucus.

39. Devin Hagerty, 'The Indo-US Entente: Committed Relationship or Friends with Benefits', in Sumit Ganguly (ed.), *Engaging the World: Indian Foreign Policy Since 1947* (New Delhi: Oxford University Press, 2016), pp. 133–66.

40. Shreya Upadhayay, 'India's Strategic Autonomy, Lost or Finally on the Right Track', *The Diplomat*, http://thediplomat.com/2016/04/indias-strategic-autonomy-lost-or-finally-on-the-right-track/.

41. The American military and diplomatic 'pivot' or 'rebalance' towards Asia became a popular buzzword after Hillary Clinton authored 'America's Pacific Century' in *Foreign Policy*. Clinton's article emphasizes the importance of the Asia–Pacific, noting that nearly half of the world's population resides there, making its development vital to American economic and strategic interests. She states that 'open markets in Asia provide the United States with unprecedented opportunities for investment, trade, and access to cutting-edge technology. Our economic recovery at home will depend on exports and the ability of American firms to tap into the vast and growing consumer base of Asia. Strategically, maintaining peace and security across the Asia–Pacific is increasingly crucial to global progress, whether through defending freedom of navigation in the South China Sea, countering the nuclear proliferation efforts of North Korea, or ensuring transparency in the military activities of the region's key players.' The 'pivot' strategy, according to Clinton, will proceed along six courses of action: strengthening bilateral security alliances; deepening America's relationships with rising powers, including China; engaging with regional multilateral institutions; expanding trade and investment; forging a broad-based military presence; and advancing democracy and human rights. https://en.wikipedia.org/wiki/East_Asian_foreign_policy_of_the_Barack_Obama_administration.

42. Ashley J. Tellis, 'India as a New Global Power', Carnegie Endowment for International Peace (2005), http://carnegieendowment.org/files/tellis.india.global.power.final.pdf.

43. S.A. Miller, 'Trump Visit to Saudi Arabia Sets New Tone for International Relations', *The Washington Post* (21 May 2017), http://www.washingtontimes.com/news/2017/may/21/donald-trumps-visit-to-saudi-arabia-sets-new-tone-/.

44. http://www.pewglobal.org/2015/06/23/1-americas-global-image/.

45. Naresh Fernandes, 'American Roots of Indian Independence', *India Ink* (14 August 2012), http://india.blogs.nytimes.com/2012/08/14/american-roots-of-the-indian-independence-movement/?_r=0.

46. http://timesofindia.indiatimes.com/india/Its-been-a-100-years-since-Komagata-Maru-climax/articleshow/43581646.cms.

47. CBC News, 'Justin Trudeau Apologises in House for 1914 Komagata Maru Incident', 18 May 2016, http://www.cbc.ca/news/politics/komagata-maru-live-apology-1.3587827.

48. Chris Ogden, *Indian Foreign Policy* (London: Polity Press, 2014), quoting McMahon Robert, *The Cold War on the Periphery: United States, India, Pakistan* (Columbia University Press, 1994).

49. 'Five Things You Should Know about Nonaligned Movement', http://www.telesurtv.net/english/analysis/5-Things-You-Need-to-Know-About-the-Non-Aligned-Movement-20160712-0032.html.

50. G-77 (the group of developing countries) was set up in June 1964 and is represented in all organizations of the UN. http://www.g77.org/doc/.

51. Shigeru Aketa, 'The Aid-India Consortium, the World Bank and the International Order of Asia, 1958–68', *Asian Review of World Histories*, 2(2): 217–48.

52. Teresita Schaffer, *India and the United States in the 21st Century: Reinventing Partnership* (Washington, DC: CSIS Press, 2009), p. 77.

53. Seymour. M. Hersh, 'On the Nuclear Edge', *The New Yorker* (29 March 1993), http://www.newyorker.com/magazine/1993/03/29/on-the-nuclear-edge.

54. Sushant Singh, '25 Years after the Gates Mission, 3 Stories and One Mystery', *The Indian Express* (21 May 2015), http://indianexpress.com/article/explained/25-yrs-after-gates-mission-3-stories-and-one-mystery/.

55. Stuart Diamond, 'The Bhopal Disaster: How It Happened', *The New York Times* (28 January 1985), http://www.nytimes.com/1985/01/28/world/the-bhopal-disaster-how-it-happened.html?pagewanted=all.

56. G. Balachandran, 'A Primer on Indian Civil Liability for Nuclear Damage Act, 2010', Institute of Defence Studies and Analyses, New Delhi, 23 September 2014, https://idsa.in/backgrounder/IndianCivilLiabilityt_gbalachandran_240914.

57. Suhasini Haidar, 'No Change in Nuclear Liability Law: MEA', *Hindustan Times* (31 August 2016), http://www.thehindu.com/news/national/mea-on-indous-negotiations-no-changes-to-the-law/article6871193.ece.

58. Anil Sai, 'Civil Liability for Nuclear Damage: Now a Dedicated Product to Cover Suppliers Risk', *The Indian Express* (25 May 2016), http://indianexpress.com/article/india/india-news-india/civil-liability-for-nuclear-damage-now-a-dedicated-product-to-cover-suppliers-risk-2817707/.

59. http://www.ibtimes.com/india-us-nuclear-agreement-india-clari-fies-says-supplier-not-directly-liable-case-1809012.

60. MEA, 'Frequently Asked Questions and Answers on Civil Liability for Nuclear Damage Act 2010 and Related Issues', Government of India, Ministry of External Affairs, 8 February 2015, http://www.mea.gov.in/index.htm.

61. 'The most dangerous place in the world today, I think you could argue is the Indian subcontinent and the line of control in Kashmir.' President Clinton, 10 March 2000, quoted by Jonathan Marcus in 'Analysis: The World's Most Dangerous Place', *BBC News* (23 March 2000), http://news.bbc.co.uk/2/hi/south_asia/681086.stm.

62. Dilip Hiro, 'The Most Dangerous Place on Earth: A Nuclear Armageddon in the Making in South Asia' (4 April 2016), http://www.huffingtonpost.com/dilip-hiro/the-most-dangerous-place-_b_9608922.html.

63. Dilip Hiro, 'The Most Dangerous Place on Earth'.

64. Dilip Hiro, 'The Most Dangerous Place on Earth'.

65. Gurmeet Kanwal, 'Next Steps in US-India Strategic Partnership: Defence Cooperation Must Be Taken to a Higher Trajectory', CSIS, 5 October 2015, https://www.csis.org/analysis/next-steps-us-india-strategic-partnership-defense-cooperation-must-be-taken-higher.

66. Rajat Pandit, 'PM Oks $1 Billion Deal with US for 4 Poseidon', *The Times of India* (2 July 2016), http://timesofindia.indiatimes.com/india/PM-oks-1bn-deal-with-US-for-4-Poseidons/articleshow/53015224.cms.

67. Sankalp Gurjar, 'India Hooked on to American Military Toys', *International Policy Digest* (5 July 2016), http://intpolicydigest.org/2016/07/05/india-s-hooked-on-american-military-toys/.

68. Manu Pubby, 'Quietly, India and US Operationalise New Military Logistic Sharing Pact', *The Print* (14 October 2017), https://theprint.in/2017/10/14/india-us-new-military-logistics-sharing-pact/.

69. Rupajyoti Borah, '5 Reasons Why India Agreed to a Logistic Agreement with the United States', *The Diplomat* (6 May 2016), http://thediplomat.com/2016/05/5-reasons-why-india-agreed-to-a-logistics-agreement-with-the-united-states/.

70. Saroj Bishoyi, 'Logistic Support Agreement: A Closer Look at the Impact on India–US Strategic Relationship', Institute of Defence Studies and Analyses, New Delhi, 2013, https://idsa.in/system/files/jds_7_1_SarojBishoyi.pdf.

71. Sushant Singh, 'India, US Sign Key Defence Pact to Use Each Other's Bases for Repairs & Supplies', *The Indian Express* (31 August 2016), http://indianexpress.com/article/india/india-news-india/mano-har-parrikar-signs-key-logistics-defence-pact-with-us-304581/.

72. Sushant Singh, 'India, US Sign Key Defence Pact to Use Each Other's Bases for Repairs & Supplies'.

73. Dmitriy Frolovsky, 'What's behind Russia's Rapprochement with Pakistan', *The Diplomat* (14 May 2016), https://thediplomat.com/2016/05/whats-behind-russias-rapprochement-with-pakistan/.

74. *INS Vikramaditya*, formerly *Admiral Goroshkov*, http://www.indian-navy.nic.in/content/about-ins-vikramaditya-newest-largest-ship-indian-navy.

75. Arun Janardhnan, 'Five Facts about Kudankulam Nuclear Power Plant', *The Indian Express* (10 August 2016), http://www.indian-navy.nic.in/content/about-ins-vikramaditya-newest-largest-ship-indian-navy.

76. Pallavi Pal, 'The Long Way Ahead in Indo-Russian Ties', Institute for Defence Studies and Analyses, New Delhi, 20 December 2010, http://www.idsa.in/idsacomments/ThewayaheadinIndoRussianties_ppal_201210.

77. John C.K. Daly, 'Tajikistan Entertains Indian Offer for Air Base', *Silk Road Reports* (17 July 2015), http://www.silkroadreporters.com/2015/07/17/tajikistan-entertains-indian-offer-for-air-base/.

78. Express News Service, 'Tajik Prez Visits India, Defence Ties to Get Boost', *The New Indian Express* (13 December 2016), http://www.newindianexpress.com/nation/2016/dec/13/tajik-prez-visits-india-defence-ties-to-get-boost-1548621.html.

79. Franz-Stefan Gady, 'Russia and Pakistan to Hold First-Ever Military Exercise', *The Diplomat* (14 September 2016), https://thediplomat.com/2016/09/russia-and-pakistan-to-hold-first-ever-military-exercise/.

80. Joy Mitra, 'Russia, China and Pakistan: An Emerging New Axis', *The Diplomat* (18 August 2015), https://thediplomat.com/2015/08/russia-china-and-pakistan-an-emerging-new-axis/.

81. Neeta Lal, 'Manmohan Singh's Legacy for India-Russia Relations', *Russia & India Report* (11 March 2014), https://in.rbth.com/eco-

nomics/2014/03/11/manmohan_singhs_legacy_for_india-russia_
relations_33641.

82. HT Correspondent, 'PM Modi says India Russia Summit "Very
    Productive', added new vigour to relations', *Hindustan Times*
    (2 June 2017), http://www.hindustantimes.com/india-news/live-
    updates-pm-narendra-modi-in-russia-modi-putin-summit/story-
    TJLAdGfGfHIAulfCiDZt3M.html.

83. Staff, 'PM Modi Visit to Russia: Bilateral Bonhomie Reiterated
    through Significant Takeaways', *Outlook* (3 April 2017), https://
    www.outlookindia.com/newsscroll/pm-modi-visit-to-russia-bilat-
    eral-bonhomie-reiterated-through-significant-takeaways/1066847.

84. Bijaya Kumar Das, 'India, Russia Sign 16 Deals, Modi Woos Russian
    Business Leaders', *India Today* (24 December 2015), http://india-
    today.intoday.in/story/india-sees-russia-as-reliable-friend-modi-to-
    putin/1/555105.html.

85. 'Narendra Modi, Putin Vow to Take Forward India-Russia Ties', *The
    Hindu* (24 June 2016), http://www.thehindu.com/news/interna-
    tional/modi-putin-at-tashkent/article8769433.ece.

86. Prakash Nanda, 'Narendra Modi in France: For true meaning of
    PM's visit look beyond headlines on climate and terror', Firstpost
    (18 October 2017), http://www.firstpost.com/india/narendra-modi-
    in-france-for-true-meaning-of-pms-visit-look-beyond-headlines-
    on-climate-and-terror-3515965.html.

87. https://www.iter.org/.

88. 'Causes for Liberation of French Colonies in India', *Wikipedia*,
    https://en.wikipedia.org/wiki/Causes_for_liberation_of_French_
    colonies_in_India.

89. Ankit Panda, 'It's Official: India and France sign $7.87 Billion Deal
    for 36 Rafale Fighters', *The Diplomat* (23 September 2016), http://
    thediplomat.com/2016/09/its-official-india-and-france-sign-
    8-7-billion-deal-for-36-rafale-fighters/.

90. 'The Emergency (India)', https://en.wikipedia.org/wiki/The_
    Emergency_(India).

91. 'In December 1975, French Minister for External Trade Raymond
    Barre visited New Delhi to "prepare" for the presidential visit. In
    his meeting with Indira Gandhi, he asked the inevitable question
    on why she had declared the Emergency. Indira Gandhi was totally
    flustered, provoking an unexpected, yet emotional response, much to
    the embarrassment of the visiting minister', Rajendra Abhyankar, *Stuff
    Happens: An Anecdotal Insight into Indian Diplomacy* (New Delhi: Har
    Anand Publications Pvt. Ltd), Chapter 1, pp. 23–27.

92. '29th G8 Summit', https://en.wikipedia.org/wiki/29th_G8_ summit.

93. 'Focus on Anti-Terror, Climate Cooperation Says Hollande', *The Hindu* (25 January 2016), http://www.thehindu.com/ news/on-day-2-of-india-visit-french-president-hollande-says-focus-is-on-antiterror-and-climate-cooperation/article8150945. ece?utm_source=InternalRef&utm_medium=relatedNews&utm_ campaign=RelatedNews.

94. 'Joint Statement at the End of the Visit to India by French President Francoise Hollande', *The Hindu* (27 January 2016), http://www. thehindu.com/news/resources/full-text-of-joint-statement-issued-by-india-france/article8151255.ece.

95. AFP, 'India Signs $ 8.8 bn Deal to Buy 36 French Rafaele Fighters', *Dawn* (27 September 2016), https://www.dawn.com/news/ 1285605.

96. UN News Centre, 'India Ratifies Paris Climate Pact at UN, Brings Its Entry "Tantalisingly Close"', http://www.un.org/apps/news/ story.asp?NewsID=55185#.V_P5Z_krJD8.

97. 'G-4 Nations', https://en.wikipedia.org/wiki/G4_nations.

98. Sanjay Baru, 'G4 Summit: Will India Utilize the Group's Strengths or Pick-Up Others' Baggage', *The Economic Times* (28 September 2015), http://blogs.economictimes.indiatimes.com/et-commentary/ g4-summit-will-india-utilize-the-groups-strengths-or-pick-up-others-baggage/.

99. Embassy of India, Berlin, 'Bilateral Relations', Embassy of India, Berlin, https://www.indianembassy.de/relationpages.php?id=37.

100. PTI, 'Modi in Berlin: India-Germany Vow "Strong Measures" against Terror Sponsors', *Hindustan Times* (30 May 2017), http:// www.hindustantimes.com/india-news/pm-modi-in-berlin-india-germany-vow-strong-measures-against-terror-sponsors/story-lvkoN9AGsJVsxFl05aRzPL.html.

101. Indrani Bagchi, 'Germany Backs India, Says Every State Has the Right to Defend Its Territory from Global Terrorism', *The Times of India* (5 October 2016), http://timesofindia.indiatimes.com/ india/Germany-backs-Indias-strikes-says-every-state-has-the-right-to-defend-its-territory-from-global-terrorism/article-show/54701421.cms.

102. John Woolley and Gerhard Peters, 'Remarks following Discussions with Chancellor Kohl of Germany and an Exchange with Reporters in Potsdam, Germany', The American Presidency

Project, 13 May 1998, http://www.presidency.ucsb.edu/ws/?pid =55942.

197

103. Mahesh Jha, 'Merkel's India Visit to Take Stock of Relations', *DW* (2 October 2015), http://www.dw.com/en/merkels-india-visit-to-take-stock-of-relations/a-18757029.

104. Katja Keppner, 'Why India and Germany Need Each Other', *DW* (6 October 2015), http://www.dw.com/en/why-india-and-germany-need-each-other/a-18764386.

105. Shubhajit Roy, '"Germany Our Natural Partner"', Says Modi After Meeting Chancellor Merkel', *Indian Express* (6 October 2015), http://indianexpress.com/article/india/india-news-india/modi-merkel-talks-germany-offers-euro-2-bln-to-india-for-solar-clean-energy/.

106. PTI, 'German Chancellor Angela Merkel Arrives for 3-day Visit', *The Hindu* (4 October 2015), http://www.thehindu.com/news/national/german-chancellor-angela-merkel-arrives-for-3day-india-visit/article7723310.ece.

107. Dhruva Jaishankar, 'India and Germany: Realising Strategic Convergence', Brookings Institution, 20 January 2017, https://www.brookings.edu/opinions/india-and-germany-realising-strategic-convergence/.

108. Hans Kudnani, 'Germany as a Geo-Economic Power', *Washington Quarterly*, 34(3): 31–45, http://www.tandfonline.com/doi/abs/10.1080/0163660X.2011.587950.

109. The Hallstein Doctrine, named after Walter Hallstein, prescribed that the Federal Republic of Germany (West Germany) would not establish or maintain diplomatic relations with any state that recognized the German Democratic Republic (East Germany) and would regard it as an unfriendly act (acte peu amical) if third countries were to recognize the German Democratic Republic or maintain diplomatic relations with it. https://en.wikipedia.org/wiki/Hallstein_Doctrine.

110. Hannes Ebert, 'India's German Policy Since 1947', in Sumit Ganguly (ed.), *Engaging the World, Indian Foreign Policy Since 1947* (New Delhi: Oxford University Press, 2016).

111. Embassy of India, Berlin, 'India-Germany Relations' (2014), http://www.mea.gov.in/Portal/ForeignRelation/Germany_Dec2014.pdf.

112. Embassy of India, Berlin, 'Bilateral Relations', Embassy of India Berlin, 20 March 2017, https://www.indianembassy.de/relation-pages.php?id=37.

113. CII blog, 'India-Germany Trade and Economic Relations', Confederation of Indian Industry, May 2017, http://ciiblog.in/india-germany-trade-and-investment-relations/.

114. 'Heiligendamm Process', https://en.wikipedia.org/wiki/Heiligendamm_Process.

115. Ministry of Foreign Affairs of Japan, 'Japan-India Bilateral Relations (Basic Data)', 25 September 2017, http://www.mofa.go.jp/region/asia-paci/india/data.html.

116. MEA, 'Visit of Prime Minister of Japan to India (13–14 September 2017)', Government of India, Ministry of External Affairs, 11 September 2017, http://www.mea.gov.in/press-releases.htm?dtl/28933/Visit+of+Prime+Minister+of+Japan+to+India+September+1314+2017.

117. Amrita Ray, 'Shinzo Abe in Gujarat Live: Japanese PM, Narendra Modi visit Sidi Sayyid Mosque in Ahmedabad', NDTV (13 September 2017), https://www.ndtv.com/india-news/live-shinzo-abe-pm-narendra-modi-to-meet-in-ahmedabad-to-boost-india-japan-ties-1749555.

118. BS Web Team, 'From Defence to Bullet Train: Where are India-Japan Ties Heading', *Business Standard* (15 September 2017), http://www.business-standard.com/article/economy-policy/from-defence-to-bullet-train-where-are-india-japan-ties-headed-117091500405_1.html.

119. MEA, 'Prime Minister's Visit to Japan for the Annual Summit Meeting (11–12 November 2016)', Government of India, Ministry of External Affairs, http://www.mea.gov.in/press-releases.htm?dtl/27548/Prime+Ministers+visit+to+Japan+for+the+Annual+Summit+Meeting+November+1112+2016.

120. FP Staff, 'India-Japan Nuclear Deal, Bullet Trains: 10 Highlights of PM Modi's Visit to the Island Nation', Firstpost (20 October 2016), http://www.firstpost.com/india/india-japan-nuclear-deal-bullet-trains-10-highlights-of-pm-modis-visit-to-the-island-nation-3101224.html.

121. Clint Richards, 'Modi-Abe Summit High on Rhetoric', *The Diplomat* (2 September 2014), https://thediplomat.com/2014/09/modi-abe-summit-high-on-rhetoric-lagging-in-agreements/.

122. Ministry of Foreign Affairs, Japan, 'Japan and India Vision 2025 Special Strategic and Global Partnership', 12 December 2015, http://www.mofa.go.jp/s_sa/sw/in/page3e_000432.html.

123. Yuki Tatsumi, 'Abe Visit Takes Japan-India Security Relations to the Next Level', *The Diplomat* (14 December 2015), http://

thediplomat.com/2015/12/abes-visit-takes-japan-india-security-relations-to-the-next-level/.

124. Aftab Seth, 'India and Japan', Atish Sinha and Madhup Mohta (eds), *Indian Foreign Policy: Challenges and Opportunities* (New Delhi: Academic Foundation, 2007), pp. 808–18.

125. 'Subhash Chandra Bose', https://en.wikipedia.org/wiki/Subhas_Chandra_Bose.

126. 'Bandung Conference of Afro-Asian Countries 1955', https://www.britannica.com/event/Bandung-Conference.

127. 'Joint Statement towards India-Japan Strategic and Global Partnership', Embassy of India, Sofia, https://www.indembsofia.org/en/joint-statement-towards-india-japan-strategic-and-global-partnership/.

128. Embassy of India, Tokyo, 'India-Japan Bilateral Brief', http://www.indembassy-tokyo.gov.in/bilateral_brief.html.

129. PIB, 'Japan's Official Development Assistance (ODA) Loan of Rs. 21590 crores to India for Financial year 2016, 17', Government of India, 31 March 2017, http://pib.nic.in/newsite/PrintRelease.aspx?relid=160362.

130. B.S. Raghavan, 'India-Japan CEPA Holds Great Promise', *The Hindu Business Line* (7 September 2011), http://www.indembassy-tokyo.gov.in/bilateral_brief.html.

131. P.S. Suryanarayana, 'Towards a Future-Oriented India-Japan Partnership', *ISAS Insights*, Institute of South Asian Studies, no. 301 (22 December 2015), http://www.isas.nus.edu.sg/ISAS%20Reports/ISAS%20Insights%20No.%20301%20-%20Towards%20a%20Future-Oriented%20India-Japan%20Partnership.pd.

132. Peter Nardin, 'United Security Council Reform', Our World, United Nations University, 1 May 2014, https://ourworld.unu.edu/en/united-nations-security-council-reform.

133. Ministry of Foreign Affairs of Japan, 'Ministerial Meeting of the G4 countries (Brazil, Germany, India, Japan) in the margins of the 68th Session of the UN General Assembly, Joint Press Release', 26 September 2016, http://www.mofa.go.jp/policy/page3e_000090.html.

134. MEA, 'Joint press Statement at the Meeting of Foreign Ministers of the G4 countries—Brazil, Germany, India and Japan—on United Nations Security Council Reform on the occasion of the 72nd Session of the UN General Assembly, New York', Ministry of External Affairs, Government of India, 20 September 2017, http://www.mea.gov.in/bilateral-documents.htm?dtl/28962/Joint+Press+Statement+at+the+Meeting+of+Foreign+Ministers+of+the+

G4+Countries+Brazil+Germany+India+and+Japan+on+United +Nations+Security+Council+Reform+on+the+occasion+of+7 2nd+Session+of+UN+General+Assembly+New+York.

135. PTI, 'G4 Nations Pitch for Expanding UNSC Permanent Members', *The Economic Times* (3 May 2016), https://economictimes. indiatimes.com/news/politics-and-nation/g4-nations-pitch-for-expanding-unscs-permanent-members/articleshow/52088145. cms.

136. Peter Nardin, 'United Security Council Reform'.

137. PTI, 'India-Japan Ties Get a Leg-Up as Modi Meets Abe' (8 September 2016), http://www.thehindu.com/news/national/ indiajapan-ties-get-a-legup-as-modi-meets-abe/article9081826. ece.

138. 'BRICS', https://en.wikipedia.org/wiki/BRICS.

139. Ian Bremmer, 'Mixed Fortunes of the BRICS Countries in Five Facts', *TIME* (1 September 2017), http://time.com/4923837/ brics-summit-xiamen-mixed-fortunes/.

140. Costa Vasquez, Supriya Roychoudhary, and Caio Borges, 'New Development Bank is BRICS' Best Card', *Financial Times* (5 September 2017), https://www.ft.com/content/cc7c7ee6-918b-11e7-a9e6-11d2f0ebb7f0?mhq5j=e5.

141. Claire Felter and Danielle Renwick, 'Mercosur: South America's Fractious Trade Bloc', Council on Foreign Relations, 13 September 2017, https://www.cfr.org/backgrounder/mercosur-south-americas-fractious-trade-bloc.

142. Pragya Pandey, '2017 BRICS Summit: Post-Doklam India, China Meet in Xiamen', *The Diplomat* (7 September 2017), https://thediplomat.com/2017/09/2017-brics-summit-post-doklam-india-china-meet-in-xiamen/.

143. 'G20 Coalition, About G20', http://www.b20coalition.org/about-g20.php.

144. Editors, 'G-20 Summit: Key Facts, Issues and Personalities of Group Which Represents Two-thirds of World Population', *Strait Times* (5 July 2017), http://www.straitstimes.com/world/europe/g-20-summit-key-facts-about-the-group-that-represents-two-thirds-of-the-world.

145. Ellie Flynn and David Hughes, 'World Leaders Summit, What is the G20, How Long is the 2017 Summit in Hamburg, Which Countries are Members, and What is on the Agenda', *The Sun* (8 July 2017), https://www.thesun.co.uk/news/1727642/g20-memebers-hamburg-summit-2017-agenda/.

146. 'India–Brazil–South Africa Dialogue Forum', http://www.ibsa-trilateral.org/about-ibsa2.
147. 'IBSA Dialogue Forum', https://en.wikipedia.org/wiki/IBSA_Dialogue_Forum.
148. Embassy of South Africa in Ethiopia, India–Brazil–South Africa Dialogue Forum, 8th Trilateral Ministerial Commission Meeting, 17 October 2017, https://www.southafricanembassyethiopia.com/?q=content/india-brazil-south-africa-dialogue-forum-8th-ibsa-trilateral-ministerial-commission-meeting.
149. PTI, 'BRICS Summit 2017: Narendra Modi, Brazilian President Michel Temer Discuss Common Global Vision, Firstpost (4 September 2017), http://www.firstpost.com/world/brics-summit-2017-narendra-modi-brazilian-president-michel-temer-discuss-common-global-vision-4007341.html.
150. PTI, 'BRICS Summit 2017'.
151. Rakesh Krishna Simha, 'Goa Liberation: How Russia Vetoed the West', *Russia and India Report* (12 December 2014), https://in.rbth.com/blogs/2014/12/12/goa_liberation_how_russia_vetoed_the_west_40297.
152. Embassy of India, Brasilia, 'Bilateral Trade', 20 March 2017, http://indianembassy.org.br/en/india-brazil/bilateral-trade/.

CHAPTER
FOUR

India in the World

*I*ndian diplomacy's success is a function of its own reposition-ing in global governance where the country is seen as an 'insider' in certain global forums. The fact that India has not always been able to recast its international behaviour in these organiza-tions often appears to do harm to its otherwise strong case for UNSC permanent membership. At the same time, India has con-sistently stressed that the democratization of global governance necessitates recognizing the growing role of emerging powers and developing countries.

Different factors, such as the rigidity of certain organizations against institutional change and the unwillingness of Western powers to change their established positions, affect India's per-ception of its activism in institutions of global governance. India's ambivalence may also derive from the fact that its foreign policy does not speak or defer to a 'grand strategy' in the changing international scenario. As a result, India is seen to be reluctant to embrace its new-found influential role in different institutions and identify new targets and possibilities for reform.

This may derive from the belief that India is yet to reach a strength in global governance institutions that will evict any backlash should it unilaterally engineer new reform proposals. India, thus, continues to take recourse to coalitions with other emerging powers and developing countries to promote reforms. India remains wedded to the working of collective interests among developing countries. It refrains from initiating any change to its initiatives in cases where the interests of other developing countries will not be served. It still sees itself as a champion of developing country interests. This idea is a running thread in India's interactions in institutions of global governance.

The UN and Its Security Council

India's latest bid at the UNSC, as a part of the G-4 aspirant countries, to push for a UNSC reform and further its claim for permanent membership suffered at the UNGA session in September 2016.[1] '... the 70th anniversary of the United Nations was not able to build up momentum with a view to reaching an agreement on this important item of the agenda of the General Assembly,' according to a joint statement with Brazil, Germany, India, and Japan. The G-4 grouping, comprising Germany and Japan—the two defeated nations of World War II—and Brazil and India—the two rising nations in the current economy—on 20 September 2017[2] resolved to encourage launching text-based negotiations during the 72nd session of the General Assembly. There is one view that India will get the permanent membership only if it becomes economically powerful.[3] However, this raises two questions: How is it that after seven decades World War II continues to cast its long shadow on the Security Council membership? Also, how important is the permanent membership of the UNSC for India?

As a founding member of the UN in 1945, India has waited a long time for the UNSC permanent membership. After more than twenty years momentum to reform, the Security Council gained momentum in 2016 when a negotiating text was adopted by the General Assembly, despite strong opposition from a small group of countries including Pakistan and Italy.[4]

India put forward, for the first time, its candidature for non-permanent membership in 1947. It has held a seat seven times, the last in 2011–2. The gradual increase in member-nations of the United Nations to 193 by 2011 has increased the complexity of the organization. India was among the original members of the United Nations that on 1 January 1942 signed the Declaration at Washington, DC. It participated in the United Nations Conference on International Organization at San Francisco from 25 April to 26 June 1945. As a founding member of the United Nations, India has supported the purposes and principles of the UN, made significant contributions in implementing the goals of the Charter and the evolution of its specialized programmes and agencies.

India participates in all of its specialized agencies and organizations as a charter member of the UN. It has contributed nearly 100,000 troops to various UN peace-keeping efforts in Korea, Egypt, and the Congo in its earlier years and in Somalia, Angola, Haiti, Liberia, Lebanon, Rwanda, and South Sudan in recent years. In addition, India is a member of all major international organizations and those at the regional and sub-regional levels.[5]

If there are countries, including some of the P-5, who support India's claim to the UNSC permanent membership there is an equally vociferous group, 'Uniting for Consensus' (UfC), led by Italy, which also includes Pakistan, who oppose it. The group steadfastly opposed the creation of a negotiating text for reform talks saying that there should first be a consensus. In a setback to the UfC and to others trying to derail the efforts to add permanent members, the UNGA in 2015 adopted a negotiating text that would kick-start meaningful discussions on reforms.[6] The adoption of the text was a breakthrough to enable meaningful negotiations.

History

As World War II was coming to an end, the United States, the United Kingdom, and the Soviet Union met in 1944 and agreed on a new framework for an international organization that would safeguard peace. Further discussions were held in San Francisco where the blueprint for a new international organization that would be at the 'heart of sustainable peace'[7] was be created to replace the failed League of Nations. While initially the General Assembly was to be the centre of gravity of the organization, the veto power accorded to the Security Council ensured that it wielded commanding power concentrated in the hands of its five permanent members. India, at that stage, had opined in favour of the veto in the expectation that it would foster the committed and impartial participation of the great powers and stave off their withdrawal from the organization.

India had reportedly played an active role in the discussions leading up to the creation of the United Nations Organization (or the UN) where it had proposed a process of nomination, rather than an election, of non-permanent members to the UNSC. India's suggestions for the selection criteria for the UNSC membership hold valid even today—relative population, industrial and economic capacity, contribution in armed forces, and so on. As a founding member of the new organization, India decided to play an active role right from the start. It accorded with Jawaharlal Nehru's sense of commitment and idealism, of a world that will not be beset by war again, where its people would have the freest possibilities of achieving their maximum potential. Despite the use of the atom bomb on Hiroshima and Nagasaki, the Indian representative to the UN, Sir Ramaswamy Mudaliar said,

> ... Are we not likely to lose all sense of proportion, even when we regard the main horror of the misuse of atomic energy, and when we fail to realize that beyond all these things there is a Power which looks upon people and upon nations and which, in its own inscrutable way, carries out its purposes for all eternity and to all eternity?

India's posture towards the UN embedded idealism which made Nehru take Pakistan's invasion of Kashmir in 1947 to the Security Council making it incumbent to accept the decision of its UN Commission on India and Pakistan. Nehru was discouraged by British Prime Minister Clement Attlee from 'direct intervention across the international border into Pakistan in exercise of the right of self-defence guaranteed under Article 51 of the Charter'.[8]

Even though the UNCIP threw the Kashmir issue into a long-term hyperbole, India saw its international prestige grow in the UN during the 1960s. It championed the causes of South Africa's anti-apartheid struggle and the decolonization of the 1960s and took initiatives in promoting global and comprehensive disarmament and assisted in the UN's programme for development and contribution to UN peace-keeping forces in the Middle East, Congo and Cyprus. Its championing of non-alignment as a policy attracted recently independent states and made India a leader within what was then referred to as the 'Third World'.

India's fall from this lofty height of international prestige was relatively sudden, the key factors being the military takeover of the Portuguese colonies of Goa, Diu, and Daman and the continuing issue of Kashmir. It further suffered with the Chinese invasion of Northeast India in 1962 by puncturing the aura of non-alignment and the sentiment then common of *'Hindi-Chini bhai-bhai'*. Many reasons are attributed for the Chinese invasion, including the sanctuary given to the Dalai Lama and as a Mao's counter-move against domestic opposition at that time. It exposed India's utter helplessness against a more powerful adversary and its unfulfilled expectation that the Western powers will come to its aid. India's contradictory position of support to the Soviet occupation of Hungary and the opposition to British, French, and Israeli military response to Nasser's nationalization of the Suez showed India's feet of clay and dented its reputation as a champion of peace.

India realized the implications of the UNSC's power structure for what it was—a power game in which India was not at the table. With brute show of force by the great powers when it suited them becoming the norm, India too shifted focus to give paramountcy to its national interest. Throughout the Cold War India found it opportune to hitch its star to the Soviet Union, particularly after the Indo-Soviet Treaty of 1971 where it received benefits from the Soviet veto on the Kashmir issue. As the Cold War ended, the Security Council firmly became the UN's centre of gravity.

In the fast-moving international changes following the Cold War, the UN became increasingly marginalized in conflicts ranging from Yugoslavia to Rwanda. The US invasion of Iraq, without UNSC mandate, proved the UN's powerlessness in the face of the leverage the great power exerted. More often than not, it is seen as a front for US-driven policies best illustrated in the cases of Libya and Syria. We also have a unique spectacle of Russia defending Syrian self-determination in the UNSC while itself breaching the principle in Crimea and Ukraine.

India in the Security Council

The seven times that India has been on the Security Council as a non-permanent member, its performance has been technically sound and nationally useful. India's handling of the Kashmir issue in the UNSC, whether it was sitting on it or not, has succeeded in ensuring that it does not come up in any fundamental way at that forum.[9] If it does, it is generally with an exhortation that the two countries should bilaterally settle the matter. The commitment to bilateral negotiations incorporated in the Shimla Agreement of 1972 holds despite Pakistan's efforts to shift the focus back to the UNSC.[10]

Ambassador Vitaly Churkin, the permanent representative of the Russian Federation to the UN and president of the UNSC for the month of October 2016, told reporters that the council 'is not discussing the issues between India and Pakistan and has no plans to do so'.[11] 'I don't want to go there. No one wants to go there,' declared Churkin during a news conference at the UN headquarters, interrupting a reporter who attempted to raise the issue. In 2017, Pakistan and India once again had a war of words on Kashmir with the Pakistan Prime Minister calling on the UNSC to appoint a special representative on Kashmir.[12] The charges were rejected by India External Affairs Minister Sushma Swaraj accusing Pakistan of backing several anti-India militant groups and helping them infiltrate Kashmir to stoke violence and carry out terrorist acts. In her speech on 23 September 2016 she targeted Pakistan by saying 'Pakistan had only built Jihadi Factories' while India was building the nation through institutions and knowledge bank.[13]

In response UN Secretary General Antonio Gutierrez at his first press conference in June 2017 stating that he had been meeting India and Pakistan on the Kashmir issue, the Indian foreign ministry stated that bilateral matters have to be dealt bilaterally.[14] The Kashmir issue appears, for the present, finessed in the UNSC;

yet India must realistically look at its effect on the prospect of its permanent membership.[15]

The UNSC has not, in the last 70 years, seen a change in its permanent membership. It indicates that even with an increase in UNSC membership and the spread and complexity of issues only the P-5, if interested, have the capability of resolving them. Yet their overwhelming power stemming from the 'veto' has so far militated against any expansion of the permanent membership.

The discussions on UNSC expansion have been hamstrung by the multiplicity of interests and proposals from the vast majority of members. Further, even in the event of a partial expansion of the UNSC the decision will require an approval by two-thirds of the UNGA membership. The P-5 knows that it is an endless road for the aspirants. India has continued its campaign for permanent membership, most recently by Prime Minister Modi in 2015 at the 47th session of the UNGA.[16] In this background, how much does permanent membership affect India? What changes in its foreign policy will become incumbent should it succeed? Will India be interested in, or have the ability, to meet these expectations?

India's activism in the UN soon after independence continued until 1962 when the Chinese invasion dealt a deathblow to the idealism that enshrined India's view of the UN. It became clear that the organization was being treated by the P-5 as the ultimate field of battle for supremacy in a world riven between countries owing allegiance to either the East (communist) or Western (capitalist) blocs and their respective military pacts.

Even though India's traumatic wake-up call cost it much in its self-esteem and international prestige, its leadership of NAM still gave it international relevance. Decolonization was continuing meanwhile, particularly in Africa, and the world witnessed countless civil wars, calling for the UN's military intervention. India was one of the few countries in a position to provide troops for peace-keeping. During the 1960s and 1970s, Indian troops provided service on behalf of the UN in Korea (1950–4), Indo-China (1954–70), Middle East (1956–67), and Congo (1960–4). In all, till date, India has participated in 43 UN peace-keeping missions, contributing up to 180,000 troops, including police personnel.

Following the 1962 Chinese aggression, India remained subdued in the UN councils until the India–Pakistan War of 1971 and
the creation of Bangladesh. India's confidence, restored after the
splitting of Pakistan, was further buoyed by its successful nuclear
test in 1974. That the Indo-Soviet Treaty of 1971 brought one
UNSC permanent member on its side was another shot in the
arm for Indian diplomacy. Both the declaration of the National
Emergency (June 1975–March 1977) and the impact of the 1974
correction of prices by oil-exporting countries, forced a stronger
sense of realism within the UN.

India continued to support all economic forums, whether
within the UN or outside, such as the North-South Dialogue,
and on questions of international security like terrorism. India
played an important role in accomplishing the agreement on
the Law of the Seas and on issues related to the financing of
development. India remained steadfast in its support to the Arab
cause even though by 1992 it had opened full-fledged relations
with Israel.

Henceforth, India would comment only on issues of direct
and indirect concern to itself or those that might secure specific
benefits. The government took a stand only on a limited number
of issues, preferring silence or abstention, except on decolonization, disarmament, military bases, and non-proliferation. This
predilection to abstention became more pronounced after 1990
when the remodelling of India's external relations and economics
demanded the building of a wider international network. The
fact that communism had ended made it even more imperative
to open relations with countries which had been kept away,
for example, Israel. At the same time, the need to build closer
relations with all the P-5, particularly the United States, became
overarching.

India's standing in the United Nations as an important member-
state has always been linked to its economic success. Its recognition as an emerging economic power was a boost in the arm while
the world keenly watched as India went through its economic
reform process. Its economic success became synonymous with its
international political stature and ability to assume responsibilities
as a UNSC permanent member. Especially since 2000, the holy

grail of permanent membership has appeared to slip from its grasp as economic growth rates have slipped.

Nevertheless, periodic boosts have kept these aspirations alive, though momentarily, India has got out of the India–Pakistan box in which both the United States and China have sought to sequester it. The 2006 India-US agreement on civil nuclear energy was one such occasion when India was seen as a power in its own right, its future more tied with that of the United States than Pakistan or China. The international recognition due to these developments has nevertheless not achieved for India the global recognition that it has always craved for. India has always felt entitled to such a status by virtue of its size, population, and ancient civilization. Even more, with the economic and political levers of the world shifting to the Asia-Pacific, India justifiably feels its importance sitting astride an India Ocean that has become an 'ocean of transit'. Should the world's fulcrum thus shift in this century, India could find itself in an enviable position—of having to choose between hitching its star to China or the United States.[17]

The role played by India and its diplomats in the councils of the UN has depended on the broad trends India has faced. It has required great drafting agility in order to ensure that pragmatic positions were maintained which would not jeopardize India's standing on a particular issue. The tendency has been to eschew statements on the burning issues of the day unless absolutely warranted. When seen in this background India's performance as a UNSC non-permanent member in 2011–2 explains itself.

India's UNSC non-permanent seat, after nearly two decades, coming at the height of the G-4 initiative, was a proving trial for a permanent seat.[18] Yet it was only a matter of perception for India was unlikely to waver from its path of speaking softly and staying away from statements on contentious issues where the P-5 were involved. India's priorities during its two-year tenure were going to be developmental concerns, eradication of poverty, Millennium Development Goals (MDGs), inclusive growth, terrorism, and Security Council reform. Nevertheless, the UNSC had to deal with a great number of contentious issues, most having to do with the aftermath of the Arab Spring and its fallout.

Nothing illustrates India's performance better than its voting on the cases of Libya and Syria. India with Brazil, South Africa, and Lebanon abstained on the UNSC vote on a resolution threatening sanctions against Syria. India's abstention on the vote was due to desire not to annoy the United States soon after it had entered the UNSC. Abstention was a calculated option as eventually 'Russia vetoed the resolution without any odium attaching to India. India also had the Libya issue in mind when the UNSC Resolution to protect "civilian areas" passed muster with the entire P-5 and degenerated into a NATO-led military operation for regime change. By abstaining India managed to avoid inserting itself into a messy diplomatic situation.'[19] It illustrated evocatively India's perspective on its tenure in the UNSC.

India's voting behaviour as a non-permanent UNSC member during 2011–2 indicated its willingness to prioritize solidarity with developing countries. India supported Iran's right to use nuclear technology for peaceful purposes and expressed its 'support for a diplomatic solution' in order 'to address all outstanding issues in restoring international confidence in the exclusively peaceful nature of Iran's nuclear programme'. India had abstained on the vote, proposing a 'no-fly zone' over Libya and stating that there was insufficient information on the impact of such a measure on the welfare of the Libyan people. The Indian position stressed the need for complete respect of sovereignty, unity, and territorial integrity of Libya. The same language was used in the case of Syria. India abstained from the vote on the UNSC resolution because it did not condemn the violence perpetrated by the Syrian opposition, nor placed any responsibility on the opposition to abjure violence and engage with the Syrian authorities. In the beginning of 2012, India voted for a new resolution on Syria on the precondition that any references to a regime change, threats of sanctions, and military intervention would be removed.

India's position in the UNSC raised scepticism on its ability to act as a responsible power in the UNSC. The alternative of adopting a pro-Western stance was seen to be highly negative in its impact on domestic public opinion. It harkened back to the Vajpayee government's unsuccessful attempt in April 2003 to keep the issue of sending Indian troops to assist the United States in northern Iraq off a parliamentary discussion or decision.

This is evident in India's position in the UNSC. Since its campaign for UNSC reform began, India has considerably increased its standing as a global power. With the exception of China, the permanent members of the UNSC all have declared their support for India's candidacy. India's approach overall reflects a 'risk-averse strategic culture'. India refuses to sacrifice any diplomatic capital with the Global South in exchange for greater recognition and endorsement by the United States and the other major powers.

India's campaign has been held hostage by the unrealistic demands of the African Group for veto-wielding permanent seats. It has also been driven to an intractable position by African states that deliberately seek to stall the reform process. An alternative strategy could focus on consolidating a strategic partnership with the United States, the one state that could change the dynamic of the reform process and mobilize greater support in favour of India. Remaining attached to the Global South diminishes the prospects of India's own campaign and renders it unsuitable for permanent membership. India's behaviour is often interpreted as a lack of commitment to the values of the liberal international order, and the Western powers perceive that granting India a permanent UNSC seat could undermine the effectiveness and legitimacy of this order.

If anything, India's latest stint at the UNSC had proved that in the face of the complex issues that beset the world, India, as a permanent member, would have to take active positions in the Council. The option of abstention would not be open. India would, thus, perforce have to take positions that could go against its own interests. Nevertheless, so long as a UNSC permanent seat remains the ultimate currency for effective international leadership, India will continue to pursue it.

India's campaign for a permanent seat was officially launched in 1994 and in collaboration with the G-4 (Brazil, Germany, Japan, and India). The G-4 campaign culminated in 2004–05 when the four states attempted to mobilize support to gain the required two-thirds majority vote in the critical General Assembly World

Summit scheduled in 2005. The G-4 demanded that the Security Council 'be expanded in both in permanent and non-permanent categories, including developed and developing countries as new permanent members'. India's coalition with the G-4 encountered numerous obstacles. India initially demanded a veto seat but then shifted to a more flexible position, accepting the possibility of a permanent seat without veto power. Its alignment with the G-4 triggered the hardening of China's stance that was opposed to Japan's bid. Most critically, India failed to rally the required support from developing countries (especially from the Africa Group) that was necessary to reach the two-thirds majority vote. The outcome of the 2005 UN Summit was ultimately a defeat for India as the G-4 failed to obtain the two-thirds majority in the General Assembly.

The G-4 members since 2005 have kept the issue of UN reforms alive with regular interaction with the L-69 of 40 African, Latin American, Asia-Pacific, and Caribbean countries and C-10 or African Union groups. The L-69 wants the UNSC expanded to include six more permanent members—four from the G-4 and two from Africa. The C-10 proposal is on similar. The three—that is G-4, L-69, and C-10—differ on the countries to be entrusted with veto powers. The impasse will persist till the multiple proposals are harmonized and even partial expansion agreed. The P-5 have a stake in prolonging this situation until such time the international situation forces a change.[20]

The tension, however, between campaigning with emerging powers and mobilizing support amongst developing countries has become evident in recent years. At the start of 2011, India with the G-4, announced the continuation of their campaign and reaffirmed their commitment to their proposed draft resolution. By July 2011, the G-4 states announced that they enjoyed the support of more than 100 states, signalling their ability to reach the required two-thirds majority of 128 votes. India appeared to succeed in gaining the endorsement of the African Group. This was assisted by the fact that the country shares age-old ties with Africa as well as the later developments with India providing large aid and suppliers' credit to African grouping such as the African Union and others. The India–Africa summits have become a fixture on the Indian foreign policy calendar. Indian President Pranab Mukherjee announced that India would remain committed to achieving reform in collaboration with the G-4.

India and the NPT

The NPT is the world's most important diplomatic tool for controlling the spread of nuclear weapons and technology. In 1968, the UN endorsed the treaty, and 62 nations signed it. India has never been a signatory to the NPT terming it as an unequal treaty.[21] One hundred and eighty-seven countries are signatories with the notable exceptions of Cuba, India, Pakistan, Israel, and North Korea (which withdrew in 2003). A large and growing number of countries, including Iran, Canada and Australia, possess the technological capability to build the bomb but have not done so. They believe that the NPT effectively prevents the uncontrolled spread of nuclear weapons.

At the same time, the world's approximately 23,300 nuclear weapons are stored at an estimated 111 locations in 14 countries, according to an overview produced by the Federation of American Scientists. Nearly half of the weapons can be operationally deployed with delivery systems capable of launching on short notice.[22]

The de facto nuclear-weapon states have developed nuclear capability for a variety of reasons other than the familiar motivations of the Cold War. For example, Israel is presumed to have the weapons for traditional threat-based deterrence while Iran expects to do so for the same reason. North Korea possesses nuclear weapons as a bargaining tool and a deterrent. India considers the balance of power with China in the latter's favour not only because of its previous lack of a nuclear deterrent but also because of China's position as a permanent UNSC member. India accepts that one of the reasons for testing its weapons was to gain the trappings of a Great Power, which is denied to India by the UN and international non-proliferation regime.

India conducted a series of nuclear tests at Pokhran, Rajasthan, on 11 and 13 May 1998, and declared itself a state armed with nuclear weapons. Before doing so, India had sought, but was denied, international guarantees that nuclear weapons would not be used against it. India's motivation was based on the unsettled border issues with Pakistan and China, their nuclear collusion, and Pakistan's own nuclear tests. It was only by 2003 that India made known its nuclear doctrine that was based on 'No First Use' (NFU).

The salient features of the government statement included the following: India will build and maintain a credible minimum deterrent; follow an NFU posture; and will use nuclear weapons only 'in retaliation against a nuclear attack on Indian territory or on Indian forces anywhere'. It was affirmed that nuclear retaliation to a first strike will be massive and designed to inflict unacceptable damage. Only the civilian political leadership through the Nuclear Command Authority will authorize retaliatory attacks; nuclear weapons will not be used against non-nuclear weapon states; and India will retain the option of retaliating with nuclear weapons in the event of a major attack against it with biological or chemical weapons.

The NFU clause in the nuclear doctrine earned India kudos in spite of being seen outside the nuclear pale. However, in the last decade, the concept has been questioned as being inapplicable in an actual war-like situation. In particular, the use of 'massive' is seen as too vague and nuclear retaliation in response to a chemical or biological attack is seen as inopportune. Furthermore, doubts have been cast on India's ability to retaliate once subjected to a nuclear attack and whether Indian cities could be kept open for a strike before a response.[23]

It has been opined that the credibility of India's nuclear doctrine needs to be substantially enhanced through a skilfully drawn signalling plan. At the same time, Defence Minister Manohar Parrikar, albeit in a personal opinion, explained the need to be unpredictable in warfare strategy. He stated, 'If a written-down strategy exists or you take a stand on a nuclear aspect, I think you're actually giving away your strength in nuclear,' Parrikar added 'why should I bind myself? I should say I am a responsible nuclear power and I will not use it irresponsibly,' Parrikar said.[24]

It may indicate that the issue is under review. India appears to have omitted the word 'minimum' from its announced doctrine of 'credible minimum deterrent' to signal a possible shift towards an open-ended arsenal. Pakistan's development of tactical nuclear weapons appear to have given it 'escalation dominance' increasing the threat of sub-conventional conflict in a nuclear environment. India's rejig of its nuclear doctrine will have to be placed in the context of its cost (estimated between USD 2.5 billion and USD 40 billion with the defence allocation in 2017–18 being USD 53.3 billion) and international fall-out on its aspiration of full membership of NSG and the civil nuclear agreement with Japan, an avowed non-nuclear power.[25]

Parallelly, India has always maintained that it remains committed to the global and nuclear disarmament. It has claimed that its acquisition of nuclear weapons was keeping in view the threat from China and Pakistan.[26] The US-India Civil Nuclear Agreement (2006) gave India facilities not usually available to a non-NPT country or to ones possessing nuclear weapons. India also saw this agreement as endorsing its view that the NPT framework established in 1968 needed to be set on a different basis.

It has opined that the existing nuclear proliferation regime has not stopped countries determined to acquire nuclear weapons such as North Korea and Iran and should the latter acquire them, in some finite time period, others will also go ahead such as Saudi Arabia and, possibly, Egypt. In this view the non-proliferation framework itself needs to be recalibrated. In a discussion between Indian and US experts, it was agreed that India and United States could work on nuclear non-proliferation, despite India unlikely to sign the NPT, by focusing on bringing India into full membership in the export control groups that form part of the larger non-proliferation system.

The two governments endorsed the proposal during the visit to India in November 2010 of US President Barack Obama. US insistence on India's membership at the NSG meetings was not in evidence. In addition, the group developed several proposals for enhancing India–US collaboration on three aspects of global non-proliferation: nuclear security, nuclear disarmament, and US–India cooperation in improving the possibilities for real progress and Indian participation in non-proliferation institutions other than the NPT itself.[27] To the extent possible, the United

States has been pushing these ideas although without much success so far.

The India–US Joint Statement released on 7 June 2015 said President Barack Obama and Prime Minister Narendra Modi 'looked forward to India's imminent entry into the Missile Technology Control Regime' and that Obama 'welcomed India's application to join the Nuclear Suppliers Group'. Yet a far cry from the Bush presidency their fulsome support seen during NSG meetings in 2016 & 2017.[28]

The groups that India needs to be a member of in order to ensure unhindered growth of its nuclear power, both for meeting climate change targets and defence, are the Missile Technology Control Regime (MTCR),[29] the NSG,[30] and the Wassenaar Arrangement.[31]

Nuclear energy is key to India's delivering on the commitments made at last year's Paris Climate Summit. The major roadblock for India to access nuclear fuel comes from China, which continues to block India's membership to the NSG. India has firmly signalled its displeasure at the tactics being used by Beijing, which firmly maintains that being a nuclear NPT signatory was necessary for joining the NSG. Meanwhile, the NSG meeting on 24 October 2017[32] failed to decide on India's entry into the group. It expects to take up in November 2017 issue of inclusion of non-NPT countries although China's position has not changed.[33]

India has grudgingly been accepted as a nuclear power although recognition by the NPT is unlikely; neither does it appear needed any longer. If the United States continues to increase its focus on the Asia-Pacific it is likely to promote India's membership to these restrictive groups of acknowledged nuclear powers, notwithstanding China's strong objections, aimed at equating India and Pakistan.

WTO

The WTO is the institution where India has been most successful to date in enhancing its influence. India's emergence as a trading power was initially forged through its campaign to forestall the launch of a new round at the 2001 Doha Ministerial Conference.

Nevertheless, it established India as a major country within the WTO. Its voice in the selection of the WTO director-general was seen to be influential in winning over the developing countries. India has insisted on the implementation of outstanding issues from the Uruguay Round and resisted the inclusion of the so-called 'Singapore Issues' (investment, competition, facilitation, and government procurement) into the negotiations. India's coalition-building strategy was focused on leading the Like-Minded Group (LMG), a group that aimed to block the Singapore Issues. India's strategy was seen as inflexible eventually forcing it to accept the Doha Development Agenda (DDA).

The 2003 Cancun Ministerial Conference witnessed India exercising its negotiating muscle with greater effectiveness, especially through its coalition-building strategy. India's leadership was the catalyst for the formation of the G-20 coalition, a group that combined the bargaining weight of emerging powers such as Brazil, China, and South Africa. The G-20 exposed the false rhetoric of the North on trade liberalization and put forward an alternative agenda that gathered broad support in the Global South.[34] India also provided leadership in other coalitions such as the Core Group and the G-33, with the former demanding the removal of the Singapore Issues from the DDA and the latter promoting greater flexibilities in food security. Along with its Southern allies, India managed to block negotiations and counterweight the US–EU agenda, ultimately causing the collapse of the Doha negotiations.

The debacle demonstrated the bargaining power of emerging powers and allowed India to substantially improve its position in the WTO.

India's recognition as a trading power enhanced during the negotiations that led to the 2004 July Framework Agreement and the 2005 Hong Kong Ministerial Conference. During this period, India consolidated its pivotal position through its participation in the Five-Interested Parties (United States, EU, Brazil, India, and Australia), and subsequently as a member of the New Quad (comprising the United States, EU, Brazil, India, also known as the G-4 of the WTO). The latter replaced the traditional West-centric Quad (the United States, EU, Japan, and Canada) that had led negotiations in the Uruguay Round. Throughout 2004–05, India played a major role in a renegotiation of the DDA that entailed removing three Singapore Issues from the agenda (and retaining only trade facilitation) and agreeing to eliminate all export subsidies by 2013. India's recognition as a leading trading power was in itself an important outcome of the Hong Kong Ministerial Conference.[35]

From the Hong Kong Ministerial onwards, India consistently participated in the inner core of the WTO decision-making process. During 2006–08, India was a part of all power configurations that led the informal process of consensus building. India's role remained largely defensive in these meetings. At a G-6 (United States, EU, Brazil, India, Australia, and Japan) meeting in 2006, the lack of agreement among the key trading parties, and especially among the United States and the EU, brought India to declare that the round was under severe threat due to the United States' lack of ambition.

At a G-4 meeting in June 2007, India, along with Brazil, refused to concede the US/EU offer on Non-Agricultural Market Access and the talks again collapsed. The Indian side blamed the United States and the EU for brinkmanship tactics that aimed at causing divisions within developing countries. India declared it would remain committed to its alliance with the G-20 and other developing countries. Finally, during a critical G-7 meeting in July 2008, Indian Commerce Minister Kamal Nath rejected a deal that seemed to be acceptable by all other key players. India's justification was that the package was inadequate in offering special developmental clauses, especially on issues of food security, and would not serve either its interests or of the developing countries.

While India was not solely responsible for the recurrent deadlock of the DDA, its image was clearly one of an obstructionist negotiator. The onset of the global financial crisis at the end of 2008 provided a new opportunity to India after it became a member of the G-20 Leaders Summit. India began proactive engagement, although its language continued to reflect ambivalence to fully embracing its apparent role as a major stakeholder. At the WTO Ministerial Conference in 2011, Commerce Minister

Anand Sharma stated, 'Decisions have to necessarily be based on multilateral consensus, regardless of the format in which negotiations take place ... I have heard suggestions for negotiating issues amongst a critical mass of members. This path is fraught with risk. Plurilateral agreements are a throwback to the days when decisions taken by a few determined the future of the rest.'[36] Reaffirming India's commitment to the global South, Sharma stressed that 'development issues, particularly those of interest to LDCs, should be the foremost priority' in the Doha Round, and noted that 'India was the first developing country to extend duty free quota access to all LDCs [least developed countries]'.

India's cautious approach finally translated into a proactive role at the 2013 Bali WTO Ministerial Conference, which focused on two major issues—food security and trade facilitation. Negotiations were largely determined by the persistence of the Indian delegation to secure a meaningful package on food security to provide flexibilities for subsistence farmers in India and other developing countries. Indian demands caused a deadlock initially but after satisfactory language on food security was agreed, India conceded to negotiating trade facilitation, effectively sealing the final agreement. The deal reflected India's willingness to engage in trade-offs, provided that clear developmental flexibilities were established. India's hard stance on food security was to settle the question of flexibility to buy and stock as much food as it wants from its farmers to ensure the implementation of the Food Security Act. Most importantly, the Bali Package showed that for the first time, India was willing to act independently of developing country coalitions (such as the G-33 that focused on issues of food security) and pursue its own path to renegotiating the DDA. The Trade Facilitation Agreement entered into force on 22 February 2017 when the WTO obtained the two-thirds acceptance of the agreement from its 164 members. India ratified the Trade Facilitation Agreement in April 2016.[37]

India and APEC

India's economy is only partly integrated into the global economy, particularly regional trade arrangements in a dynamic Asia-Pacific.

The Asia-Pacific Economic Cooperation (APEC),[38] founded in 1989, has 21 members representing all the major economies—the United States, China, Russia, Canada, Australia, Chile, Mexico, Peru, and all of ASEAN. In terms of manufacturing, it covers almost 70 per cent of the world's industrial capacity. APEC's criterion for membership is that the member is an economy, rather than a state. As a result, APEC uses the term 'member economies' rather than 'member countries' to refer to its members. One result of this criterion is that membership of the forum includes Taiwan (officially the Republic of China, participating under the name 'Chinese Taipei') alongside PRC, as well as Hong Kong, which entered APEC as a British colony but is now a Special Administrative Region of the PRC. APEC also includes three official observers—ASEAN, the Pacific Islands Forum, and the Pacific Economic Cooperation Council.

The emergence of regional trade agreements such as the still-born Trans-Pacific Partnership (TPP), if it comes to fruition, threatens to further distance India from the global supply chains critical to Prime Minister Modi's 'Make in India' initiative. President Trump's abandoning of TPP,[39] signalling a more inward-looking policy, gives India a breather to consider its international trade strategy. India's entry into APEC, which accounts for nearly 60 per cent of the global GDP, would provide a pathway for greater integration into the region's economy. It would also ensure that trade remains a unifying force in the region, where competing trade regimes are straining ties. India, with an observer status, needs to take advantage of the opening of APEC membership as a gateway to other larger trade opportunities. Failing this, India will be left behind in international agreements currently being negotiated.

India's joining APEC will facilitate the attainment of its ambitious target of creating one million jobs each month under the 'Make in India' and 'Skill India' programmes of the government. It will help to integrate the Indian economy into global supply chains that lie at the base of the new generation trade agreements already negotiated like the TTP and the Trans-Atlantic Trade and Investment Partnership (TTIP) between the United States and the EU.

India's entry into APEC also holds multiple benefits for the existing members as it will open up a new market of 600 million in a few years. India will by 2030 become the fifth largest consumer market in the world. By making available a large pool of skilled workforce it will help to meet the employment targets assumed by the Indian government. More importantly, the opening of the Indian economy, if it is to join APEC, will further enable domestic economic liberalization. It has been estimated that India's staying out of APEC will subject it to a huge level of trade diversion once China and other ASEAN countries join the arrangement. India's growth target of 10 per cent per annum requires it to be a part of APEC since it will keep open the most important markets for its products. APEC is, thus, the critical entry point for India to participate in the new generation of trade agreements.

With its Act East policy India appears to have no alternative but to make efforts to join APEC. Even more so, if the ambitious bilateral US–India trade target of USD 500 million is to be achieved. It, thus, involves a bigger ambition than that of finalizing a bilateral investment treaty. For the same reason, the US' intention to pull India into a group, which will pull down trade barriers, will be good for India–US economic interest. From a strategic perspective, closer economic relationship with the United States will make it a force against China's economic strength.

India's acceptance into APEC depends on its industry being able to accept the standards required by the intellectual property and environmental standards of its members. The coming into force by July 2017 of the Goods and Services Tax (GST) will harmonize the national market. The resulting integration of the domestic market could itself raise potential growth to 10 cent per annum. Any accretion of the growth rate will align its tax, incentives and regulatory systems enabling it to join the APEC. With support from Russia, China, and the US, India had targeted the APEC meeting on 11-12 November 2017 in Vietnam for its entry into the organization.[40] With the setback to the TPP, it is more than likely that APEC would welcome India into its fold. At the same time, the uncertainty introduced by the Trump

IFIs—The IMF and the World Bank

India's campaign for reforming the voting and quota shares of IFIs is a feature of its role in these institutions. Although some success has been achieved, Indian officials have often claimed that substantial obstacles remain in integrating emerging powers in the global financial governance.

In September 2006, India suffered a decrease in its influence in the IMF. Its voting share dropped from 1.95 to 1.91 per cent (though its quota share remained unchanged) at the same time when four developing countries (China, Mexico, South Korea, and Turkey) witnessed an increase in their voting shares. India had previously allied with Argentina, Brazil, and Egypt in a campaign against this reform process. The four countries had jointly stated that the tendency of increasing voting shares of some developing countries by reducing those of others was disturbing and unacceptable. Twenty-three developing countries, including India, voted against the 2006 reform plan but lost the vote. Despite this setback, India declared its commitment to continue its campaign for reforming the IFIs. India argued that the voting pattern must reflect the economic strength of the emerging powers and be determined by GDP (on a Purchasing Power Parity basis), GDP growth rate, and foreign exchange reserves. India's global ranking in all three indicators was higher compared to its IMF voting position.

In April 2008, a new round of reforms saw India ascending to the 11th position in the IMF. India's quota share increased from 1.92 to 2.44 per cent, while its voting share increased to 2.34 per cent. India intensified its campaign for further reform. At the 2010 Annual Meeting of the IFIs, India called for a 5–6 per cent shift of quota shares from advanced to developing countries to restore the Fund's legitimacy. India also bought USD 10 billion of IMF bonds, signalling its willingness to participate in the burden sharing of the Fund and further support its reform campaign. Coming as it did after the economic and financial crisis of

2008–09, it created a positive vibe among the developed countries. In October 2010, a new round of IMF reforms, promoted this time through the G-20 Leaders Summit, further improved India's IMF position from 11th to 8th, increasing its quota share from 2.44 to 2.75 per cent.

India's diplomacy in the IFIs has relied extensively on coalition-building. The G-24 has served as India's preferred platform for pursuing reform. The coalition, established in 1971, has traditionally coordinated action on issues of finance and development and holding biannual sessions before the IMF and World Bank sessions. Its leadership of the G-24 allowed India to mobilize support for its proposal for a 5–6 per cent transfer of quotas from advanced to emerging economies in the IMF. The language and positions articulated in G-24 communiqués were very close to India's reform agenda. India also mobilized the G-15 group[41] to promote reform that has allowed members to coordinate positions between more advanced developing countries to pursue joint strategies in trade, investment, and finance. In recent years, India has increasingly promoted IMF/World Bank reform through the BRICS coalition given that the group's geopolitical weight provides greater advantage. More recently, the BRICS states have provided funds (USD 100 billion) for the formation of their own development bank, a new institution perceived as a potential rival to the IMF and the World Bank. Similarly, the Chinese-sponsored AIIB is yet another attempt by the emerging economic powers to change the global financial agenda.[42]

Climate Change Agreement

A worldwide pact to battle global warming, the Paris Agreement, entered into force on 4 November 2016.[43] It represents a new international initiative in global governance which, for the first time, brings all nations to undertake ambitious efforts to combat climate change and adapt to its effects with enhanced support to assist developing countries. The significance of India's support to the climate pact lies in the fact that India accounts for over 4 per cent of global emissions, behind the world's top polluters, United

States and China. Its agreement was crucial to cross the threshold mark of 55 per cent. India has a major role to play in the future evolution of this global platform.

The Paris Agreement's central aim is to strengthen the global response to the threat of climate change by keeping global temperature rise, in this century, below 2°C above pre-industrial levels and to pursue efforts to limit the temperature increase even further to 1.5°C. Additionally, the agreement aims to strengthen the ability of countries to deal with the impacts of climate change. To reach these ambitious goals, appropriate financial flows, a new technology, and an enhanced capacity-building framework will be put in place, thus, supporting action by developing countries and the most vulnerable countries in line with their own national objectives. The agreement also provides for enhanced transparency of action and support through a more robust transparency framework.

The Paris Agreement required all parties to put forward their best efforts through 'nationally determined contributions' (NDCs) and to strengthen these efforts in the years ahead. This requires that all parties report regularly on their emissions and on their implementation efforts. In 2018, parties will take stock of the collective efforts in relation to progress towards the goal set in the Paris Agreement. There will also be a global stock-taking after every five years starting with 2023 to assess the collective progress towards achieving the purpose of the agreement and to inform further individual actions by its signatories.

The Paris Agreement is the first-ever agreement binding all the world's nations, rich and poor, to a commitment to cap global warming caused mainly by the burning of coal, oil, and gas. This means drastically and urgently cutting emissions that requires both political commitment and considerable financial investment. By 2030, according to the UN Environment Programme, annual emissions will be 12 to 14 billion metric tons of carbon dioxide equivalent (CO_2-e) higher than the desired level of 42 billion tons. The 2014 level was about 52.7 billion tons. The year 2016 contrary to expectation saw a small improvement in emissions over 2015 giving hope for movement towards the 2 degrees C global target.

The historic agreement was endorsed in Paris in December 2015, after years of complex and divisive negotiations, though remarkably ratification was reached with record speed. All countries submitted voluntary, non-binding, carbon-cutting targets towards this goal. According to the International Energy Agency, implementing the pledges would require investments of USD 13.5 trillion by 2030 in efficient low-carbon and energy technology, almost 40 per cent of total energy sector spending.

India formally ratified the Climate Change Agreement on 2 October 2016 to mark Mahatma Gandhi's birth anniversary. India currently produces about 4.5 per cent of the world's greenhouse gas (GHG) emissions. The Paris Agreement requires all countries who ratify it to come up with a national plan to limit global temperature rise. As part of its plan, India has set a goal of producing 40 per cent of its electricity with non-fossil fuel sources by 2030. India also promised to plant trees or preserve enough tree cover to act as a sink for at least 2.5 billion tons of carbon dioxide and has called on the United States and other developed countries to share technologies that help decrease emissions.

India's Obligations

India has tried to balance its carbon emissions with its economic growth objectives by not setting an outright pollution reduction goal. Being a part of the global climate change regime, India will have significant obligations under the treaty. The country will have to reduce its carbon footprint from its 2005 levels by 33 to 35 per cent by 2030.

A key result area for India will come in the form of the reduction of emission intensity targets which is the volume of emissions per unit of the GDP. The country will have to diversify its power generation sources and shift them significantly towards renewable energy sources to reduce volumes of emissions per unit of the GDP. In numbers, by 2025, India will need a 175 gigawatt-power production capacity from non-fossil fuel sources. To achieve these targets, the government would need to initiate steps on several fronts.

India decided to ratify the Climate Change Agreement after initial uncertainty stemming from India seeking *quid pro quo* with its membership of the NSG. In deciding to do it on 2 October 2016, the Indian government was guided by important considerations, first, the fact that it is one of the largest global polluters; and second, the improvement in US–India relations. The likely positive effect on India's UNSC membership would have also been foreseen. India benefited from being a part of the first negotiation round under the Paris Agreement which was held during the meeting of the Committee of Parties (COP 22) in Marrakesh on 8 November 2016.[44] It brought more clarity on the details of the Paris Agreement and on the application of 'Equity' and 'Common but Differentiated Responsibility' concepts in which India has a vital interest.

Ratification was also enabled by the fact that climate action on the ground in India has begun since 2008 when India adopted a Climate Action Plan.[45] It comprises eight national missions: Solar Mission; Water Mission; Missions on Enhanced Energy Efficiency, on Sustainable Habitat, on Sustaining Himalayan Ecosystems, on Sustainable Agriculture, on Strategic Knowledge for Climate Change; and Green India Mission.

India announced a revised Climate Action Plan that incorporated its NDCs to the global climate targets under the Paris Agreement.[46] India is investing in actions to tackle climate change while addressing critical issues such as poverty, food security, and access to healthcare and education. India's NDC builds on its goal of installing 175 gigawatts of renewable power capacity by 2022 and by setting a new target to increase its share of non-fossil-based power capacity from 30 per cent to about 40 per cent by 2030 (with the help of international support). The plan also prioritizes efforts to build resilience to climate change impacts and gives a broad indication of the amount of financing necessary to reach its goals.

India's plan sends a clear signal for clean energy with an ambitious target for 2022 of 175 gigawatts, mostly from solar energy. Yet coal and other fossil fuels will continue to play a major role in India's energy mix. Its Green India Mission is expected to increase carbon sequestration, creating an additional carbon sink of 2.5 to

3.0 billion tonnes of carbon dioxide through additional forest and tree cover.

Yet India emphasizes on adaptation in order to protect sensitive sectors, including agriculture, water, and health. It estimates that it will require, from 2015 to 2030, USD 206 billion for action on 'adaptation' of climate-friendly industrial technologies and processes. India has expressed its commitment to a strong climate agreement which has strengthened its claim for UNSC permanent seat.

India went to Marrakesh with a draft Framework Agreement on International Solar Alliance, which 26 countries signed. The agreement will take the shape of an international treaty once 15 countries that have signed ratified it. About 120 countries lie, either fully or in part, between the Tropics of Cancer and Capricorn, and are potential members of the treaty. Some 80 countries had supported the declaration of the alliance last year. The creation of climate-proof agriculture in Africa was a major initiative of the conference. It will promote sustainable soil management, better water management, effective risk mitigation strategies and clean energy technologies.[47]

Terrorism

When 9/11 happened, India felt vindicated in its stand that terror knew no boundaries and needed to be tackled globally. India's two decades' experience of cross-border terrorism made it a willing partner in the global war on terror. Yet India has continued to suffer as it refused to accept a distinction between 'good' terrorist and 'bad' terrorists. This is the crux of the difference in the way India and the United States along with the West view the issue.

Another difference is India's philosophy when dealing with domestic insurgent groups. India has always kept the door open to bring the militant groups back into the national mainstream. With a growing diversity of insurgent and militant groups in the country, the effort has always been to bring them in, rather than keeping them out. This is not a sign of weakness—India took strong steps in Punjab and against some insurgent groups in the Northeast.

For India, the fight against terrorism became essential in the late 1990s after the forced withdrawal of the Soviet Union from Afghanistan. The Afghan mujahideen,[48] funded and provisioned by the United States and controlled by Pakistan, was abandoned by the former but not the latter. For Pakistan, they represented a ready-made trained insurgent group that could be re-deployed against the Indian government, and its Army, in Kashmir and add a new dimension to its fruitless fight to capture the state. The transformation of the mujahedeen of the 1980s into the Taliban of the 1990s represented a tightening of Pakistan's control on these insurgent groups, aimed at gaining the avowed 'strategic depth'[49] in Afghanistan. India had waged a lonely battle for a very long time in the UN and with the United States to secure the recognition of Pakistan's sponsorship of terrorist attacks in Kashmir and in India. But until 9/11, nobody heard India.

The United States will continue to see Pakistan as crucial so long as they remain in Afghanistan, even if it means ignoring that country's tendency to nurture terrorist groups, majority based in Pakistan, which have continued to target not only India but major capitals and cities in the Western world. Despite the announcement at the end of 2014 of the withdrawal of US and NATO forces from Afghanistan, US continues to maintain 8,500 of its troops in that country. Contrary to his pre-election speeches President Trump announced a commitment of up to 4,000 more troops to combat a resurgent Taliban. In response to his suggestion the UK will be adding 85 experts to their 585 troops.[50] In his speech Pakistan has come under particular criticism from him and other US officials, who argue Islamabad should be doing more to combat the growth of extremism in the region. It is unlikely in this situation the US will change its position on Pakistan.

International Action

In 2016, at the UN, India called for the early adoption of the Comprehensive Convention on International Terrorism[51] that it had proposed as early as 1996. After two decades, it remains in the open-ended group for deliberation. At the fifth review on 1 July 2016 of the UN Global Counter-Terrorism Strategy India again reiterated that the international community to adopt the CCIT.[52]

The global strategy is a unique instrument to enhance national, regional, and international efforts to counter terrorism. Through its adoption, all member states have agreed, for the first time, to a common strategic and operational approach to fight terrorism, by not only sending a clear message that terrorism is unacceptable in all its forms and manifestation but by also resolving to take practical steps individually and collectively to prevent and combat it. These practical steps include a wide array of measures ranging from strengthening state capacity to counterterrorist threats to a better coordination throughout the UN system's counterterrorism activities.

Yet international action has remained stymied by the considerations of realpolitik on the part of the major powers. The United States is still unable to take determined action against the nurturing of terror groups by Pakistan.[53] It will continue to need Pakistan so long as it continues to have an interest in Afghanistan. Similarly, China has found technical reasons to avoid the inclusion of LeT[54] in the UN list of terrorist organizations because of its growing economic interest in the port of Gwadar and the road linking it to the Chinese hinterland.[55] When the matter came up again in 2016, China was the only country seeking an extension of the technical hold on the LeT in the UN list. India had opined that the sanctions committee was taking a 'selective approach' in tackling terrorism and had made a strong call for the reform of the 'subterranean universe' of the UNSC's sanctions regimes. It went on to criticize the lack of transparency in their functioning and said that the principles of 'anonymity and unanimity' adopted by UNSC members absolved individual members of accountability.[56]

In this background, India will have to continue fighting terrorism on its own. After the Pathankot and Uri attacks, it has become certain that at best India could expect sympathy, and possibly commiseration, but no hard action will be taken by the international community.

The dilemma of maintaining a Third World identity and simultaneously acting as a responsible global power lies at the core of India's diplomacy. India has strived to balance between these roles by engaging with the West while committing to the founding principles of its foreign policy—non-intervention, non-aggrandizement, non-alignment, and strategic autonomy. External factors, such as the persistent deadlocks among major players in the WTO negotiations and the complexity of the UNSC reform process, allow India to transfer responsibility for the lack of reform to other parties. India's increasing need for material resources will also expose the disconnect between India's search for major power status and its claim to leadership of the Global South. India's unwillingness to go away from the principles of non-alignment will, therefore, determine the nature of its future repositioning in global governance.

India has historically been a strong advocate of multilateralism since these institutions have allowed India to punch above its weight and overcome the limitations of its material power. It has developed an array of bilateral relations with established and emerging powers that allow for directly engaging in balance of power politics. Yet India refrains from strong alliance-building and strategic partnerships with major powers.

India feels its own sovereignty and development must be safeguarded before it can adopt a proactive stance and shape negotiating outcomes. 'This condition means that India, like other emerging powers, understands its role in global governance through the lens of defending national power rather than providing leadership.'[57] India, therefore, favours a 'defensive multilateralism' that facilitates its relocation while minimizing costs in terms of autonomy and self-sufficiency. Such multilateralism is characterized by a preference to remain a 'selective rule-taker' while establishing India's authority to act as 'rule-maker'. India is reluctant to fully engage with global governance processes, remaining a reactive and cautious player that proactively participates only in select international fora and on particular issue areas. India's modest record in providing public goods across different regimes and its persistence to operate as a veto player do not demonstrate its intention to assume international responsibilities.

Defensive multilateralism reflects the view that the country has not yet reached a position in which it has the power to unilaterally engineer and promote reform in one international institution, without facing a backlash in another, or in jeopardizing its chances for permanent membership in the UNSC. The Indian elite considers that Indian diplomacy alone cannot shape global governance. It limits to India's capacity for effecting structural change in the international system. India is equally mindful of the resistance from the G-7 states to attacks on their privileged international positions. India's reform diplomacy, practiced through the purpose-built coalitions continue to offer improved sectoral bargaining advantage for all its member-states.

India's emergence has generated heightened expectations in the West that it can operate as a system-shaper in a multipolar order. According to Washington's perspective, inviting India to act as 'responsible stakeholder' is necessary now that India occupies a pivotal position in regimes on trade, security, energy, and the environment. In the WTO, US officials urge India and other BRICS countries to refrain from acting as 'elephants hiding behind mice', which seek to be treated as developing countries although they now share little with less-developed states. The IMF and the World Bank have also endorsed the economic success of the BRICS and have aspired to promote a new form of 'global developmental liberalism' that propels India and other emerging economies to act as drivers of the global economy and as legitimizers of the neoliberal order.

Indian officials, however, perceive that such heightened expectations only act as a mechanism for imposing further responsibilities upon India which will force it to undertake commitments that it is not yet ready to assume. India's foreign policy establishment has not yet developed its own vision of how India's newly acquired power could influence global governance. While embracing its new-found position in the WTO and the IFIs, India refuses to abide by Western expectations for proactively contributing to the management of these regimes and committing the financial resources required for providing global public goods.

The divergent expectations held by India and the West became apparent during the former's term as a UNSC non-permanent member during 2011–2. The West expected India to demonstrate 'responsible leadership' and promote policy changes in regimes with which it maintained friendly relations, such as Iran, Libya, and Syria. This was expected to contribute to the UNSC and enhance India's future prospects for permanent membership. In the view of some of India's strategic experts such expectations only represent subordination to US preferences. It substantiates the view that India is yet to become part of the established power structure.

Solidarity with the Global South

India's attachment to the collective causes of the Global South determines the adaptability and flexibility of its reform agenda. Indian foreign policy has historically projected a sense of altruism and exceptionalism that has allowed India to defend the interests of weaker states. Non-alignment and non-intervention has been the cornerstone of India's multilateral engagement in both the political and economic spheres. Indian diplomacy still maintains aspects of non-alignment that often resurface in India's international reform agenda, especially in initiatives to overcome the marginalization of developing countries.

India has adopted a more selective coalition-building strategy and has shown a willingness to lead flexible alliances that vary across different institutions. Smaller groups such as the Like Minded Group[58] and the G-20 in the WTO, and the G-24 in the IFIs, maintain aspects of bloc diplomacy but are more proactive and issue-focused compared to the missionary stance of the NAM and the G-77. India has increasingly cooperated with other emerging powers such as Brazil and South Africa in the IBSA Dialogue Forum, and Germany and Japan in the joint campaign for UNSC reform. Participation in these transcontinental alliances augments India's capacity to shape international outcomes and strive for the redistribution of existing resources and the recognition of their status.

India faces the challenge of achieving the recognition of its status within institutional structures that have historically marginalized developing countries. In attempting to manage conflicting expectations over its own role, 'India maintains the same reform agenda even after certain of its own demands have been met. When India's agenda appears ineffective in promoting institutional change, India is content with maintaining the same approach since it escapes the dilemma of adopting a proactive approach that could require its detachment from the global South'.[59] Yet this approach has embedded within it a reluctance to re-evaluate and re-order new strategies for promoting institutional change in keeping with its rising stature.

Notes

1. 'India's Push for UN Security Council Reforms Suffers Setback', *The Times of India* (28 July 2016), http://timesofindia.indiatimes.com/india/Indias-push-for-UN-Security-Council-reforms-suffers-setback/articleshow/53435140.cms.

2. Geman Federal Foreign Office, 'Joint Press Statement of the Foreign Ministers of the G4 countries-Brazil, Germany, India and Japan—on United Nations Security Council Reform', 21 September 2017, http://www.auswaertiges-amt.de/EN/Infoservice/Presse/Meldungen/2017/170921_VN%20Reform.html.

3. R. Jagganathan, 'India's Permanent UNSC Membership Will Only be Possible in 2020–25 Despite Modi's Pitch', Firstpost (27 September 2015), http://www.firstpost.com/world/despite-modis-pitch-indias-permanent-unsc-membership-will-only-be-possible-in-2020-25-2446222.html.

4. NDTV, http://www.ndtv.com/india-news/indias-security-council-permanent-seat-hope-receives-setback-1437293.

5. Ministry of External Affairs, Government of India, 'Briefs on Multilateral Relations', http://www.mea.gov.in/regional-organisations.htm.

6. 'India's UN Security Council Permanent Seat Bid Selfish: Pakistan', *Hindustan Times* (31 October 2015), http://www.hindustantimes.com/world/india-s-un-security-council-permanent-seat-bid-selfish-pakistan/story-rPgWma4B7CvrOT0csBvCsI.html.

7. Manu Bhagavan, 'India and the United Nations or Things Fall Apart', in David M. Malone, C. Raja Mohan, and Srinath Raghavan (eds), *The Oxford Handbook of Indian Foreign Policy* (New Delhi Oxford University Press, 2015), pp. 596–608.

8. Chinmaya R. Gharekhan, 'India and the United Nations', in Atish Sinha and Madhup Mohta (eds), *Indian Foreign Policy: Challenges and Opportunities* (New Delhi: Academic Foundation, 2007), pp. 193–215.

9. 'India–Pakistan Relations', 1 October 2016, http://internationalrelations.org/india-pakistan-relations/.

10. Edwin Mora, 'Russia-led UN Security Council Plans to Ignore India-Pakistan Kashmir Crisis', 5 October 2016, http://www.breitbart.com/national-security/2016/10/05/russia-led-un-security-council-ignoring-india-pak-clashes-kashmir/.

11. Staff Writer, 'Security Council Not Discussing India-Pak Issue', *The Hindu* (1 November 2016), http://www.thehindu.com/news/international/south-asia/%E2%80%98Security-Council-not-discussing-India-Pak-issue%E2%80%99/article15425786.ece.

12. Devjyot Ghoshal, 'Pakistan Keeps It Predictable at the UN: Hostility for India, Love for China', *Quartz India* (21 September 2017), http://www.thehindu.com/news/international/south-asia/%E2%80%98Security-Council-not-discussing-India-Pak-issue%E2%80%99/article15425786.ece.

13. Blogs, Nazia Memon, 'The United Nations and Pak-India Dispute over Jammu and Kashmir', Samaa. Tv, 26 September 2017, https://www.samaa.tv/pakistan/2017/09/united-nations-pak-india-dispute-jammu-kashmir/.

14. PTI, 'Indo-Pak Matters have to be Resolved Bilaterally: MEA', *DNA* (22 June 2017), http://www.dnaindia.com/india/report-indo-pak-matters-have-to-be-resolved-bilaterally-mea-2480560.

15. Stanley Kochanek, 'India's Changing Role in the United Nations', Pennsylvania State University, January 1980, http://www.jstor.org/stable/2756961?seq=1#page_scan_tab_contents.

16. 'India-led Efforts Give Boost to UN Security Council Reforms in 2015', *NDTV* (5 December 2015), http://www.ndtv.com/india-news/india-led-efforts-give-boost-to-un-security-council-reforms-in-2015-1258948.

17. Rajesh Singh, 'India in the UNSC: Quest for Permanent Foothold', *The Pioneer* (4 November 2016), http://www.dailypioneer.com/sunday-edition/sunday-pioneer/special/india-in-unscquest-for-permanent-foothold.html.

18. Archis Mohan, 'India and the United Nations', Ministry of External Affairs, Government of India (23 September 2013), http://mea.gov.in/in-focus-article.htm?22231/India+and+the+United+Nations.

19. Rajeev Sharma, 'Behind India's Syria Diplomacy', *The Pioneer* (5 October 2011), http://thediplomat.com/2011/10/behind-indias-syria-diplomacy.

20. Archis Mohan, 'India and the United Nations', Ministry of External Affairs, Government of India, 20 September 2013,

http://mea.gov.in/in-focus-article.htm?22231/India+and+the+United+Nations.

21. Baker Spring and Robert Dillion, 'Nuclear India and the Non-Proliferation Treaty', The Heritage Foundation, 18 May 2006, http://www.heritage.org/research/reports/2006/05/nuclear-india-and-the-non-proliferation-treaty.

22. Hans M. Kristensen, 'Estimated Nuclear Weapons Locations 2009', Federation of American Scientists, 25 November 2009, http://fas.org/blogs/security/2009/11/locations/.

23. Gurmeet Kanwal, 'India's Nuclear Doctrine: Need for a Review', Center for Strategic and International Studies, 5 December 2014, https://www.csis.org/analysis/india%E2%80%99s-nuclear-doctrine-need-review.

24. '"Why Bind Ourselves to No First Use Policy" Says Defence Minister Parrikar on India's Nuclear Doctrine', The Times of India (10 November 2016), http://timesofindia.indiatimes.com/india/Having-a-stated-nuclear-policy-means-giving-away-strength-says-Parrikar/articleshow/55357107.cms.

25. Nishant Rajeev, 'A Holistic Approach to India's Nuclear Doctrine', The Diplomat (24 May 2017), https://thediplomat.com/2017/05/a-holistic-approach-to-indias-nuclear-doctrine/.

26. Akhilesh Pillalamarri, 'India's Nuclear Weapons Programme: 5 Things You Need to Know', The National Interest (22 April 2015), http://timesofindia.indiatimes.com/india/Having-a-stated-nuclear-policy-means-giving-away-strength-says-Parrikar/articleshow/55357107.cms.

27. 'India and the Non-Proliferation System', NTI-Center for Strategic and International Studies, 5 January 2012, http://www.nti.org/analysis/reports/india-and-non-proliferation-system/.

28. Edit, 'NSG Members Fail to Decide on India's Entry', The Tribune (25 October 2017), http://www.tribuneindia.com/news/nation/nsg-members-fail-to-decide-on-india-entry/427196.html.

29. Kelsey Davenport, 'Established in April 1987, the voluntary Missile Technology Control Regime (MTCR) with 35 members aims to limit the spread of ballistic missiles and other unmanned delivery systems that could be used for chemical, biological, and nuclear attacks. It urges them to restrict their exports of missiles and related technologies capable of carrying a 500-kilogram payload at least 300 kilometres or delivering any type of weapon of mass destruction.', 'Missile Technology Control Regime at A Glance', Arms

Control Association, August 2016, https://www.armscontrol.org/factsheets/mtcr.

30. Kelsey Davenport, 'The Nuclear Suppliers Group (NSG) is a group of 48 nuclear supplier countries that seeks to contribute to the non-proliferation of nuclear weapons through the implementation of two sets of Guidelines for nuclear exports and nuclear-related exports. The NSG Guidelines also contain the so-called "Non-Proliferation Principle", adopted in 1994, whereby a supplier, notwithstanding other provisions in the NSG Guidelines, authorises a transfer only when satisfied that the transfer would not contribute to the proliferation of nuclear weapons. The NSG Guidelines are consistent with, and complement, the various international, legally binding instruments in the field of nuclear non-proliferation. These include the Treaty on the Non-Proliferation of Nuclear Weapons (NPT), the Treaty for the Prohibition of Nuclear Weapons in Latin America (Treaty of Tlatelolco), the South Pacific Nuclear-Free-Zone Treaty (Treaty of Rarotonga), the African Nuclear-Weapon-Free Zone Treaty (Treaty of Pelindaba), the Treaty on the Southeast Asia Nuclear-Weapon-Free Zone (Treaty of Bangkok), and the Central Asian Nuclear-Weapon-Free Zone Treaty (Treaty of Semipalatinsk).' Arms Control Association, August 2017, https://www.armscontrol.org/factsheets/NSG.

31. Daryl Kimball, 'The Wassenaar Arrangement, formally established in July 1996, is a voluntary export control regime whose 41 members exchange information on transfers of conventional weapons and dual-use goods and technologies. Through such exchanges, Wassenaar aims to promote "greater responsibility" among its members in exports of weapons and dual-use goods and to prevent destabilizing accumulations.' 'The Wassenaar Arrangement at a Glance', Arms Control Association, October 2012, https://www.armscontrol.org/factsheets/wassenaar,https://www.armscontrol.org/factsheets/wassenaar.

32. Kimball, 'The Wasenaar Arrangement at a Glance'.

33. 'China Leads Opposition to India's Joining Nuclear Suppliers Group', *The Indian Express*, http://indianexpress.com/article/india/india-news-india/india-nsg-bid-membership-china-nuclear-weapons-2843901.

34. Charalampos Efstathopoulos, 'India and Global Governance: The Problem of Ambivalent Reform', *International Politics*, 53(2): 239–59, http://link.springer.com/article/10.1057/ip.2015.44.

35. Sungjoon Cho, 'Half Full or Half Empty': The Hong Kong WTO Ministerial Conference has Delivered an Interim Deal for the Doha Round Negotiations' America Society of International Law, 9(39), https://www.asil.org/insights/volume/9/issue/39/half-full-or-half-empty-hong-kong-wto-ministerial-conference-has.

36. WTO, 'Statements by Members and Observers at the Plenary Session', WTO Eighth Session of the Ministerial Conference, 15–17 December 2011, https://www.wto.org/english/thewto_e/minist_e/min11_e/min11_statements_e.htm.

37. 'India–US Resolve Food Security Deadlock: Here's What the Fight Was about,' Firstpost (12 November 2014), http://www.firstpost.com/economy/india-us-resolve-food-security-deadlock-heres-what-the-fight-was-about-1981991.html.

38. Australian Government, Department of Foreign Affairs and Trade, Asia Pacific Economic Cooperation (APEC), http://dfat.gov.au/international-relations/regional-architecture/apec/pages/asia-pacific-economic-cooperation-apec.aspx.

39. Peter Baker, 'Trump Abandons Tran-Pacific Partnership, Bama's Signature Trade Deal', *The New York Times* (23 January 2017), http://www.thehindu.com/news/international/us-welcomes-indias-interest-in-joining-apec/article8535711.ece.

40. 'US Welcomes India's Interest in Joining APEC', *The Hindu* (29 April 2016), http://www.thehindu.com/news/international/us-welcomes-indias-interest-in-joining-apec/article8535711.ece.

41. 'Group of 15', https://en.wikipedia.org/wiki/Group_of_15.

42. https://en.wikipedia.org/wiki/Asian_Infrastructure_Investment_Bank.

43. https://ec.europa.eu/clima/policies/international/negotiations/paris/index_en.htm.

44. 'Outcomes of UN Climate Change Conference in Marrakesh', Center for Climate and Energy Solutions (7–8 November 2016), https://www.c2es.org/international/negotiations/cop22-marrakech/summary.

45. 'National Action Plan on Climate Change', Ministry of Environment, Government of India, http://www.moef.nic.in/downloads/home/Pg01-52.pdf.

46. Apurba Mitra, Thomas Damassa, Taryn Franken, Fred Stolle, and Kathleen Mogelgaard, '5 Key Takeaways from India's New Climate Plan (INDC)', World Resources Institute, 2 October 2015,

http://www.wri.org/blog/2015/10/5-key-takeaways-india%E2%80%99s-new-climate-plan-indc.

47. Amitabh Sinha, 'What Marrakesh Achieved, What's Ahead in Climate Change Fight Now', *The Indian Express* (30 November 2016), http://indianexpress.com/article/explained/marrakesh-climate-conference-global-warming-paris-agreement-4402172/.

48. Nashin Arbabzadeh, 'The 1980s Mujahideen, the Taliban and the Shifting Idea of Jihad', *The Guardian* (28 April 2011), https://www.theguardian.com/commentisfree/2011/apr/28/afghanistan-mujahideen-taliban.

49. Anand Arni and Abhimanyu Tondon, 'The Genesis of Pakistan's "Strategic Depth"', *Afghanistan Fair Observer* (2 June 2014), http://www.fairobserver.com/region/central_south_asia/the-genesis-of-pakistans-strategic-depth-in-afghanistan-88910/.

50. Barney Henderson and Kae McCann, 'Donald Trump Commits More US Troops to Afghanistan and Calls on Britain to Follow Suit', *The Telegraph*, 22 August 2017, http://www.telegraph.co.uk/news/2017/08/21/donald-trump-address-nation-outline-new-afghanistan-strategy/.

51. 'What Is the Comprehensive Convention on International Terrorism', *Livemint* (28 September 2016), http://www.livemint.com/Politics/Ee84kLhbyP5NJ9mFnMzkKO/Will-Sushmas-speech-at-the-UNGA-give-fresh-push-to-antiter.html.

52. https://www.un.org/counterterrorism/ctitf/en/un-global-counter-terrorism-strategy.

53. https://en.wikipedia.org/wiki/Pakistan_and_state-sponsored_terrorism.

54. Ankit Panda, 'Why China Snubbed India on a Pakistan-Based Terrorist at UN', *The Diplomat* (25 June 2015), http://thediplomat.com/2015/06/why-china-snubbed-india-on-a-pakistan-based-terrorist-at-the-un/.

55. Bruce Reidel, 'China-Pakistan Axis and Lashkar-e-Taiba', Brookings Institution, 26 June 2015, https://www.brookings.edu/opinions/the-china-pakistan-axis-and-lashkar-e-taiba/.

56. 'China's Technical Hold on Masood Azhar's UN Terror Listing Already Extended', *The Indian Express*, http://indianexpress.com/article/world/world-news/chinas-technical-hold-on-masood-azhars-un-terror-listing-already-extended-3059989/.

57. 'China's Technical Hold on Masood Azhar's UN Terror Listing Already Extended', *The Indian Express*, http://indianexpress.com/

article/world/world-news/chinas-technical-hold-on-masood-azhars-un-terror-listing-already-extended-3059989/.

58. 'Like Minded Group', https://en.wikipedia.org/wiki/Like_Minded_Group.

59. 'Like Minded Group', https://en.wikipedia.org/wiki/Like_Minded_Group.

CHAPTER
FIVE

India's Groupings
with Emerging Countries

Brazil: The 'Eastern Brother'[1]

The last decade has seen Brazil and India come together in three limited purpose-built groupings—BRICS,[2] IBSA,[3] and G4.[4] Following the Cold War, India and Brazil joined forces in opposing to the agendas of developed countries because the WTO (which included them) spoke for the interests of the First World and did not cater to their post–economic liberalization interests. Three reasons[5] have been adduced for the trans–continental cooperation between India and Brazil:

1. Identity-based: This refers to the shared history of colonialism and exploitation. 'The diplomatic approximation between the two countries began during the Cold War despite their opposing alignment.'[6] Although the two nations had different alignments, 'Brazilian and Indian policymakers adopted increasingly non-aligned position[s] in their international policies as their respective ISI (import substitution industrialization) strategies gained momentum. In the context of the oil shocks of the 1970s and in the aftermath of decolonization, both countries became increasingly proactive in the economic arena.'[7] During the 1980s, Brazil, amidst economic turmoil triggered by the debt crisis, retreated from

active international participation, weakening its ties with developing countries including India. Brazil and India made a made a fresh start on the international stage after the end of the Cold War.

2. Interest-based: This refers to the India–Brazil partnership which 'revolv[es] around their alliances for reforming global governance in issue areas other than trade'[8] that was forged during the WTO Uruguay Round[9] negotiation and then in the WTO Doha Round issues.[10] This 'interest base' led them to seek reform in the UNSC for permanent membership which was done through the G-4 grouping along with Germany and Japan. Clearly, it was their estimate that short of changing the UN system itself the first step would be to secure permanent membership. From this point of view, they appeared to have chosen to join the 'global oligarchy', possibly to the detriment of their long-standing identity as representatives of the developing world in all international organizations.

3. To balance domestic interests: Brazil has a 'mini-India' in which two-thirds of 17 per cent of the workforce, much larger in India, is dependent on subsistence agriculture and rural activity. With the vagaries of domestic politics, the small farmers' lobby could potentially prevent Brazil from championing liberalization of trade in international forums.

History

Brazil remained relatively distant from its eastern brother, India, until the second half of the 1990s, just before both countries began to draw increasing attention from international relations analysts as the 21st century's most prominent emerging powers. Brazil's championing of developing world causes was overshadowed by the country's need to regain the West's confidence as it faced domestic economic turmoil. 'By the end of the 1990s, Brazil had once again realigned itself with several partners in the Global South. The country diversified its economic ties after being left by the West at the margins of international society.'[11]

> The emergence of Brazil-India partnership in the multilateral system of trade can be traced to the Informal Group of Developing Countries (IGDC) in the General Agreement on Tariffs and Trade (GATT). Later the IGDC 'converted into the G10 and, aligned with the European Community, contributed to limiting the

launched in 1986. Nonetheless, as the negotiations evolved, the group dissipated, in part because Brazil and India opted for divergent paths in light of changes in their economic interests'.[12]

It was only after the launch of the DDA that 'Brazil and India converged again to leverage strength against the "rich men's side" in the WTO, as they led efforts, along with South Africa, to secure the TRIPS [Trade-Related Intellectual Property] declaration on the right to grant compulsory licensing pharmaceuticals.'[13]

Two years later, during the Cancun Ministerial Conference[14] Brazilian and Indian diplomats successfully built the G-20. Brazil considers that 'India is the only emerging power with analogous diplomatic experience in the multilateral trading system'.[15] Being a coalition of developing nations, mostly with interests in agricultural exports, the G-20 managed to counter the 'business as usual' proposals of the US and EU negotiators—proposals that would have failed to tackle the price distortions that farm subsidies in the developed world cause in international markets. In the 2000s, Brazil was working to turn away from its Third World mindset and reinforce relationships with the United States and EU. At the same time, Brazilian foreign policy focused on fostering regional integration with Argentina, Paraguay, and Uruguay through the Common Market of the South (MERCOSUR).[16]

However, going through a boom in commodity exports, Brazil became interested in opening markets not only in the developed world but also in the Global South. Nonetheless, it acquiesced with the balanced approach that India developed as the Round evolved, placing particular emphasis on the inclusion of Special Safeguard Measures [SSM] in the Agreement of Agriculture (AoA).[17] Such balance did not prevent India from clashing with Brazil's fundamental economic interest in expanding market access for commodities.[18]

The magnitude of disagreement between India and Brazil was not evident until 'Indian diplomacy turned its attention to the G33, a further coalition of developing countries that had as a primary goal the defence of their domestic farming communities from eventual food import surges'.[19] 'The successive attempts to revive the DDA negotiations since then, including

Bali ministerial [conference, 3–7 December 2013],[20] demonstrate that Brazil was untroubled by India's concerns in 2008.' Although Brazil projected proactive diplomatic participation, in reality Brazilian 'diplomats report that, during the Cardoso years, Brasilia's instruction to diplomats in Geneva was to avoid being portrayed in the international press being on the side of more critical delegations, in particular the Indian one'.[21] In 2001, Brazil, Russia, India, and China came together as the BRIC and later expanded to include South Africa to form BRICS.

2001–16

The India-Brazil relationship is now extensive and comprehensive,[22] covering every important segment of interaction at three levels: bilateral; multilateral in forums such as IBSA, BRICS, BASIC[23], G-4, and G-20; and in the larger multilateral arena such as the UN, WTO, United Nations Educational, Scientific and Cultural Organization (UNESCO), World Intellectual Property Organization (WIPO), etc. Their bilateral relations have acquired the dimension of a strategic partnership in the last decade with regular high-level visits from both sides.[24]

In 2014, Indian exports to Brazil were USD 22.60 billion while imports were USD 11.14 billion. There have been two-way investments between India and Brazil. As per Department of Industrial Policy and Promotion (DIPP) statistics on FDI, dated October 2013, cumulative equity inflows from Brazil into India during the period April 2000–October 2013 have been USD 23 million, representing 0.01 per cent of the total equity inflows of USD 206 billion.

While Brazilian companies have invested in automobiles, IT, mining, energy, biofuels, and footwear sectors in India, Indian companies have invested in sectors such as IT, pharmaceutical, energy, agri-business, mining, and engineering/automobiles. The total FDI by Indian companies in Brazil from July 2007 to December 2013 was USD 103.25 billion. The FDI from Brazil to India from 1995 to 2017 was USD 3353 million and included companies like Infosys, Pidilite, RSB, Fomento, Inox, and Unichem.

Brazil's identity as an emerging power is the glue that brings together its interests with India's. Even without shared interests in the DDA negotiations, Brazil and India have, for their own reasons, preserved their alliances in various groupings. During the Cold War, India, the 'Eastern Brother', had stronger stances on the reform of the world order. India is ranked higher on any given international scale of power, given its geopolitical location near China and the strategic partnership it has developed with the United States through the civil nuclear agreement.

> While it would be wrong to say that Brazil considers relations with India to be more promising than those with China, the example of IBSA shows that there are some issue areas for which Brazilian policy makers deem cooperation with India to be more promising. This has to do with both countries' openness and the nature of their political regimes. In addition, Brazil regards the types of challenges India faces as somewhat similar to those Brazil has to confront, such as high-income inequality and lack of social inclusion. On the international front, both Brazil and India seek to change the balance of power of international institutions such as the UN Security Council, while China is presently a status-quo power ... IBSA allows for interaction among equals, while the BRICS alliance is clearly dominated by China.[25]

South Africa: Politics of Multilateralism[26]

Prime Minister Narendra Modi's visit to South Africa on 7–8 July 2016 was more than a ritual that all Indian prime ministers have observed to pay homage to Mahatma Gandhi's time there and the proximity Indian political leadership has felt to Nelson Mandela.[27] Four agreements were signed during the India–South Africa Joint Commission held during the visit. They were MoU/Agreements on ICT, establishment of grassroots innovation in the area of science and technology, tourism and a Programme of Cultural Cooperation.[28] There was also an understanding on stepping up cooperation in defence, energy, agro-processing, HRD, infrastructure, and development of science and technology. South Africa supported India's entry into the Nuclear Suppliers Group (NSG). President Zuma's visit to Delhi to attend the 3rd India–Africa Summit Forum[29] held from 26–29 October 2015 was recalled and their participation in BRICS, IBSA, and IORA was reviewed.

The organization of BRICS is also indicative of South African perceptions that it needs India in the grouping to actively 'confront the assumed political and economic hegemony of the United States and Europe by attempting to shift the global political and economic center from developed world to regional players in the Global South'.[30]

The IBSA Dialogue Forum initiative in June 2003 aimed at promoting international partnership among these emergent countries as a 'tri-continental enterprise' of significant players within Asia, Latin America, and Africa, respectively. The catalyst was to form a coordinated response among the three major aspirants for representation in the UNSC. IBSA has since moved beyond this to address the development challenges of preserving economic growth, continued unemployment, and income inequality. It has played an important role in raising the Global South's voice in world-governing institutions such as the UN and its agencies like the World Bank, the IMF, and the WTO. IBSA was the first significant inclusion of South Africa into this recurrent pattern.

History

India and South Africa share a history defined by mutual experiences of British imperialism, shared patterns of intercontinental migration and commerce, and, most significantly, rich traditions of political activism against forms of colonial rule during the 20th century. The contemporary views of India from the vantage point of South Africa must be understood through the historical relationship going back to the 19th century. Furthermore, South Africa-Indian relations must also be set against a backdrop of varying multilateral relationships across time[31] 'and the political light cast by Gandhi, Mandela, and other influential figures in both countries during the twentieth century'.[32]

Relations between South Africa and India began during the colonial period before these territories became the recognized entities they are today.

With control came settlement. British immigrants started arriving in the Cape Colony [South Africa] during the first decades of the nineteenth century, a trend that, in addition to new foreign state control, encouraged pre-existing settlers of Dutch descent to move in to the interior, resulting in the founding of two Afrikaner republics, the Orange Free State and the South African Republic (also known as the Transvaal Republic).

'Parallel to this process of white settlement was the migration and settlement of Indian indentured labourers in Natal, starting in 1860. During the next 50 years, approximately 150,000 indentured workers arrived.'[33] The outcome was the establishment and growth of an Indian population, now numbering one million, which remains one of the largest Indian communities outside of India today—a fact that explains the enduring bond between both the countries.

Yet this bond was also shaped by politics. Mahatma Gandhi was among those migrants to Natal during the late 19th century when he arrived as a young attorney. 'Facing the everyday effects of racial discrimination in a new context, Gandhi participated in the founding of the Natal Indian Congress (NIC) in 1894, an organization through which he developed *satyagraha*, a political philosophy and strategy that emphasized the possibilities and effectiveness of non-violent resistance to achieve political change.'[34] The African National Congress (ANC) in 1923 actively drew upon the example of the NIC with Nelson Mandela embracing the principles of *satyagraha* during the Defiance Campaign of the early 1950s.

The Bandung Afro-Asian Conference[35] from 8–24 April, 1955 with the presence of 29 representatives from Africa and Asia had a profound influence on the relations between the two countries. The primary issue was maintaining the sovereignty of recently liberated nation states without being sucked into the burgeoning Cold War and continuing decolonization, particularly in Africa. Jawaharlal Nehru recognized the importance of multilateralism as a strategy to balance the Western powers and the Soviet Union. The non-aligned agenda reflected the sense of urgency within the overlapping contexts of global decolonization and the Cold War. Nehru also viewed Bandung as an occasion to consolidate India's standing among its regional neighbours and in Africa.

Non-alignment informed India's relations with apartheid South Africa. Indeed, it positioned India as a global leader and ultimately as a protector and mentor of South African anti-apartheid activists in the years to come. The final communiqué that stated the desire for economic cooperation and cultural exchange among Afro-Asian states and the recognition of new and future forms of imperialism (Final Communiqué of the Asian-African Conference, 1955).[36]

The Bandung Conference was a crucial, and often neglected, moment in the development of South African perceptions of India during the second half of the 20th century. It provided a vital early occasion for South Africa's anti-apartheid activists to meet foreign diplomats and political leaders to publicize their struggle, particularly in the postcolonial world. It was an important moment in establishing the global scope of the anti-apartheid struggle. In a similar fashion, the conference presented a forum for Nehru and India to express public support on this issue before an intercontinental audience.[37]

Post-apartheid Era

South Africa-India relations must be understood as part of a broader set of multilateral relationships between Asian and African countries after World War II. They strengthened with India granting the ANC full diplomatic status in 1967, despite its ban in South Africa itself.[38] In 1995, after the collapse of apartheid, an India–South Africa Joint Ministerial Commission was established to organize and approve a number of legal agreements, business arrangements, educational exchange, and cultural activities. It met six times between 1995 and 2005. While important issues, such as energy, have remained on the sidelines, other issues, such as defence and military matters, have faced complexities that have produced limited cooperation.

On nuclear weapons, the two nations have different positions. While South Africa supports non-proliferation, having closed down its nuclear facilities, India, as a declared nuclear power, has

Trade and Contact

Trade and people-to-people contact are the most important issues
for the future. India and Africa have one-third of the world's
population with a majority being below 35 years of age. Of all of
South Africa's non-traditional partners in the 'Emerging South',
the relationship with India is the most active and holds the most
promise.

Trade between India and Africa has increased annually at
approximately 32.8 per cent between 2005 and 2011, with the
expansion centring on natural resources, as well as on Indian
capital investment and business in telecommunications, IT,
and automobiles. 'A study conducted in collaboration with the
Confederation of Indian Industry (CII) and the WTO concluded
that South Africa, Nigeria, Angola, Egypt, Algeria, and Morocco
accounted for 89 per cent of total African exports to India.'[41]
The annual India–Africa Summits have become the vehicle for
building mutually cooperative relations between India and the
countries of the African continent.[42]

Their bilateral trade turnover stood in 2015 at USD 15 billion and is targeted to cross USD 20 billion by 2018.[43] Two-way
investments are substantial. Major Indian investors in South Africa
include Tata (automobiles, IT, hospitality, and ferrochrome
plant), UB Group (breweries, hotels), Mahindra (automobiles),
and a number of pharmaceutical companies, including Ranbaxy,
CIPLA, etc. There are IT companies as well and some investments
in the mining sector. SAB Miller (breweries), ACSA (upgrada-
tion of Mumbai airport), Sanlam and Old Mutual (insurance),
ALTECH (set-top boxes), Adcock Ingram (pharmaceuticals), and
Rand Merchant Bank (banking) lead South African investments
in India. First National Bank, a leading bank in South Africa,
opened its branch in Mumbai in April 2012. In 2017 (August),
724,000 Indian tourists visited South Africa while approximately
51,922 South African tourists visited India in 2015. The two
countries have wide-ranging relations, which emphasize on

cultural exchanges, particularly for the Indian-origin community numbering 1.5 million members.[44]

'Relations between South Africa and India have provided a key anchor to these different developments, building upon a long-standing history as well as providing a sense of continuity in membership between these formations.'[45] 'South Africa has looked to India for assistance in its re-emergence in the global community after apartheid. But this relationship has been shaped, and complicated, by the influence and legacies of the Cold War that still remain.'[46]

Competition in Africa

The huge demand from the world's most populous countries—China and India–for resources and raw materials will continue to be a driving force for Africa's development.[47] Growing resource-driven competition between China and India—at times friendly, at times tense—to garner the attention of many African countries includes South Africa as well.[48]

> As for India and China in Africa, in terms of investment and trade statistics, there is little competition. In 2014, China's trade with Africa was at $200 billion, while trade between India and Africa was at $70 billion. As for investment, leaving aside the Mauritius tax haven, Chinese investment in Africa outweighs India's. However, India-Africa relations are growing and the October summit has signaled India's long-term engagement with the continent.[49]

The trading pattern of India and China with Africa has generally been marked by import of raw materials from Africa and export of finished products to the continent. This colonial trading pattern may not necessarily mean that Indian and Chinese capital in Africa was unleashing colonial exploitation like earlier times.

India has been able to leverage its historical relationship with the continent especially through non-alignment and its steadfast anti-apartheid stance and support to the African National Conference and Nelson Mandela. Yet it remains true that while Chinese FDI has been accused of bringing in a lot of Chinese labour, Indian entrepreneurs have been more conscious of their investments providing jobs for the local population. Indian investment, given its historical origins, has also gone in retail trading ventures, agricultural plantations, particularly coffee and small industries especially in East Africa.

The resources war in Africa is being presently waged through financial resources and development sops. Given the tremendous rise in African population coupled with a low level of effective governance, it may not stay the same.

Mauritius, as a tax haven, continues to account for the bulk of Indian investments in Africa but does not contribute to African development as it is round-tripped back to India. Indian investment in Africa is characterized by large-scale investment by a few public sector companies in oil, gas, and mining sectors by making energy security the critical pull factor. Indian companies are also involved with mining of yellow cake a raw material for the nuclear industry. However, Indian public sector companies have not been able to weave in development cooperation features into their investments. Indian investments are largely concentrated in East and North Africa. Elsewhere Indian companies have primarily relied on the government's credit and suppliers' credit facilities to make an entry. Conceived as a crutch to launch Indian companies in Africa it has become the only entry vehicle without any growth beyond. It has not always led to the best outcome either for the host country or India. These are issues which will need to be addressed as India moves up in the investment stakes in Africa.[50]

While the configuration of India and South Africa in each of the formations differs, their cooperation builds the premise that multilateralism presents the best strategy for politically and economically weaker countries to critique and generate an alternative to industrialized countries.

Russia: A Constant Friend?

Prime Minister Narendra Modi's latest visit to Moscow from 30 May to 2 June 2017 came at a time of flux and major changes in international relations. The visit for the 18th annual Russia-India Annual Summit served to establish the importance with which the two countries hold the relationship.[51] Modi participated in the St Petersburg International Economic Forum (SPIEF) on June 2, where India and Serbia were the guest countries. Modi and Putin spoke about '70 years of strong ties' between the two countries after which Modi said the two countries have adopted the St Petersburg declaration.[52]

In the statement titled 'A vision for the 21st century', India and Russia also urged all countries to stop cross-border movement of terrorists. Its highlights included a commitment to bilateral reliability although Russia India relations have increasing moved from psychological and ideological to transactional as indeed has happened with the US as well. Five agreements were signed including the general framework agreement and credit protocol for Units 5 & 6 of the Kudankulam nuclear power plant. It was also agreed that Russia will advance nuclear manufacturing under the Make in India project. The two countries agreed to step up their trade in keeping with the target of USD 30 billion by 2030.

Yet it did not alleviate India's concern with Russia's increasing cultivation of Pakistan both for strengthening its position in Afghanistan and in supplying armaments to the latter. The joint military exercises with Pakistan was ultimately aimed at selling equipment in which a start was made with the sale of Mi-35 attack-cum-transport helicopters. Russia has observed the growing closeness between India and the US including an increase in defence purchases.

It reiterated the sentiments expressed by both sides on 16 October 2016, during the eighth summit of the BRICS countries in Goa. India and Russia had worked at re-establishing 'the special and privileged nature' of their strategic partnership by signing 16 agreements.[53] It was very different from the steadfast relationship that the two countries had established after the signing of the Treaty of Peace and Friendship in 1971.[54]

Russia's relationship with India must be seen in its historical context and in the context of the changes provoked by the end of the Cold War and the break-up of the Soviet Union. Even more, rapid changes in the international system in the 21st century have ushered in an era marked by the move towards increasing

countries super-imposed on the international system. Russia and
India interact with each other bilaterally, multilaterally through
the UN and its agencies, and through limited purpose groupings such as the BRICS,[55] SCO,[56] and the grouping of Russia,
India, and China (RIC).[57] The possibility of the two countries
interacting within the Collective Security Treaty Organization
(CSTO)[58] is for the future.

Even after the break-up of the Soviet Union, India has maintained a high level of relations with Russia, which has been subject to changes in the international situation, including the rise of
China and the near closing of US military presence in Iraq and
Afghanistan. These changes have created new opportunities for
both the countries.

History

The close relationship between the two countries from India's
independence until the end of the Cold War was a remarkable
exercise in statecraft by both sides. It stood India well in the 1971
India–Pakistan War which created Bangladesh and thereafter.
The Soviet Union became India's major source of defence armaments, which by the 1980s accounted for 85 per cent of India's
imports and heavy industry. 'USSR became India's principal
source of weaponry and military training and played a peerless
role in helping develop Indian defence industries by transferring
military technology and authorizing the licensed production of
weaponry.'[59] Russia still remains India's major supplier of defence
material.

The end of the Cold War and the break-up of the Soviet Union
into the independent states of Central Asia and Eastern Europe
was as much as a shock to India as to other countries. 'Yet few
were forced to reassess their foreign policy more thoroughly as a
result.'[60] India had to contend with Russia's diminished power
and the instability within, which had affected India's own sense
of security. The India-Russia relationship went through several
phases due to the loss of sustained cooperation that was the hall-
mark of the Cold War era. Russia, in coming to grips with its

new positioning in a fast globalized world, also lost its seemingly clear focus on building relations with India based on the supply of defence material which secured its legitimacy as a great power. This uncertainty in the bilateral relationship immediately after the end of the Cold War was largely fuelled by India's Soviet-era debt and its disposal.

Russia's struggle to retain its earlier status by building its relations with Europe, the United States, and China also came in the way of India resurrecting its earlier close relations. It was only after Vladimir Putin's first presidency (2000–14) that India regained its importance in Russia's world view, now tempered by NATO's expansion and the West's attempts to encroach on its traditional hinterland in Central Asia, Eastern Europe, and Ukraine. The signing of the Indo-Russian strategic partnership in 2000 was an important step in rebuilding the momentum in the bilateral relationship.

Yet it could not still the reverberations that would affect India–Russia relations. For Russia, the need to cultivate the West, China, and Pakistan became important determinants of its new status in the world. With China, Russia was enmeshed in the SCO where India's full membership is an accomplished fact.[61] Furthermore, as India's relationship with the United States, including defence purchases, gained momentum after 2000, Russian overtures to Pakistan became inevitable.

During Vladimir Putin's first presidential term, Russia grew interest in participating in the G-8 and strengthening ties with both China and India, seeing them as Asia's 'rising powers'.[62] It also led to RIC meetings on Afghanistan,[63] given their common interest, as religiously diverse countries, in curbing Islamic fundamentalism and terrorism. Nevertheless, between 2000– and 2008 India-Russia relations remained mired owing to Russian concerns on India's growing relations with the United States, including the finalization of the India–US civil nuclear agreement and its decision to build India as a global power.

Russia's military exercises with Pakistan and the likely sale of defence aircraft to that country set off alarm bells in India.[64] This changing phase of Russia-Pakistan relations is not new, since Russia has sold defence equipment to Pakistan before 1970.

Yet this development should be seen in the context of growing
India–US relations, including the purchase of high-value defence
aircraft. Whether it poses a challenge to New Delhi's time-tested
strategic partnership with Moscow remains moot. While it may
indicate that India–Russia ties may no longer be defined by
Moscow's ties with Islamabad it could also be the former's way of
serving India notice.

> Russia has not joined Chinese efforts to shield Pakistan. It
> has, however, changed its position on the Afghan Taliban
> and has joined China in initiating peace negotiations between
> the Taliban and the Afghan government. There is no reason
> for India to object to this. However, it is true that Russia has
> recently improved relations with Pakistan and entered into a
> military hardware relationship with it for the first time in several
> decades. This is a matter of concern for India and should be
> clearly conveyed to our Russian friends. Our response should
> be to enhance our engagement with Russia rather than react by
> limiting it.[65]

Decade Beyond 2000

In this context, Vladimir Putin's visit to Goa for the 2016 BRICS
Summit appeared to reassure India on the durability of the relationship. To allay Indian concerns, Russian officials made it clear
that Moscow has not signed any contracts and has no plans to
sign any military-related deals with Pakistan. The two states also
reiterated their common opposition to terrorism. Prime Minister
Narendra Modi underlined that 'Russia's clear stand on the need
to combat terrorism mirrors our own'.[66]

Important agreements signed and operationalized included
laying the foundation for the third and fourth units of
India's Kudankulam nuclear power plant. On the energy front,
the two sides announced an agreement by which a group led
by Russian state-controlled oil giant Rosneft would pay USD
13 billion for a controlling stake in both India's Essar Oil and the
port facilities that it owns.

Energy cooperation between the two countries is a major
growth area with India being the fourth largest importer of oil in

the world. With Russia becoming a petro-state, this augurs well for India. Russia is the second largest producer of oil in the world with 10.2 million barrels/per day of which 7 million is exported. It is also the second largest producer of natural gas in the world, most of which goes to Turkey and Europe. Trade remains a weak link between the two countries.[67] Although ONGC Videsh has important shares in the Sakhalin-I oil projects it is still a marginal player in the Russian oil and gas industry. Russia's agreement of 2010 to build 18 nuclear plants in India and supply technology and fuel for India's reactors is an important plank in bilateral energy cooperation.

Russia's relations with India will remain important in the 21st century not only because of the latter's growing status as a rising economic power but also for three other reasons.[68] First, because of Russia's need for strategic counterbalance to China, both regionally and internationally; second, to bolster Russia's claim to global leadership; and third, 'the normative strength that Russia gains from aligning with both India and China on issues relating to sovereignty and self-determination'[69] from Syria to Chechnya, Kashmir, and Xinjiang. On the other hand, for India, the time for a strategic alignment with United States and Russia becomes inevitable in the context of the unbridled rise of China.

Whether Russia will, through its BRICS membership, secure the means to enhance its global economic and political influence depends on the intersecting triangles of relationships that the grouping engenders. In this context, India and Russia confront four dynamic intersecting triangles: United States–India–Russia, Russia–India–Pakistan, United States–India–China, and Russia–India–China. Whether their joint participation enhances their global and bilateral standings will depend on the effort each one is prepared to make to build long-term synergy.

Common Indian and Russian interests in the future of Afghanistan are an excellent hook on which to anchor the relationship. Yet both countries will have to build their bilateral relationship in the background of their historical proximity and current mutuality of interests, particularly in oil and gas and defence supplies and their common stand against religious fundamentalism and terrorism. Their commonality of views on Libya and Syria indicates that so long as Russia is prepared to stand for principles of non-intervention and sovereignty it can expect India's voice on its side. Yet it is ironical that while Russia defends Syrian sovereignty in the UNSC, it is itself in violation of these principles in Crimea and eastern Ukraine. India did not castigate Russia for its annexation of Crimea and its action in eastern Ukraine just as it was the only Third World country to not condemn the Soviet's invasion of Afghanistan in 1979.

There appears no immediate likelihood of the United States or any other power replacing Russia as the principal supplier of defence material to India, coupled as it is with the licensing of the equipment for production in India. In this context, the Russia decision to intensify defence cooperation, joint manufacturing, co-production including of S-400 air defence systems is important. In addition, Russia is expected to transfer the GLONASS satellite navigation system,[70] which has military applications, to India together with its source codes. It beats the US-controlled Global Positioning System (GPS) system that India uses or the EU-controlled Galileo system,[71] with the source codes to either remaining inaccessible to India. This has implications for India's defence posture vis-à-vis Pakistan and China.

Politically Russia and India have considerable synergies that emanate from their strong position on terrorism. Yet, at the BRICS Summit in 2016, both Russia and China ring-fenced their concerns on Pakistan, given their interests in seeking Pakistan's cooperation in Xinjiang and Chechnya, and did not agree to a discussion on the terrorist attack on the Uri military camp.[72] The St. Petersburg Declaration of 1 June 2017 however corrected this position. India and Russia have continued to maintain common stances in the UNSC on Libya and Syria and have common concerns about China's aggressive posturing in the South China Sea. Yet Russia's support of China's OBOR project was the result of Russia's aim to strengthen synergy with China.

With Russia's tactical alignment with China 'states more apprehensive about China's growing power than Russia will gain in strategic significance for India.'[73] The two countries have mutual confidence that the 'bilateral relationship will not be hostage to disruptions and surprises'.[74] There is a substantial convergence of their world view and common stake in preserving the relationship. Russia supports India's claim to UNSC permanent membership, supported its elevation in the SCO and backed India's admission to APEC.[75] 'Unless the strategic environment changes radically (think an overtly revisionist China that will drive India into an American embrace; a tighter Russia-Pakistan nexus in the context of Moscow's desire to influence Afghan developments; or a seamless Sino-Russian anti-American condominium) the Indo-Russian relationship is unlikely to wither on the vine.'[76]

China: Cooperation between Adversaries?

> One week can be a long time in inter-state relations. In a week's time, India and China had kissed and made up after their armies stood eyeball to eyeball at the Doklam Plateau for more than two months. The trouble at the India-Bhutan-China tri-junction began on June 16 when Indian soldiers detected construction activity on what is considered disputed territory on the Doklam Plateau.[77]

The BRICS Summit from 3–5 September 2017 at Xiamen provided the opportunity for ending the long standoff as it would have made it difficult for Prime Minister Modi to attend it and reduced Xi's intention to project China as a global player in the context of the forthcoming 19 session of the CPSU. One of the major highlights of the summit from India's point of view was that for the first time the group's declaration specifically named Pakistan-based terror groups like Lashkar-e-Taiba (LeT), Jaish-e-Mohammad (JeM), and the Haqqani network. Whether China follows it up by removing its hold in the UN Security Council remain uncertain. Yet BRICS provides India with a platform to keep China engaged multilaterally as well as working with other members on matters of shared concern. In a reversal of sorts, BRICS for India today has become an instrument to manage the externalities—positive and negative—of China's exponential rise. The success and failure of

To understand the parameters which determine India–China cooperation in international fora and smaller, 'purpose-built' groupings it would be instructive to look at the way China has played the nuclear issue vis-à-vis India.

India–China Nuclear Conundrum

The interaction between India and China on the nuclear issue from 1974 to 2008 demonstrates the following:

1. Ever since India's first nuclear test—the peaceful nuclear explosion—in 1974, China has largely dealt with the nuclear issue at the international level. By talking the nuclear issue bilaterally, it would have appeared to equate the two countries. It also gave China relative latitude in continuing to extend nuclear assistance to Pakistan.

2. China has promoted itself as a status-quo nuclear power and India as an outsider and spoiler with its conduct needing international scrutiny. China has not forgotten that most of the pressure on China—which staged its first test in 1964–came from the United States, Britain, France and the Soviet Union, then the four established nuclear powers. China objected to the nuclear double standard practiced by the magisterial powers.

3. China harboured the conviction that US withdrawal of sanctions on India and promoting India's entry into the NSG and other related bodies signalled its intention to build India as a counterweight to itself.

4. Unlike the United States, China did not apply sanctions on India after the 1998 tests and worked behind the scene at mending its relations. The trade between the two countries was equally important to China.

5. Much like with the United States, the nuclear tests were also a turning point in India-China relations.

China's position on India's rise as a nuclear weapon power has evolved over 30 years since India's first nuclear test[79] to those conducted on 11–13 May 1998[80] and the 2008 NSG waiver.[81,82] One of China's main strategies in dealing with a nuclear India has been to downplay India's credentials as a de facto nuclear weapon state.

China initially downplayed India's 1974 peaceful nuclear explosion as a response to its own nuclear test of 1964 and sought to portray it as an assertion of India's sovereignty in favour of a peaceful use of nuclear energy. It was only thereafter that it dismissed it as 'nonsense', asserting that a test was a test. China saw it as a sign of Indian expansionism to contain Pakistan and, by implication, China. It explains China's receptivity to Pakistan on cooperation in missile and nuclear technology.[83] Both China and Pakistan continue to deny that their cooperation is anything but peaceful and within IAEA guidelines.[84]

Following India's example, Pakistan decided to initiate a nuclear weapons programme and turned to China for help.[85] More recently, A.Q. Khan's revelations confirmed Chinese nuclear weapons assistance in the 1980s which included the production of fissile material and information on a nuclear warhead and missile design.[86]

India's five underground nuclear tests between 11–13 May 1998 (followed by Pakistan's five underground tests on 28 May 1998 and a fifth on 30 May 1998) provoked a studied reaction, with China expressing grave concern about this being against the international trend and detrimental to peace in South Asia. It was in line with its intention to portray itself as a status-quo nuclear power. However, following the leaked letter from Prime Minister Vajpayee to US President Bill Clinton citing China as the reason for the tests, the latter took umbrage. It refuted the charge as war-mongering by the then India defence minister George Fernandes.

China came up with three explanations for India's nuclear tests: first, this shored up the BJP's hold on Indian politics; second, it reflected India's ambition for regional hegemony and great power status; and third, this attempted to balance neighbouring capabilities beyond Pakistan and China, including the United States in the Pacific. China also stated that it would undermine the institutional integrity of the global nuclear order. The aim was to project India as an outsider and a spoiler. China's perception of the threat posed by India in the medium term depends on three factors, which all have uncertain trajectories: foreign support for India's great power aspiration, the enhancement of India's conventional military capability, and the character of China's interactions with India with regard to border disputes and Tibet.[87]

At the same time, China did not impose sanctions on India although it facilitated UNSC Resolution 1172 that included sanctions on both India and Pakistan. With the United States, China issued a statement asking India and Pakistan to cease testing and join the NPT and CTBT. Yet China also worked behind the scenes to improve bilateral relations with India.

This was possibly in recognition of the fact that the United States was more interested in accommodating India in the nuclear order, which Beijing remained adamantly opposed. The issue came up with the 2005 US–India Civil Nuclear Cooperation Agreement.[88] With the US championing India's 'waiver' from the NSG, this would allow India to trade in nuclear materials. China opposed it, firstly, because it questioned the applicabity of testing and safeguards. Secondly, it viewed the waiver as setting a bad example of double standards, undermining efforts with Iran and North Korea. More importantly, the agreement gave India recognition as a 'responsible nuclear power' that has never indulged in proliferation. Eventually, China's efforts to filibuster NSG approval, by winning smaller states to its side and to seek a general statement of the 'waiver' so that Pakistan would be covered, did not succeed. Under US pressure, China attended the meeting but abstained from the vote, giving it the effect of a unanimous decision.

☙

Strategic considerations, in particular, the need to preserve broader relations with the United States and India, might account for this disjuncture; however, a division within China's assessment of relations with India may also be at play. Mindful of its commercial interests in India, China consistently sought to differentiate itself from India as a nuclear actor. In seeking beneficial relations with India, China has continued to emphasize the border and Tibet issues in bilateral interactions. Keeping these issues active retains India in the South Asian box.

Nevertheless, China has found reason to work with India in 'purpose-built' groupings where its perceived self-interest has been served. China, together with India, is a member of BRICS, SCO, and the BASIC grouping in the climate fora. India too has responded to China's pragmatism in equal measure.

BRICS

Differences cropped up between India and China regarding the inclusion of a few Pakistan-based terror groups on the UN list at the Goa Summit of BRICS,[89] which almost threatened the survival of the grouping.[90] At the same time, surprisingly, India and China pledged to work together within the organization on issues such as energy security, energy security, and anti-terrorism.[91] These differences came out in the open, eventually leading to a general statement on terrorism without mentioning Pakistan. The presence of all members of the BIMSTEC grouping, which excludes Pakistan, was indicative of India playing hardball as much as China had.[92] The 2016 BRICS Summit has once again brought issues regarding the cohesiveness of the grouping and its value to India.[93]

BRICS' political agenda of multilateralism in international relations, respect for sovereignty, and non-interference in internal affairs brought these five countries from three continents together. Their extensive economic agenda has been the driver. It includes, among others, energy, e-commerce, narcotics, education, youth affairs, interbank cooperation, culture, agriculture, science and technology, innovation, telecommunications, disaster management, anti-corruption, media, and legal cooperation.

Trade and Banking

In 2015, BRICS countries accounted for a total nominal GDP of USD 16.92 trillion, which was 23.1 per cent of the world GDP. Their territories combined are home to 3.073 billion inhabitants (53.4 per cent of the world population). The groups' exports amounted to USD 3.48 trillion in 2014. Imports in that same year amounted to USD 3.03 trillion. Since 2001, BRICS members have more than doubled their share of world exports. In that year, the group represented 8.1 per cent of world's total exports; in 2015, they accounted for 19.1 per cent of that total.

Between 2006 and 2015, intra-BRICS trade increased by 163 per cent, from USD 93 to USD 244 billion. In the same period, Brazil's exports to other BRICS countries increased by 202 per cent, from USD 14.25 to USD 43.05 billion. Imports have increased by 249 per cent, from USD 10.84 to USD 37.87 billion. In 2015, Brazil recorded a positive trade balance of USD 5.1 billion with the BRICS.[94]

BRICS' biggest success has been in the setting up of the NDB, earlier BRICS Bank.[95] The initial authorized capital of the bank was USD 100 billion, divided into one million shares with a par value of USD 100,000 each. The initial subscribed capital of the NDB was USD 50 billion divided into paid-in shares (USD 10 billion) and callable shares (USD 40 billion). The initial subscribed capital of the bank was equally distributed among the founding members. The agreement on the NDB specifies that the voting power of each member will be equal to the number of its subscribed shares in the capital stock of the bank. It has already disbursed USD 911 million in 2016 for projects in all its member states.

Although the BRICS countries comprise over one-fifth of the global economy, together they wield about 11 per cent of the votes at the IMF. Long-standing dissatisfaction with Bretton-Woods institutions has pushed BRICS towards developing-country alternatives in global development finance. The rising economic strength of the BRICS countries has outpaced increases in their voice at the World Bank and the IMF. South-South economic cooperation has expanded dramatically in the recent years. Brazil now has more embassies in Africa than it does in the United Kingdom. China too has become Africa's most important trading partner.

The value of South-South trade now exceeds North-South trade by some USD 2.2 trillion—over one-quarter of the global trade. Low-income countries have also seen unprecedented growth in South-South foreign aid with China, Brazil, and India becoming major donors. Therefore, these BRICS institutions like the NDB are the result of a two-decade-long process of greater economic engagement by and among developing nations.[96]

While the NDB has got off to a good start, it could be overshadowed by the China-financed AIIB[97] that will finance projects in the Asia-Pacific, particularly along China's OBOR project which will link China with Europe in a reverse replication of the old Silk Road.

All five BRICS governments, representing almost half the world's population, have committed to work nationally, regionally, and globally to ensure universal health coverage, a need felt most urgently in all countries.[98] Other areas in which the BRICS countries are making strides are in knowledge production and inward and outward FDIs.

In order to become the driving force of the world economy by the end of the 21st century the BRICS countries have to promote and integrate financing in their institutions of higher learning. While recruitment to institutions of higher learning has increased, a greater effort is needed to improve the quality of education.

An unprecedented combination in 2008—a profound financial crisis among developed countries, paired with relative economic stability among emerging powers—caused a legitimate crisis in the international financial order, which led to an equally unprecedented cooperation among emerging powers. The BRIC countries—South Africa was yet not a part of the grouping—were able to use their temporarily increased bargaining power to become agenda-setters. This culminated in the IMF quota reforms agreed in 2010. The BRIC platform forms part of the landscape of global governance. Second, intra-BRIC cooperation in the area of international finance enhanced trust among the BRICS countries and led to a broader type of cooperation. Intra-BRICS cooperation is, therefore, likely to continue, even after the conditions that facilitated its genesis—the crisis in the West—have disappeared.'[99]

SCO

The PRC, Kazakhstan, Kyrgyzstan Republic, Russia, Tajikistan, and Uzbekistan founded the SCO, an intergovernmental

1. strengthen relations among the member states;
2. promote cooperation in political affairs, economics and trade,
    science and technology, energy, transportation, tourism, cultural
    and educational spheres, and environmental protection;
3. safeguard regional peace, security, and stability; and
4. create a democratic, equitable, international, political, and
    economic order.

With assistance from the ADB and the United Nations Economic
and Social Commission for Asia and the Pacific, SCO members
have developed an intergovernmental agreement on facilitating
international road transport. A programme for multilateral trade
and economic cooperation, signed in September 2003, defines
the basic goals and objectives for economic cooperation within
the SCO framework. It also lays out the priorities and achiev-
able steps for cooperation, the free movement of goods, capital,
services, and technologies over two decades. On 15 January 2004,
the SCO Secretariat was established in Beijing.[100]

The SCO emerged from Shanghai 5 (China, Russia,
Kazakhstan, Kyrgyzstan, and Tajikistan) which emerged following the demarcation of China's borders with the four newly
independent states that appeared after the collapse of the Soviet
Union in 1991. It transformed into the SCO with the induction
of Uzbekistan as a new member at the Shanghai Summit in 2001.
Having been created at China's behest, with Russian support, the
SCO is still grappling to evolve as a well-knit entity. Nevertheless,
'the significance of the SCO cannot be underestimated because
of the presence of large territorial and economic powers such as
Russia and China, as well as the geopolitical space that the grouping
occupies.'[101]

The most significant incentive for China's setting up the
organization was the strength and inflow from Central Asia of
terrorism, separatism, and religious extremism that it feared in
its Xinjiang region.[102] Russia's support as the successor state was
manifest. Although India was interested in membership because of
the same fears, it was only able to apply when membership opened

in 2014. At the SCO Ufa Summit in 2015, the organization, despite strong opposition from China, decided to bring in both India and Pakistan. Although it was expected that the membership would become operative from the SCO Tashkent Summit on 23–4 June 2016 all that could be achieved was agreements for entry by India and Pakistan. India became a full member at the SCO meeting in June 2017 in Astana, Kazakhstan.

India's primary interest in the organization is its anti-terror component. India's attribution of most terror attacks to alleged Pakistani state-sponsored groups is a potential point of contradiction within the SCO. The SCO's regional anti-terrorism structure (RATS) is still an enticing security mechanism for a country facing a large and ever-growing terror threat.[103] It could also be useful to India in the context of India's development of Iran's Chabahar port to meet its growing economic involvement in the region. Yet it may provoke the SCO, backed by China, to muscle a role for itself in Kashmir. Even more important is the fact that India, to keep the bilateral dialogue going, should be a member of any organization in its extended neighbourhood, even if it includes Pakistan.

India and Pakistan's accession has raised the SCO's prestige and lent the body a greater legitimacy, despite concern that continuing differences between the two nations could forestall closer cooperation among the member states. Analysts point to the case of SAARC which was set up to advance relations among South Asian nations.[104] Nevertheless, the smaller SCO member states have looked with unease at being eclipsed by both Beijing and Moscow. The inclusion of India and Pakistan provides them an opportunity to wean off their heavy reliance on China and Russia for trade and investment flows.

BASIC: Climate Change Negotiations

The Climate Change Agreement of 2015 sets out a global action plan to put the world on track to avoid dangerous climate change by limiting global warming to well below 2°C. The Paris Agreement is a bridge between today's policies and climate neutrality before the end of the century.[105] It became operational

Change (UNFCCC) Conference (Committee of Participants 22) in Marrakesh on 3 November 2016.[106]

Many observers expressed surprise at the emergence of the BASIC group—Brazil, China, India, and South Africa—and its unity during COP15[107] in 2009. In the decisive days of the Copenhagen Conference, the four countries coordinated their positions on 'an hourly basis', according to Indian Environment Minister Jairam Ramesh. Their tight and functional cooperation in the heat of the chaotic Committee Of Parties (COP) 15 showed a greater level of unity—for example, issuing joint statements before a key conference—than had been usual in South–South climate diplomacy.

Two key factors help explain the BASIC countries' bond. The first is their membership in the G-77 group of developing countries and in the BRICS group where they have all played key roles for decades and where strands of a common identity have been formed. The second is the increasing rise of these countries in world economic and political affairs, triggering concerted efforts by industrialized countries to impose an obligation for GHG emission reductions on the larger emerging economies, particularly China and India, and to link this obligation to a future global climate agreement. Together, these two factors have drawn these countries together at COP15 and since.

The four BASIC countries represent roughly 40 per cent of the world's population, and each is indisputably a regional power. South Africa's economy accounts for around 31 per cent of Sub-Saharan Africa's total GDP; Brazil accounts for 38 per cent of the GDP in Latin America and the Caribbean, and India accounts for 80 per cent of the GDP in South Asia. China is a developing superpower, with a population of 1.379 billion, 35 per cent contribution to GDP in the East Asia and Pacific region, and a permanent seat on the UN Security Council. All four BASIC countries have substantial and fast-growing GHG emissions, and in absolute terms (total tonnes of emissions per year), China remains the world's largest GHG emitter. In 2005, the four BASIC countries collectively accounted for nearly 60 per cent of the total annual GHG emissions from non–Annex 1 countries[108] (with no binding commitments) and almost 29 per cent of total global emissions, of which China alone produced almost 17 per cent.[109]

The 'positive' aspect of the agenda—interpreted charitably but rarely stated in such explicit terms by BASIC itself—was to act as a bridge between the industrialized North and the developing South in climate negotiations; defend equity in climate actions and burden-sharing against Northern pressure; and demand a legally binding global climate agreement. The 'negative' or conservative and 'inward-looking' aspect of the agenda is aimed at resisting binding climate obligations or quantitative caps on the BASIC countries even at the cost of promoting an ineffectual climate agreement.[110]

After President Trump's announcement of US withdrawal from the Climate Accord the Trump administration is considering staying in the Paris agreement to fight climate change 'under the right conditions,' offering to re-engage in the international deal after President Donald Trump said the U.S. would pull out if it didn't find more favourable terms.[111] Rescinding on the agreement was not in his first 100 days' programme reflecting the stringent conditions for withdrawal. With the agreement in force since November 2016, it would take at least three years from the date the United States entered into the agreement, plus an additional year. Backing out of an international agreement that the United States had previously entered into could be an unwise move from a public relations standpoint. It would invite a strong negative reaction globally.

Even though China and India are the first and third largest polluters, their sticking together to insist on a 'common but differential treatment' for developing countries was largely responsible for maintaining cohesion among the developing countries throughout the negotiations leading to the Paris Agreement.

At the same time, when China and the United States jointly declared their national emission targets in advance of the negotiations in Paris in 2015 it diluted the goal of 2°C set in the Kyoto Protocol and the negotiations that led to the Paris Agreement. As a result, the Paris Agreement is an amalgam of individual country targets, individually arrived at even though the global target of 2°C has been maintained.

With the US withdrawal from the Climate Agreement the burden of keeping the agreement in force falls on the EU, Russia, and the BASIC group, apart from most of the other signatories. Thus, the value of the BASIC group will endure now that the Paris Agreement is in force.

RIC; Russia, India, China

The grouping came into being in response to the developments in Afghanistan following the US invasion and the latter's efforts to bring in a governance free of radical Islamic parties, particularly the Taliban. Russia, India, and China, which form the RIC, span two continents, link three oceans, and represent 40 per cent of the global population and over 22 per cent of the globe's territorial surface. They are also non-Islamic and secular countries that have Muslim populations. They are, thus, open to radical Islamic influences from Pakistan, Saudi Arabia, and Afghanistan.

Although the relations between any two, except Russia and India, have not always been of the best their common interests—anti-terrorism, radical Islam, and global governance—have brought them together. Furthermore, all RIC countries are focused on developing their own economies but also have substantial differences in resources and policies.

While India and China are the largest consumers of oil and gas Russia is the supplier with one of the largest reserves. For example, while China and India are projected to consume respectively 13 trillion and 3.4 trillion cubic feet of gas, Russian natural gas production is expected to be around 29 trillion cubic feet. There are possibilities of trilateral cooperation in agriculture, manufacturing, defence, and space.[112]

The strongest commonality is their interest in keeping the international system multipolar and opposing attempts to intervene in the internal affairs of nation states and provoking 'regime change'. The UNSC's consideration of Libya earlier and Syria currently brought out these commonalities in a stark manner.

Apart from their common interest in promoting a stable and secure Afghanistan, RIC has a number of potential development areas such as energy cooperation, expanded security cooperation, counterterrorism, and cyber-security, and aims to enter into a strategic dialogue focusing on security and growth.[113] In 2015, RIC issued a joint statement recommending India's inclusion in APEC forum. India is still knocking on the doors primarily because its economy is not considered open enough.

At the 14th meeting of the foreign ministers at the RIC Forum, held on 18 April 2016 in Moscow, the countries vowed to deepen cooperation in combating terrorism and discussed various aspects of trilateral cooperation on global and regional issues.[114] They also pitched for setting up of a broad counterterrorist front with the UN playing a central role and stepping up efforts to combat global drug threat. They also discussed creating a new security and cooperation architecture in the Asia–Pacific region.[115] The next meeting of the trilateral forum is scheduled in New Delhi.[116]

The RIC forum provided one more restricted forum for the three countries to discuss bilateral issues. For India, this is important with respect to its relations with China.

OBOR[117]

China's One Belt One Road initiative, announced by President Xi Jinping, is aimed at developing the country's hinterland and connecting it to Europe overland and by sea. It equally has strategic underpinning as it gives China a stake in the development of the region across all of Europe. It comes at a time when Chinese foreign policy has become increasingly assertive. It also pre-supposes that there exist no political or strategic issues with the EU making it possible to expand trade, investment, and cultural exchanges.

The overland routes from Beijing ends in Rotterdam while the maritime route ends in Venice and takes it to all of India's neighbours to the south—perhaps why it is also touted as the New Silk Road. The China–Pakistan corridor is considered the flagship project of OBOR. The Chinese-founded AIIB is the instrument by which countries along the route will be provided funding for joining the project. None of the countries along the route are excluded from participation in the OBOR project.

Despite reservations by many countries on the strategic motives which underlie the project many are accepting participation. It plays on the existing levels of underdevelopment not only in the Chinese region, which will be its fulcrum, but also in the countries along the route. The opportunity to connect their economies to the world is an opportunity too good to miss.

Apart from a lack of political trust between China and a number of important OBOR target countries, there are problems of inadequate investable-level credit ratings of some of these countries and the over-leveraging of the Chinese banking system. India believes that OBOR is a unilateral initiative and it could not commit to participation without substantial consultations. The China–Pakistan corridor, which goes through Aksai Chin, is a major obstacle to India's participation. The current strategic mistrust between Delhi and Beijing will make it very difficult for Indian policymakers to accept the OBOR initiative in its present form.[118]

India and China have kept their bilateral contact going not only through regular bilateral fora but also through these restricted groupings. It is evident that China will continue to associate with India in multilateral groupings, regardless of the stances it will take bilaterally and in multilateral groupings. It is persuaded by its major interest in trading with India and also the fact that India is an important ally on issues where it needs support in international fora. Largely, the Chinese stance on dealing with India in these forums is self-serving with the latter not always getting the quid pro quo it expects. The question for India is whether the gain from joining these groupings outweighs its disadvantages.

Each of these groupings—whether BRICS, BASIC, RIC— came into being based on the strength of their common advantage in coming together without minimizing the bilateral issues that exist. India's participation in these groups has increased its role as a global agenda-setter[119] and given it the experience to take on global leadership. Furthermore, to the extent that these restricted groupings discuss issues of concern, India benefits from the views of its peers. Being a part of these groupings also creates additional pegs in its claim for a permanent UNSC membership.

1. Vinicius Rodrigues Viera, 'The "Eastern Brother": Brazil's View of India as a Diplomatic Partner in World Trade', in Kate Sullivan (ed.), *Competing Visions of India in World Politics* (Palgrave Macmillan, 2015): pp. 111–27.

2. https://en.wikipedia.org/wiki/BRICS. BRICS, is the acronym for an association of five major emerging national economies: Brazil, Russia, India, China, and South Africa. The BRICS members are all leading developing or newly industrialized countries, but they are distinguished by their large, sometimes fast-growing economies and significant influence on regional affairs; all five are G-20 members. Since 2009, the BRICS nations have met annually and India hosted the 8th BRICS conference in Goa on 15–16 October 2016. As of 2015, the five BRICS countries represent over 3.6 billion people, or half of the world population. They have a combined nominal GDP of USD 16.6 trillion, equivalent to approximately 22 per cent of the gross world product, combined GDP (PPP) of around USD 37 trillion and an estimated USD 4 trillion in combined foreign reserves.

3. 'IBSA Dialogue Forum', https://en.wikipedia.org/wiki/IBSA_Dialogue_Forum The IBSA Dialogue Forum (India, Brazil, South Africa) is an international tripartite grouping for promoting international cooperation among these countries. It represents three important poles for galvanizing South-South cooperation and greater understanding between three important continents of the developing world namely, Africa, Asia, and South America. It is playing an increasingly important role in the foreign policies of India, Brazil, and South Africa and has become instrumental for promoting ever closer coordination on global issues between three large multicultural and multiracial democracies of Asia, South America, and Africa, and contributed to enhancing trilateral cooperation in sectoral areas.

4. 'G 4 Nations', https://en.wikipedia.org/wiki/G4_nations The G-4 nations comprise Brazil, Germany, India, and Japan which support each other's bids for permanent seats on the UNSC. Although the G-4's primary aim is permanent member seats in the Security Council they have also started cooperating beyond it to enhance trade and investments between them. India has been the main beneficiary of investments coming from Germany and Japan. All

four countries have been elected non-permanent members of the Security Council since the UN's establishment. Their economic and political influence has grown significantly in the last decades, reaching a scope comparable to the permanent members (P-5). However, the G-4's bids are often opposed by Uniting for Consensus movement, and particularly their economic competitors or political rivals in their regions.

5. Viera, 'The "Eastern Brother"'.

6. Viera, 'The "Eastern Brother"', p. 117.

7. Viera, 'The "Eastern Brother"', p. 117.

8. Viera, 'The "Eastern Brother"', p. 117.

9. 'Uruguay Round', https://en.wikipedia.org/wiki/Uruguay_Round.

10. WTO, 'Breifing Note on Some of the Main Issues of the Doha Round', World Trade Organization, https://www.wto.org/english/tratop_e/dda_e/status_e/brief00_e.htm.

11. Viera, 'The "Eastern Brother"', pp. 112–13.

12. Viera, R. de S. Farias (2009) O Brasil e o GATT (1973–93): Unidades Decisorias e Politica Externa (Curitiba: Jurua)' in 'The "Eastern Brother"', p. 114.

13. Viera, 'The "Eastern Brother"', p. 114. R. de S. Farias (2009) O Brasil e o GATT (1973–93): Unidades Decisorias e Politica Externa (Curitiba: Jurua).

14. Ram Mohan R. Yallapragada, William Roe, Madhu Parchuri, and Alfred Toma, ' The Collapse at Cancun: The Fifth Ministerial Conference of the World Trade Organisation', http://swer.wtamu.edu/sites/default/files/Data/65%20-%2070-229-852-1-PB.pdf.

15. Viera, 'The "Eastern Brother"', p. 114. R. de S. Farias (2009) O Brasil e o GATT (1973–93): Unidades Decisorias e Politica Externa (Curitiba: Jurua).

16. Viera, 'The "Eastern Brother"', p. 115. M. Hirst, 'The Foreign Policy of Brazil: From Democratic Transition to Its Consolidation', in H. Munoz and J. S. Tulchin (eds), *Latin American Nations in World Politics* (Boulder: Westview Press, 1996), pp. 197–224. https://books.google.com/books?id=85YMCgAAQBAJ&pg=PT269&lpg=PT269&dq=The+foreign+Policy+of+Brazil:+From+Democratic+Transition+to+Its+consolidation,+in+H.+Munoz+and+J.+S.+Tulchin,+eds,+Latin+American+Nations+in+World+Politics+(Boulder:+Westview+Press),+197–224.&source=bl&ots=NYarxXVxm2&sig=EKIyqgNEsTq_kNrlAY0sXG0BI2w&hl=en&sa=X&ved=0ahUKEwjnnIuzxYLXAh.

17. Kaliappa Kalirajan & Kanhaiya Singh, 'India and the WTO's Agreement on Agriculture(A-o-A)', http://ageconsearch.umn.edu/bitstream/25366/1/ip06ka01.pdf.

18. Viera, 'The "Eastern Brother"', p. 115. M. Hirst, *The Foreign Policy of Brazil*.

19. Viera, 'The "Eastern Brother"', p. 115. M. Hirst, *The Foreign Policy of Brazil*.

20. WTO, 'Ninth WTO Ministerial Conference', World Trade Organization, https://www.wto.org/english/thewto_e/minist_e/mc9_e/mc9_e.htm.

21. Viera, 'The "Eastern Brother"', p. 115. M. Hirst, *The Foreign Policy of Brazil*.

22. Ministry of External Affairs, Ministry of External Affairs, Government of India, 'India-Brazil Relations', https://www.mea.gov.in/Portal/ForeignRelation/Brazil__May_2014.pdf.

23. 'Basic Countries', https://en.wikipedia.org/wiki/BASIC_countries.

24. Embassy of India Brasilia, 'Bilateral Relations', http://indianembassy.org.br/en/india-brazil/bilateral-relations/.

25. Oliver Stunkel, 'Seeing India through Brazilian Eyes', *Seminar 630* (February 2012), http://freepdfhosting.com/dbbbfc48b5.pdf.

26. Christopher J. Lee, 'From Imperial Subjects to Global South Partners: South Africa, India and the Politics of Multilateralism', in Kate Sullivan (ed.), *Competing Visions of India in World Politics: India's Rise beyond the West* (Palgrave Macmillan, 2015), chapter 5, pp. 79–93.

27. IANS, 'Modi in Africa: After South Africa Tour PM Leaves for Tanzania', Firstpost (9 July 2016), http://www.firstpost.com/world/modi-in-africa-after-south-africa-tour-pm-leaves-for-tanzania-2884064.html.

28. MEA, 'India-South Africa Joint Commission during the Visit of Prime Minister to South Africa', Ministry of External Affairs, Government of India, 8 July 2016, http://www.mea.gov.in/bilateral-documents.htm?dtl/27001/IndiaSouth+Africa+Joint+Statement+during+the+visit+of+Prime+Minister+to+South+Africa.

29. Nivedita Ray, 'Third India-Africa Forum Summit: Priorities, Proposals and Prospects', Indian Council of World Affairs, 16 November 2015, http://www.icwa.in/pdfs/IB/2014/ThirdIndiaAfricforumsummitIB16112015.pdf.

30. David Harris and Simona Vittrini, 'What Does 'Development Cooperation Mean? Perceptions from India and Africa', in Kate Sullivan (ed.), *Competing Visions of India in World Politics: India's Rise beyond the West* (Palgrave Macmillan, 2015), chapter 6, pp. 94–110.

31. The Wire Staff Report, 'The India Africa Relationship is beyond Strategic Considerations'.

32. The Wire Staff Report, 'The India Africa Relationship is beyond Strategic Considerations'.

33. The Wire Staff Report, 'The India Africa Relationship is beyond Strategic Considerations'.

34. The Wire Staff Report, 'The India Africa Relationship is beyond Strategic Considerations'.

35. 'Bandung Conference', https://en.wikipedia.org/wiki/Bandung_Conference.

36. Ena. Iu, 'Final Communique of the Asian-African Conference of Bandung (24 April 1955)', *European Navigator*, http://ecf.org.il/media_items/1128.

37. Staff, 'The India Africa Relationship is Beyond Strategic Considerations', The Wire, 24 October 2015, https://thewire.in/13932/the-india-africa-relationship-is-beyond-strategic-considerations/.

38. 'The India Africa Relationship is Beyond Strategic Considerations', The Wire.

39. 'Treaty on Non-proliferation of Nuclear Weapons', https://en.wikipedia.org/wiki/Treaty_on_the_Non-Proliferation_of_Nuclear_Weapons.

40. 'Comprehensive Nuclear Test Ban Treaty', https://en.wikipedia.org/wiki/Comprehensive_Nuclear-Test-Ban_Treaty.

41. Harris and Vittrini, 'What Does 'Development Cooperation Mean? Perceptions from India and Africa', in *Competing Visions of India in World Politics*, p. 92. CII/WTO (Confederation of Indian Industry/ World Trade Organization) (2013) India-Africa: South-South,http://www.wto.org/english/tratop_e/devel_e/a4t_e/global_review 13prog_e/india_africa_report.pdf [access 14 May 2014].

42. The Wire Staff Report, 'The India Africa Relationship is beyond Strategic Considerations', *The Wire* (24 October 2015), http://thewire.in/13932/the-india-africa-relationship-is-beyond-strategic-considerations/.

43. PTI, 'South Africa-India Trade to Reach $20 Billion by 2018: Minister', *Business Standard* (8 January 2015), http://www.business-standard.com/article/pti-stories/south-africa-india-trade-to-reach-20-bn-by-2018-minister-115010800936_1.html.

44. Embassy of India, Pretoria, Ministry of External Affairs, 'India-South Africa Relations', July 2013, https://www.mea.gov.in/Portal/ForeignRelation/India-SouthAfrica_Relations.pdf.

45. Embassy of India, Pretoria, Ministry of External Affairs, 'India–South Africa Relations'.

46. Embassy of India, Pretoria, Ministry of External Affairs, 'India–South Africa Relations'.

47. Yu Lintao, 'Competition in Africa? India and China Both Aim to Exchange Resources and Promote Development', *Beijing Review*, 1, http://www.bjreview.com/World/201601/t20160104_800045934.html.

48. Harris and Vittrini, 'What Does 'Development Cooperation Mean? Perceptions from India and Africa', in *Competing Visions of India in World Politics*, p. 91.

49. Daouda Cisse, 'China and India in Africa', *The Diplomat* (13 November 2015), https://thediplomat.com/2015/11/china-and-india-in-africa/.

50. Malancha Chakravarty, 'Indian Investments in Africa: Scale, Trends and Policy Recommendations', Observer Research Foundation, New Delhi, Working Paper, 19 May 2017, http://www.orfonline.org/research/indian-investment-africa-scale-trends-and-policy-recommendations/.

51. Editors, 'Modi Visit to Russia: Bilateral Bonhomie Reiterated through Significant Takeaways', *Outlook* (3 June 2017), https://www.outlookindia.com/newsscroll/pm-modi-visit-to-russia-bilateral-bonhomie-reiterated-through-significant-takeaways/1066847.

52. Express Web Desk, 'Full Text: Saint Petersburg Declaration between Russia and India', *The Indian Express* (2 June 2017), http://indianexpress.com/article/india/full-text-saint-petersburg-declaration-between-russia-and-india-narendra-modi-vladimir-putin-4685818/.

53. Harsh V. Pant, 'Viewpoint: Brics Sees Rekindling of India–Russia Romance', *BBC* (17 October 2016), http://www.bbc.com/news/world-asia-india-37675341.

54. 'Indo-Soviet Treaty of Friendship', https://en.wikipedia.org/wiki/Indo-Soviet_Treaty_of_Friendship_and_Cooperation.

55. 'BRICS', https://en.wikipedia.org/wiki/BRICS.

56. 'Shanghai Cooperation Organisation', https://en.wikipedia.org/wiki/Shanghai_Cooperation_Organisation.

57. 'A Role for the RIC Trilateral', *The Hindu* (17 November 2010), http://www.thehindu.com/opinion/editorial/a-role-for-the-ric-trilateral/article892179.ece.

58. GlobalSecurity.org, 'Collective Security Treaty Organisation', http://www.globalsecurity.org/military/world/int/csto.htm.

59. Rajan Menon, 'India and Russia: The Anatomy and Evolution of a Relationship', in David M. Malone, C. Raja Mohan and Srinath Raghavan (eds), *The Oxford Handbook of Indian Foreign Policy* (New Delhi: Oxford University Press, 2015), Part V, Chapter 37, pp. 508–21.

60. Menon, 'India and Russia: The Anatomy and Evolution of a Relationship', in *The Oxford Handbook of Indian Foreign Policy*, p. 512.

61. Catherine Putz, 'What's Happening at the 2016 SCO Summit in Uzbekistan? Depends on Who You Ask', *The Diplomat* (24 June 2016), http://thediplomat.com/2016/06/whats-happening-at-the-2016-sco-summit-in-uzbekistan-depends-on-who-you-ask/.

62. Natasha Kuhrt, 'Russian View of India in the Context of Afghanistan', in Kate Sullivan (ed.), *Competing Visions of India in World Politics: India's Rise beyond the West* (Palgrave Macmillan, 2015), Chapter 11, pp. 175–89.

63. Ankit Panda, 'Foreign Ministers of Russia, India, China Meet in Mocsow', *The Diplomat* (19 April 2016), http://thediplomat.com/2016/04/foreign-ministers-of-russia-india-china-meet-in-moscow/.

64. Umair Jamal, 'Russia Wants to De-Hyphenate India and Pakistan: Should Delhi Worry?' *The Diplomat* (27 September 2016), http://thediplomat.com/2016/09/russia-wants-to-de-hyphenate-india-and-pakistan-should-delhi-worry/.

65. Kallol Bhattacherjee, 'Early Visit of PM Modi to the US would have a Positive Impact', *The Wednesday Interview, The Hindu* (5 March 2017), http://www.thehindu.com/opinion/interview.

66. Rajesh Mohapatra and Jayanth Jacob, 'Old friend' Russia's Stand on Combating Terrorism Mirrors Our Own', *Hindustan Times* (16 October 2016), http://www.hindustantimes.com/india-news/russia-s-stand-on-combating-terrorism-mirrors-india-s-says-modi/story-rc3crMpJUJMHTIk7HnEFVP.html.

67. India–Russia trade is about USD 11 billion (2012) whereas India–China bilateral trade is USD 38 billion and India–US trade USD 35 billion in the same period.

68. Kuhrt, 'Russian View of India in the Context of Afghanistan'.

69. Kuhrt, 'Russian View of India in the Context of Afghanistan'.

70. NovAtel, 'GLONASS: An Introduction to GNSS (Global Navigation Satellite System', http://www.novatel.com/an-introduction-to-gnss/chapter-3-satellite-systems/glonass/.

71. European Space Agency (ESA), 'Galileo Navigation', http://www.esa.int/Our_Activities/Navigation/Galileo/What_is_Galileo.

72. Praveen Swami, 'BRICS Summit: Why China and Russia did not Name Pakistan on Terrorism', *Indian Express* (18 October 2016), http://indianexpress.com/article/opinion/web-edits/brics-summit-why-china-and-russia-did-not-name-pakistan-on-terrorism-3087651/.

73. Menon, 'India and Russia: The Anatomy and Evolution of a Relationship'.

74. Menon, 'India and Russia: The Anatomy and Evolution of a Relationship'.

75. APEC Secretariat, 'Asia Pacific Economic Grouping' (APEC), http://www.apec.org/About-Us/About-APEC/Member-Economies.aspx.

76. Vidya Nadkarni, 'India and Russia: A Special Relationship?' in Sumit Ganguly (ed.), *Engaging the World: Indian Foreign Policy since 1947* (New Delhi: Oxford University Press, 2016), Part II, Chapter 7, pp 195–221.

77. Harsh V. Pant, 'China and India May have Pulled Back on the Himalayan Frontier but the Bilateral Chill is Real', *Quartz India* (18 September 2017), https://qz.com/1079868/doklam-standoff-india-and-china-may-have-pulled-back-on-the-himalayan-frontier-but-the-bilateral-chill-is-real/

78. Pant, 'China and India May have Pulled Back on the Himalayan Frontier but the Bilateral Chill is Real'.

79. 'Smiling Buddha', https://en.wikipedia.org/wiki/Smiling_Buddha

80. 'Pokharan II', https://en.wikipedia.org/wiki/Pokhran-II

81. 'Nuclear Suppliers Group', https://en.wikipedia.org/wiki/Nuclear_Suppliers_Group

82. 'Nuclear Suppliers Group Gives India "Waiver" but Only after Row between Delhi and Beijing'. https://www.wsws.org/en/articles/2008/09/nucl-s17.html

83. J. Garver, *Protracted Contest, Sino-Indian Rivalry in the Twentieth Century* (Seattle and London: University of Washington Press, 2001).

84. Garver, *Protracted Contest, Sino-Indian Rivalry in the Twentieth Century*.

85. Burr, W, 'China, Pakistan, and the Bomb: The Declassified File on US Policy 1977–1997', *National Security Archive Electronic Briefing Book No. 114* (5 March 2004), http://www.gwu.edu/~nsarchiv/NSAEBB/NSAEBB114/index.htm [accessed 2 May 2011].

86. D. Albright, P. Brannan, and A. Scheel Stricher, 'Self-serving Leaks from the A Q Khan Circle', *ISIS Report* (9 December 2009).

87. Xiaoping Yang, 'China's Perceptions of India as a Nuclear Weapons Power', Carnegie Endowment for International Peace, 30 June 2016, http://carnegieendowment.org/2016/06/30/china-s-perceptions-of-india-as-nuclear-weapons-power-pub-63970.

88. 'India–United States Civil Nuclear Cooperation Agreement', https://en.wikipedia.org/wiki/India%E2%80%93United_States_Civil_Nuclear_Agreement.

89. 'India–United States Civil Nuclear Cooperation Agreement', https://en.wikipedia.org/wiki/India%E2%80%93United_States_Civil_Nuclear_Agreement.

90. PTI, 'India, China Discord Among Issues that Could Capsize BRICS', *The Economic Times* (21 October 2016), http://economictimes.indiatimes.com/news/politics-and-nation/india-china-discord-among-issues-that-could-capsize-brics/articleshow/54975316.cms.

91. Xinhuanet, 'China, India Vow to Advance Cooperation among BRICS nations', *English.news.cn* (15 September 2016), http://news.xinhuanet.com/english/2016-09/15/c_135689868.htm.

92. Saul Moross, 'BRICS Caught between India and Pakistan', *Global Risks Insights* (24 November 2016), http://globalriskinsights.com/2016/11/brics-caught-india-china/.

93. Kanwal Sibal, 'Stronger China, Losing Russia: India's BRICS Story in Trouble', DailyO (10 November 2016), http://www.dailyo.in/politics/brics-goa-china-pakistan-russia-unsc-nsg-cpec-masood-azhar/story/1/13347.html.

94. Ministry of Foreign Affairs, Brazil, 'BRICS Economic Data and Trade Statistics', http://brics.itamaraty.gov.br/about-brics/economic-data

95. 'New Development Bank', https://en.wikipedia.org/wiki/New_Development_Bank.

96. Raj M. Desai and Raymond Vreeland, 'What the New Bank of BRICS is All About', 17 July 2014, https://www.washingtonpost.com/news/monkey-cage/wp/2014/07/17/what-the-new-bank-of-brics-is-all-about/.

97. 'Asian Infrastructure Investment Bank', https://en.wikipedia.org/wiki/Asian_Infrastructure_Investment_Bank.

98. Robert Marten, et al. 'An Assessment of Progress Towards Universal Health Coverage in Brazil, Russia, India, China and South Africa (BRICS)', *The Lancet*, 384(9960): 2164–71.

99. Oliver Stuenkel, 'The Financial Crisis, Contested Legitimacy, and the Genesis of Intra-BRICS Cooperation', in *Global Governance:*

A Review of Multilateralism and International Organizations, 19(4): 611–30.

100. 'Shanghai Cooperation Organisation (SCO)', Asian Regional Integration Center, https://aric.adb.org/initiative/shanghai-cooperation-organization.

101. Ashok Sajjanhar, 'India and the Shanghai Cooperation Organisation', *The Diplomat* (19 June 2016), http://thediplomat.com/2016/06/india-and-the-shanghai-cooperation-organization/.

102. Josh Ye, 'Massive Show of Force Staged in China's Xinjiang Region after Terrorist Attacks', *South China Morning Post* (17 February 2017), http://www.scmp.com/news/china/policies-politics/article/2071788/massive-show-force-staged-chinas-xinjiang-region-after.

103. Daniel Urchick, 'The Potential for Sino-Indian Tension in the SCO', Geopoliticalmonitor.com (27 June 2016), https://www.geopoliticalmonitor.com/the-potential-for-sino-indian-tension-in-the-sco/.

104. Srinivas Mazumdaru, 'India, Pakistan and the SCO Expansion', *DW Akademie* (22 June 2016), http://www.dw.com/en/india-pakistan-and-the-sco-expansion/a-19347657.

105. European Commission, 'Climate Action: Paris Agreement', https://ec.europa.eu/clima/policies/international/negotiations/paris/index_en.htm.

106. Keith Bradsher, 'The Paris Agreement on Climate Change is Official. What Now', *New York Times* (3 November 2016), http://www.nytimes.com/2016/11/04/business/energy-environment/paris-climate-change-agreement-official-now-what.html?_r=0.

107. C2ES, 'Fifteenth Session of the Conference of Parties to the United Nations Framework Convention on Climate Change, Center for Climate and Energy Solutions, 7–18 December 2009, https://www.c2es.org/international/negotiations/cop-15/summary.

108. C2ES, 'Outcomes of the UN Climate Change Conference in Paris', Center for Climate and Energy Solutions, 31 November–12 December 2015, https://www.c2es.org/international/negotiations/cop21-paris/summary.

109. Karl Halding et al, 'Together Alone: Brazil, South Africa, India, China (BASIC) and the Climate Change Conundrum', Stockholm Environment Institute, https://www.sei-international.org/mediamanager/documents/Publications/Climate/sei-basic-preview-jun2011.pdf.

110. Praful Bidwai, 'The Emerging Economies and Climate Change: A Case Study of the BASIC Grouping', TNI Working papers, https://www.tni.org/files/download/shifting_power-climate.pdf.

111. Emre Peker, 'Trump Administration Seeks to Avoid Withdrawal from Paris Climate Accord', *The Wall Street Journal* (17 September 2017), https://www.wsj.com/articles/trump-administration-wont-withdraw-from-paris-climate-deal-1505593922.

112. Samir Saran, 'India's Contemporary Plurilateralism', in David M. Malone, C. Raja Mohan, and Srinath Raghavan (eds), *The Oxford Handbook of Indian Foreign Policy* (Delhi: Oxford University Press, 2015), Part VI, Chapter 45, pp. 623–34.

113. Samir Saran, et al., 'A Roadmap for RIC', Observer Research Foundation, New Delhi, February 2014, https://samirsaran.files.wordpress.com/2014/02/orf-policy-perspective.pdf.

114. Konstantin Zavrazhin, 'The RIC Core of BRICS Meets in Moscow', *Russia and India Report* (20 April 2016), http://in.rbth.com/world/2016/04/20/the-ric-core-of-brics-meets-in-moscow_586377.

115. Ankit Panda, 'Foreign Ministers of Russia, India, China Meet in Moscow', *The Diplomat* (19 April 2016), http://thediplomat.com/2016/04/foreign-ministers-of-russia-india-china-meet-in-moscow/.

116. Ministry of External Affairs, Government of India, 'Joint Communique of the 14th meeting of the Foreign Ministers of the Russian Federation, the Republic of India and the People's Republic of China', 18 April 2016, http://mea.gov.in/bilateraldocuments.htm?dtl/26628/Joint_Communiqu_of_the_14th_Meeting_of_the_Foreign_Ministers_of_the_Russian_Federation_the_Republic_of_India_and_the_Peoples_Republic_of_China.

117. Peter Cai, 'Understanding China's Belt and Road Initiative', Lowy Institute for International Policy, March 2017, https://www.lowyinstitute.org/publications/understanding-china-s-belt-and-road-initiative.

118. Peter Cai, 'Why India is Wary of China's Silk Road Initiative', Huffpost, http://www.huffingtonpost.com/peter-cai/india-china-silk-road-initiative_b_11894038.html.

119. Samir Saran, 'India's Contemporary Plurilateralim' in David Malone, C. Raja Mohan, and Srinath Raghavan (eds), *The Oxford Handbook of Indian Foreign Policy* (Delhi: Oxford University Press, 2015).

CHAPTER SIX

New Horizons

*I*ndian foreign policy went through a process of churning in the early 1990s that created the basis of the economic policies of the country. It was only through a foreign policy outreach that India could hope to maintain and enhance its economic growth at home and political interests abroad. Never before had India's foreign policy been tasked in such a demanding manner. With the end of the Cold War and the ensuing economic crisis, India faced a forced reorientation of foreign policy to cover regions and countries that had remained neglected or caught up in a historical straitjacket.

Africa Outreach

India, in the decades after independence, earned considerable goodwill from its championing of decolonization in Africa, offering a 'third choice' of non-alignment to the newly liberated African countries. India's participation in UN peace-keeping forces in trouble spots in Africa helped to enhance India's prestige in those countries and the region. India has contributed troops to UN peace-keeping missions in Congo, Mozambique, Somalia, Rwanda, Angola, Sierra Leone, Ethiopia and Eritrea, Sudan and South Sudan, Ivory Coast, and Liberia, of which four are ongoing.[1]

Until the end of the Cold War, the relationship remained largely confined to the political level, except for countries with substantial India-origin populations such as Ghana, Nigeria, South Africa, Kenya, Tanzania, and Uganda.

In these countries the status of a largely prosperous, yet insular, Indian community became more a cause for apprehension, particularly after forced evacuation of the Indian community in Uganda in 1972.[2] Prior to 1972 there was 80,000 persons of Asian descent (Indians and Pakistanis); by 2003 the figure had dwindled to 15,000. Although the Indian community is back in Uganda, the memory of those events still make it difficult for the community to truly become a bridge to the Ugandans to promote mutually beneficial economic, investment, trade and people-to-people relations. Till 1990 and its economic transformation, neither did India need to nor did it possess the wherewithal to economically exploit the goodwill generated by the Indian community in different African countries for its own economic growth.

India's foreign policy, and its diplomacy on the ground, has made remarkable progress in building mutually beneficial relations in Africa. In a general sense, Indian initiatives towards Africa fell between the liberal interventionist Western model and the business-oriented and non-interventionist Chinese model.[3] As the champion of the developing world interests, India has promoted itself as the preferred partner. Although Indian investment still ranks behind that from Europe and China, it has gained from the perception that Indian companies are more willing to engage local resources and local personnel. Furthermore, India has also tried to ensure that its projects and investments in Africa respond to local needs and are not predetermined.[4] Neither does Indian investment, unlike the Chinese, go into large prestige projects. More importantly, Indian trade with Africa has also grown from USD 3 billion in 2000 to USD 90 billion by 2015, which augurs well for the projected rise in the African population.[5]

By the year 2050, according to the UN, annual increases in Africa's population will exceed 42 million people per year and the total population will have doubled to 2.4 billion.[6] The traditional argument advanced for the lack of industrial growth in Africa no longer holds true. In its relatively industrially pristine state, Africa becomes the ideal venue and market for green technologies for a world trying to cope with rising carbon emissions.

The rapid growth of the Indian economy after the economic reforms from 1991 brought about a new interest in Africa.[7] Indian diplomacy became the driver of the country's outreach to Africa which went beyond countries in East Africa. Sharing its development experience and promoting beneficial development in fellow developing countries has always been a guiding factor of India's projection towards Africa. After 1990, India has been equally guided by other factors that impinged on its rapid growth in the two following decades.

Two considerations guide the Indian thrust towards Africa: first, the needs of each country for its own economic growth and second, the need to build wider and deeper relations in Africa given their weight in international councils. The former includes the search for resources, boosting trade and investment, securing the sea-lanes of communication, and the role of the Indian diaspora in Africa. The latter includes the need for the African continent's support in India's bid for a UNSC permanent membership and its support on other issues that come up in the UNSC and other UN and regional bodies. Should eventually the countries in Africa get two seats, which they will rotate, in the UNSC India will need to greatly intensify its relations with each of the countries in that vast continent. Furthermore, building closer relations with African countries also emphasizes the qualitative difference between Indian and Chinese investments in Africa.[8]

India and Africa's partnership has entered a new era. Close political relationships are being invigorated by a flourishing trade and investment relationship. This new trade and investment relationship could be crucial in the struggle to lift millions out of poverty. India's renewed and rejuvenated focus on Africa was exercised through the regular India–Africa Summits[9] and a wide variety of financial and technical instruments focusing on specific groups of African countries.

The refocused Indian Technical and Economic Cooperation (ITEC)[10] programme was the instrument until the 1990s for sharing the Indian development experience as part of South-South cooperation. It included the deputing of technical industry experts and training candidates from Africa in a large number of technical disciplines in Indian institutions. It also included scholarships for African students in Indian universities. Yet another connect with Africa has been through the IBSA Forum aimed at emphasizing the common interests of the three continental countries in the international arena. After the post-economic liberalization thrust to Africa, the ITEC programme was expanded to include the funding for pilot projects in specific areas and to cover feasibility studies.

This was coupled with grants and lines of suppliers' credit through the EXIM (Export-Import) Bank of India. Indian technical and financial assistance was made available through the CII–EXIM Bank India-Africa Project Partnership[11] with programmes such as partnership with African Union's New Partnership for Africa's Development (NEPAD),[12] the Techno-Economic Approach for Africa–India Movement (Team-9)[13] which was directed at the franco and lusophone countries in Africa like Burkina Faso, Chad, Equatorial Guinea, Ghana, Guinea-Bissau, Ivory Coast, Mali, and Senegal.

Each India–Africa Forum Summit (IAFS) the last held in New Delhi in November 2015[14] has been used to further enhance Indian contributions to the growth and development in Africa through these instruments, together with assistance directed through the African Union[15] and regional organizations such as the Economic Community of West African States (ECOWAS).[16] A total of USD 10 billion has so far been committed to Africa. The result these efforts has also been an increase in the ITEC programme[17] budget to USD 2 billion (2012),[18] a contribution of USD 3 million to the World Food Programme, and 167 open credit lines of EXIM Bank amounting to USD 8.57 billion (2013) covering all the major African countries.

India still has some distance to traverse to become a major player in Africa. Its bilateral trade was USD 90 billion (2015),[19] the fourth largest compared with China's USD 180 billion (2015).[20] India's development assistance was USD 289 million (2014) compared with USD 75 billion from China (2000–2012), USD 90 billion from the United States (2012),[21] and USD 53.789 billion (2013)[22] from the OECD's Development Assistance Committee. Yet India's assistance is regionally broader and more diversified. India's relative proximity to East Africa has made that region the entry point for the country's thrust to the rest of the continent. Given the need to combat piracy on the sea-lanes of communication India has also increased its naval presence in the IOR and promoted military training at its institutions, particularly with countries in East Africa.

In comparison with China, India's major difference is the greater participation of the private sector in these projects. Largely, India is looked at favourably in comparison to the West and China and has been less susceptible to controversy. India has been able to leverage its historical role in supporting anti-colonial movements in Africa and has aimed to foster greater regional integration and multilateral cooperation. In a subtle way, India has also tried to promote its multicultural model of democracy.

How has Africa reacted to India's activism? India's stance of considering 'sovereignty as sacrosanct and developmental hectoring or even tutoring as anathema'[23] has generated a favourable image in Africa. India has integrated well the various domestic markets in Africa, with 597 Indian companies who have invested USD 5 billion over 2008–16, It includes majors like ONGC Videsh, GSPC, Birla, Bajaj, Airtel, Essar Group, and Tata group. The top 11 companies account for 80 per cent of investment flows into African countries.[24] India is offering capacity-building training in its institutions under its ITEC programme, which has been a boon because of its low cost and high standard.

Given its 'relative flexibility and less didactic stance'[25] India is getting it right in Africa. Much of the credit for this forward movement goes to the three-way cooperation between India's government, diplomacy, and business.

Initiatives in Central Asia

Prime Minister Modi's momentous visit, in June 2015, to five Central Asian Republics-Kazakhstan, Kyrgyzstan, Tajikistan, Turkmenistan, and Uzbekistan-was aimed at giving a renewed focus to India's relations based on five imperatives—security cooperation, connectivity, creating strategic space, reviving cultural contact, and building partnerships.[26] The growth of the arc of terror in that region centring on Xinjiang in China, Chechnya in Russia, and the Fergana valley split between Uzbekistan, Kyrgyzstan, and Tajikistan threatens that region and peace in Afghanistan and India. Modi's visit signalled India's intention to step up its relations with the north-western end of its extended neighbourhood.

India's initiatives towards the CAR's predate their independence. India has had historical relations going back to antiquity with each of these countries. The leadership of the Soviet Union saw as benign India's cultivation of these Soviet republics. Since breaking away from the USSR in 1990, India has yet to take full advantage of its historic relations to develop trade, investment, defence relations, and bring these countries into the Indian neighbourhood sphere.[27]

> All Central Asian States are well endowed with mineral and water resources. Kazakhstan with the world's second largest reserves ... of uranium ... has deposits in commercially exploitable quantities of iron-ore, coal, oil, gas, gold, lead, zinc, and molybdenum.... Uzbekistan has large reserves of gas, uranium, and gold. Turkmenistan is endowed with world's fourth largest reserves of natural gas. Tajikistan and Kyrgyzstan have huge hydroelectric potential while the latter is also rich in gold deposits. India's momentum towards the Central Asian Republics is motivated, firstly, by securing access to these resources, and secondly, to rejuvenate people-to-people relations.[28]

The absence of common borders and of transit through Pakistan is an important reason for its 'listless state of bilateral relations'[29] with the CARs. It has prevented the expansion of economic, commercial, energy relations, and tourism. India's only access to the CAR is either through China, Turkey or through northern Europe. In this context, India's renovation and development of Iran's Chabahar port through a trilateral agreement could be a game changer.[30] Chabahar port, in south-eastern Iran's Sistan-Baluchistan, and its linkage through Afghanistan to Central Asia and beyond will be a major instrument for intensifying India's relations with Central Asia. India has allocated USD 500 million to develop the port and its hinterland as a regional trade hub.

It competes directly with Pakistan's Gwadar port, only 100 kms away, that China is developing with a road and railway link to its border for transportation of crude oil and other minerals. It will be an important fulcrum in China's OBOR project.

India, Iran, and Afghanistan have also agreed on a three-nation pact to build a transport-and-trade corridor through Afghanistan that could halve the time and cost of doing business with Central Asia and Europe.

The second connectivity project that India is working on is the INSTC, a multi-modal trade transport network that includes rail, road, and water transport from Mumbai via Bandar Abbas in Iran to Moscow in Russia. It could be used to explore further options for developing connectivity with Turkey, for example, or other countries in Eastern Europe. For India, the INSTC holds much potential to help develop its economic and strategic importance in Eurasia and Central Asia. It could facilitate India's economic integration with Eurasian economies and other countries in surrounding regions.[31]

India's ITEC programme has been effectively used for training in Indian institutions and for financing pilot projects like the setting up of a dairy in Kyrgyzstan and a machine tool training facility in Turkmenistan. Young professionals from the CAR also seek training in areas such as banking, remote sensing, agriculture, rural development, information technology, and learning English. It is an important instrument in India's armoury to intensify its relations with the CAR. The absence of authentic and up-to-date information on potential and possibilities has kept economic and commercial relations from growing. Significant opportunities exist for Indian companies to undertake projects for building infrastructure related to rail network, roads, highways, power stations, transmission lines, renewable energy, and nuclear power in these countries. Several areas present excellent opportunities for enhancing bilateral trade and economic cooperation.

India has been actively building institutional linkages to facilitate trade and investment. Regular meetings of bilateral joint commissions have helped to move cooperation forward, assisted by bilateral double tax avoidance agreements and representation of Indian banks in all the CAR countries. Although bilateral trade with the CAR is still small, Indian companies have taken advantage of their privatization process and have set up major ventures.

Barring a few major companies majority of trade and investment is dominated by smaller companies. A plant in Kazakhstan, owned by ArcelorMittal, produces steel for the Chinese market and employs 50,000 workers. Similarly, Punj Lloyd has established a name in pipeline construction with the British Petroleum (BTC) pipeline from Azerbaijan through Turkey to the Mediterranean. The company has also provided similar services to the Tengiz and Kashagan offshore oil projects in Kazakhstan. Indian companies, under the Indian lines of credit, have also set up small industrial projects.

The crowning piece in the bilateral relationship with the region is the Turkmenistan–Afghanistan–Pakistan–India (TAPI) gas pipe-line[32,33] that will bring Turkmenistan gas to India via Afghanistan and Pakistan. Proposed in 1996 by Union Oil Company of California (UNOCAL), the former US oil major, the project has now been taken over by the ADB. The pipeline is expected to come on stream in 2019. From India's point of view, a major issue remains without a solution. The pipeline will not be viable unless the natural gas reaches the Indian market, but there is no assurance that this will happen without interruptions *en route* to the Indian border. Tension between India and Pakistan, and the control of the Taliban on its stretches in Afghanistan, increases the uncertainty of both the security of the pipeline and of uninterrupted deliv-ery of crude oil to India. A host of energy projects in the region remain uncertain because of continuing political uncertainty in Afghanistan[34] and Pakistan.

India's diplomacy will bear the onus of responsibility for mov-ing the relationship forward in a region beset by problems of connectivity, security, and financial resources. In this context, the expansion of the SCO to include India and Pakistan will shift its focus to trade and economics which will open up opportunities for India.[35] The continuing importance of Russia in the CAR demonstrates the failure of their 'multi-vector' foreign policy aimed at balancing their ties with Russia, the US, China, as well as other key countries in the region.[36] This underlines the need for India, in its thrust towards Central Asia, to strengthen synergies with Russia. The projected use by India of the airfield at Gissar or Ayni, near Dushanbe in Tajikistan, is an example.[37] Although

India had refurbished the airfield under a bilateral agreement with Tajikistan, Russia still holds the rights over civil aviation space in Central Asia. Only Russian cooperation will make it possible for India to use the airfield.

Much depends on the infrastructure facilities being available for an exponential rise in India's relations with the Central Asian region. The major projects are already in place. It will be left to India's diplomacy to keep carving out new avenues to intensify its presence in the region.

India and ASEAN

During the 14th India–ASEAN Dialogue held in September 2016, Prime Minister Narendra Modi transformed the 'Look East' policy to 'Act East' policy which showcased India's greater commitment in the region. India emphasized the need to combat terrorism jointly. They also discussed a plan of action (PoA) to implement the ASEAN–India Partnership for Peace, Progress, and Shared Prosperity (2016–20), adopted on 5 August 2015 in Kuala Lumpur, by the leaders of ASEAN and India at the PMC Plus One Session. The PoA 2016–20 spells out and sets the course of joint action, practical cooperation, and concrete projects and activities. It comprises three broad areas, namely political and security cooperation, economic cooperation, and sociocultural cooperation. Projects and activities conducted under the PoA 2016–20 include annual meetings/visits, seminars and workshops, training courses, and exchange programmes.[38]

India's relationship with ASEAN is a key pillar of its foreign policy and the foundation of its re-modelled Act East' policy. The promotion of the relationship into a Strategic Partnership in 2012 was a natural progression since India became a Sectoral Partner of the ASEAN in 1992, Dialogue Partner in 1996, and Summit-Level Partner in 2002. There are 30 dialogue mechanisms between India and ASEAN, cutting across various sectors.[39]

In addition to ASEAN, India has taken other policy initiatives in the region that involve some members of ASEAN such as BIMSTEC[40] and the MCG.[41] India is also an active participant in several regional forums such as the Asia-Europe Meeting (ASEM),

East Asia Summit (EAS), ASEAN Regional Forum (ARF), ASEAN Defence Ministers' Meeting+ (ADMM+), and Expanded ASEAN Maritime Forum (EAMF).

India and Southeast Asia have shared historical and civilizational relations since thousands of years. After India's independence in 1947 and the adoption of non-alignment as the basis of its foreign policy, its first major external foray was the 1955 Bandung Conference of Afro-Asian states.[42] Yet even before at the Asian Relations Conference, held in Colombo in 1947, India had viewed the countries of Southeast Asia as its natural partners given the long historical and civilizational contact among their people. Prime Minister Nehru had said the following at that conference:

> We have no designs against anybody; ours is the great design of promoting peace and progress all over the world. Far too long have we, of Asia, been petitioners in Western courts and chancelleries. That story must now belong to the past. We propose to stand on our legs and to cooperate with all others who are prepared to cooperate with us. We do not intend to be the playthings of others.

India's independence movement had been a stimulant to the anti-colonial struggle in Southeast Asia. Leaders such as Sukarno, Norodom Sihanouk, Aung San Suu Kyi, and Ho Chi Minh admired Indian personalities like Mahatma Gandhi, Rabindranath Tagore, and Jawaharlal Nehru. Many leaders from Southeast Asia had attended the sessions of the Indian National Congress and had met Indian leaders during the freedom movement. It is during this time that Indian leaders proposed the concept of Asianism and emphasized the spiritualism of Asia over the materialistic West. They called upon a common Asian identity in opposition to the West. The Indian leadership supported the national movements of the Southeast Asian countries during the anti-colonial period.

Yet India's emphasis on its cultural links did not always go down well in Southeast Asia with the countries, liberated after decades of colonization, wary and apprehensive of yet another country taking over the mantle of the colonizers, albeit in a different garb. As a result, despite the friendships that Nehru maintained with Indonesia's Sukarno, Cambodia's Norodom Sihanouk, and other leaders, bilateral relations between India and Southeast Asian countries did not move ahead. This became more difficult since India's policy of non-alignment did not accord with the treaties that these countries entered into with either of the power blocs during the Cold War period. Equally, Southeast Asia no longer figured in India's foreign policy priorities except in the context of their membership in the G-77 countries in the UNCTAD.

The end of the Cold War brought about a sea change in the fortunes of Southeast Asian countries. The 10 countries of Southeast Asia have a combined GDP of USD 1.9 trillion (larger than India), a population of almost 600 million people (nearly twice that of the United States), and an average per-capita income which almost matches China's. Over the last decade, the countries have averaged a growth rate of more than 5 per cent per year. If Southeast Asia were one country, it would be the world's ninth largest economy. It would also be the most trade dependent, with a trade-to-GDP ratio in excess of 150 per cent, and one of the world's consistently good performers.

All 10 Southeast Asian nations belong to ASEAN—a 45-year-old regional organization that has promoted economic integration and decided to create an economic community with a single market for goods, services, investments, and skilled labour in 2015.[43] The AEC aspires to go beyond typical trade agreements, aiming to create a single market and production base with equitable development across its 10 member countries. While ASEAN has made some significant political achievements during the past five decades,[44] its economic integration project is still very much a work-in-progress, and could remain so for many years or even decades to come. The only clear success ASEAN can claim is the reduction of tariffs among member countries with 99 per cent of the tariff lines being reduced to zero. The use of non-tariff measures, however, continues.

The drastic changes in India's internal and external policies after the end of the Cold War also compelled a redesign of its foreign policy towards the Southeast Asian region. India's Look East policy, launched in 1991 by Prime Minister Narasimha Rao,[45] over the last two decades has strengthened the country's economic, political, civilizational, and security links with the rest of Asia. In order to cope with the global financial turmoil, India needs to become even more persistent and proficient in deepening its linkages with the rest of Asia. The success of the policy depends on the commitment of the Indian government to implement the proposed plans and projects and give a role to the north-east region.[46] India is now a member of the EAS, comprising 16 countries, which includes the 10 members of the ASEAN, Japan, China, Republic of Korea, Australia, and New Zealand.

The Look East policy has substantively achieved its goal to connect economically with the ASEAN region and to counter China in that region. Its limitations arise from delays in connectivity projects between India and the ASEAN and the fact that it has yet to substantially benefit Northeast India. The progress on security cooperation, particularly with Thailand, has helped to track Pakistan-based terror groups that use some ASEAN countries for sanctuary and succour.

An anecdote from the first India–ASEAN Summit in 2002 colourfully brings out the reason India commands the interest it does. Addressing the members present at the summit Singapore Prime Minister Goh Chong Tok said,

> We see ASEAN like a jumbo aircraft; its one wing is China, and the other India. We want India to be entrenched in our region for the sake of our prosperity and stability.

Thus, both countries' participation in ASEAN guarantee its stability and prosperity. India's strength also derives from the non-intrusive way in which it practices its foreign relations. With China taking a belligerent stance in the South China Sea, it has put pressure on ASEAN.[47] An international tribunal in The Hague ruled that China's expansive claim in the South China Sea and the construction of an artificial island had no legal basis under UNCLOS. Yet it did not prescribe any particular action for China. Although the case was registered by the Philippines, Vietnam has an equal interest in the area. However, while the former is actively building its relations with China under President Duterte, the latter has remained mute after the decision. ONGC Videsh, India's oil major, is a minor partner in an offshore oil exploration bloc in the South China Sea with British Petroleum as the major partner. The further evolution of this issue impinges indirectly on India as well.

ASEAN is an area where India has considerable stakes in the changing strategic environment in the Asia Pacific. China's aggressive stances and the United States' continued interest in the area give reason for India also to intensively look into the region. Prime Minister Modi's Act East policy aims to meet these objectives. Indian diplomacy will once again be the vanguard for realizing it.

Israel

Prime Minister Narendra Modi's visit Israel from 4 July 2017 to 6 July 2017 was the first by any Indian prime minister, and marked 25 years of bilateral relations. That even the possibility of such a visit is being mentioned in the media marks a major change in the way India–Israel relations are viewed in the country and the world.[48] The prospect of a Modi visit to Israel breaks the long-standing barrier that the relationship faced externally in the Arab world. Internally, it signifies that the relations between the two countries have finally become politically bi-partisan with both the Congress and the BJP on board. In effect, developments in India–Israel relations are no longer the reason for ventilating of views by various groups in the country or in the Islamic world. During the visit India and Israel signed seven agreements in key areas like space, water management, energy, and agriculture. A Memorandum of Understanding was signed to set up USD 40 million worth India–Israel Industrial Research and Development (R&D) and Technical Innovation Fund.[49]

With this visit India's relations with Israel have acquired a veneer of normalcy that had been lacking so far. The visit came at a time when international relations are in a state of flux. The ongoing conflicts in Syria, Iraq, and Yemen have seen an unprecedented realignment of forces in the Arab world. The possibility of alliance between Israel, Saudi Arabia, and Egypt[50] has changed the strategic context and removed the need for strident postures in the Arab world. India–Israel relations are now an issue of management rather than rhetorical broadsides. It has equally rendered India free to develop its relations with Israel as with any other country.

For two countries which became independent nearly seventy years ago it has taken India (August 1947) and Israel (May 1948) a long time for the relationship to become stable. Following India's independence and its emergence as a secular democracy, one of the first foreign policy decisions it was confronted with was the kind of relations it would have with the recently established state of Israel, a majoritarian democracy. India's small and dwindling Jewish community, one of the oldest in the world, has never suffered persecution.

Fresh out of the trauma of partition and the continuing controversy on the nature of the Indian state, the government decided to recognize the state of Israel but only allowed consular relations on a non-reciprocal basis. From then on until 1992, despite sporadic attempts to move the relationship forward, India and Israel had no state-to-state relations. India opened full diplomatic relations with Israel in May 1992 following the commencement of the 1992 Madrid Peace Process[51] and the imperative to restructure its international relations following the demise of the Soviet Union and the United States' emergence as the sole superpower.

In the context of its economic reform programme imposed by the country's straitened economic circumstance, Indian diplomacy became the instrument for opening to the larger world beyond its circle of non-aligned and developing countries. Israel became an important element in this restructuring for two reasons, first, its value as a major weapons supplier that it soon became and second, to underpin forward movement in India's relations with the United States.

Besides changes in the global economic and political environment after the Cold War, the fact that India's neighbourhood had become increasingly dangerous dictated that defence and security issues, and indeed supplies, became and remained the fulcrum of the relationship during the 1990s. It was only after 2000 that the relationship expanded to include trade, industry, information, technology, investment, and people-to-people contact.

In contrast to the fallow decades since the independence of the two countries, the last two decades have seen an explosive growth in the diversity of contact between them. 'A confluence of structural, domestic, and individual factors has been responsible for a radical shift in Indo–Israeli strategic relations.'[52]

Present

The supply of military hardware and software remains the cornerstone of the relationship, with Israel emerging as the second largest supplier of armaments to India with annual defence sales of over USD 1 billion. Other areas have included 'counter-terrorism, border management, upgrading of Soviet inventories, surveillance, small arms and ammunition, missile defence and early warning systems'.[53]

During the visit of Prime Minister Modi to Israel contracts valued at USD 3 billion are likely to be finalized. They include the acquisition of 164 'Litening-4' targeting pods—targeting designation tools used by ground-attack aircraft—for Indian Air Force fighter jets such as the Sukhoi-30MMKIs and an undisclosed number of Spice 250 precision-guided bombs with a standoff range of 100 kilometres (62 miles).[54] Three missile deals worth USD 2.6 billion were signed. The Indian air force also expects 2 Phalcon airborne surveillance radars at the cost of USD 1.6 billion and the army for S 356 spike anti-tank guided missiles along with 321 launchers for nearly USD 500 million. India also seeks advanced missiles and drones.[55]

At the same time bilateral trade, though still bulking in favour of diamonds, reached USD 4.52 billion in 2014.[56] FDI inflows from Israel to India from April 2000 to March 2011 totalled USD 53.14 million, placing it at 38th rank (0.04 per cent of the total FDI inflows to India). These figures, however, may not accurately reflect the FDI from Israel as a number of Israeli companies also invest in India through the US and Europe route.[57] In 2016, Israel invested nearly USD 5 billion in Israeli start-ups. There are 300 multinational R&D centres in the country. It is a leader in cyber-security, homeland security, drone technology, robotics, machine learning, precision agriculture, digital printing, autonomous vehicles and computer vision and healthcare. 'A combination of Israeli innovation, India's market share and its growing might in digital services is a great recipe for success.'[58]

During President Rivlin's recent visit to India, Israel sought an FTA to boost bilateral trade.[59] An interesting feature of bilateral economic relationship is the role of Indian state governments in promoting the relationship. State governments have used Israeli technologies and products in agriculture, horticulture, irrigation, desertification, water management, desalinization, and infrastructure.[60] In medical technology, in particular, there has been good cooperation between Israeli start-ups and Indian counterparts, mainly for testing and validation, an essential requirement for US Food and Drug Administration (FDA) approval and global launch.[61]

The development of the relationship beyond defence based on the natural talents of the two peoples augurs well for its future despite its political and security imperatives. The relationship appears destined to grow out of the clouds of the past yet it is important to realize that despite considerable synergy there are equally important differences of perspective between the two countries. Two need mention.

First is the Pakistan factor in the bilateral India–Israel matrix.[62] Pakistan appeared to be an important influence in shaping India's relationship with Israel until the 1990s because of the partition and the Kashmir issue.[63] India's intention to secure the support of the Arab and Islamic world was an important reason for keeping the relationship with Israel on hold. It was only thereafter that the constellation of circumstances, particularly the inauguration of the Middle East Peace Process in Madrid in 1991, created favourable conditions for establishing full diplomatic relations. Israel labelled its relationship with India as 'special', implying that it would keep away from Pakistan. This was an unwritten factor in Israel becoming India's major arms supplier.

Nevertheless, Israel had not abandoned the possibility of opening relations, at an opportune moment, with Pakistan, the largest country in the Islamic world. This appeared to have come soon after the US invasion of Iraq in 2003. It was reflected in Israel, for the first time, in prevaricating in September 2003 on the text relating to Kashmir in the Delhi Declaration issued at the end of Prime Minister Ariel Sharon's visit to India. India preferred to have no mention of Kashmir in the declaration so that Israel would be held to its earlier statement. This highlights the fact that Israel, pursuing its national interest, will continue to find an opening to Pakistan whenever conditions are suitable. In that eventuality

India would have to re-evaluate its defence acquisitions from that country.

Second, India and Israel do not have any adversaries in common. While Pakistan is not in the circle of threats that Israel faces, Iran is not in India's circle. This has meant that in discussions on counterterrorism the two countries are speaking parallel to each other. The only possibility of cooperation on counterterrorism is on the techniques of interception, warning, and in dealing with terrorism. Both countries have much to learn from each other, for example, the Israeli law on incitement India needs to look at its value in the Indian context.

Both sides are now poised to grow their bilateral relations mindful of the changing perspectives that the ongoing war in the Arab world has brought. As both the countries are outside what is essentially a struggle within Islam, this has become the most important basis for intensifying the synergies.

Indian Diaspora

When Prime Minister Modi addressed the Indian diaspora at Madison Square Gardens on his first visit to the United States, he was greeted with thunderous applause, according to an article on 28 September 2014 in *Wall Street Journal*.[64] That honeymoon with the Indian diaspora, particularly in the United States, still continues. It was indeed a moment of glory for someone who had personally faced, over a decade, ostracization by the US establishment and the denial of visa for their understanding of his culpability in the 2002 Godhra killings. Modi has shown a high degree of equanimity and purpose in letting the matter rest.

The Indian diaspora numbers 20 million in 136 countries, making it the largest in the world, although UN figures place the number a little lower.[65] It has become an important part of India's foreign policy projection in certain advanced countries, particularly in the United States, and counts as a major source of foreign exchange. The extent to which it has secured a voice in domestic policy is moot. Yet the influence of the diaspora is seen in sectors such as ICT and industry. Their influence on Indian state elections remains a matter of conjecture.

The importance of Indian diaspora in its external projection is very different from the advice Jawaharlal Nehru gave Indian communities abroad. He exhorted them to identify with their country of residence and not look towards the home country for succour and help. It went against the interest and activism of Indian diaspora in fighting for India's independence. The Indian National Congress, during the independence movement, had taken up with the British sovereign government the case of discrimination against Indians settled in other colonial dominions. Most importantly, Mahatma Gandhi was quintessentially 'diasporic' as he had practised his concept of 'satyagraha' in South Africa.

During Jawaharlal Nehru's prime ministership, the policy vis-à-vis Indian diaspora was clear: Indian-origin populations outside India had a duty to the countries where they resided since they had gone there voluntarily. Nehru's injunction to them was to completely 'associate with the indigenous people of the country of adoption, to "cooperate" with them, not demand any "special rights and privileges", and extend their undivided "loyalty" to the country of residence.'[66]

This issue came up in connection with the grant of citizenship to Indian Tamil plantation workers taken by the British to work on Sri Lankan tea plantations. Successive Sri Lankan governments had not granted them this right. Prime Minister Lal Bahadur Shastri eventually reached an agreement on citizenship with the Bandaranaike government.[67] Similarly, the case of Indians being denied equal treatment and their eviction by the Burmese government became a cause célèbre with opinion ranged on both sides.[68]

This was equally true in east African countries like Kenya and Uganda and South Africa where the Indian diaspora seemed at odds with the African national movements and their social and economic struggles. India's forward foreign policy for African independence and anti-apartheid stance created an ambivalence, and even antipathy, to India within East and South African Indian communities, many of whom felt abandoned by India in the face of prejudice within their adopted homelands, as witnessed in Uganda in 1972.[69] Even in societies where local Indian populations occupied less controversial places, Delhi's relations with overseas Indians atrophied.

India's spreading economic outreach in Iraq and the Gulf countries in the 1980 meant a movement of Indians for employment to these countries. It forced the Indian government to distinguish between PIOs who represented long-settled Indian communities abroad and NRIs, a primarily tax concept, to denote Indian nationals going abroad for work. The issue of the Indian government's responsibility towards NRIs came up with the Iraq–Iran War which began in September 1980 (1980–88), leaving nearly 22,000 Indian skilled and unskilled workers and professionals stranded.

In line with the extant government policy, the Indian government refused to think of evacuating the stranded Indians until the exacerbation of the war caused a reversal of policy by Prime Minister Indira Gandhi.[70] The change in policy was provoked by the need to bring fellow nationals back home in times of distress and in recognition of their growing contribution to the national exchequer through remittances.[71] By 2015, remittances from overseas Indians were contributing USD 69 billion, according to the World Bank. Since the Iraq–Iran War the Indian government has evacuated Indian nationals from Iraq (again), the Gulf countries, Lebanon, Libya, and Lebanon. Evacuation of Indian nationals working abroad has now become a part of the embedded policy.

Post Cold War

The dire state of national finances that led to the economic reform programme in 1991 also emphasized the indispensability of remittances received from the Indian communities (both PIOs and NRIs) living abroad. The next stage of the Indian government's interaction was to find the basis for leveraging strengths of the diaspora for the good of the community and the country. The setting up of a dedicated Ministry of Overseas Indians, in 2004, was an important first step. It helped the Indian government to look to alleviating problems faced in India by the India's overseas communities. In return, the government also paid attention to the way in which they could enhance India's political and economic interests.

Indian diplomatic missions abroad, particularly in the United Kingdom and the United States, encouraged 'political activism' by the Indian expatriate communities, both to pursue their own interests and those of India. The tremendous success of this exercise in the United States was based on the example of the Jewish lobby in that country.[72] Indian Americans number about 3 million in the United States. According to the 2010 United States Census, the Asian Indian population in the country grew from almost 1,678,765 in 2000 (0.6 per cent of the US population) to 2,843,391 in 2010 (0.9 per cent of the US population), a growth rate of 69.37 per cent—one of the fastest growing ethnic groups in that country. Their household income is 25 per cent higher than the US national average and educational level is 70 per cent higher. One out of six doctors in the United States is of Indian origin, and the Asian American Hotel Owners Association owns 49 per cent of hotel properties (by rooms). The tremendous success achieved by Indian Americans in ICT has been widely recognized.

The greatest success of Indian diplomacy was the painstaking way in which the Congressional Caucus in the US House of Representatives and the US Senate was built up in 1999.[73] It is the largest single country caucus in the US House and Senate. With the increasing entry of Indian origin politicians in the US administration and legislature, and in the states an increase in the effect of these caucuses is inevitable. Similarly, in the UK Parliament[74] and the European Parliament, Indian delegation[75] has helped to move the relations forward at the government and popular levels. These groups are the counterpart of political action committees of the Indian diaspora in the United States.

In the United Kingdom, the British Indian community, numbering 1.4 million, some of whom were there before Indian independence, is economically affluent and primarily forms the middle class. A 2011 study by the Joseph Rowntree Foundation found British Indians have among the lowest poverty rates among all ethnic groups in Britain, second only to the White British. Studies have shown that Indians are more likely, than other ethnic minorities, to be employed in professional and managerial occupations, including financial services. In the EU the Indian diaspora[76] was 1.2 million (2015). Although not as politically active as Indians in the United States, since 2011 they grouped themselves under the 'Indian Diaspora in Europe' organization.

With the growing activity of the Indian diaspora worldwide, the government at home has taken important steps to meet their expectations. Apart from setting up a separate department in the government which deals with Indian communities abroad, Pravasi Bharatiya Divas (PBD) is celebrated annually on 9 January since 2000 to commemorate Mahatma Gandhi's return to India.[77] The 14th PBD was held from 7 January 2017 to 9 January 2017 in Bengaluru.[78]

In order to understand the issues of the Indian diaspora and leverage their strengths the government in 2000 set up a high-level committee on Indian diaspora which submitted its report on 8 January 2002. The thrust of the committee's vision was that rather than pursue a hub-and-spoke relationship with its diaspora the government must have a policy framework to forge a web relationship. The committee felt that creating a network of people of Indian origin that strengthens the diaspora would also strengthen India and have a positive relation with the host country. While most of its recommendations were implemented, the issue of granting dual citizenship remains elusive. As a via media, the government issues an Overseas Citizen of India (OCI) card which gives the holder the same rights as an Indian resident citizen, excepting the buying of land and voting in the elections.

The relationship between India and its diaspora, over the last 15 years, has developed into one of mutual benefit with both the sides of the matrix gaining from it. It has secured India a continuous source of funds for its development while connecting the overseas community with their roots. As a result, Indian states such as Kerala, Andhra Pradesh, Gujarat, Tamil Nadu, and Maharashtra have seen greater exodus of its people abroad and have also started celebrating PBD at the state level to garner investments for tourism. This laudable development has, to some extent, differentiated between PIOs—the diaspora that went earlier and has settled abroad—from the NRIs who are generally expected to return back to India. The distinction is in the nature of the issue. While PIOs have to be nurtured to bring them closer to India, NRIs, who are certain to return to return, have a greater value as contributors to the Indian exchequer. There may still be the need to connect with Indian communities in countries where they continue to face difficulties of status due to cultural differences.

~&~

This chapter has taken selected issues to demonstrate the verve and vitality of India's diplomatic effort in countries and sectors of actual and potential importance. There are a host of other areas and regions that will require extraordinary effort by India's diplomacy if it is to assert its leadership in the world. The most important are the outstanding issues like Kashmir that will continue to demand a studied diplomatic effort. There are new areas of growth and power like international action on consequences of climate change; the creation of new models in world trade like APEC and the still-born TPP, and other new trading arrangements, that excludes India; and the creation of access to technologies and resources for exploration of the space, the seabed, and the ocean floor. India's diplomatic effort is the first point from which this quest must begin.

Notes

1. 'Indian Army United Nations Peace-keeping Missions' https://en.wikipedia.org/wiki/Indian_Army_United_Nations_peacekeeping_missions.

2. Palash Ghosh, 'Uganda: Forty Years after Idi Amin Expelled Asians', *International Business Times* (8 June 2012), http://www.ibtimes.com/uganda-forty-years-after-idi-amin-expelled-asians-739228.

3. David Harris and Simona Vettori, 'What Does Development Cooperation Mean? Africa, India and the Politics of Multilateralism', Kate Sullivan (ed.), *Competing Visions of India in the World India's Rise beyond the West* (Palgrave Macmillan, 2015), pp. 94–110.

4. Kabir Taneja, 'India in Africa: Learning from China's Mistakes', *The Wire* (23 November 2015), http://thewire.in/16099/india-in-africa-learning-from-chinas-mistakes/.

5. Alioune Ndiaye, 'India's Investment in Africa: Feeding Up an Ambitious Elephant', International Centre for Trade and Sustainable Development, 15 September 2016, http://www.ictsd.org/bridges-news/bridges-africa/news/india%E2%80%99s-investment-in-africa-feeding-up-an-ambitious-elephant.

6. Joseph J. Bish, 'Population Growth in Africa: Grasping the Scale of the Challenge', *The Guardian* (11 January 2016), https://www.theguardian.com/global-development-professionals-network/2016/jan/11/population-growth-in-africa-grasping-the-scale-of-the-challenge.

7. African Development Bank Group, 'India's Economic Engagement with Africa', 2, 6 (11 May 2011), http://www.afdb.org/fileadmin/uploads/afdb/Documents/Publications/India's%20Economic%20Engagement%20with%20Africa.pdf.

8. Tandit Kundu and Ritika Mazumdar, 'Are China and India the New Colonial Powers in Africa?' *Live Mint* (29 March 2017), http://www.livemint.com/Opinion/egDrI1HjeM4j5PWXkwgpjP/Are-China-and-India-the-new-colonial-powers-in-Africa.html.

9. Ruchira Beri, '3rd India Africa Forum Summit: Rejuvenating Relations', Institute of Defence Studies and Analyses, 29 October 2015, http://www.idsa.in/idsacomments/3rd-india-africa-forum-summit_rberi_291015.

10. Ministry of External Affairs, Government of India, 'Indian Technical and Economic Programme', 29 November 2016, http://itec.mea.gov.in/.

11. CII, '12th CII EXIM Bank Conclave', http://www.ciiafricaconclave.com/AboutUs.aspx.

12. African Development Bank Group, 'New Partnership for Africa's Development', http://www.afdb.org/en/topics-and-sectors/initiatives-partnerships/nepad/.

13. Arndt Michael, 'Pivot to Asia: India's Evolving Sub-Saharan Africa Engagement', Center for Advanced Study of India, University of Pennsylvania, 11 August 2014, https://casi.sas.upenn.edu/iit/arndtmichael.

14. Suhasini Haidar, 'The India Africa Summit: Beyond the Event', *Hindustan Times* (9 November 2015), http://www.thehindu.com/opinion/columns/indiaafrica-summit-beyond-the-event/article7862362.ece.

15. Wikipedia 'Africa Union', https://en.wikipedia.org/wiki/African_Union.

16. 'Economic Community of West African States', http://www.ecowas.int/member-states/.

17. MEA, 'About ITEC, Indian Technical and Economic Cooperation Programme', Ministry of External Affairs, Government of India, https://www.itecgoi.in/about.php.

18. Embassy of India, Yemen, 'Indian Technical and Economic Cooperation Programme', http://eoisanaa.org/indian-technical-and-economic-cooperation-itec-programme-2/.

19. 'India–Africa Relations', https://en.wikipedia.org/wiki/Africa%E2%80%93India_relations.

20. Eleanor Albert, 'China in Africa', Council on Foreign Relations, 12 July 2017, https://www.cfr.org/backgrounder/china-africa.

21. The Conversation Africa, 'How and Why China Became Africa's Biggest Aid Donor', HuffPost (26 April 2016), https://www.huffingtonpost.com/the-conversation-africa/how-and-why-china-became_b_9775722.html.

22. OECD, 'Development Aid At a Glance, Africa', 2016 edition, https://www.oecd.org/dac/stats/documentupload/2%20Africa%20-%20Development%20Aid%20at%20a%20Glance%202016.pdf.

23. David Harris and Simona Vettori, 'Indian Technical and Economic Cooperation Programme'.

24. Malancha Chakrabarty, 'Indian Investments in Africa: Scale, Trends and Policy Recommendations' Observer Research Foundation, 17 May 2017, http://www.orfonline.org/research/indian-investment-africa-scale-trends-and-policy-recommendations/.

25. David Harris and Simona Vettori, 'Indian Technical and Economic Cooperation Programme'.

26. Jayanth Jacob, 'Five Underlying Themes of PM Modi's Central Asia Trip', *Hindustan Times* (6 July 2015), http://www.hindustantimes.com/india/five-underlying-themes-of-pm-modi-s-central-asia-trip/story-U1xVM2SjpU7bCQEnuJ3RnI.html.

27. Ashok Sajjanhar, 'India–Central Asia Relations: Expanding Vistas of Partnership', *Raisina Debates*, Observer Research Foundation, 22 June 2016, http://www.orfonline.org/expert-speaks/india-central-asia-relations-expanding-vistas-of-partnership/.

28. Sajjanhar, 'India–Central Asia Relations'.

29. Sajjanhar, 'India–Central Asia Relations'.

30. 'India, Iran and Afghanistan Sign Chahbahar Port Agreement', *Hindustan Times* (26 May 2016), http://www.hindustantimes.com/india/india-iran-afghanistan-sign-chabahar-port-agreement/story-2EytbKZeo6zeCIpR8WSuAO.html.

31. Bipul Chatterji and Surendar Singh, 'An Opportunity for India in Central Asia', *The Diplomat* (4 May 2015), http://thediplomat.com/2015/05/an-opportunity-for-india-in-central-asia/.

32. 'Turkmenistan-Afghanistan-Pakistan-India Pipeline' https://en.wikipedia.org/wiki/Turkmenistan%E2%80%93Afghanistan%E2%80%93Pakistan%E2%80%93India_Pipeline.

33. 'Afghan Taliban Offer to Protect Infrastructure Projects Including the TAPI Pipeline', *Hindustan Times* (30 November 2016), http://www.hindustantimes.com/world-news/afghan-taliban-offer-to-protect-infrastructure-projects-including-tapi-pipeline/story-0O8VK1ORfNrrvsMprOX2RM.html.

34. Zabiullah Muddabber, 'Afghanistan's Role in Central Asia–South Asia Energy Projects', *The Diplomat* (12 July 2016), http://thediplomat.com/2016/07/afghanistans-role-in-the-central-asia-south-asia-energy-projects/.

35. Pierre-Olivier Bussiers, 'New Alliances in Central Asia', *The Diplomat* (9 February 2016), http://thediplomat.com/2016/02/new-alliances-in-central-asia/.

36. Nivedita Das Kundu, 'India and Central Asia: Friendly Interactions', Valdai Discussion Club, 7 June 2016, http://valdaiclub.com/a/highlights/india-and-central-asia-friendly-interactions/.

37. Victoria Panfilova, 'Tajikistan May Hand over Aini Airfield to India', *Vestnik Kavkaza* (13 July 2015), http://vestnikkavkaza.net/analysis/Tajikistan-may-hand-over-Aini-airfield-to-India.html.

38. Association of South East Asian States, 'Overview ASEAN-India Dialogue Relations', 19 August 2016, http://asean.org/storage/2012/05/Overview-ASEAN-India-as-of-19Aug16-r3fn.pdf.

39. Ministry of External Affairs, Government of India, 'ASEAN-India Relations', November 2016, http://www.mea.gov.in/aseanindia/20-years.htm.

40. 'Bay of Bengal Initiative for Multi-Sectoral Technical and Economic Cooperation', https://en.wikipedia.org/wiki/Bay_of_Bengal_Initiative_for_Multi-Sectoral_Technical_and_Economic_Cooperation.

41. Ministry of External Affairs, Government of India, 'Mekong-Ganga Cooperation (MGC)', November 2016, http://mea.gov.in/aseanindia/about-mgc.htm.

42. US Department of State, 'Bandung Conference', https://history.state.gov/milestones/1953–1960/bandung-conf.

43. Vikram Nehru, 'Southeast Asia: Crouching Tiger or Hidden Dragon?' Carnegie Endowment for International Peace, 7 July 2011, http://carnegieendowment.org/2011/07/07/southeast-asia-crouching-tiger-or-hidden-dragon-pub-44964.

44. Somkiat Tangkitvanich and Saowary Rattanakhomfu, 'Assessing the ASEAN Economic Community', East Asia Forum, 21 March 2017, http://www.eastasiaforum.org/2017/03/21/assessing-the-asean-economic-community/.

45. Anna Louise Strachan, Harnit Kaur, and Tuli Sinha, 'India's Look East Policy: A Critical Assessment', IPCS South East Asia Research Programme, New Delhi, October 2009, http://www.ipcs.org/pdf_file/issue/SR85-SEARPInterview-Sikri1.pdf.

46. A. Sundaram, 'Look East Policy', *International Journal of Advancement in Research and Technology*, 2(5), http://www.ijoart.org/docs/Look-East-Policy.pdf.

47. Jane Perlez, 'Tribunal Rejects Beijing's Claims in South China Sea', *The New York Times* (12 July 2016), http://www.nytimes.com/2016/07/13/world/asia/south-china-sea-hague-ruling-philippines.html.

48. 'The Most Important New Alliance in Asia', *Tower Magazine* (18 September 2016), http://www.jewishpress.com/indepth/analysis/the-most-important-new-alliance-in-asia/2016/09/18/.

49. Express Web Desk, 'Modi in Israel: All that Happened During the PM's Historic Visit', *Indian Express* (6 July 2017), http://indianexpress.com/article/india/pm-narendra-modi-in-israel-benjamin-netanyahu-reuven-rivlin-all-that-you-should-know-about-this-historic-trip-4739085/.

50. Ben Caspit, 'Is Israel Forming an Alliance with Egypt and Saudi Arabia?' *Al-Monitor* (13 April 2016), http://www.al-monitor.com/pulse/originals/2016/04/israel-al-sisi-egypt-saudi-arabia-islands-transfer-alliance.html.

51. Rajendra Abhyankar, 'The Evolution and Future of India-Israel Relations', Harold Hartog School of Government and Policy, Tel Aviv University, Research Paper No. 6 (March 2012).

52. Nicholas Blarel, 'The Partnership That Dare Not Speak Its Name', in Sumit Ganguly (ed.), *Engaging the World: Indian Foreign Policy since 1947* (New Delhi: Oxford University Press, 2016), pp. 352–74.

53. P.R. Kumaraswamy, 'Israel: A Maturing Relationship', in David Malone, C. Raja Mohan, and Srinath Raghavan (eds), *The Oxford Handbook of Indian Foreign Policy* (London and New Delhi: Oxford University Press, 2015), pp. 539–51.

54. Fraz-Stefan Gady, 'Revealed: India Close to Signing $ 3 Billion Defence Deal with Israel', *The Diplomat* (10 February 2016), http://thediplomat.com/2016/02/revealed-india-close-to-signing-3-billion-defense-deal-with-israel/.

55. Ian Marlow, N.C. Bipindra, and Michael Arnold, 'On Israel Trip PM Modi has Massive Drone, Missile Deals', NDTV (4 July 2017), https://www.ndtv.com/india-news/on-israel-trip-pm-modi-has-massive-drone-missile-deals-to-consider-1720250.

56. Embassy of India, Tel Aviv, 'Bilateral Trade Relations', Embassy of India, Tel Aviv, January 2016, https://www.indembassy.co.il/pages.php?id=14#.WD3d9rIrKpo.

57. Israel Ministry of Economy and Industry, Foreign Trade Administration, 'Overview of India-Israel Bilateral Trade and Economic Relations', http://itrade.gov.il/india/israel-india/.

58. Sindhuja Balaji, 'Israeli Investors See Big Opportunities in India's Start-Up Community', Forbes (10 July 2017), https://www.forbes.com/sites/sindhujabalaji/2017/07/10/israeli-crowdfunding-platform-sees-big-opportunity-in-indias-start-up-community/#794a0db78716.

59. 'Israel Seeks FTA with India to Boost Trade', The Hindu (18 November 2016), http://www.thehindu.com/business/Israel-seeks-FTA-with-India-to-boost-trade/article16666692.ece.

60. P.R. Kumaraswamy, 'Israel: A Maturing Relationship', in David M. Malone, C. Raja Mohan, and Srinath Raghavan (eds), The Oxford Handbook of Indian Foreign Policy (New Delhi: Oxford University Press, 2015) http://www.oxfordhandbooks.com/view/10.1093/oxfordhb/9780198743538.001.0001/oxfordhb-9780198743538-e-39?mediaType=Article.

61. Israel Trade and Economic Office, Embassy of Israel India, 'Business Opportunities for Indian and Israeli Companies in the ICT Domain', http://itrade.gov.il/india/2016/09/08/business-opportunities-for-indian-and-israel-companies-in-the-ict-domain/.

62. Noor Dahri, 'Pakistan's Military Cooperation with Israel', The Times of Israel (7 February 2016), http://blogs.timesofisrael.com/pakistans-military-cooperation-with-israel/.

63. Kumaraswamy, 'Israel: A Maturing Relationship'.

64. Niharika Mandhana, 'Narendra Modi Taps Indian Diaspora in the US', Wall Street Journal (28 September 2014), http://www.wsj.com/articles/narendra-modi-taps-indian-diaspora-in-u-s-1411946161.

65. Somini Sengupta, 'Indian Diaspora Is the World's Largest at 16 m: UN', The Times of India (14 January 2016), http://timesofindia.indiatimes.com/world/us/Indian-diaspora-is-worlds-largest-at-16m-UN/articleshow/50569762.cms.

66. 'India's Policy towards Her Diaspora and Diasporic Issues in the Region', Chapter 5, p. 158, shodhganga.inflibnet.ac.in/bitstream/10603/16671/10/10_chapter%205.pdf.

67. 'Sirima-Shastri Pact', https://en.wikipedia.org/wiki/Sirima%E2%80%93Shastri_Pact.

68. V. Suryanarayana, 'The Indian Community in Myanmar', *Defence India Forum* (DFI), Paper No. 352, 26 November 2009, http://defenceforumindia.com/forum/threads/the-indian-community-in-myanmar.7100/.

69. 'Expulsion of Asians from Uganda', https://en.wikipedia.org/wiki/Expulsion_of_Asians_from_Uganda.

70. Rajendra Abhyankar, *Stuff Happens: An Anecdotal Insight into Indian Diplomacy* (New Delhi: Har Anand Publications Pvt. Limited, 2013), pp. 212–22.

71. 'India World's Largest Remittance Recipient in 2015, World Bank', *The Times of India* (14 April 2016), http://timesofindia.indiatimes.com/business/india-business/India-is-top-remittance-recipient-of-2015-World-Bank/articleshow/51822766.cms.

72. Neela Banerjee, 'In Jews, Indian Americans See a Role Model in Activism', *The New York Times* (2 October 2007), http://www.nytimes.com/2007/10/02/us/02hindu.html.

73. 'India Caucus a Pillar of Support for India–US Ties: Ambassador Arun Singh', *The Economic Times* (11 June 2015), http://economictimes.indiatimes.com/news/politics-and-nation/india-caucus-a-pillar-of-support-for-india-us-ties-ambassador-arun-singh/articleshow/47624978.cms.

74. 'Record Number of Indian-Origin MPs Elected to UK Parliament', *The Times of India* (8 May 2015), http://timesofindia.indiatimes.com/nri/other-news/Record-number-of-Indian-origin-MPs-elected-to-UK-parliament/articleshow/47207051.cms.

75. European Parliament, 'India Delegation', http://www.europarl.europa.eu/delegations/en/d-in/home.html?page=3#delegation_menu.

76. 'British Indian', https://en.wikipedia.org/wiki/British_Indian.

77. Ministry of External Affairs, Government of India, 'Pravasi Bharatiya Divas', https://www.mea.gov.in/pravasi-bharatiya-divas.htm.

78. Bengaluru Bureau, 'Pravasi Bharatiya Divas 2017', *The Hindu* (10 January 2017), http://www.thehindu.com/news/cities/bangalore/Pravasi-Bharatiya-Divas-2017/article17017220.ece.

CHAPTER
SEVEN

India's Diplomatic Apparatus

*T*he first time that a foreign policy issue was discussed in the public arena was in March 2013 during the US invasion of Iraq. 'The division in the United Nations Security Council meant that the US had to go it alone. A number of approaches were made to the Indian government, both officially and publicly, which led the entire issue to finally come out in the Indian media and on the streets of New Delhi, Lucknow and elsewhere.'[1]

Three months after the fall of Baghdad, in its newfound ardour for India, the Bush administration mounted relentless pressure on the Indian government to send troops to northern Iraq to help them with policing and other security tasks. There was little appreciation of the different contexts of region, religion, politics, economics, and society that any government in India would have to wrestle with in taking such decisions.

The Indian government was in a difficult situation. There was a division in Prime Minister Atal Bihari Vajpayee's inner cabinet. There was also no clear assessment of the *quid pro quo* of sending Indian troops, at Indian expense, in an area of Iraq where the troops could come into confrontation with Iraqi militia. The issue involved not only India's close relations with Iraq but also had to deal with the anger on the Indian street against the United States. Important questions arose on how the government would handle public pressure if even one Indian soldier was killed or if Indian troops were placed under foreign command.

This was complicated by the Bush administration's initiatives to build India's global standing, eschewing the negativity in the bilateral relationship after India's 1998 nuclear tests. The issue became a matter of public debate as various opposition political parties, and other interests saw it as a peg on which to hang their anti–US and anti–BJP stance. While the Vajpayee government was engaged in looking for a way out of this dilemma, it was also concerned that the parliament should not take any decision that would adversely affect the government's flexibility of action. No amount of filibustering was able to obviate a discussion with the political parties represented in parliament.

The heated debate in the media and public demonstrations forced the government to call for a meeting of all political parties to explore a *via media*. The situation was dire for a government that was looking at electoral successes in the heartland states of Uttar Pradesh and Bihar. The two points of discussion in the all-party meeting were the manner in which the US action was to be referred to in the parliamentary resolution and whether India could send troops to Iraq as part of the United States army. A heavily acrimonious meeting eventually led to an agreement on a resolution which 'deplored', rather than 'condemned', the US invasion of Iraq and decreed that Indian troops could go to Iraq only under a UN mandate and command.[2] US' Iraq invasion was not under a UN mandate and hence it closed the option for then and in the future.[3]

The debate over sending Indian troops to Iraq on Indian streets was demonstrative of an increasing trend of foreign policy moving from the rarefied echelons of the government into India's body politic. Henceforth it became de rigueur for political parties in the government and the opposition to exploit the public sphere to determine foreign policy discussions and decisions by the parliament. At the same time, Indian elections are rarely decided on foreign policy issues. Neither are issues of alliances, grand strategies, international stature, weapon development, acquisitions, and alliances discussed in the public domain unless the issue has the potential to politically embarrass the ruling party or can be politically exploited by the opposition.

The only exception was the Bofors acquisition[4] that became a cause célèbre, leading to the downfall of the Rajiv Gandhi government. In the last three decades, there has been an increasing watering down of the belief that 'historically, the lack of salient foreign policy issues within wider Indian political culture and the insularity and elitism of Indian foreign policymaking processes have positioned Indian foreign policy elites as the primary, though not exclusive, producers of India's foreign policy discourse'.[5] The number of players in the foreign policy sphere has also increased.

The Parliament

It is not surprising that discussions on the making of the Indian constitution had no dedicated session on foreign policy.[6] It could have been due to Jawaharlal Nehru's commanding presence in the making and implementation of India's foreign policy and the fact that the subject was assigned to the Union List in the Constitution. Dr. B R. Ambedkar, who as Law Minister was the architect of the Indian Constitution, had very definite and contrary views on India's foreign policy precepts. He was critical of some of the foreign policy initiatives of Nehru and put forth alternative thoughts on foreign policy. He spoke of China's insidious intentions and importance of building ties with America.[7]

In the last two decades, the two houses of the Indian Parliament—the Lok Sabha and the Rajya Sabha—have seen foreign policy issues being taken up by opposition parties more to embarrass the government than to discuss a matter of substantive policy. Neither has there been an effort by any political party in office to inform the house, and the country, on any particular issue through a White Paper. Only in limited cases, where it was incumbent on the government either to avoid or dissipate controversy that governments have resorted to *suo moto* statements on specific issues in the house.

The traditional relationship of partnership between the government and the opposition in parliament, as the highest body, to provide a full rationale for an integrated view of foreign and domestic policies has withered. The parliament has become a reactive player in foreign relations and not 'an avant garde organization which seeks a widening of political opportunities both at home and abroad by visualizing foreign policy, as an area of accommodation and legitimate compromise, to clarify the consequences of new developments in scientific, technological, cultural and educational spheres, apart from the purely political and strategic developments'.[8] Similarly, the parliament's Consultative Committee on External Affairs has dealt more with the Ministry of External Affairs (MEA)'s budget and cultural outreach than discussed policy. Yet, as described below, at times the parliament has proved effective in reining in, or setting exacting standards, for the government in power on specific foreign policy issues.

History

Soon after independence, there was no discussion on the parliament's role in foreign policy though much time was spent on the discussion of India's joining the Commonwealth. As foreign policy was in the Union List, with the central government having complete powers on its making and implementation, there appeared to be no incentive to discuss the subject. Furthermore, since the Indian constitution provides no parliamentary approval for ratification of treaties or on the declaration of war, these opportunities were also not open to the members to debate or approve. Only in case of the government's action to cede or acquire territory is it necessary to secure a two-thirds approval in both houses of parliament. Some important instances follow in successive paragraphs.

Soon after the Chinese invasion in 1962, public opinion forced the government to place the full correspondence between Jawaharlal Nehru and Zhou Enlai, the Chinese prime minister, on the table of the house. The government was also required to do the same for granting China concessions for the use of Aksai Chin (which they eventually captured militarily) and on the possibility of swapping Aksai China for NEFA, now the state of Arunachal Pradesh.

Similarly, despite India–Pakistan talks in 1962–63, on exchanging enclaves located in a small section of the India-East Pakistan (now Bangladesh) borderland in the former princely state of Cooch Behar (now the name of a district in the Indian state of

West Bengal), no progress could be made as it needed a two-thirds vote in both the houses of the parliament. It was only in 2013 that the 19th Constitutional Amendment was enacted to settle the matter with Bangladesh.

The long period seen in the case of the Bangladesh enclaves was indicative of the fractured composition of the parliament in the intervening years and the difficulty of getting two-thirds majority in both houses. India and Bangladesh formally exchanged 162 enclaves on 1 August 2015, ending a century-old territorial anomaly and completing a process of land and population exchange that began in the 1950s.[9] The same situation will arise if ever India and Pakistan decide to have substantive discussions on Kashmir. The inalienable nature of Kashmir's accession to India is a matter of a Lok Sabha resolution. Only a two-thirds majority can reverse it if there is call to give up India's claim to PoK.

The other remarkable instances were the 12th Amendment Act to the Constitution incorporating Goa into Indian territory and the 36th Amendment Act recognizing Sikkim as India's 22nd state.

Present

In the last decade, although the US–India Agreement on Civil Nuclear Cooperation did not need parliamentary approval it led to a no-confidence motion in the Lok Sabha against the United Progressive Alliance (UPA) government following the withdrawal of the CPM from the government coalition. In their view, the agreement was the thin end of the wedge in bringing India into a treaty-type relationship with the United States. The no-confidence motion could be defeated only after the Congress was able to persuade the BJP and Samajwadi Party (SP) to vote for the agreement.[10]

The Civil Liability for Nuclear Damage Act 2010 or the Nuclear Liability Act, a highly debated and controversial act that aims to provide civil liability for nuclear damage, was passed by both the houses of the Parliament after considerable controversy. This was one of the final steps to activate the 2008 Indo–US civilian nuclear agreement. American nuclear reactor manufacturing companies will require the liability bill to get insurance in their home state. The act provides for prompt compensation to the victims of a nuclear incident through a no-fault liability to the operator, appointment of claims commissioner, the establishment of a Nuclear Damage Claims Commission, and for matters connected therewith or incidental thereto.

> This was followed by New Delhi's intent to have a nuclear insurance pool to take care of the liability of operators and suppliers. The insurance pool of Rs 1,500 crore was launched in June 2015 with some Indian insurance companies and a British insurance partner. Beyond Rs 1,500 crore, the liability will be borne by the Indian government up to Rs 2,610 crore and beyond that, India will be able to access international funds under the CSC [Convention on Supplementary Compensation for Nuclear Damage]. This step has opened the doors to India's nuclear commerce.[11]

The act effectively caps the maximum amount of liability in case of each nuclear accident at Rs 5 billion (USD 74 million) to be paid by the operator of the nuclear plant, and if the cost of the damages exceeds this amount, special drawing rights up to USD 300 million will be paid by the central government.[12] The opposition insisted, this time with resonance on both sides of the house, on specifying the extent of damages liability on the foreign contractor because of the allegedly meagre compensation (USD 470 million) paid for the gas disaster in Bhopal on 2–3 December 1984 leading to the death of 2,259–3,787 persons (estimates vary) and 558,125 injuries including 38,478 temporary partial blindness and 3,980 severe and permanent disability. The genetic defects from the tragedy were in some cases carried forward to future generations.[13,14]

Parliament has also become the scene for inter-party jousting on a foreign policy issue. An example was when Prime Minister Manmohan Singh had to withdraw from attending the 2013 Commonwealth Summit to placate the Tamil party Dravida Munnetra Kazhagam (DMK)[15] which had taken a hard stand on the LTTE–Sri Lanka government war. The government and opposition parties have used, more often than not, foreign policy in parliament as a hook to assert their point of view rather than a *suo moto* examination of its content and direction on a specific foreign or defence policy issue. The tradition set up since Jawaharlal

Nehru, of foreign and defence policies being the prerogative of the prime minister, has kept the discussion out of public debate.

The 'surgical strike' in June 2015 by Indian commandos on Naga insurgent camps in Myanmar[16] and the Indian Army's similar attack on 28 September 2016 against terrorist camps in PoK[17] became the subjects of controversy. With the Pakistan government denying the strike inevitably it became controversial in the Indian parliament. While the government did disclose details of the strike, the opposition appeared intent to debunk the government. This demonstrated a new tendency on part of the opposition parties to question government action in such cases, which proved the absence of unity on national security issues.

Regional Interests

With regard to regional interests as well, political parties, whether in power or opposition, have used foreign policy issues to extract their pound of flesh in domestic political terms rather than contribute positively to policy-making. Largely, the state legislatures have had no direct role in the making of foreign policy that remains firmly within the competence of the union government. Nevertheless, legislatures in Indian states have served the purpose of regional political parties to agitate, seek action, filibuster, or exact a quid pro quo from the Union government for people from their states abroad. It has been most in evidence in states neighbouring SAARC countries, like Tamil Nadu on the Sri Lanka Tamil issue, West Bengal on the water issue, border, and illegal migration from Bangladesh, or Kerala on Malayali populations working abroad when they are in distress.

Thus, despite close people-to-people relations between Tamil Nadu and Sri Lanka, or Bihar and Uttar Pradesh and Nepal and Bhutan, there has been little attempt to incorporate them into the foreign policy framework. As a result, these states have become disruptors rather than constructors of the bilateral relationships with the contiguous states.

The Government

The Indian cabinet is finally responsible for the formulation, clearance, and implementation of India's foreign policy. The Cabinet

Committee on Security headed by the prime minister has ministers responsible for External Affairs, Defence, Home, and Finance as its members.

MEA

The government's primary instrument is the MEA for proposing and executing India's foreign policy. The MEA[18] maintains 171 Indian Missions (2010) abroad, largely manned by officers of the IFS. It is relatively less prone to outside political influence as it is primarily run by the bureaucracy. It continues to suffer from important handicaps stemming from a shortage of trained officers.

Although the MEA has had a policy planning division since the 1970s, often led by eminent people such as G. Parthasarathy[19] at its head, the division has been unable to catalyse independent thinking and research on medium- and long-term issues facing India. A part of the problem arises from turf issues, with the 'territorial divisions' unwilling to interact in a meaningful way with the policy planning division. The graver difficulty arises from the fact that there is an unclear demarcation of the relationship between the territorial and policy planning division. No amount of effort and ideas has succeeded in finding a workable and beneficial solution to this issue.

The ministry primarily relies on its territorial divisions to drive the bilateral relationship. Depending on the countries included in each territorial division, the chain of command may run up to the foreign secretary or one of the other secretaries responsible. The secretaries themselves report directly to the minister of External Affairs. The foreign secretary as *primus inter parus* heads the ministry at the bureaucratic level. Government action to make good the long-standing criticism that the IFS[20] was understaffed has sought to be corrected in recent years.

The increase in the annual intake of officers to service, coupled with the increase in the entry age limit has brought about salutary changes. First, most entrants to the IFS are not, as earlier, from large cities and well-known universities. The intake is broader now, based on regional, language, and economic diversity, and is truly reflective of an integrating India. Second, the increase in entry age means that a majority of new officers have previously held other jobs and been in other professions, mainly in medicine, industry, and consultancy, making them more aware of the country they will represent. Third, a majority of entrants have acquired their university degrees in engineering and management, sciences and medicine, increasing the need for focused instruction in foreign affairs and diplomacy. These changes have gone a long way in the effort to build a foreign service that will be able to handle India's needs in the 21st century.[21]

Yet the complexity of relationships covering a wide range of subjects has meant that other ministries and departments of the government also have a crucial role. Further, at least with India's major partners, the Prime Minister's Office (PMO) has become the formulator, collator, director, and decision-maker on major foreign policy initiatives. At least since 1998, major foreign policy decisions have become concentrated in the hands of the national security adviser to the prime minister. He has also become the focal point of inter-ministerial consultations on issues dealing with the P-5 members, particularly, the United States, China, Israel, and Pakistan and the Islamic countries. The government has also resorted to nominating special envoys when it feels that a particular region or an issue needs regular special handling beyond the bureaucratic level. There have been special envoys on West Asia, Pakistan, and on US-India Nuclear Agreement and climate change. There have also been special missions set up to the WTO and to the Committee on Disarmament in Geneva. At the same time, the MEA has not incorporated the practice of recruitment through 'lateral entry' at different levels although pressure in its favour is building up. It raises questions of inter se seniority and future career prospects of the IFS officers. The prime minister's prerogative to appoint ambassadors from outside the service has, however, continued.

The making and implementation of Indian foreign policy depends on the relative ranking of a country in India's foreign policy. Four circles of countries invariably get continuous high-level attention through a channel starting from the foreign secretary to the NSA to the prime minister. The inner-most circle is that of India's neighbours encompassed within SAARC—countries that

have an immediate and direct impact on India and on populations in contiguous Indian states. The next circle comprises the
P-5 who as permanent members of the Security Council have a
major impact on Indian foreign policy and their policy vis-à-vis
countries in the first circle and others with whom India has
important relations. The third circle comprises countries that have
close relations with India vis-à-vis politics, trade, and investments
such as the members of the G-4 grouping, EU and ASEAN.

The fourth circle covers countries in India's extended neighbourhood in the Persian Gulf, including Iran and Iraq because
of historicity and the intensity of current contact based on politics, religion, oil, investment, and people-to-people relations. The
fifth circle comprises countries of Africa and their organizations
like the African Union, of Central Asia, and others in the Asia-
Pacific, Europe, and South America. In the case of this circle, more
often than not, the MEA does the running on the making and
implementation of foreign policy, except when a head of state or
government visit is being planned.

With a plethora of ministries dealing with the formulation
of foreign policy, the common criticism relates to the cumber-
some and time-consuming structure that militates against quick
decisions; the lack of institutional capacity to plan, monitor, and
synthesize policy; and the insular and opaque nature of decision-
making. As a result, Indian foreign policy has been called status
quo-ist and suffers from 'cognitive disability' or unwillingness to
break the mould. As explained above, after nearly three decades of
pursuing an 'internationalist' mind-set, Indian foreign policy has
embraced a growing sense of 'realism' in emphasizing areas and
issues that directly affect the interests of the country and people.

Media

Cable News Network's (CNN) almost blow-by-blow coverage of
the first Gulf War 1991 was a watershed moment in news report-
ing, particularly of war and terrorism, which quickly enough got
imitators.[22] Suddenly, no source of information could deliver
news faster than CNN. It raised a new challenge to the foreign
policy establishment by instantaneously bringing both news and

opinions from the far corners of the world. The subsequent multi-plication of satellite-based news channels tested the limits of exist-ing methods of foreign policymaking. With time, this got even more complicated by the easy access to social networking sites such as Facebook and Twitter. It provided an instantaneous means to anyone with an access to a computer or smartphone the ability to put out an opinion—right or wrong.

It has been a mixed blessing for India. The plethora of print and electronic media and social networking sites has facilitated the dissemination of the government's views on a specific issue while making it easy for anyone to voice an opinion on a foreign policy issue. However, Indian foreign policy-makers have found the new media to be overall beneficial. Everyone—from Prime Minister Modi to the ministers heading important ministries—has taken to the new media. Remarkably, Foreign Minister Sushma Swaraj has effectively used these channels to act on urgent issues distressing Indians abroad.[23]

At the same time, the lack of India's own news assets abroad has meant an excessive reliance on foreign news media. An attempt was made during the second Gulf War, with some success, but not longevity, to set up an Indian television channel called the Third Eye airing on Doordarshan, the government-owned TV's foreign news channel, to project Indian views internationally.[24] This remains a major lacuna in India's news projection overseas. The reasons are not far to seek. In spite of having 82,237 daily newspapers (2011) in Hindi, English, and other major languages;[25] 190 government television channels; and 1,970 permitted private satellite TV channels,[26] the Indian public shows no great inter-est in foreign affairs except in countries with important Indian diaspora.

Neither have Indian media and TV channels aimed at building up viewership based on informing and shaping public opinion. It has been more disruptive, often forsaking national interest, as in the case of the Tamil Tigers in the 1980s, the Mumbai terror attack or the terrorist incident at Pathankot airbase most recently. During the Mumbai terror attack it was 'equally horrifying on November 26 2008 other than the attack of course was watching the scores of television journalists trying to outdo each other in terms of

Breaking News, knowing very little that they were doing nothing but compromising national security. The handlers in Pakistan who were in the control room at Karachi got live updates of the operations and they kept improvising as a result of which the operation dragged on for hours together.'[27]

Countries like the United Kingdom have a 'D Notice' policy that is observed by all news media even in these days of digital media and social networking sites.[28] Once the government puts out a D Notice about any news item all media is required to stop any reports on that subject. The need for such a procedure in India remains a felt need.

In general, Indian media has followed the government's lead on particular foreign policy issues, though not always. During the various stages till the final steps which led to the India-US Civil Nuclear Agreement (2008), the media was supportive of the government, while it took a contrary view on the India-Pakistan Statement at the Sharm El-Sheikh[29] which seemed to give credence to Indian intelligence activity in Balochistan. The strong opposition in the media to the statement saw Prime Minister Manmohan Singh's attempt to revive India-Pakistan talks fail. On the other hand, despite the media blowing up the issue of Chinese incursions across the LoAC (2007–08), the government continued its low-key non-confrontational policy in line with the 1993 agreement to maintain tranquillity on the India-China border.[30]

Prime Minister Modi's outreach to people and countries, ignored or taken for granted by New Delhi, has changed the practice of Indian diplomacy. Although there are more news and TV coverage of his visits abroad, and of other leaders visiting India, it remains largely true that most issues are no longer exclusively viewed through the prism of Pakistan. The Modi government has clearly charted a path where it seeks to engage the world on India's terms, and not let Pakistan dominate the narrative of India's perception of the world.[31]

In a broad sense, the influence of media over foreign policymaking is limited because it does not have adequate access to information while the quality of reportage veers on the sensational rather than placing premium on analytical reportage.

Think Tanks and Universities

It is only in the last decade that Indian think tanks have become more prolific in putting out research on foreign policy issues of concern to the decision-making levels of the government. The Indian Council of World Affairs, the oldest think tank on foreign policy in India, is an adjunct of the MEA and serves as its connection to the academic community on foreign policy. Yet in these cases too they have been hamstrung by the fact that most think-tanks, especially the Delhi-based ones, rely on funding from government ministries or agencies. The only privately funded think tanks are the Ambani-financed Observer Research Foundation and the Thapar-funded Ananta Aspen Centre, Centre for West Asian Studies, Jamia Millia Islamia, in Delhi, Gateway House, Indian Council on Global Relations in Mumbai, the Kunzru Centre for Defence Study and Research, Pune, and a few others in Pune, Chennai, and Bengaluru.

The backward linkage between the think tanks and universities and their forward linkage to the MEA still needs to be built up. So far, as the academia—universities with international relations department and study centres focusing on different regions—is concerned, academic writing on foreign policy issues is largely theoretical and not always policy oriented. It detracts from their usefulness for foreign policy-making. It is still not possible for the National Archives of India (NAI) and the Nehru Memorial Museum & Library (NMML) to give unbridled access to Nehru's papers which still are the best sources for details on the early formation of Indian foreign policy.

The MEA has made limited effort through its public policy and policy-planning divisions to bring in specialists to work on different areas and subject issues and create a greater awareness by arranging lectures at selected universities on specific subjects. It also has a dedicated officer of the rank of Joint Secretary to foster and manage relations with the states of the Indian Union.

Public Opinion

In the foreign policy sphere, public opinion is used *ex ante* to prepare the ground and *ex post facto* to inform, convert, or justify a particular policy or action. From this perspective, public participation in India is flawed because the public is neither aware, nor interested in a set of values by which to judge a foreign policy action—and equally importantly, nor is it given a range of policy options to choose from.[32]

The only time that the public can express its opinion on a foreign policy issue is at election time—but this topic has rarely been deciding factor in the outcome of the elections. Nevertheless, a foreign policy issue can be used to stir up the support of vote banks which can affect state or general elections. The best example is the Sri Lanka Tamil issue used since 1983 in Tamil Nadu state elections by both the DMK and the AIADMK (All India Anna Dravida Munnetra Kazhagam)[33] to not only win the state but also, between 1983 and 2014, to achieve posts in central government coalitions.[34] Clearly, the exploitation of the Sri Lanka Tamil issue in the state elections has rarely yielded major dividends to that community in their struggle for civic and political rights.[35] Similarly, the issue of fishing rights for Tamil fishermen in the Palk Strait, around the island of Katchatheevu which was ceded to Sri Lanka as part of the 1974 Indo Sri Lanka Maritime Boundary Agreement also generates political steam, particularly during the time of elections in the state.[36]

Similarly, relations with Bangladesh have played an important role in public opinion and state elections in West Bengal and Assam. The issue of the sharing of river water has always been used by political parties in West Bengal both to filibuster agreements as well as to garner favours from the party and government at the centre.[37] The issue of illegal migration, which affects both Assam and West Bengal, has always been a plank in state elections, and has been used both by state and national parties.[38] The inflow of Myanmar's Rohigya Muslims, through Bangladesh, to India has become the latest issue to be agitated in the press after Prime Minister Modi's position during his visit to Myanmar from 5–7 September 2017.[39]

India's relations with Nepal have always underpinned the discourse during state elections in Bihar, because the state gets water from Nepal's dams and, more recently, when the Madhesis, residents of the Nepali flatlands bordering Bihar, felt ignored during the country's constitutional crisis.[40]

In J&K, when an India–Pakistan dialogue is ongoing, or is expected, it has a favourable effect on the electoral turnout and the fortunes of major national political parties; however, disruption of dialogue or terrorist attacks favour local parties.[41] The Indian government's position, after the Uri terror attacks, that it would only talk on terrorism with Pakistan has had much airing in the media.[42]

Nevertheless, the perceived fear of public opinion—whether sectional or national—has deterred the government at times from pursuing dialogue or concessions with China, Bangladesh, Pakistan, and Sri Lanka. The government has to also keep in view the sensitivities of certain states and sections of the population before embarking on negotiations or new initiatives with any of India's neighbours. This was evident in the DMK pressure on the central government on its decision on Sri Lanka in the UN Human Rights Council (2008), the West Bengal government's pressure on signing the Teesta Accord, or pressure from the Kerala government in the case of Italian marines jailed for killing Indian fishermen off the Kerala coast (2011). The arrest of Indian diplomat Devyani Khobragade by New York police in 2013 led to a period of bitter acrimony and downturn in India-US relations. It demonstrated that regardless of the country the impact on anticipated public opinion in encouraging or disrupting relations has to be factored in.

India faces considerable challenges in its neighbourhood with outstanding issues, particularly border agreements with China and Pakistan, the issue of Kashmir, and others with Sri Lanka and Nepal. An important reason for the long delay in settling the issue of adverse possession of enclaves with Bangladesh was due to perceptions of public opinion. Interestingly, the government finds itself in a catch-22 situation: settling an outstanding issue improves overall tenor of public opinion, while catering to it can prevent that solution. Even the best conjuncture for moving forward could be blocked by the force of public opinion.

With continuous political and social ferment in the country, other ministries, media, political debate, and public opinion have begun to erode the traditional insularity and isolation of the foreign policy elite. The fact that foreign policy has descended into the public space will not only enable diverse views to be articulated as inputs to foreign policy-making but engender greater government accountability.

Notes

1. Rajendra Abhyankar, *Stuff Happens: An Anecdotal Insight into Indian Diplomacy* (New Delhi: Har Anand Publications Pvt. Limited, 2013), p. 167.

2. Devirupa Mitra, 'How India Nearly Gave in to US Pressure to Enter the Iraqi Killing Zone', *The Wire* (8 July 2016), http://thewire.in/50028/india-nearly-gave-us-pressure-join-iraq-war/.

3. Amit Baruah, 'No Troops for Iraq without Explicit UN Mandate: India', *The Hindu* (15 July 2003), http://www.thehindu.com/2003/07/15/stories/2003071505870100.htm.

4. 'Bofors Scandal', https://en.wikipedia.org/wiki/Bofors_scandal.

5. J. Bandyopadhyaya, *The Making of India's Foreign Policy*, Second Edition (New Delhi: Allied Publishers Ltd, 1979).

6. Rudra Chaudhuri, 'The Parliament', in David Malone, C. Raja Mohan, and Srinath Raghavan (eds), *The Oxford Handbook of Indian Foreign Policy* (London and New Delhi: Oxford University Press, 2015), p. 220.

7. Harish Parvathaneni, 'What if Ambedkar Had Shaped India's Foreign Policy', *The Indian Express* (14 March 2009), http://indianexpress.com/article/opinion/columns/what-if-ambedkar-had-shaped-indias-foreign-policy/. The author is working on a study of Ambedkar's views on foreign policy.

8. M.L. Sondhi, 'Parliament and Indian Foreign Policy', 24 July 1976, http://mlsondhi.org/Indian%20Foreign%20Policy/PARLIAMENT%20AND%20INDIAN%20FOREIGN%20POLICY.htm.

9. Hosna J. Shewly, 'India and Bangladesh Swap Territory, Citizen in Landmark Enclave Exchange', Migration Policy Institute, 9 March 2016, http://www.migrationpolicy.org/article/india-and-bangladesh-swap-territory-citizens-landmark-enclave-exchange.

10. Bidyut Chakrabarty and Sugato Hazra, *Winning the Mandate* (New Delhi: SAGE Publications, 2016).

11. Subhajit Ray, 'Ratifying Nuclear Convention: Road from "Intent" to "Commitment"', *The Indian Express* (15 February 2016), http://indianexpress.com/article/explained/ratifying-n-convention-road-from-intent-to-commitment/.

12. 'Nuclear Liability Act', https://en.wikipedia.org/wiki/Nuclear_Liability_Act.

13. 'Bhopal Disaster', *Encyclopedia Britannica* (11 November 2015), https://www.britannica.com/event/Bhopal-disaster.

14. 'Bhopal Disaster', https://en.wikipedia.org/wiki/Bhopal_disaster.

15. 'Dravida Munnetra Kazhagam', https://en.wikipedia.org/wiki/Dravida_Munnetra_Kazhagam.

16. 'Maynmar Operations: 70 Commandos Finish Task in 40 Minutes', *The Hindu* (10 June 2015), http://www.thehindu.com/news/national/myanmar-operation-70-commandos-finish-task-in-40-minutes/article7302348.ece.

17. Bill Rogio, 'Indian Commandos Strike Terrorists inside Pakistan-occupied Kashmir', *Threat Matrix* (29 September 2016), http://www.longwarjournal.org/archives/2016/09/indian-commandos-strike-terrorists-inside-pakistan-occupied-kashmir.php.

18. Government of India, Ministry of External Affairs organizational chart. It gives basic information on the work distribution and levels in the Ministry of External Affairs, http://www.mea.gov.in/divisions.htm.

19. A.P. Venkateshwaran and Kapila Vatsyayana, 'Remembering GP, the Gentle Colossus', *The Hindu* (7 July 2012), http://www.the-hindu.com/opinion/op-ed/remembering-gp-the-gentle-colossus/article3610515.ece.

20. Prakash Nanda, 'Indian Foreign Service in Desperate Need of Reform Particularly When It Is Losing Relevance', Firstpost (9 August 2016), http://www.firstpost.com/world/indian-foreign-service-in-desperate-need-of-reform-particularly-when-it-is-losing-relevance-2943924.html.

21. Sudha Ramachandran, 'The Indian Foreign Service: Worthy of an Emerging Power?' *The Diplomat* (12 July 2013).

22. Ali Abunimah and Hussein Ibish, 'The CNN of the Arab World Deserves Our Respect', *Los Angeles Times* (22 October 2001), https://electronicintifada.net/content/cnn-arab-world-deserves-our-respect/3960.

23. Washington Post, 'Sushma Swaraj: Social Media Savvy Indian Foreign Minister Excels as "Supermum of State"', *Gulf News* (22 November 2016), http://gulfnews.com/news/asia/india/sushma-swaraj-social-media-savvy-indian-foreign-minister-excels-as-supermum-of-state-1.1885872.

24. 'Allies Hound Saddam with Bunker-Buster Bombs', *The Tribune* (9 April 2003), http://www.tribuneindia.com/2003/20030409/main1.htm.

25. 'India Has 82237 Newspapers, 4853 Registered in 2010–11', Yahoo News (29 December 2011), https://in.news.yahoo.com/india-82237-newspapers-4853-registered-2010-11-121003100.html.

26. 'List of Television Stations in India', https://en.wikipedia.org/wiki/Lists_of_television_stations_in_India.

27. One India staff writer, '26/11 Mumbai Terror Attack: More Horrifying than the Attack was the TV Coverage', *One India* (26 November 2014), https://www.oneindia.com/feature/26-11-mumbai-terror-attack-media-role-responsibility-1572960.html.

28. Naomi Grimley, 'D for Discretion: Can Modern Media Keep a Secret?' *BBC* (22 August 2011), http://www.bbc.com/news/uk-politics-14572768.

29. Liz Mathew, 'Rewind to Sharm el-Sheikh Statement 2009: Shame, Compromise Said BJP When Manmohan Used B-Word', *The Indian Express* (16 August 2016), http://indianexpress.com/article/india/india-news-india/pm-narendra-modi-balochistan-independence-day-bjp-manmohan-singh-2977533/.

30. Manoj Joshi, 'The Media in the Making of Indian Foreign Policy', in David Malone, C. Raja Mohan, and Srinath Ranganathan (eds), *The Oxford Handbook of Indian Foreign Policy* (New Delhi: Oxford University Press, 2015), pp. 259–70.

31. Sunil Raman, 'PM Modi's Foreign Policy Breaking New Grounds: Is the Current Media Coverage Enough?', Firstpost (1 November 2015), http://www.firstpost.com/india/pm-modis-foreign-policy-breaking-new-grounds-is-the-current-indian-media-coverage-enough-2490802.html.

32. Devesh Kapur, 'Public Opinion', in David Malone, C. Raja Mohan, and Srinath Raghavan (eds), *The Oxford Handbook of Indian Foreign Policy* (London and New Delhi: Oxford University Press, 2015), pp. 298–311.

33. Kumar Chellappan, 'Lanka a Non-Issue as TN Goes to Polls Tomorrow', *The Sunday Times*, Colombo (14 May 2016), http://www.sundaytimes.lk/160515/news/lanka-a-non-issue-as-tn-goes-to-polls-tomorrow-193909.html.

34. T. Ramakrishnan, 'Sri Lanka Interest in TN Politics Wanes', *The Hindu* (23 April 2016), http://www.thehindu.com/elections/tamilnadu2016/sri-lankas-interest-in-tn-politics-wanes/article8510265.ece.

35. *Eye Sri Lanka*, 'TN Leaders Asked Not to Ese Tamil Issue' (26 April 2016), http://www.eyesrilanka.com/2016/04/26/tn-leaders-asked-not-to-use-tamil-issue/.

36. V. Suryanarayana, 'The India-Sri Lanka Fisheries Dispute: Creating a Win-Win in Palk Bay', *Carnegie India* (9 September 2016), http://carnegieendowment.org/files/Suryanaryanan_Fisheries_Dispute_.pdf.

37. Harun ur Rashid, 'West Bengal and Assam Election Results and Its Impact on Bangladesh', *South Asia Monitor* (26 May 2016), http://southasiamonitor.org/detail.php?type=vign&nid=17261.

38. Aparna Chandrashekhar, 'Migration from Bangladesh: A Humanitarian Issue Highly Politicized in West Bengal', Firstpost (15 April 2016), http://www.sundaytimes.lk/160515/news/lanka-a-non-issue-as-tn-goes-to-polls-tomorrow-193909.html.

39. Prabhash K. Dutta, 'How Rohingyas Reached India and Why Government is Not Ready to Let Them Stay', *India Today* (7 September 2017), http://indiatoday.intoday.in/story/rohingya-muslims-myanmar-india-aung-san-suu-kyi-narendra-modi/1/1042724.html.

40. Kathmandu, 'Bihar and Blockade', *Republica* (4 November 2015), http://admin.myrepublica.com/opinion/story/30634/bihar-and-blockade.html.

41. 'Unrest in Kashmir Steps India and Pakistan on Edge', STRATFOR (5 April 2016), https://www.stratfor.com/analysis/unrest-kashmir-sets-india-and-pakistan-edge.

42. Dhritiman Ray, 'Government Should Initiate Dialogue with Pakistan on Kashmir, says Sushil Kumar Shinde', *Times of India* (26 May 2017), https://timesofindia.indiatimes.com/india/government-should-initiate-dialogue-with-pakistan-on-kashmir-says-sushil-kumar-shinde/articleshow/58861644.cms.

CHAPTER
EIGHT

Setting Course for the Future

The Making of Foreign Policy

The theme of this book has been to assess the extent to which India has gone beyond its operating principle of 'strategic autonomy', which is defined as 'relating to or characteristic of strategy.'[1] 'Strategic Autonomy refers to a foreign policy posture, whereby a nation maintains independent outlook and orientation in foreign affairs with respect to the issues defining her core strategic interests.'[2] Only a state with overwhelming superior power has the wherewithal to exercise complete strategic autonomy. The practice of strategic autonomy is equally dependent on the power capabilities of a state in a particular historical era in international relations.

In a multipolar world characterized by shifting international relations, as at present, even a superpower's ability to dictate outcomes becomes relative. The greater the multipolarity in international relations, the greater does it benefit powers like India. At the same time, an operating principle has meaning only in the context of an avowed strategy.

The earlier chapters have highlighted that India has finally gone beyond its avowed operating principle of strategic autonomy by stating the goals which it has sought to achieve. Prime Minister Manmohan Singh articulated a set of goals that would guide the practice of India's foreign policy practice. Prime Minister Narendra Modi has carried the idea forward in re-calibrating goals of India's foreign policy. The epilogue makes an assessment of the success that India has achieved in meeting its stated goals.

There is no gainsaying the fact that India's status as a global player today entirely due to its sustained high annual rate of economic growth since 1996. Without it, India would still be mired in the development trap of the 1960s and 1970s. By the same token, unless India capitalizes on the window that it now has, the danger of regressing into that trap, like Argentina in the 1960s and Brazil in the 1970s, is real.

Non-Alignment

India had to structure its foreign policy in the light of the changing circumstances both internationally and nationally. Was India's commitment to non-alignment real or a posture? How much did India use it to promote its self-interest? After independence, India managed to avoid joining the Cold War power blocs and becoming enmeshed in their power struggle. Pakistan's joining the Western pacts with alacrity strengthened India's resolve. Indian leaders were left with trying an as-yet untried option of staying equidistant.

Non-alignment, which had its origin in India's colonial experience and the non-violent independence struggle, made it possible for India to be the master of its fate in an international system dominated politically by Cold War alliances and economically by Western capitalism and Soviet communism. The idea of being the master of its fate has always been the beacon guiding Indian's foreign policy projection ever since.

The policy of non-alignment articulated by Nehru and his successors and the refusal to align with any bloc or alliance were meant to preserve India's freedom of action internationally; in fact, Indian leaders preferred non-violence and international cooperation as a means of settling international disputes. After Independence in 1947 non-alignment became an identifying feature of Indian foreign policy and enjoyed a strong, almost unquestioning, support among the Indian elite. It was not until the 1955 Bandung Conference of Afro-Asian States that the idea of a non-aligned movement of countries, not belonging to either of the power blocs, came to fruition.[3] It was in 1961 that the first conference of non-aligned countries was held, in Belgrade.

On the plank of non-alignment, India was able to attract other recently liberated countries as well who wished to concentrate on their internal policies rather than become aligned with either superpower. India remains committed to achieving peace through the legitimate framework of the UN and is one of the highest global contributors of peace-keeping troops, a status marker frequently invoked when arguing for increased participation, including permanent membership of the UNSC. Traditionally non-alignment has remained the chosen principle of India's for-eign policy although there have been changes of emphasis under succeeding Indian prime ministers. The 1974 nuclear test under Indira Gandhi and Rajiv Gandhi's activist policy towards Sri Lanka or Manmohan Singh's opening up to the United States were not always underwritten by the Indian elite.

After the Cold War

After 1990, India's foreign policy projection had to adapt to the United States' overarching status as the only superpower and leader of the global order. It led to the introduction of a realistic tilt in its *soi-disant* non-aligned foreign policy. At the same time, it brought home that India's foreign policy would have to relate to its multidimensional character. India also recognized that the responsibility for the security of one billion people rested solely with the Indian government. Neither would India benefit from a nuclear umbrella, unlike Australia, New Zealand, or Israel.

Its interpretation of non-alignment, however, did not exclude India taking measures to enhance its own security or develop-ment agendas. Thus, despite its continuing moral opposition to nuclear weapons and support for a peaceful global order, India tested nuclear weapons in 1974 and again in 1998. The latter tests were the watershed. Even the India–US Civil Nuclear Agreement would not have been possible without India's impeccable record on the use of nuclear power. The nuclear tests of 1998 unlocked relations with the US and like-minded Western countries as it 'destroyed the illusion that New Delhi could somehow be coaxed out of pursuing the ultimate currency of great power status. Once the illusion evaporated the US and India could begin to relate to one another on a more realistic footing'.[4] More importantly, it changed the way in which the world looked at India and led to an upward spurt in relations with other major powers and those of West Asia, the Gulf, and ASEAN.

The movement away from non-alignment, in its strictest sense, has also been seen in India's defence posture. India had always been aware that the nexus between China and Pakistan had resulted in its neighbourhood becoming progressively dangerous. The clandestine development of nuclear weapons by Pakistan, its export of nuclear technology to North Korea, Libya, and Iran, and the nuclear and missile nexus between China and Pakistan threatened India. Accordingly, India was forced to enhance its defence profile by upgrading, planning, and cooperating in defence and defence procurement and export with selected countries, including the P-5. For the first time, in 2004, India started a regular interaction with NATO which had started its 'out-of-area-role' in Afghanistan.[5] Since then, despite the EU's strides in building its defence profile, NATO has become a corollary of EU membership and in some cases has preceded its membership. India's defence cooperation agreements and MoUs cover selected countries and include joint exercises on land, sea, and air. Some of these agreements have also led to the acquisition of advanced defence weaponry, particularly from the United States and Israel, diversifying its sourcing away from Russia.

India also devoted its resources to expanding the reach of Indian naval power into the Gulf and the Malacca Strait. Until the IOR becomes a fulcrum of India's foreign policy posture and until it learns to manage its north-western and north-eastern strategic priorities effectively, without turning them into declarations in IOR politics, India's global diplomatic persona will still look incomplete.

India's membership in restrictive groupings such as the G-4, BRICS, and the New Quad in the WTO signifies its intention to be a part of alliances that further its interests even though

they are exclusionary for the majority of the Global South.
The inclusion of the BRICS and other purpose-built groups in global hierarchies has partially legitimized these structures; yet there is an increasing awareness that India will need to temper its 'duality' in major groupings. Such selective coalition-building and the willingness to lead these flexible alliances have stood India well. These organizations have created a new paradigm for cross-continental cooperation between emerging economies and impart a degree of dynamism to the international order. It could help to give a new impetus to finding solutions to global issues such as climate change, pandemics, trade, energy, security, and resource scarcity.

At the same time, the dilemma of adopting a proactive approach, which will detach it from the Global South, remains. The dilution of its image as a spokesman for the developing countries demonstrates a streak, missing earlier, of overtly pursuing its self-interest. Yet India's proactive stance in these groupings augments its capacity to shape international outcomes.

Similarly, the G-20 Leaders' Summit also reflects a North–South configuration of power that is more pluralist compared with the G-7/G-8. The G-20 process equally enhances the collective perceptions of exclusion and marginalization on the part of small developing states.

The 'cognitive disability' from which India has suffered since the Cold War was articulated by Brajesh Mishra, national security adviser, when he suggested that India needs 'a new organizing principle'[6] for the practice of its foreign policy. India's joining selective groupings has shown that it is no longer afraid of doing deals which enhance its security and growth with new partners across the economic, political, and military spectrum.[7] It demonstrates a movement towards defining the core content of its foreign policy which will be guided by the principle of strategic autonomy,[8] which means an independence of orientation in its core interests.[9] Prime Ministers Manmohan Singh and Narendra Modi have tried to delineate the goals which India's foreign policy must achieve.

Manmohan Singh's five principles[10] gave primacy to India's economic development in stating that it shaped India's relations with the world. Indian foreign policy's objective, therefore, was to 'to create a global environment conducive to the well-being of our great country.'[11] India will seek greater integration with the world economy to benefit its people and seek stable, long-term, and mutually beneficial relations with all major powers. It will promote greater regional cooperation and connectivity in South Asia, acknowledging its shared destiny. Finally, India's foreign policy will be defined as much by its values as by creating a plural, secular, and liberal democracy.

In clearly enunciating the connection between India's development and security Prime Minister Manmohan Singh placed India's foreign policy as one instrument in the government's armoury to achieve its goals. The great reliance on globalizing India's path to its economic growth and enhanced status, at whatever the cost, went against previous ideas of autonomy more geared to restriction and self-sufficiency. India's entry into the nuclear club through the US–India agreement on civil nuclear cooperation was entirely due to Manmohan Singh's courage in pushing the deal in the parliament despite domestic opposition. Yet the landmark development was dissipated as India didn't move forward on operationalizing it until this was accomplished by Narendra Modi.

The low rate of economic growth marked by high inflation and fall in the rupee value during Manmohan Singh's second term was equally responsible for a lacklustre performance in India–US relations. Two visits to India by President Obama kept the relationship coasting along without any major developments, and India still remained excluded from restrictive nuclear regimes. Manmohan Singh's foreign policy doctrine nevertheless established that an activist Indian foreign policy, driven by its democratic values, would be a net positive for regional and global security. The vision it represented made up for the lacunae in India's foreign policy stemming from the absence of a clear set of goals against which to match outcomes. The growing proximity to the US did not find favour with the Indian public.

India had benefited from the economic turbulence which shook the world economy in 2008 and whose effects still linger. It enabled India to assert its economic power seen in its role in the G-20 as well as in smaller groupings such as IBSA, BRICS, and G-4; Bangladesh, Bhutan, India, and Nepal (BBIN); BIMSTEC- and

ASEAN-based groupings like the EAS, ARF, ADMM, and MGC; and other groupings like SCO, GCC, FIPIC, and CELAC. India's plurilaterals with Russia and China, Brazil and South Africa, Japan and Australia, and Iran and Afghanistan showed a willingness to interact with partners on common interests and issues without hoping for an understanding across-the-board. India's foreign policy projection had diversified to keep up with the prevailing international setting.

Narendra Modi's foreign policy activism, since he took office in May 2014, has been remarkable and continued a forward path. He has made 56 foreign tours[12] of which the US four times, eight countries twice and 36 countries once. He visited Afghanistan and Nepal twice; China, France, and Russia (among the UNSC permanent members); Japan (part of the G-4); Singapore (South-east Asia); and Uzbekistan twice. His visits were either bilateral or for attending conferences of international or regional groupings of which India is a member. Often these visits have incorporated both elements. The intensity with which India has tried to develop its bilateral relations with these countries would classify Modi as a 'foreign policy prime minister'. Modi's foreign tours have been seen as the fulcrum of his government's foreign policy, aimed at increasing India's international profile and garnering development FDI, technology inputs, and creating limited groups to move India's foreign policy goals forward.

Prime Minister Modi sought to explain the goals and motivation behind his activism in the foreign policy domain in 2017 at the second edition of the Raisina Dialogue[13] considered analogous to other regional security forums, including the Shangri-La Dialogue and the China-hosted Xiangshan Forum. This was further elucidated by Foreign Secretary Dr. Subrahmanyam Jaishankar at the same conference.[14] The current uncertainty in international relations arises from 'a global stock-taking going on and must approach it with empathy, rather than anxiety. We should also recognise that this is not so much global change, as change with global implications.'[15] Taken together, the two speeches lay down the foreign policy focus of the country in a difficult international situation which has been marked by volatility in growth with dangers from unstoppable migration and protectionist attitudes. It has put the gains of globalization at risk.

In United States since the Trump presidency and in Europe in general there is a fatigue with 'openness' and a tendency to close international initiatives in trade and migration fuelled by terrorism and 'unequal' trade arrangements. There is a lack of commitment to tackle global issues such as terrorism, climate change, the security of weapons of mass destruction and cyber-security—all of which have become major dangers to settled polities.

Narendra Modi, like his predecessor, gives primacy to the role of foreign policy in India's transformation, recognizing that the external context is integral to its development and security. Thus, 'rebuilding connectivity, restoring bridges to immediate and extended geographies',[16] and 'shaping relations networked with India's economic priorities'[17] through 'development partnerships'[18] spanning the globe becomes its overarching goal. Interestingly, Modi's view of India's foreign policy goals specifically mentions 'building India as a human resource power and creating Indian narratives on global challenges and helping to reconfigure and rebuild global institutions and organisations'.[19]

In specifically highlighting the need to make India an international human resource power, Modi has focused on the enmeshing of India's security and foreign policy to attain an ever-expanding capability and prosperity of the Indian people. This appears to derive from Amartya Sen's 'human development approach',[20] further elaborated by Martha Nussbaum[21] as 'creating and enhancing, in its widest sense, the capabilities of the people'. The application of the capabilities approach to the practice of India's foreign and security policy acknowledges that providing secure and sustainable economic, political, and social development to India's population is an overarching goal of the government. It equally highlights that jobs and security will remain the priority focus.

In stating that India will take a role in rebuilding global institutions and organizations and create Indian narratives on global challenges, Modi has given a proactive character to Indian foreign policy. It recognizes that world politics is in transition from bipolarity to a new as yet indeterminate international order

and the possibility of China rising to the top is not in the too
distant future. China's rejection of the international award on
the South China Sea is the first sign. A new version of bipolarity
may be on the cards. Will India and China be able to continue
their dual projection of a developed and a developing country?
India's giving up its earlier hesitation in activism in global governance increasingly reflects its determination that it has a role
to play at the global level and in its own interest.

As Modi put it, 'Institutions and architectures built for a different world, by a different world, seem outdated.'[22] In further
elaboration, it was stated that

> the absurdity of the main multilateral decision-making body
> being more than 70 years old—and due for retirement anywhere
> in the world—is obvious to all except those with a vested
> interest. There can be no getting away from the myriad of global
> challenges that will eventually require a credible multilateral
> response. The pressures to reform the UN will only grow with
> each passing day.[23]

It would also appear to convey India's intention to take on a role in
keeping with its international ambitions. It gets away from India's
outsider mentality which derived from a reluctance to assume
roles that are not reflective of its identity as a leading developing
country. The Indian system will henceforward be more focused
on finding an outcome rather than sticking to a forum or formal
arrangement.[24] India expects to count on broad support from
many nations, regions, and groupings with whom it has built up
relations of support and mutual benefit.

Prime Minister Modi has made specific comments on various
regions, particularly on South Asia and China. With neighbours,
rebuilding connectivity and bringing India closer to them remains
a primary objective. This will have to be achieved by ensuring that
their right to development is not abridged but nurtured. It would
also include removing long-standing problems as was done with
Bangladesh. India will have to proactively be a force for development in the neighbourhood rather than pursue the exclusion
of other powers from the region. Similarly, India needs to keep
its focus on the Gulf countries where the remittances by seven

million Indians working there equals that of India's exports of IT products.

The growth in China's power will remain a dynamic factor in Asia and India will have to deal with it. Despite major differences on the border and the China–Pakistan nexus in nuclear and missile technology, the two countries have been working together in BRICS and on climate-change negotiations. China's OBOR project and the 'string of pearls' strategy to place its ports in the waters surrounding India have created a new challenge. India will need to intensify its arc of influence in the IOR well beyond its littoral limits. India's initiative on Security and Growth for All in the Region initiative (SAGAR) is intended to deepen its maritime relations and freedom of navigation.

It is accepted that it is not unnatural for two large neighbouring powers to differ in the management of their relations, yet it remains moot whether China will accept India's contention that both countries need to show sensitivity and respect for each other's core interests. The visit to Arunachal Pradesh from April 4 to 11, 2017 of the Dalai Lama is clearly a red rag to China. It has responded by threatening to make a solution to the border issue more difficult.[25] The decision to welcome the Dalai Lama in Arunachal Pradesh has been seen as New Delhi's way of showing its resentment towards China's intransigence on the issues of listing Pakistan-based cleric Masood Azhar in a UN list of terrorists, India's entry into the NSG, and the movement of the China-Pakistan Economic Corridor (CPEC) despite New Delhi's concerns that a few projects under it will be in PoK.[26]

Notwithstanding Modi's two visits to Beijing, India-China relations will continue to be tense despite growth in bilateral trade. China's growing power, extending into the ASEAN and the Gulf countries, has become an important component of India's threat perception. India has normalized its trade relations with China and ensured tranquillity on the India-China border while developing a separate track for the boundary question. If the Trump administration continues with increase in US involvement in the Asia-Pacific, India will need to look at creating space between the United States and China rather than being forced to take sides at this stage. Its seeming strategic ambivalence towards China is rooted in the fact that for India, taking a side now could impact peace and tranquillity on the India–China border.

India has maintained good defence relations with Russia and still considers it a trusted and strategic partner, especially in defence. This is notwithstanding Russia's recent overtures to Pakistan in holding military exercises and supply of defence hardware. Russia's reluctance at the BRICS meeting in Goa in joining in the condemnation of terrorism sponsored from Pakistan was telling. The most recent in a string of spiralling retaliation was the rejection by China of the Russian proposal to hold a meeting of defence ministers of the three countries belonging to the RIC grouping. This came on the heels of the visit by Dalai Lama to Arunachal Pradesh.[27]

India recognizes that deep fissures between the United States and Europe leading to the erosion of unity in the Western camp could signal the strengthening of multi-polarity. To a considerable extent, these fissures can be traced to the on-going war in Syria in which the West has taken different positions—both of principle and on the ground. The resulting massive refugee crisis, an increase in terrorist attacks in Europe and United States attributed to the ISIS, and a good number of American and European youth joining the ISIS have deeply impacted these countries. Yet India has cemented its relations with the United States, the United Kingdom, and France although its 'reluctance to enter into military alliances and interfere in the affairs of other states' continues.[28] India is unlikely to shift to wholesale alignment with powerful countries, particularly those in the west.

Despite Nawaz Sharif's presence in May 2014 at Modi's swearing-in ceremony and the latter's impromptu visit to Lahore on 25 December 2016 there is no likelihood of the bilateral dialogue between the two countries recommencing. As Prime Minister Modi has said, 'India alone cannot walk the path of peace. It has also to be Pakistan's journey to make. Pakistan must walk away from terror if it wants to walk towards dialogue with India.'[29] India's relations with Pakistan have continued in a see-saw fashion despite the sense that under the Modi government an inflexion has been introduced to assert Indian position. Early indications in the UNSC following the first India–Pakistan War (1947) made it clear that India was unlikely to find much joy there on the Kashmir issue. The Shimla Agreement by its exclusive reliance on bilateralism continues to assist India whenever the issue comes up in the Security Council.

Nevertheless, the continuing issue of 'hyphenation' between India and Pakistan by the United States and the United Kingdom continues despite monumental differences between the two countries on economic potential, nuclear capabilities, the practice of stable democracy, and a large dynamic middle class. On any matrix, Pakistan does not exceed 15 per cent of any of India's attributes. It has continued to support and direct terrorist groups targeting India and Afghanistan, patronized the Taliban in Afghanistan, and leaked nuclear weapon and missile technology information to North Korea and Iran.

The US 'hyphenation' between India and Pakistan, barring the Bush years (2001–09), has continued throughout the last decade. Pakistan will continue to measure itself against India in the future as well. India has got beyond the India–Pakistan box. It is a legacy of partition which cannot be overcome. In these circumstances the international preoccupation with the question of a nuclear war between India and Pakistan is inevitable. The sooner India comes to terms with it the better it will be for developing a robust Pakistan policy which could include calibrated retaliation to terror attacks, including readiness to cross the LoC, 'isolating' Pakistan internationally as an ongoing strategy, examining the possible leverage available through the Indus Waters Treaty, and the revocation of the NFU commitment.

At the same time, massive and immediate efforts are needed to bring Kashmir's population into the national mainstream. The fact that in April 2017 only 2 per cent of the population voted in the state bypoll in Srinagar is a matter of deep concern.[30] The Indian government on 24 October 2017 has appointed Dineshwar Sharma as interlocutor on Kashmir 'to initiate and carry forward a dialogue with elected representatives, various organisations and concerned individuals in the state of Jammu and Kashmir'.[31] The reactions to the appointment are mixed raising the question of whether it is tactical or substantive and whether it can succeed without a parallel dialogue with Pakistan.[32]

Continuing US interest in Afghanistan makes its transactional relationship with Pakistan inevitable. India will perforce have to work around it. While the United States has broadly accepted 'Indian exceptionalism', the Indian tilt towards the former that emerged after Pokharan II, also currently appears irreversible. Bilaterally, India's intensive relationship with the United States that transformed after the Clinton visit (2000) still shows signs of buoyancy assisted by the increasing political awareness of the Indian diaspora in the United States, India's prowess in IT, and the growing acquisition of defence materials from US manufacturers. At the same time, the India–US 'global partnership' has not moved to reduce the salience of the Pakistan factor.

The India–US Civil Nuclear Agreement and the United States' intention to work with India on three aspects of global non-proliferation—nuclear security, nuclear disarmament, and bilateral cooperation—to ensure India's entry into nuclear regimes such as the NSG, Missile Technology Control Regime (MCTR), and the Wassenaar group did not progress during the Obama years (2008–16). A number of other issues were also left without resolution during the Obama years like the goals of non-proliferation, defence agreements and procurement, the use of genetically modified foods, the openness of the Indian economy in the context of APEC, and the now in limbo, Trans-Pacific Partnership (TPP).[33] Much will depend on the stance which President Donald Trump will take. India's growing proximity to the United States has nevertheless had its influence on most other countries, increasing its salience in their policy. Apart from the countries in East Asia like Japan and South Korea and Australia and New Zealand one most notices this in India's relations with the Islamic world.

India's ambivalence to position itself as a prominent global actor appears to have been eclipsed. It still considers that the key challenge in engaging the world 'is to reconcile a quest for recognition from established major powers with a desire to maintain relations of solidarity with developing country allies of the Cold War era'.[34] It remains moot to what extent this duality of goals dilutes India's commitment and purpose. Nevertheless, India's nuclear tests in 1974 and 1998 and its being part of restricted purpose-built groups like G 20 or BRICS and IBSA is akin to 'great power mimicry'.[35] How long this will work remains moot.

> This strategy can be understood in terms of two competing, and at times overlapping, rising power practices, compliance with, and resistance to, the hegemonic norms and institutions of the existing international political and economic order.[36] Rising states, such as India, are therefore in the complicated position of needing to conform, at least partially, to the structure of power that has historically subordinated them.[37]

India's steadfast quest to secure a permanent seat in the UNSC has, nevertheless, been seen at variance with its championing third world issues. It has been read by some as acceptance of international oligarchy casting doubt about India's message that it was uniquely positioned to solve the problem of representativeness in the UNSC. India's claim to seek a permanent UNSC seat and to represent better the developing countries may sound hollow to developing countries, just as it could sound moralizing to the established powers. Yet given the present divisiveness in the interests of major global players and the unstable state of international relations, India's best option lies in pursuing its claim to the UNSC as presently structured and work from within.

Like the rest of the BRICS countries, India's emergence is inextricably linked to integrating to the institutions of the liberal order. Decision-making processes in these institutions favour a formal (IMF/World Bank) or informal (WTO) hierarchical structure where major powers dominate negotiating outcomes.

In this background, India's foreign policy ambition has been elucidated[38] thus:

- India's aspires to bridge global divides through 'non-aligned and multilateral engagement in a globally interdependent and economically integrated world.'[39] India acts as a bridge between the different regions of the world, serves to conceptually tether India to allies of the past and future, and introduces an element of dynamism through its synthesizing ability. India has used it to good effect in the G-4, G-20, BRICS, and IBSA, demonstrating its active engagement with a broad spectrum of stakeholders crucial to the country's global and domestic ambitions.

- Second, India's claim to knowledge leadership is based on its demographic dividend—a vast, young human capital that is considered the key to its continued productivity and growth.[40] In a vision of its soft power,[41] India sees itself as a norm-setter by example, rather than coercion, and as an innovator or inflector of particular forms of global knowledge and values.
- Third, India sees itself as an alternative power which seeks legitimacy both from the established powers and its developing country partners.[42] India's model of a secular democracy is expected to appeal as much to the Western liberal democracies as to democratic aspirations in the Arab and Muslim world. The concept of a 'civilian power' used for Germany[43] fits well within India's goal of transitioning into a global power which will perforce have to assume global responsibilities.

The cardinal idea behind the practice of India's foreign policy has been well summed up by India's National Security Adviser Shivshankar Menon (2011) of 'a power that works for development, peace and international understanding, in its own interest and in that of its friends and partners abroad'. Its dynamic element comes from 'its use of multilateral institutions and economic cooperation to achieve its foreign policy goals, its aversion to [the] use of military force, only in a multilateral context and in limited circumstances, thereby helping to strengthen international norms'.[44]

As emerging powers, like India, climb to ascendency they can be expected to chafe at or question existing rules and norms. They will require, as Henry Kissinger said, to devise an international agreement on 'the nature of workable arrangements about permissible aims and methods of foreign policy'.[45] It may be time for India to initiate this dialogue.

In coping with the process of establishing for itself a niche in the transforming world, India's mechanism for strategic thinking has increasingly harnessed its equities in different parts of the world and taken a cohesive view, in terms of its foreign policy goals, of the practice of its foreign policy. A more robust strategic consciousness and readiness to accept linkages across issues will further its goals. This will have to be achieved within a continually growing economy by developing the greatest synergy between its foreign policy and domestic policies.

India will always remain fixed in the global consciousness. India's profile in the world is unique. In today's fractious world India has a lot to contribute. Its ethos of consultation and compromise has kept India together. The problems that beset India are its own—whether it is poverty or infrastructure or security—and India will have to tackle them on its own. India may have something to learn from others but it has to find its own solutions. India has to seize the moment, otherwise, the momentum will dissipate. India's mind-set has to change. Making India a world power is going to be a huge exercise. It has to be done now. Will India seize the opportunity to lead? After the post–Cold War shift from defensive unilateralism and hegemony to forward-looking multilateral leadership, India's organizing principle for its foreign policy must conform to its status as an emerging power.

To sum up: Indian diplomacy, in responding to an unstable world, needs to elucidate and articulate the goals of its foreign policy. Admittedly, some will be unmutable like non-aggression, non-intervention, and a steadfast recourse to peaceful solutions. Other goals will need to articulate India's foreign policy priorirties within a timeframe: be it five years or ten. Without the enunciation of these goals, the principle of strategic autonomy is at best an operating methodology of illusory impact.

Notes

1. English Dictionary and Thesaurus, English Collins Dictionary, http://dictionary.reverso.net/english-definition/strategic%20 autonomy.
2. Arunoday Bajpai, 'What is Meant by Strategic Autonomy with Respect to India's Foreign Policy?' *Quora* (6 October 2016), https://www.quora.com/What-is-meant-by-Strategic-Autonomy-with-respect-to-Indias-foreign-Policy.
3. 'The Non-Aligned Movement: Description and History', 12 December 2015, http://internationalrelations.org/non-aligned-movement/.
4. Devin H. Hagerty, *South Asia in World Politics* (New York: Rowan & Littlefield, 2005).
5. Hriday Ch. Sarma, 'India & NATO: Partners in Arms?', *The Diplomat* (30 November 2016), http://thediplomat.com/2016/11/india-and-nato-partners-in-arms/.

6. MEA, 'Global Security: An Indian Perspective-Presentation at National Defence Institute, Lisbon by Brajesh Mishra', Ministry of External Affairs, Government of India, 13 April 2000, http://mea. gov.in/in-focus-article.htm?18909/Global+Security+an+Indian+P erspective++A+Presentation+At+National+Defence+Institute+Li sbon+by+Mr+Brajesh+Mishra.

7. David Brewster, 'End of Strategic Autonomy', *The Indian Express* (18 November 2014), http://indianexpress.com/article/opinion/ columns/end-of-strategic-autonomy/.

8. Kanwal Sibal, 'Strategic Autonomy as an Indian Foreign Policy Option', *The Indian Panorama* (8 May 2015), https://www.thein-dianpanorama.news/featured/strategic-autonomy-as-an-indian-foreign-policy-option-article-35231.html#.WOz3flXyupo.

9. Varghese K. George, 'Modi in America: "Strategic Autonomy", "Nonalignment" in His Diplomatic Lexicon', *The Hindu* (5 June 2016), http://www.thehindu.com/opinion/Modi-in-America-%E2%80%98 Strategic-autonomy%E2%80%99-%E2%80%98non-alignment% E2%80%99-in-his-diplomatic-lexicon/article14386295.ece.

10. Ankit Panda, 'Did India's Manmohan Doctrine Succeed?' *The Diplomat* (6 November 2013), http://thediplomat.com/2013/11/ did-indias-manmohan-doctrine-succeed/.

11. Ankit Panda, 'Did India's Manmohan Doctrine Succeed?'

12. PTI, 'Narendra Modi Made 56 Foreign Visits as PM: MEA', PTI, New Delhi, 5 April 2017, http://www.hindustantimes.com/india-news/narendra-modi-made-56-foreign-visits-as-pm-mea/story-tpzZvkjL6HeZ7BRDQwFTZO.html.

13. FP Staff, 'PM Narendra Modi Inaugurates Second Raisina Dialogue: Here the Full Text of the Speech', Firstpost (17 January 2017), http://www.firstpost.com/india/pm-modi-inaugurates-raisina-dialogue-in-delhi-read-full-speech-here-3208182.html.

14. PTI, 'China's Power Dynamic Factor in Asia: Full Text of Foreign Secretary Jaishankar's Speech at Raisina Dialogue', *Hindustan Times* (24 January 2017), http://www.hindustantimes.com/india-news/china-s-power-dynamic-factor-in-asia-full-text-of-foreign-secretary-jaishankar-s-speech-at-raisina-dialogue/story-g7 Fxz82vcDzRnvkqHrqemK.html.

15. MEA, 'Speech by Foreign Secretary at Second Raisina Dialogue' Ministry of External Affairs, Government of India, 18 January 2017, http://mea.gov.in/Speeches-Statements.htm?dtl/27949/Speech_ by_Foreign_Secretary_at_Second_Raisina_Dialogue_in_New_ Delhi_January_18_2017.

16. 'PM Narendra Modi Inaugurates Second Raisina Dialogue: Here's the Full Text of the Speech', Firstpost (17 January 2017), http://www.firstpost.com/india/pm-modi-inaugurates-raisina-dialogue-in-delhi-read-full-speech-here-3208182.html.

17. 'PM Narendra Modi Inaugurates Second Raisina Dialogue: Here's the Full Text of the Speech', Firstpost.

18. 'PM Narendra Modi Inaugurates Second Raisina Dialogue: Here's the Full Text of the Speech', Firstpost.

19. 'PM Narendra Modi Inaugurates Second Raisina Dialogue: Here's the Full Text of the Speech', Firstpost.

20. Amartya Sen, *Development as Freedom* (Anchor Books, 2000).

21. Martha Nussbaum, *Creating Capabilities: The Human Development Approach* (New York: Belknap Press, 2013).

22. 'PM Narendra Modi Inaugurates Second Raisina Dialogue: Here's the Full Text of the Speech', Firstpost.

23. 'PM Narendra Modi Inaugurates Second Raisina Dialogue: Here's the Full Text of the Speech', Firstpost.

24. Hindustan Times.

25. K.J.M. Verma, 'Dalai Lama's Arunachal Visit Negatively Impacts Border Dispute, says China', *Live Mint* (13 April 2017/28 October 2017), http://www.livemint.com/Politics/HKJs8LIGHbl2e9r6d07BiK/China-says-it-will-take-further-action-after-Dalai-Lamas.html.

26. Sutirtho Patranobis, 'Dalai Lama's Arunachal Visit Likely to Hurt India-China Ties Say Experts', *Hindustan Times* (8 April 2017), http://www.hindustantimes.com/india-news/chill-ahead-in-india-china-ties-over-dalai-s-arunachal-visit-experts-warn/story-cwHN-fOfGTmIOiDpu00IXlK.html.

27. Alexander Korablinov, 'China Snubs Russian Request for Trilateral Defence Meetings with India', *Russia Beyond the Headlines* (12 April 2017), http://rbth.com/international/2017/04/12/china-snubs-russian-request-for-trilateral-defense-meeting-with-india_740367

28. Sumit Ganguly (ed.), *India as an Emerging Power* (London: Frank Cass, 2003), http://discuss.forumias.com/uploads/FileUpload/6a/167cf4808d926ab3a30abc965da92f.pdf.

29. 'PM Narendra Modi Inaugurates Second Raisina Dialogue: Here's the Full Text of the Speech', Firstpost.

30. 'Srinagar By Poll: Only 2% Turnout Recorded after Re-polling in Kashmir', *Hindustan Times*, http://www.hindustantimes.com/india-news/srinagar-by-election-only-2-02-voter-turnout-recorded-after-repolling-in-kashmir/story-3lCTvA4P1sYB4eXo4EeRjM.html.

31. PTI, 'Dineshwar Sharma Formally Appointed Centre's Interlocutor for Jammu and Kashmir', *The Economic Times* (25 October 2017), https://economictimes.indiatimes.com/news/politics-and-nation/dineshwar-sharma-formally-appointed-centres-interlocutor-for-jammu-and-kashmir/articleshow/61220284.cms.

32. Manoj Joshi, 'The History of Dialogue in Kashmir Does Not Inspire Confidence in Delhi's Latest Move', Observer Research Foundation, 25 October 2017, http://www.orfonline.org/research/the-history-of-dialogue-in-kashmir-does-not-inspire-confidence-in-delhis-latest-move/.

33. Kevin Granville, 'What is TPP? Behind the Trade Deal that Died', *New York Times* (23 January 2017), https://www.nytimes.com/interactive/2016/business/tpp-explained-what-is-trans-pacific-partnership.html.

34. Kate Sullivan, 'India's Ambivalent Projection of Self as a Global Power: Between Compliance and Resistance', in Kate Sullivan (ed.), *Competing Visions of India in World Politics: India's Rise beyond the West* (London: Springer, 2015), http://www.palgrave.com/us/book/9781137398659, p. 15.

35. Phillip Nell, Dirk Nabers, and Melanie Hanif, 'Regional Powers and Global Redistribution', Routledge, 22 March 2016, https://books.google.com/books?id=w73OCwAAQBAJ&pg=PA100&lpg=PA100&dq=great+power+mimicry+in+international+relations&source=bl&ots=_MwSSMTf7G&sig=30CMoOQ1rWhXLyXOZjUE4emJ350&hl=en&sa=X&ved=0ahUKEwjcpdyo1pHXAhUIw1QKHSo6Bp0Q6AEITjAH#v=onepage&q=great%20power%20mimicry%20in%20international%20relations&f=false.' Once a state reaches the level of middle power or emerging great power theory and practice show that they tend to behave in a way which maintains the status quo-calling for incremental reform or within-change at times but shying away from systemic or transformational change which could ultimately be detrimental to themselves.' 'India no longer needs the comfort of third world solidarity.... Making the old radicalism unnecessary.'

36. Sullivan, 'India's Ambivalent Projection of Self as a Global Power: Between Compliance and Resistance'.

37. Sullivan, 'India's Ambivalent Projection of Self as a Global Power: Between Compliance and Resistance'.

38. Sullivan, 'India's Ambivalent Projection of Self as a Global Power: Between Compliance and Resistance'.

39. Sullivan, 'India's Ambivalent Projection of Self as a Global Power: Between Compliance and Resistance'.

40. N. Nilekani, *Imagining India: Ideas for the New Century* (New Delhi: Penguin, 2003), https://www.amazon.in/Imagining-India-Ideas-New-Century/dp/0143067079.

41. Joseph S. Nye Jr, *Soft Power the Means to Success in World Politics* (New York: Public Affairs, 2004), www.publicaffairsbooks.com/book/soft-power/jr-nye/9780786738960.

42. Sullivan, 'India's Ambivalent Projection of Self as a Global Power: Between Compliance and Resistance'.

43. 'Civilian power' in the German context means that unlike a great power, Germany uses multilateral institutions and economic cooperation to achieve its foreign policy goals and avoids the use of military force except in limited circumstances and in a multi-lateral context. It thus helps to 'civilize' international relations by strengthening international norms. India and Germany, approaching their common ideas from either end, have both espoused non-aggrandizement, eschewing the use of force, maintaining the sovereignty of other countries and supporting a multilateral international power structure. As India moves into the ranks of the global economic powers it could well adopt the categorization of a 'civilian power' instead of non-alignment as perfectly incorporating what it stands for in the 21st century. H. Kudnani, 'Germany as a Geo-Economic Power', *Washington Quarterly*, 34(3), https://csis-prod.s3.amazonaws.com/s3fs-public/legacy_files/files/publication/twq11summerkundnani.pdf.

44. H. Kudnani, *The Paradox of German Power* (Oxford: Oxford University Press, 2015), https://global.oup.com/academic/.../the-paradox-of-german-power-9780190245504.

45. Henry Kissinger, *World Order* (Penguin, 2014), https://www.penguinrandomhouse.com/books/316669/world-order-by-henry-kissinger.

Epilogue: Indian Foreign Policy under Narendra Modi

> James Hacker: Foreign affairs are a complicated business, aren't they?
> Sir Humphrey Appleby: Yes, indeed, Prime Minister. That's why we
> leave it to the Foreign Office.
> *From the British serial 'Yes, Minister', 1980*

Since assuming the office in May 2014, Prime Minister Narendra Modi has devoted much of his time and effort to the practice of India's foreign policy rather than leaving it to his Ministry of External Affairs.[1] At his inaugural address to the second Raisina Dialogue held on 17 January 2017 in New Delhi, Modi articulated the foreign policy goals his government has pursued while maintaining that India's 'choices and actions are based on the strength of our national power'.

India's strategic intent will be based on the 'civilizational ethos' of 'realism, co-existence, cooperation and partnership'.[2] On the basis of this operating principle determining its strategic choices he went on to delineate the foreign policy goals which his government has aimed at:

- Rebuilding connectivity, restoring bridges, and re-joining India with our immediate and extended geographies.

- Shaping relationships networked with India's economic priorities.
- Making India a human resource power to be reckoned with, by connecting our talented youth to global needs and opportunities.
- Building development partnerships that extend from the islands of the Indian Ocean and Pacific to the islands of the Caribbean and from the great continent of Africa to the Americas.
- Creating Indian narratives on global challenges.
- Helping re-configure re-invigorate and rebuild global institutions and organizations.
- Spreading the benefits of India's civilizational legacies, including Yoga and Ayurveda, as a global good. Transformation, therefore, is not just a domestic focus. It encompasses our global agenda.[3]

In over the three years that he has been in office, Indian foreign policy has seen a proactive stance[4] based on these goals with some successes and other noticeable misses. It will be appropriate to analyse whether this has meant a change of substance or merely of a nuance. Modi has said that 'our foreign policy is only about "India First"'.[5] In his period in office up to March 2017 he has visited 56 of which 36 countries once, eight twice, and the United States four times. By any reckoning, this is a remarkable achievement. Has the tenor of India's foreign policy changed in any way? In overall terms what does it mean for the way forward?

Goals

While comparing the foreign policy goals enunciated by Manmohan Singh and Narendra Modi[6] it is clear that the basic thrust of foreign policy remains the same; indeed it cannot be otherwise. Both have gone beyond the principle of strategic autonomy and emphasised that the security and prosperity of India's population have to be its primary target. Yet we see is a difference in emphasis and priorities. For Modi, an equally important goal is to enhance India's status in a world order going through major transformation in order that its development and growth targets continue to be realized. India's domestic objectives are woven into the practice of its foreign policy to confront major challenges it faces on the home front.

According to the World Bank 23.6 per cent or approximately 300 million people remain Below Poverty Line (BPL). The proportion of youth is bulging with 65 per cent of the population below the age of 35. This could be a time bomb waiting to happen 'if annually 12 to 15 million new jobs are not created for the next 20 years'.[7] India's status as a major human resource power, for the first time, has become a stated aim of its foreign policy. This means that major challenges are delivering high-quality formal education to seven million additional children each year, developing infrastructure which will require USD 200 billion annually, improve healthcare access, and cope with climate-change targets. All these will require a sustained long-term annual growth rate of 14 per cent in the non-agricultural sector. Much will, therefore, depend on the success of the 'Make in India' and 'Skill India' programmes.

What Did Not Work?

In the light of the foregoing narrative, a look at some of the major criticisms of Modi's foreign policy forays will set the scene for making a judgement. Some commentators have opined, largely because of the major failure in understanding the nature of civil violence in Kashmir, that the existing policy has been dismantled without putting anything in its place. That 'while using armed force to deal with the militant groups, there is need to simultaneously engage the political elements, either in Hurriyat or the National Conference in a dialogue process aimed at restoring normality to the state'.[8] Pakistan continues to provide political, moral, and material support to militancy and carries on a proxy war through jihadi armies—which have now concentrated on the Indian Army and police positions—which is only one aspect of a complex problem. The other, and possibly more important, problem is 'the rise of militant active in the Valley. According to Jammu and Kashmir police 80% of the militants in the north are not locals while in the south they comprise 80–90%'.[9]

The appointment on 24 October 2017 of Dineshwar Sharma, formerly head of India's internal intelligence agency, Intelligence Bureau, has two advantages over earlier interlocutors: first, there is a clear authority to whom he will report, and second, he is totally familiar with the Kashmir issue having dealt with it throughout his career. It suffers from three negatives: first, it is not clear whether this appointment is merely tactical to ward off international pressure; second, the absence of a parallel track dialogue with Pakistan given its varied potential to disrupt any such initiative; and third, whether an intelligence officer will have the breadth of vision needed to bring a viable solution to the table. It is also not known at this stage whether he has any ideas to offer underwritten by the government. Through this appointment the government, which continues a hard policy against militancy in Kashmir and talks with Pakistan, appears to convey that only the government can deliver improvement in prospects, within the Indian constitution, for Kashmir and its people. The government intends to continue its muscular policy towards the terrorists and the Army has stated that it will not affect its operations in Kashmir.

Pakistan's continuing cross LOC forays have neither been deterred by the 'surgical strike' nor has the effort to isolate the country been successful, largely because of its continuing relevance to the United States in Afghanistan and the fact that an increase of terrorist attacks in Turkey and various cities Europe has reduced the salience of the Indian situation. At the same time, India has found no joy from China, despite two visits by Modi, on its crucial concerns—the settlement of the border, the support for India's NSG membership, and the demand to proscribe Masood Azhar. Further, China, as an upper riparian state, with the origin of India's major rivers, including the Indus and Brahmaputra, in the Tibetan plateau has continued its dam-building activity to divert the Brahmaputra–Tsangpo waters to feed Beijing. This powerful weapon will also have to be taken into account should India decide to consider action against Pakistan to assert its position on the Indus Waters Treaty.

To make the Indian economy more attuned with receiving FDI and foreign investments under the 'Make in India' scheme, demonetization and the introduction of the Goods and Services Tax 'to replace(s) more than a dozen federal and state levies and unifying a $2 trillion economy and 1.3 billion people into one of the world's biggest common markets' was completed.[10] Despite the perceived negative fallout of both measures India's rate of growth in 2016–17 has been pegged at 7 per cent per annum.[11] The massive victory in the Uttar Pradesh state elections has buoyed the government's resolve to isolate Pakistan and has also seen rising impatience with China. The former is seen in the abandonment of any attempt to dialogue with Pakistan and the latter in disconcerting China with the presence of the prime minister of the Tibetan government-in-exile at Modi's swearing-in in 2014, the Doklam issue and the allowing of the Karmapa and the Dalai Lama to go to Tawang in 2017.

'Modi's foreign policy has been criticized as highly unpredictable and marked by flip-flops in relations with critical countries in the neighbourhood ... [he has also been accused] of making India dependent on the US.'[12] In 2016, India's relations with Pakistan and China went sour, or returned to normal, depending on the perspective. 'The year began with Pathankot and ended with the worst LoC violence in eight years.'[13] That 'Beijing, traditionally wary of taking stances on Indo-Pakistani disputes ... openly toes the Islamabad line'[14] can be explained by the fact that its major projects, such as the linking of Gwadar port, are coming on stream and prevarication on India's concerns matters less. At the formal meeting of OBOR countries on 14 May 2017 China said that it will still persuade India to join with Chinese President XI Jinping praising the USD 46 billion China-Pakistan Economic Corridor CPEC—which India has said violates its sovereignty—as its 'flagship' project, while promising to respect the territorial integrity of different countries.[15]

At the same time, in the four visits that Modi made to the United States and the two that President Obama made to New Delhi, the two leaders developed a rapport with the latter calling it the defining relationship of the 21st century. In the American view, the signing, at long last, of the LEMOA agreement which allows both the sides to access each other's military bases has not received enthusiastic support from Indian opinion-makers and analysts, notwithstanding the government's clarification that it is not a defence agreement and does not bind India. The fact remains that it will be the United States which will be using Indian military base facilities more. India's purchase of US defence equipment to the extent of USD 13 billion also introduces a new dimension in the bilateral relationship. When it comes to President Trump, however, India has received mixed signals on the bilateral relationship. For him, 'China is enemy number one ... and to contain it has already opened up the Taiwan card.... In Trump's worldview, India is almost non-existent.'[16]

Trump has made it clear that he would ban or make it hard for companies who engage in outsourcing and stop visa for foreign workers if they are a threat to American jobs. His upward review of minimum compensation for H1B visas and reducing their annual quota will affect India's IT service companies. It is unlikely that India will get much joy on increasing H1B and L1 visas for Indian professionals and continuing to allow social security payments to be repatriated to India after the visa holders' return. It hits at one of the innovative goals of India's foreign policy. Nevertheless, the Indian government continues to raise the issue most recently at the first U.S.–India bilateral Trade Policy Forum (TPF) under the Trump administration on 27 October 2017.[17]

'Trump has also made a U-turn on his promised harsher action against Pakistan'[18] mainly because of the decision to keep and increase US troops in Afghanistan. On a broader view it continues the prevailing level of insecurity for the country. 'After berating Pakistan for supporting terrorist groups in Afghanistan in a major foreign policy speech in August, US President Donald Trump seems to have softened his rhetoric after Islamabad facilitated the release of a Canadian-American family from militant-infested Waziristan over the weekend.'[19]

> While Trump-led America shows no sign of siding with India, India has lost the trust of an old and reliable friend like Russia and has ruined a working relationship and instead got engaged in an open confrontation vis-à-vis China. Since the Uri attack, Modi and his government have been boasting of isolating Pakistan internationally. The election of Donald Trump has brought that danger to India itself....[20]

Although Trump had expressed his desire to mediate the Kashmir dispute before he was elected speculation believes that with US naming on 27 July 2017 Hizbul Mujahideen chief Syed Salahuddin as 'Specially Designated Global terrorist Trump may have been taking steps to mediate in Kashmir.'[21] Reiterating

ment India responding to US UN Ambassador Nikki Haley said
India rejected the comments by the US ambassador to the UN
suggesting a proactive role for America in India–Pakistan ties,
saying the outstanding issues between the sub-continental neighbours should be sorted out bilaterally. 'The government's position
for bilateral redressal of all India–Pakistan issues in an environment free of terror and violence hasn't changed', the Indian
government said.[22]

What Succeeded?

Foreign policy initiatives take time to work out and are greatly
dependent on the ambient circumstances being favourable. In this
regard, the unsettled state of international relations provides the
setting to judge the results of Modi's foreign policy as the prime
mover of the practice of India's foreign policy.

> In a move of great symbolism emphasizing India's goal of building
> new relationships to meet India's international and domestic
> goals, Modi did not attend the 17th Nonaligned Summit from
> September 13-18, 2016 despite host Venezuela's repeated attempts
> to woo him. Instead he despatched Vice-president Hamid Ansari.
> Following Charan Singh in 1979, Modi was the second prime
> minister to miss the summit since the country co-founded the
> movement.... He has gradually but decisively shifted Indian foreign
> policy in directions which few would have dared to try before.[23]

As the Minister of External Affairs Sushma Swaraj has said,
'There is an overall loosening of relationships and even countries
that are formal allies are now hedging.'[24] Modi has decided, in
line with his enunciated goals that in the present state of international relations India has to pursue a policy of multiple alignments
strengthening its relations with all major powers and its neighbours. The successes of his foreign policy can be grouped under
the bridging of diplomacy and development, stressing relations
in the neighbourhood, stepping up interactions with the major
powers, and using purpose-built groupings to achieve India's
salience and broaden their scope to cater to its developmental
needs. The last three years have seen some important initiatives

in foreign policy aimed at pushing the strands of Modi's foreign policy goals.

India's 'initiative to create a forum for the fourteen members of the Pacific Island Forum (FIPIC) and the pledging to it of USD 1 billion for mitigating the effects of climate change emphasizes the principle that size is not a factor in the councils of the world.'[25] It has changed India's status in that grouping of island developing countries from being a dialogue partner of the PIC (Pacific Island Forum). This will prove to be important if and when the UNSC permanent membership comes to a vote.

With his invitation to SAARC leaders (and Mauritius) at his swearing-in ceremony in May 2014 it was clear that Narendra Modi was going to be a 'foreign policy prime minster', an activist in Jawaharlal Nehru's mould but not always in sync with established norms. In the evolution of his foreign policy, he has shown pragmatism in introducing a dose of realism, an ability to shake up moribund structures, and 'an instinctive understanding of power in the conduct of world affairs'.[26]

What is interesting is that in pushing his foreign policy goals he has not hesitated in playing to his nationalist base as in the case of the Land Boundary Agreement with Bangladesh. In going against the long-held concept of inviolability of the Indian borders, Modi focused his attention on the strengthening of the border against infiltration 'and appealed to the Hindu religious nationalism of his domestic political base by linking the border settlement to a crackdown on illegal Muslim immigration'.[27]

The recognition that diplomacy has to serve as the handmaiden to India's development has been embedded into the practice of foreign policy. On all his visits abroad, this has been a major item for bilateral interaction. The leveraging of international partnerships, including by giving new momentum to groupings like BRICS, G-4, IBSA, and others, has had a salutary effect on the commitment of FDI, technology access, and securing access to natural resources needed for development. In this regard, major steps have been taken in using India's ITEC programme and Lines of Credit to actively pursue mutually beneficial relations with countries of the African continent.

True to his own statement, Modi's foreign policy has focused on building bridges with countries in India's neighbourhood.

He has visited all the SAARC countries except Maldives, some more than once. India has equally become more forthcoming in providing assistance and capacity building or in providing humanitarian assistance such as in Nepal, Sri Lanka, and the Maldives. Despite the lack of agreement on the Teesta River water the visit of Bangladesh President Sheikh Hasina in April 2017 has gone a long way in correcting the tenor of bilateral relations. External Affairs Minister Sushma Swaraj visited Dakha on October 22, 2017 for the joint consultative committee to review bilateral relations. She met both President Sheikh Hasina and Opposition leader Begum Khalida Zia. India's stand on the repatriation of Rohingyas and the perpetual delay in the Teesta Agreement due to obduracy of West Bengal chief minister has caused disappointment on the part of Sheikh Hasina who is facing pressure for early general elections. During Swaraj's meeting with met Begum Khalida Zia she said she expects the elections to be 'participatory and credible. The meeting was criticised by the ruling Awami League while other speculated that India might be hedging its bet.'[28]

The emphasis, both to the east and west, has been on building connectivity with each of India's neighbours going beyond SAARC. The investment committed to developing the Chabahar port in Iran through a trilateral agreement with Iran and Afghanistan will be a landmark development in opening a route to Afghanistan and Central Asia. However with President Trump having denied certification for the Iran Nuclear agreement the possibility of US pressure on India to curb relations with Iran could affect the project.[29] Similarly, the long-delayed Kaladan multi-modal project with Myanmar to the east will help to connect the eastern states of India to the region.

An important initiative is the exploration of the full potential of the intra-SAARC groupings like BBIN and going beyond to include the Mekong-Ganga Cooperation (MGC) and ASEAN groupings. At the same time, despite two visits to Nepal, India has not been able to assert its earlier position. The revision of the India-Nepal Treaty has become the touchstone of the health of the relationship. It has been further complicated by China's moves to build and strengthen its road and rail link with Nepal.

Of the SAARC countries although considerable progress has been made in shoring up relations with the Maldives the relationship has yet to come back to its earlier proximity. Here again, the growing presence of China and radical Islamic groups presents new challenges. At the same time, India will remain the 'default' power for the Maldives illustrated by its assistance in 2014 during the 'drinking water crisis'.[30] Similarly, India has established itself as the 'first responder' in any humanitarian or natural disaster in the SAARC region, including Myanmar. India responded to the earthquake in Nepal, the landslide in Sri Lanka, and the evacuation of stranded citizens and others during hostilities in Yemen.

The continuation of terrorism from the soil of Pakistan has led to a phase of no dialogue, and people-to-people interactions have withered. The Indian government is now committed to pursuing its projects within SAARC even if it means going through a trilateral or bilateral route. In the evolving configuration of the neighbourhood, as US policy towards the region and its constituents gets clarified, India will have to evaluate its own options. In this matrix, the evolution of bilateral relations with China becomes even more important. The overt display of the China–Pakistan nexus will remain a matter of concern.

India's policy towards the Gulf countries, as well as those in its proximate neighbourhood has remarkably acquired a personal dimension as well. Nothing illustrates this better than the developments with Saudi Arabia and the UAE. Modi's visit to Riyadh was remarkable as he was given the country's highest national honour,[31] the King Abdulaziz Sash, the first such award given to a visiting Indian prime minister. It demonstrated Saudi Arabia's intention to step up the closeness of the bilateral relationship. It remains debatable whether it demonstrated that Modi's hard-line Hindu image was seen by the hard-line Islamic Saudi regime as someone they could do business with. That Modi's visit came a few days after the United States and Saudi Arabia together had issued joint sanctions on LeT, the perpetrator of the 2008 Mumbai attack, also demonstrated the Saudi intention to build bilateral relations with India on a different basis. It signalled the changing international stance of the Saudi royal family including its opening relations with Israel.[32]

With Modi's visit in April 2015,[33] which came after 34 years, and the return visit on 25 January 2017 of Crown Prince Mohammed bin Zayed Al Nahyan as the chief guest at the Republic Day, it signalled the growing closeness between the two countries. Among a series of UAE-India deals and agreements the most important was the one concerning the setting up of a strategic oil reserve in India.[34] The setting up of a national crude oil reserve has been a major requirement given that India's ever increasing appetite for oil while its reserves are depleting. The closeness which Sheikh Mohammed has imparted to the bilateral relationship was well illustrated by the draping in lights of the Indian tricolour on the Republic Day of Burj Khalifa in Dubai—the world's tallest building.

Modi's initiatives towards Saudi Arabia and UAE reflects an acknowledgement of India's political, economic, and strategic importance to the Gulf emirates. The commitment of billions of dollars during these visits is an earnest desire on their part to link their countries with India. At the same time, India has made it clear that it has no interest in getting enmeshed in the ongoing sectarian wars in the region in which Saudi Arabia and some other Gulf countries are major players, given that, at its heart, it is a struggle within Islam. India fears that the outcome of this strife will be long in coming and, as a result, has to ensure that its effects are not felt domestically.

Modi has equally firmed up a new relationship with Africa with bilateral trade amounting to over USD 100 billion and is looking at long-term collaboration in energy, raw materials, and security. Fifty-four countries from the continent attended the third India Africa Forum Summit (IAFS) from 26–29 October 2015. Touted as the most spectacular diplomatic exercise hosted by India since the 1983 NAM Summit, this meeting provided an opportunity for India to rejuvenate relations with the continent.[35] It met a key goal of building development-oriented partnerships. Modi has visited Mozambique, South Africa, Tanzania, and Kenya so far. Unfortunately, recent isolated attacks on Africans in New Delhi threaten to disrupt the positive evolution of the relationship unless action is taken to educate and deal with the disruptive elements.[36]

The government has also increased the salience of the IOR in its foreign and defence policy realizing that its core strengths can be harnessed to increase its profile in the region. India has become an important player in the IORA with the goal of developing a blue economy. It recognizes that in this region it can leverage its strengths in the face of growing Chinese presence.[37] The Act East policy, which is another landmark in Modi's conception of foreign policy goals, has opened new vistas of cooperation between India and not only the ASEAN countries but beyond, such as with Australia, Japan, and Vietnam. It needs to be assiduously pursued, especially in regard to the commitments made.[38]

While the Modi government has greatly intensified its relations with the major powers it is clear that the greatest movement has been vis-à-vis the United States followed by Japan and Germany. The so-called Modi–Obama 'bromance', though mystifying, has indeed stepped up the United States as India's foremost superpower partner. 'The signing of the joint vision statement for Asia Pacific and Indian Ocean regions, apart from the LEMOA military exchanges agreement' are important successes.[39] The clarity of US policy during the Obama years is not yet seen with President Trump. This is an area which will have to be worked on.

The visit on 26 October 2017 to Delhi of US Secretary of State Tillerson revealed that the US is working hard to shore up the relations especially with Trump increasing US troops in Afghanistan.[40] In the context of Trump's statement requiring India to step up its participation in Afghanistan Sushma Swaraj said 'everything could be done if Pakistan could be brought to heel'.[41] Tillerson criticized Pakistan for the safe havens it provides to terrorist groups but did not mention attacks on India. Neither was the name of Hafez Saeed, the mastermind of the Mumbai attack, included in the list of 75 persons handed over by him in Islamabad. It indicated that the US is totally focussed on its own concerns in Afghanistan and not with those of India. Despite the bonhomie India will continue to be at variance with the US on many issues other than Pakistan like Iran and the extent of play to be given to the defence relationship.

Following Tillerson visit to Delhi a new momentum has gathered in favour of expanding the India-US-Japan grouping to include Australia. Tillerson has said that the US sees the four countries as anchors to balance growing Chinese thrust in the Asia-Pacific. India has indicated that it 'is open to working with like-minded countries on issues that advance our interests and promote our viewpoint. We are not rigid in this regard'.[42]

Fast mutating international relations have also led to Russia's growing closeness to China and building parallel relations, including the supply of defence equipment, to Pakistan. India will have to tread warily to keep intact the parameters on which these relations have been based.

An Assessment

The major challenges to Indian foreign policy will arise from the unpredictability which has become a feature of international relations, in the main, due to changes in Washington and Beijing. Increasingly, the need to preserve a multipolar and multilateral environment has become paramount. As articulated by Narendra Modi, India's foreign policy goals will be activist aiming to build relationships with multiple players. In doing so, India projects its faith in multi-polarity not only as a regulator of international relations but also as the best way for India to realize its development and security goals.

As Modi continues his domestic economic reforms—buoyed by confidence gained from his party's success in state elections in some major states—he will be motivated by the twin considerations of keeping the country on the growth path and securing his position for the next general elections in 2019. Foreign policy could play a major role if it brings in the resources for development and smoothens the crinkling international environment which India faces. Much will, in the end, depend on the success of domestic economic reforms in ensuring a sustained high rate of annual growth far above the projected 7 per cent per annum. It will require being able to work with the opposition and in ensuring that the agenda is not disrupted by religious hardliners. The country cannot afford to lose its focus from providing jobs and incomes to the 65 per cent population below the age of 30 years.

In achieving his foreign policy goals it has been opined that he is likely to be hamstrung by 'the obduracy of India's foreign policy establishment'[43]and the 'entrenched frameworks of foreign policy ideas'.[44] The idea of going beyond the concept of strategic autonomy is the theme of this book. From my recounting of the changes in foreign policy practice it is clear that changes both of substance and nuance have been initiated. For much of these changes Modi will rely on the support of his core constituency. That itself introduces an element of doubt about their longevity.

Despite manifest misses and disappointments in the face of changing equations, which pose new international challenges, the Modi government has done well in giving more in-depth attention to the practice of India's foreign policy. Negatives in the domestic political discourse on foreign policy—from needless polarization to extreme positions and the media cacophony on Pakistan-bashing—have detracted from its continuity vis-à-vis its aims. 'Politics ought to end at the water's edge.'[45] The advancement of India's national interests, in a world which, after 1991, is again witnessing major changes, depends on spelling out its priorities and goals. This is what the Narendra Modi government has achieved.

Notes

1. 'Foreign Policy of the Modi Government', https://en.wikipedia. org/wiki/Foreign_policy_of_the_Narendra_Modi_government.
2. MEA, 'Inaugural Address by Prime Minister at Second Raisina Dialogue, New Delhi (January 17, 2017)', Ministry of External Affairs Government of India, January 17, 2017, http://mea.gov. in/Speeches-Statements.htm?dtl/27948/Inaugural_Address_by_ Prime_Minister_at_Second_Raisina_Dialogue_New_Delhi_ January_17_2017.
3. MEA, 'Inaugural Address by Prime Minister at Second Raisina Dialogue, New Delhi (January 17, 2017)'.
4. Iain Marlow, 'PM Modi's Aggressive Foreign Policy Cancels Old Traditions: Foreign Media', *Bloomberg* (15 November 2016),

http://www.ndtv.com/india-news/economic-box-ticked-pm-modis-assertive-foreign-policy-foreign-media-1625536.

5. 'Foreign Policy, Good Governance: Top 10 Quotes from PM Modi's Town Hall Event', *Hindustan Times* (6 August 2016), http://www.hindustantimes.com/india-news/from-foreign-policy-to-good-governance-top-10-quotes-from-pm-modi-s-town-hall-event/story-dkfPG5NKdieaFnWRvG2NRO.html.

6. See Chapter 8.

7. Nandan Unnikrishnan and Uma Purushothaman, 'India in the Modern World/Indian Foreign Policy: Priorities and Imperatives', Draft of paper published in *Russia in Global Affairs Journal*. The final paper is in Russian. http://www.globalaffairs.ru/number/I-vse-zhe-po-zavetam- Neru17845https://www.researchgate.net/publication/301620523_Modi's_Foreign_Policy.

8. Manoj Joshi, 'The Modi Government Has Dismantled India's Foreign Policy', The Wire (23 December 2016), https://thewire.in/88490/modi-government-foreign-policy/.

9. Joshi, 'The Modi Government Has Dismantled India's Foreign Policy'.

10. Rajesh Kumar Singh, 'India Launches New Economic Era with Sales Tax Reform', Reuters Business News (30 June 2017), http://www.reuters.com/article/us-india-tax/india-launches-new-economic-era-with-sales-tax-reform-idUSKBN19L2UM.

11. Tim Worstall, 'World Bank-India's Demonetisation has Hit Growth Down to 7% for Fiscal 2016-17', Forbes (1 January 2017), https://www.forbes.com/sites/timworstall/2017/01/11/world-bank-indias-demonetisation-has-hit-growth-down-to-7-for-fiscal-2016-2017/#aa3d50262ed8.

12. Ashok Swain, 'How Donald Trump's Election Has Exposed Modi's Foreign Policy Blunder', DailyO (12 December 2016), http://www.dailyo.in/politics/donald-trump-narendra-modi-foreign-policy-pakistan-china-russia-obama/story/1/14640.html.

13. Pramit Pal Chaudhri, '2016: End of Modi's Foreign Policy Honeymoon', *Hindustan Times* (28 December 2016), http://www.hindustantimes.com/opinion/2016-end-of-modi-s-foreign-policy-honeymoon/story-1xpfEYoNtgWjI8bYjDA5MI.html.

14. Chaudhri, '2016: End of Modi's Foreign Policy Honeymoon'.

15. Saibal Dasgupta, 'China-Pakistan Economic Corridor Plan is OBOR Flagship: Chinese President Xi Jinping', *The Times of India* (15 May 2017), https://timesofindia.indiatimes.com/world/china/

china-pakistan-economic-corridor-plan-is-obor-flagship-chinese-president-xi-jinping/articleshow/5867.

16. Swain, 'How Donald Trump's Election Has Exposed Modi's Foreign Policy Blunder'.

17. PTI, 'H1B, L1 Visas Issue Taken up "Very Strongly" with US Says Union Minister Suresh Prabhu', *The Hindu* (28 October 2017), http://www.thehindu.com/news/national/india-very-strongly-raises-h1b-visa-issue-with-us-prabhu/article19937770.ece.

18. Swain, 'How Donald Trump's Election Has Exposed Modi's Foreign Policy Blunder'.

19. Elizabeth Roche, 'Has Donald Trump Softened Stance on Pakistan after Hostages Rescue?', *LiveMint* (28 October 2017), http://www.livemint.com/Politics/bH79Cpg4Vky97zkxtKrErJ/Has-Donald-Trump-softened-stance-on-Pakistan-after-hostages.html.

20. Swain, 'How Donald Trump's Election Has Exposed Modi's Foreign Policy Blunder'.

21. Hamid Mir, 'By Naming Syed Salahuddin, is Trump Mediating in Kashmir', *The Indian Express* (28 June 2017), http://indianexpress.com/article/opinion/by-naming-salahuddin-is-trump-mediating-in-kashmir-4725194/.

22. TNN, 'India Rejects US Offer to Mediate with Pakistan on Kashmir Issue', *The Times of India* (5 April 2017), https://timesofindia.indiatimes.com/india/india-rejects-us-offer-to-mediate-with-pakistan-on-kashmir-issue/articleshow/58018616.cms.

23. Harsh V. Pant, 'How India-US Ties Were Modi-fied', *The Diplomat* (8 January 2017), http://thediplomat.com/2017/01/how-india-us-ties-were-modi-fied/.

24. Chaudhri, '2016: End of Modi's Foreign Policy Honeymoon'.

25. Unnikrishnan and Purushothaman, 'India in the Modern World/ Indian Foreign Policy'.

26. Dhruva Jaishankar, 'India's Five Foreign Policy Goals: Great Strides, Steep Challenges', The Wire (26 May 2016), https://thewire.in/38708/indias-five-foreign-policy-goals-great-strides-steep-challenges/.

27. Manjari Chatterji Miller and Kate Sullivan de Estrada, 'Has India Seen a Foreign Policy Reset under Narendra Modi', *International Affairs* (15 January 2017), https://blog.oup.com/2017/01/india-foreign-policy-reset-modi/.

28. Edit, 'Sushma Swaraj Arrives in Dhaka on Two-day Visit', *The Tribune* (22 October 2017), http://www.tribuneindia.com/news/nation/sushma-swaraj-arrives-in-dhaka-on-two-day-visit/485408.html.

29. Mark Lander and David E. Sanger, 'Trump Disavows Nuclear Deal but Doesn't Scrap It', *The New York Times* (13 October 2017), https://www.nytimes.com/2017/10/13/us/politics/trump-iran-nuclear-deal.html.

30. Ankit Panda, 'Maldives Faces Drinking Water Crisis', *The Diplomat* (5 December 2014), https://thediplomat.com/2014/12/maldives-faces-drinking-water-crisis/.

31. Subajit Ray, 'Terror, Investments the Focus as PM Modi Lands in Saudi Arabia', *The Indian Express* (3 April 2016), http://indian-express.com/article/india/india-news-india/pm-modi-in-saudi-arabia-to-boost-ties-deepen-counter-terror-cooperation/.

32. Samuel Ramani, 'Israel Is Strengthening Its Ties with Gulf Monarchies', The World Post, http://www.huffingtonpost.com/samuel-ramani/why-israel-is-strengthening_b_11946660.html.

33. Shubhajit Ray, 'PM Narendra Modi's UAE Visit: Quick Take', *The Indian Express* (18 August 2015), http://indianexpress.com/article/india/india-others/pm-narendra-modis-uae-visit-quick-take/.

34. Hemendra Mohan Kumar, 'Energy Security Leads Series of UAE-India Deals and Agreements', The National (16 April 2017), http://www.thenational.ae/business/economy/energy-security-leads-series-of-uae-india-deals-and-agreements.

35. Ruchita Berry, 'Third India-Africa Forum Summit: Rejuvenating Relations', Institute of Defence Studies and Analyses, 29 October 2015, http://www.idsa.in/idsacomments/3rd-india-africa-forum-summit_rberi_291015.

36. Murali Krishnan, 'India Rejects Racism behind Attacks on Africans', *DW* (5 April 2017), http://www.dw.com/en/india-rejects-racism-behind-attacks-on-africans/a-38312666.

37. Rajiv Bhatia, 'A Review of Narendra Modi's Foreign Policy', Newslaundry (30 May 2016), https://www.newslaundry.com/2016/05/30/a-review-of-narendra-modis-foreign-policy.

38. Ashok Sajjanhar, '2 Years on, Has Modi's "Act East" Policy Made a Difference for India', *The Diplomat* (3 April 2016), http://thediplomat.com/2016/06/2-years-on-has-modis-act-east-policy-made-a-difference-for-india/.

39. Suhasini Haidar, 'The Voice of Modi's Foreign Policy', *The Hindu* (25 January 2017), www.thehindu.com/news/national/The-voice-of-Modi%E2%80%99s-foreign-policy/article17089963.ece.

40. Manoj Joshi, 'Tillerson Visit: India Needs to Learn from China, Pak on US Ties', Observer Research Foundation, 27 October 2017,

http://www.orfonline.org/research/tillerson-visit-india-needs-to-learn-from-china-pak-on-us-ties/.

41. Manoj Joshi, 'Tillerson Visit: India Needs to Learn from China, Pak on US Ties'.

42. Indrani Bagchi, 'India Wary as Japan, US Seek Quadrilateral with Australia', *The Times of India* (28 October 2017), https://timesofindia.indiatimes.com/india/india-wary-as-japan-us-seek-quadrilateral-with-australia/articleshow/61281250.cms.

43. Miller and Estrada, 'Has India Seen a Foreign Policy Reset under Narendra Modi', *International Affairs*, http://www.academia.edu/30962737/Has_India_Seen_a_Foreign_Policy_Reset_Under_Narendra_Modi.

44. Miller and Estrada, 'Has India Seen a Foreign Policy Reset under Narendra Modi'.

45. Jaishankar, 'India's Five Foreign Policy Goals'.

Select Bibliography

Abidi, A.H.H. 1995. 'Relations between India and Iran, 1947–1979'. *Iranian Journal of International Affairs*. 7: 877–902.

Abidi, A.H.H. 1995. 'Iranian Perspective on Relations with India'. *International Studies*. 32(3): 315–25.

Abraham, R. 2012. 'India and Its Diaspora in the Arab Gulf Countries: Tapping into Effective "Soft Power" and Related Public Diplomacy'. *Diaspora Studies*. 5(2): 124–46.

Acharya, A. 2008. *China & India: Politics of Incremental Engagement*. New Delhi: Har Anand Publications.

Acharya, S. and R. Mohan. 2011. *India's Economy: Performance and Challenges: Essays in Honour of Montek Singh Ahluwalia*. Oxford: Oxford University Press.

Ahmed, A. 2014. *India's Doctrine Puzzle: Limiting War in South Asia*. India: Routledge.

Aiyar, P. 2012. *Smoke and Mirrors: An Experience of China*. New Delhi: HarperCollins Publishers.

Al-Habbas, K.N. 2011. 'Saudi-Indian Relations: Past Difficulties, Present Opportunities and Future Prospects'. *Journal of King Abdulaziz University: Economics and Administration*. 25(1): 297–317.

Alden, C. and M.A. Vieira. 2005. 'The New Diplomacy of the South: South Africa, Brazil, India and Trilateralism'. *Third World Quarterly*. 26(7): 1077–95.

Allen, D. 2013. 'The EU and India: Strategic Partners but Not a Strategic Partnership', in Christiansen, T., E. Kirchner, and P. Murray, *The Palgrave Handbook of EU-Asia Relations*. Basingstoke: Palgrave.

Ali, E. and D.K. Talukder. 2009. 'Preferential Trade among the SAARC Countries: Prospects and Challenges of Regional Integration in South Asia'. *JOAAG*. 4(1): 47–59.

Ansari, H. 2007. *India and the Persian Gulf; Indian Foreign Policy: Challenges and Opportunities*. New Delhi: Foreign Service Institute/Academic Foundation.

Ashraf, S. 2011. 'India–Pakistan Relations: Common Ground and Points of Discord'. *ECSSR (Abu Dhabi). Emirates Lecture Series*. (88): 58.

Ashraf, T. 2015. 'The Pakistan-India Conundrum: A Historical Survey'. *Pakistan Journal of Social Sciences*. 35(1): 309–20.

Athwal, A. 2007. *China-India Relations: Contemporary Dynamics (Vol. 3)*. New York: Routledge.

Auner, E. 2013. 'Indian Missile Defense Program Advances'. *Arms Control Today*. 43(1): 33–4.

Aung, T.T. and S. Myint. 2001. 'India–Burma Relations', in Arnott, D. (ed.), *Challenges to Democratization in Burma: Perspectives on Multilateral and Bilateral Responses*. International IDEA (accessed on 12 June 2016) http://www.burmalibrary.org/docs3/challenges_to_democratization_in_burma-Chaptr4.pdf

Bandyopadhyay, S. 2007. 'India and New Zealand: A Sixty-Year Roller Coaster'. *New Zealand International Review*. 32(4): 10–14.

Banerjee, D. 2012. *India and R2P: Reconciling the Tension between Intervention and State Sovereignty. The Responsibility to Protect–From Evasive to Reluctant Action?* Johannesburg: Hanns Seidel Foundation.

Bagai, M. 2015. 'India Australia Relations: Retrospect and Prospect'. *Global Journal of Human-Social Science Research*. 15(5): 39–45.

Bagla, P. 2006. 'Breaking Up (a Nuclear Program) Is Hard to Do'. *Science*. 311(5762): 765–6.

Bajpai, K. 2000. 'India's Nuclear Posture after Pokhran II'. *International Studies*. 37(4): 267–302.

Bajpai, K.P. 2009. 'Obstacles to Good Work in Indian International Relations'. *International Studies*. 46(1–2): 109–28.

Bajpai, K.P. and H.V. Pant. 2013. *India's National Security:A Reader*. Oxford and New York: Oxford University Press.

Bajpai, K.P. and S. Mallavarapu. 2005. *International Relations in India: Bringing Theory back Home*. New Delhi: Orient Longman,

Bajpai, K.P. and A. Mattoo. 1996. *Securing India: Strategic Thought and Practice*. New Delhi: Manohar.

Bajpai, K.S. 1992. 'India in 1991: New Beginnings'. *Asian Survey*. 32(2): 207–16.

Bajpai, U.S. 1986. *India and Its Neighbourhood*. New Delhi: Lancer International in association with India International Centre.

Bal, S.N. 2004. *Central Asia:A Strategy for India's Look-North Policy*. India: Lancer Publishers.

Bala, M. 2002. *India-Australia Trade and Investment Relations in the 1990s. Australia in the Emerging Global Order: Evolving Australia-India Relations.* New Delhi: Shipra Publications.

Ban, C. and M. Blyth. 2013. 'The BRICs and the Washington Consensus: An Introduction'. *Review of International Political Economy.* 20(2): 241–55.

Bandyopadhyaya, J. 2003. *The Making of India's Foreign Policy.* New Delhi: Allied Publishers.

Bandyopādhyāya, Ś. 2004. *From Plassey to Partition: A History of Modern India.* New Delhi: Orient Blackswan.

Bardhan, P. 2012. *Awakening Giants, Feet of Clay: Assessing the Economic Rise of China and India.* UK and USA: Princeton University Press.

Baru, S. 2009. 'The Influence of Business and Media on Indian Foreign Policy'. *India Review.* 8(3): 266–85.

Baruah, A. 2007. *Dateline Islamabad.* New Delhi: Penguin.

Basant, R. and S. Morris. 2000. 'Competition Policy in India: Issues for a Globalizing Economy'. *Economic and Political Weekly.* 35(31): 2735–47.

Basrur, R.M. 2009. 'Theory for Strategy Emerging India in a Changing World'. *South Asian Survey.* 16(1): 5–21.

Bass, G.J. 2015. 'The Indian Way of Humanitarian Intervention'. *Yale J. Int'l L.* 40: 227–95.

Basu, B.B. 1999. 'Indo-Russian Defense Cooperation'. *Strategic Analysis.* 23(3); 503–05.

Basu, B.B. 2000. 'Putin's Visit and Future of India-Russia Defense Cooperation'. *Strategic Analysis.* 24(9): 1763–9.

Basu, P.K., B. Chellaney, P. Khanna, and S. Khilnani. 2005. *India as a New Global Leader.* London: Foreign Policy Centre.

Batabyal, A. 2006. 'Balancing China in Asia a Realist Assessment of India's Look East Strategy'. *China Report.* 42(2): 179–97.

Bayne, N. and S. Woolcock (eds). 2011. *The New Economic Diplomacy: Decision-Making and Negotiation in International Economic Relations.* England and USA: Ashgate Publishing, Ltd.

Behera, N.C. 2008. *International Relations in South Asia: Search for an Alternative Paradigm.* New Delhi: SAGE Publications.

Behuria, A.K., S.S. Pattanaik, and A. Gupta, A. 2012. 'Does India Have a Neighbourhood Policy?'. *Strategic Analysis.* 36(2): 229–46.

Belfiglio, V.J. 1972. 'India's Economic and Political Relations with Bhutan'. *Asian Survey.* 12(8): 676–85.

Beri, R. 2003. 'India's Africa Policy in the Post-Cold War Era: An Assessment'. *Strategic Analysis.* 27(2): 216–32.

Beri, R. 2008. 'IBSA Dialogue Forum: An Assessment'. *Strategic Analysis*. 32(5): 809–31.

Bhagavan, M. 2010. 'A New Hope: India, the United Nations and the Making of the Universal Declaration of Human Rights'. *Modern Asian Studies*. 44(02): 311–47.

Bhagavan, M. 2013. *India and the Quest for One World: The Peacemakers*. UK: Palgrave Macmillan.

Bhardwaj, S. 2003. 'Bangladesh Foreign Policy vis-à-vis India'. *Strategic Analysis*. 27(2): 263–78.

Bhashin, M. 2008. 'India's Role in South Asia–Perceived Hegemony or Reluctant Leadership?'. *Indian Foreign Affairs Journal*. 3(4).

Bhatia, V. 2012. 'The US–India Nuclear Agreement: Revisiting the Debate'. *Strategic Analysis*. 36(4): 612–23.

Bhattacharya, S., Shilpa, and M. Bhati. 2012. 'China and India: The Two New Players in the Nanotechnology Race'. *Scientometrics*. 93(1): 59–87.

Bisht, M. 2012. 'Bhutan–India Power Cooperation: Benefits beyond Bilateralism'. *Strategic Analysis*. 36(5): 787–803.

Biswas, B. 2012. 'New Directions in India's Foreign Policy'. *India Review*. 11(2): 134–8.

Blank, J., J.D. Moroney, A. Rabasa, and B. Lin. 2015. *Look East, Cross Black Waters: India's Interest in Southeast Asia*. California: Rand Corporation.

Blank, S. 2003. 'India's Rising Profile in Central Asia'. *Comparative Strategy*. 22(2): 139–57.

Bloomfield, A. 2016. *India and the Responsibility to Protect*. Surrey: Ashgate Publishing, Ltd.

Blank, S. 2005. *Natural Allies? Regional Security in Asia and Prospects for Indo-American Strategic Cooperation*. USA: DIANE Publishing.

Blarel, N. 2012. 'India's Soft Power: From Potential to Reality? India: The Next Superpower'. LSE IDEAS London School of Economics and Political Science. Available at http://eprints.lse.ac.uk/43445/.

Bonnor, J. 2008. 'Australia–India: An Important Partnership'. *South Asian Survey*. 15(1): 165–77.

Borah, R. 2011. 'Japan and India in the Changing East Asian Equation'. *Journal of Contemporary Eastern Asia*. 10(2): 25–33.

Borah, R. 2011. 'Japan and India: Natural but Wary Allies'. *New Zealand International Review*. 36(4): 23–8.

Bourantonis, D., K. Ifantis, and P. Tsakonas. 2007. *Multilateralism and Security Institutions in an Era of Globalization*. Abingdon/New York: Routledge.

Brewster, D. 2011. 'Indian Strategic Thinking about East Asia'. *Journal of Strategic Studies.* 34(6): 825–52.

Brewster, D. 2012. *India as an Asia Pacific Power (Vol. 18).* New York and London: Routledge.

Brewster, D. 2014. 'Beyond the "String of Pearls": Is There Really a Sino-Indian Security Dilemma in the Indian Ocean?' *Journal of the Indian Ocean Region.* 10(2): 133–49.

Brewster, D. 2014. *India's Ocean: The Story of India's Bid for Regional Leadership.* New York and London: Routledge.

Broadman, H. G. 2007. *Africa's Silk Road: China and India's New Economic Frontier.* Washington, D.C.: The World Bank.

Broinowski, R. 2000. 'India, China and Australia: The Fractured Triangle'. *South Asia: Journal of South Asian Studies.* 23(s1): 141–50.

Brunatti, A. and D.M. Malone. 2009. 'India's West Asia Approach: A Triumph of Bilateralism'. *Indian Foreign Affairs Journal.* 4(4): 43–62.

Brunatti, A.D. and D.M. Malone. 2010. 'Fading Glories? India's Relations with Western Europe and Russia'. *International Relations.* 24(3): 341–70.

Bruneau, R. 2006. 'Engaging a Nuclear India: Punishment, Reward, and the Politics of Non-Proliferation'. *Journal of Public and International Affairs.* 17: 27–46.

Brobst, P.J. 2005. *The Future of the Great Game: Sir Olaf Caroe, India's Independence, and the Defense of Asia.* United States: University of Akron Press.

Bullion, A. 1997. 'India and UN Peacekeeping Operations'. *International Peacekeeping.* 4(1): 98–114.

Burgess, S. 2013. 'A Pivot to India? The US–India Strategic Partnership and Multi-Polarity in Asia'. *US Air War College:* 1–19.

Burke, S.M. 1973. 'The Postwar Diplomacy of the Indo-Pakistani War of 1971'. *Asian Survey.* 13(11): 1036–49.

Burns, R.N. 2007. 'America's Strategic Opportunity with India: The New US–India Partnership'. *Foreign Affairs.* 86(6): 131–46.

Buzan, B. 2002. 'South Asia Moving towards Transformation: Emergence of India as a Great Power'. *International Studies.* 39(1): 1–24.

Cameron, F., A. Berkofsky, M. Bhandari, and D. Halley. 2005. 'EU–India Relations'. *EPC Issue Papers.* 35: 1–47.

Carpintero, Ó., I. Murray, and J. Bellver. 2016. 'The New Scramble for Africa: BRICS Strategies in a Multipolar World', in *Analytical Gains of Geopolitical Economy.* Emerald Group Publishing Limited, 191–226.

Carranza, M.E. 2007. 'From Non-Proliferation to Post-Proliferation: Explaining the US–India Nuclear Deal'. *Contemporary Security Policy*. 28(3): 464–93.

Carranza, M.E. 2016. *India-Pakistan Nuclear Diplomacy: Constructivism and the Prospects for Nuclear Arms Control and Disarmament in South Asia*. UK: Rowman & Littlefield.

Carter, A.B. 2006. 'America's New Strategic Partner?' *Foreign Affairs*. 85(4): 33–44.

Chacko, P. 2013. *Indian Foreign Policy: The Politics of Postcolonial Identity from 1947 to 2004*. London and New York: Routledge.

Chacko, P. 2015. 'The New Geo-Economics of a "Rising" India: State Transformation and the Recasting of Foreign Policy'. *Journal of Contemporary Asia*. 45(2): 326–44.

Chacko, P. 2016. 'Foreign Policy, Ideas and State-Building: India and the Politics of International Intervention'. *Journal of International Relations and Development*: 1–26.

Chakma, B. 2012. 'Bangladesh-India Relations: Sheikh Hasina's India-Positive Policy Approach'. *S. Rajaratnam School of International Studies*, Nanyang Technological University (accessed on 11 April 2016) https://www.rsis.edu.sg/wp-content/uploads/rsis-pubs/WP252.pdf.

Chambers, M.R. (ed.). 2002. *South Asia in 2020: Future Strategic Balances and Alliances*. Carlisle, Pennsylvania: Strategic Studies Institute, US Army War College.

Chamling, D.R. 1978. *India and the United Nations*. New Delhi: Associated Publishing House.

Chanda, R. and S. Gopalan. 2009. 'Understanding India's Regional Initiatives with East and Southeast Asia'. *Asian-Pacific Economic Literature*. 23(1): 66–78.

Chandra, B., M. Mukherjee, and A. Mukherjee, 2000. *India after Independence: 1947–2000*. New Delhi: Penguin.

Chari, P.R. 2014. *Indo-US Nuclear Deal: Seeking Synergy in Bilateralism*. India and UK: Routledge.

Chaudhuri, R. 2014. *Forged in Crisis: India and the United States since 1947*. UK: Oxford University Press.

Chaulia, S.S. 2002. 'BJP, India's Foreign Policy and the "Realist Alternative" to the Nehruvian Tradition'. *International Politics*. 39(2): 215–34.

Cheema, P.I. 2006. 'The Contribution of Track II towards India-Pakistan Relations'. *South Asian Survey*. 13(2): 211–33.

Cheema, S.A. 2010. 'India–Iran Relations Progress, Challenges and Prospects'. *India Quarterly: A Journal of International Affairs*. 66(4): 383–96.

Cheema, S.A. 2014. 'India–Iran Relations in the Post–Cold War: A Neo-Realist Analysis'. *India and Iran in Contemporary Relations*. 1: 1–13.

Chellaney, B., 2009. 'India: Regional Security Challenges'. *Security politics in Asia and Europe*. 6(3): 166–71.

Chenoy, A.M. 2008. 'India and Russia Allies in the International Political System'. *South Asian Survey*. 15(1): 49–62.

Cheru, F. and C. Obi. 2010. *The Rise of China and India in Africa: Challenges, Opportunities and Critical Interventions*. London: Zed Books/Nordiska Afrikainstitutet.

Cheru, F. and C. Obi. 2011. 'India–Africa Relations in the 21st Century: Genuine Partnership or a Marriage of Convenience', in Mawdesley, E. and G. McCann (eds) *India in Africa: Changing Geographies of Power*. Cape Town, Dakar, Nairobi, and Oxford: Pambazuka Press.

Chin, G.T. 2015. 'The State of the Art: Trends in the Study of the BRICS and Multilateral Organizations', in *Rising Powers and Multilateral Institutions*. UK: Palgrave Macmillan, 19–41.

Chiriyankandath, J. 2004. 'Realigning India: Indian Foreign Policy after the Cold War'. *The Round Table*. 93(374): 199–211.

Choden, T. 2004. 'Indo–Bhutan Relations Recent Trends'. *Perspectives on Modern South Asia–A Reader in Culture, History, and Representation*: 298–302.

Chopra, V.D. 2006. *India's Foreign Policy in the 21st Century*. Delhi: Gyan Publishing House.

Chung, T. and P. Uberoi. 2008. *Rise of the Asian Giants: The Dragon-Elephant Tango*. London: Anthem Press.

Ciociari, J.D. 2011. 'India's Approach to Great-Power Status'. *Fletcher F. World Aff.* 35: 61–90.

Cooper, A. and A. Farooq. 2015. 'Testing the Club Dynamics of the BRICS: The New Development Bank from Conception to Establishment'. *International Organizations Research Journal*. 10(2): 32–44.

Cooper, A.F. and T. Fues. 2008. 'Do the Asian Drivers Pull Their Diplomatic Weight? China, India, and the United Nations'. *World Development*. 36(2): 293–307.

Crossette, B. 2010. 'The Elephant in the Room'. *Foreign Policy*. 177: 29.

Dahiya, R. 2015. 'India and West Asia: Challenges and Opportunities'. *Indian Foreign Affairs Journal*. 10(4): 324–30.

Damodaran, A.K. and U.S. Bajpai. 1990. *Indian Foreign Oolicy, the Indira Gandhi Years*. New Delhi: Radiant Publishers.

Das, P. 2013. 'India Myanmar Border Problems: Fencing Not the Only Solution'. *IDSA Comment*. 15: 313.

Dasgupta, S. and S.P. Cohen. 2011. 'Is India Ending Its Strategic Restraint Doctrine?' *The Washington Quarterly*. 34(2): 163–77.

Datta, S. 2002. 'Indo–Bangladesh Relations: An Overview of Limitations and Constraints'. *Strategic Analysis*. 26(3): 427–40.

Datta, S. 2008. 'Bangladesh Factor in the Indo–Myanmarese Gas Deal'. *Strategic Analysis*. 32(1): 103–22.

Datta, S. 2008. *India and Bangladesh: Stuck in a Groove? India's Neighbourhood: Challenges Ahead*. New Delhi: IDSA and Rubicon Publishers.

Datta-Ray, D. 2014. *The Making of Indian Diplomacy: A Critique of Eurocentrism*. New York: Oxford University Press.

Datta-Ray, S.K. 2009. *Looking East to Look West: Lee Kuan Yew's, Mission India*. Singapore: Institute of Southeast Asian Studies.

Daulet Singh, Z. 2010. 'Thinking about an Indian Grand Strategy'. *Strategic Analysis*. 35(1): 52–70.

Dellios, R. and R.J. Ferguson. 2011. 'Sino-Indian Soft Power in a Regional Context'. *Culture Mandala: The Bulletin of the Centre for East-West Cultural and Economic Studies*. 9(2): 15–34.

Destradi, S. 2011. *Indian Foreign and Security Policy in South Asia: Regional Power Strategies*. New York: Routledge.

Destradi, S. 2012. 'India as a Democracy Promoter? New Delhi's Involvement in Nepal's Return to Democracy'. *Democratization*. 19 (2): 286–311.

Dietl, G. 2012. 'India's Iran Policy in the Post-Cold War Period'. *Strategic Analysis*. 36(6): 871–81.

Dittmer, L. 2005. *South Asia's Nuclear Security Dilemma: India, Pakistan, and China*. New York and London: ME Sharpe.

Dixit, J.N. 2001. *India's Foreign Policy and Its Neighbours*. India: Gyan Books.

Dixit, J.N. 2005. *Indian Foreign Service: History and Challenge*. Delhi: Konark Publishers.

Dossani, R. and S. Vijaykumar. 2005. 'Indian Federalism and the Conduct of Foreign Policy in Border States: State Participation and Central Accommodation since 1990'. *APARC Working Paper*.

Druckman, D., A.A. Benton, F. Ali, and J.S. Bagur. 1976. 'Cultural Differences in Bargaining Behavior India, Argentina, and the United States'. *Journal of Conflict Resolution*. 20(3): 413–52.

Dubey, M. 2007. 'SAARC and South Asian Economic Integration'. *Economic and Political Weekly*: 1238–40.

Dukkipati, U. 2009. 'India-Japan Relations: A Partnership for Peace and Prosperity'. *South Asia Monitor*. 134: 1–3.

Efstathopoulos, C. 2011. 'Reinterpreting India's Rise through the Middle Power Prism'. *Asian Journal of Political Science*. 19(1): 74–95.

Efstathopoulos, C. 2015. *Middle Powers in World Trade Diplomacy: India, South Africa and the Doha Development Agenda*. UK and USA: Palgrave Macmillan.

Efstathopoulos, C. 2016. 'India and Global Governance: The Politics of Ambivalent Reform'. *International Politics*. 53(2): 239–59.

Efstathopoulos, C. and D. Kelly. 2014. 'India, Developmental Multilateralism and the Doha Ministerial Conference'. *Third World Quarterly*. 35(6): 1066–81.

Egreteau, R. 2008. 'India and China Vying for Influence in Burma—A New Assessment'. *India Review*. 7(1): 38–72.

Egreteau, R. 2008. 'India's Ambitions in Burma: More Frustration Than Success?'. *Asian Survey*, 48(6): 936–57.

Egreteau, R. 2011. 'A Passage to Burma? India, Development, and Democratization in Myanmar'. *Contemporary Politics*. 17(4): 467–86.

Egreteau, R. 2012. 'The China–India Rivalry Reconceptualized'. *Asian Journal of Political Science*. 20(1): 1–22.

Fair, C.C. 2007. 'India and Iran: New Delhi's Balancing Act'. *Washington Quarterly*. 30(3): 145–59.

Fair, C.C. 2007. 'Indo-Iranian Ties: Thicker Than Oil'. *Middle East*. 11 (1): 41–58.

Fair, C.C. 2010. 'India in Afghanistan and Beyond: Opportunities and Constraints'. *The Century Foundation* (accessed on 2 October 2017) https://papers.ssrn.com/sol3/papers.cfm?abstract_id=1681753.

Ferdinand, P. 2014. 'Rising Powers at the UN: An Analysis of the Voting Behaviour of BRICS in the General Assembly'. *Third World Quarterly*. 35(3): 376–91.

Fidler, D.P. and S. Ganguly. 2010. 'India and Eastphalia'. *Indiana Journal of Global Legal Studies*. 17(1): 147–64.

Flemes, D. 2009. 'India-Brazil-South Africa (IBSA) in the New Global Order Interests, Strategies and Values of the Emerging Coalition'. *International Studies*. 46(4): 401–21.

Follath, E. 2012. 'India at Crossroads on Path to Superpower Status'. *Spiegel Online International* (accessed on 24 November 2016) http://www.spiegel.de/international/world/india-caught-between-super-power-dreams-and-harsh-realities-a-851247.html.

Franda, M.F. 2002. *China and India Online: Information Technology Politics and Diplomacy in the World's Two Largest Nations*. Maryland: Rowman & Littlefield.

Freedberg, S.J. 2007. 'The Kabul-New Delhi Axis'. *National Journal Washington DC*. 39(19): 60–4.

Gahlaut, S. 2009. 'South Asia and the Nonproliferation Regime', in Busch, N. and D. Joyner (eds), *Combating Weapons of Mass Destruction: The Future of International Nonproliferation Policy*. Athens and London: University of Georgia Press.

Ganguly, S. 2003. *The Kashmir Question: Retrospect and Prospect*. Great Britain: Frank Cass and Company Limited.

Ganguly, S. 2010. *India's Foreign Policy: Retrospect and Prospect*. UK: Oxford University Press.

Ganguly, S. 2013. *Conflict Unending: India-Pakistan Tensions since 1947*. United States: Columbia University Press.

Ganguly, S. and D. Mistry. 2006. 'The Case for the US-India Nuclear Agreement'. *World Policy Journal*. 23(2): 11–19.

Ganguly, S. and M.R. Kraig. 2005. 'The 2001–2002 Indo-Pakistani Crisis: Exposing the Limits of Coercive Diplomacy'. *Security Studies*. 14(2): 290–324.

Ganguly, S. and M.S. Pardesi. 2009. 'Explaining Sixty Years of India's Foreign Policy'. *India Review*. 8(1): 4–19.

Ganguly, S. and N. Howenstein. 2009. 'India-Pakistan Rivalry in Afghanistan'. *Journal of International Affairs*. 63(1): 127–40.

Garver, J.W. 2002. 'The China-India-US Triangle: Strategic Relations in the Post-Cold War era'. *National Bureau of Asian Research*.

Gaur, M. 2011. 'Focus: India's Look East Policy'. *Foreign Policy Research Centre Journal*. 8: 1–40.

Gauri, F.N. 2013. 'Indo-Saudi Trade Relation'. *Arabian Journal of Business and Management Review* (Nigerian Chapter). 1(2): 45–57.

Gayer, L. 2010. 'From the Oxus to the Indus: Looking Back at India-Central Asia Connections in the Early Modern Age', in *China and India in Central Asia*. Palgrave Macmillan US, 197–214.

Ghosh, A. 2009. *India's Foreign Policy*. India: Pearson Education.

Ghosh, P.S. 2011. 'Changing Frontiers Making Deeper Sense of India–Bangladesh Relations'. *South Asia Research*. 31(3): 195–211.

Gilboy, G.J. and E. Heginbotham. 2012. *Chinese and Indian Strategic Behavior: Growing Power and Alarm*. UK: Cambridge University Press.

Goldstein, A., N. Pinaud, and H. Reisen. 2006. 'The Rise of China and India'. *Policy Insights*. 19: 1–2.

Gordon, A.S. 2007. *Widening Horizons: Australia's New Relationship with India*. Australia: Australian Strategic Policy Institute.

Gordon, S. 1995. 'South Asia after the Cold War: Winners and Losers'. *Asian Survey*. 35(10); 879–95.

Gordon, S. 2014. *India's Rise as an Asian Power: Nation, Neighborhood, and Region*. Washington, D.C.: Georgetown University Press.

Grace, F. and A. Mattos. 2001. *Indian and Asean: The Politics of India's Look East Policy*. New Delhi: ISEAS.

Guha, R. 2007. *India after Gandhi: The History of the World's Largest Democracy*. New York: HarperCollins.

Guha, R. 2012. 'Will India Become a Superpower?' *India: The Next Superpower*. LSE IDEAS London School of Economics and Political Science. Available at http://eprints.lse.ac.uk/43442/1/India_will%20india%20become%20a%20superpower%28lsero%29.pdf.

Guihong, Z. 2006. 'The Rise of China. India's Perceptions and Responses'. *South Asian Survey*. 13(1): 93–102.

Gupta, A. 2005. *The US-India Relationship: Strategic Partnership or Complementary Interests?* USA: DIANE Publishing.

Gupta, A. 2012. 'India Can Play a Stabilizing Role in the Region'. *Indian Foreign Affairs Journal*. 7(4): 379–87.

Gupta, B.S. 1997. 'India in the Twenty-First Century'. *International Affairs (Royal Institute of International Affairs 1944)*: 297–314.

Gupta, K.R. and V. Shukla. 2009. *Foreign Policy of India*. New Delhi: Atlantic Publishers & Dist.

Gupta, U.N. 2007. *International Nuclear Diplomacy and India*. New Delhi: Atlantic Publishers & Dist.

Haacke, J. 2006. *Myanmar's Foreign Policy: Domestic Influences and International Implications*. UK: Routledge.

Haacke, J. 2006. 'Myanmar's Foreign Policy towards China and India'. *Adelphi Paper* 46(381): 25–39.

Hall, I. 2012. 'India's New Public Diplomacy'. *Asian Survey*. 52(6): 1089–110.

Hanif, M. 2009. 'Indian Involvement in Afghanistan: Stepping Stone or Stumbling Block to Regional Hegemony?'. *German Institute of Global and Area Studies*. 98: 5–30.

Hansel, M. and Möller, M. 2015. 'Indian Foreign Policy and International Humanitarian Norms: A Role Theoretical Analysis'. *Asian Politics & Policy*. 7(1): 79–104.

Haokip, T. 2011. 'India's Look East policy: Domestic Concern or Foreign Apprehension'. *Foreign Policy Research Centre Journal*. 8: 227–34.

Haokip, T. 2015. 'India's Look East Policy: Prospects and Challenges for Northeast India'. *Studies in Indian Politics*. 3(2): 198–211.

Harden, B.E. 2014. 'The Diplomatic Ambitions of the BRIC States: Challenging the Hegemony of the West'. *Journal of International Relations and Foreign Policy*. 2(2): 1–18.

Harmer, A., Y. Xiao, E. Missoni, and F. Tediosi. 2013. '"BRICS Without Straw"? A Systematic Literature Review of Newly Emerging

378   Economies Influence in Global Health'. *Globalization and Health.* 9 (15): 1–11.

Harrison, S.S. and G. Kemp, 1993. *India & America after the Cold War: Report of the Carnegie Endowment Study Group on US-India Relations in a Changing International Environment.* Washington: Brookings Institute Press.

Harshe, R. and K.M. Seethi. 2005. *Engaging with the World: Critical Reflections on India's Foreign Policy.* New Delhi: Orient BlackSwan.

Hirst, M. 2008. 'Brazil India Relations: A Reciprocal Learning Process'. *South Asian Survey.* 15(1): 143–64.

Hoffmann, S.A. 2004. 'Perception and China Policy in India', in Frankel, F.R. and H. Harding (eds), *The India-China Relationship: What the United States Needs to Know.* Washington, D.C.: Columbia University Press.

Hoffmann, S.A. 1990. *India and the China crisis (Vol. 6).* UK and USA: University of California Press.

Holslag, J. 2013. *China and India: Prospects for Peace.* USA: Columbia University Press.

Holslag, J. 2009. 'The Persistent Military Security Dilemma between China and India'. *The Journal of Strategic Studies.* 32(6): 811–40.

Hong, Z. 2007. 'China and India Courting Myanmar for Good Relations', in Kok-Kheng Yeoh, E. (ed.), *Facets of a Transforming China.* Malaysia: Institute of China Studies, University of Malaya, 64.

Hopewell, K, 2015. 'Different Paths to Power: The Rise of Brazil, India and China at the World Trade Organization'. *Review of International Political Economy.* 22(2): 311–38.

Hossain, I. 1998. 'Bangladesh-India relations: The Ganges Water-Sharing Treaty and Beyond'. *Asian Affairs: An American Review.* 25(3): 131–50.

Hosur, P. 2010. 'The Indo-US Civilian Nuclear Agreement: What's the Big Deal?' *International Journal.* 65(2): 435–48.

Hoyt, T.D. 2006. *Military Industry and Regional Defense Policy: India, Iraq and Israel.* London and New York: Routledge.

Hurrell, A. and A. Narlikar. 2006. 'A New Politics of Confrontation? Brazil and India in Multilateral Trade Negotiations'. *Global Society.* 20(4): 415–33.

Hussain, T.K. 1996. *China, India and Southeast Asia after the Cold War. India and Southeast Asia: Challenges and Opportunities.* New Delhi: Konark Publishers Pvt. Ltd.

Hussain, M. 2012. 'Indo-Iranian Relations during the Cold War'. *Strategic Analysis.* 36(6): 859–70.

Hussain, Z. 2013. 'India and the United Arab Emirates: Growing Complementarities in the 21st Century'. *IUP Journal of International Relations*. 7(1): 45–59.

Hymans, J.E. 2002. 'Why Do States Acquire Nuclear Weapons? Comparing the Cases of India and France', in Sardesai, D.R. and R.G. Thomas (eds), *Nuclear India in the Twenty-First Century*. USA: Palgrave Macmillan, 139–60.

Inbar, E. and A.S. Ningthoujam. 2012. *Indo-Israeli Defense Cooperation in the Twenty-First Century*. Israel: Begin–Sadat Center for Strategic Studies, Bar-Ilan University.

Isaksen, K.A. and K. Stokke. 2014. 'Changing Climate Discourse and Politics in India. Climate Change as Challenge and Opportunity for Diplomacy and Development'. *Geoforum*. 57: 110–19.

Jacob, H. 2010. *Shaping India's Foreign Policy: People, Politics, and Places*. New Delhi: Har Anand Publications.

Jacobs, L.M. and R. Van Rossem. 2014. 'The BRIC Phantom: A Comparative Analysis of the BRICs as a Category of Rising Powers'. *Journal of Policy Modeling*. 36: 47–66.

Jacques, K. 1999. *Bangladesh, India, and Pakistan: International Relations and Regional Tensions in South Asia*. New York: Macmillan Press.

Jaganathan, M.M. and G. Kurtz. 2014. 'Singing the Tune of Sovereignty? India and the Responsibility to Protect'. *Conflict, Security & Development*. 14(4): 461–87.

Jain, B.M. 2004. 'India–China Relations: Issues and Emerging Trends'. *The Round Table*. 93(374): 253–69.

Jain, B.M. 2009. *Global Power: India's Foreign Policy, 1947–2006*. United Kingdom: Lexington Books.

Jain, B.M. 2010. *India in the New South Asia: Strategic, Military and Economic Concerns in the Age of Nuclear Diplomacy (Vol. 45)*. London and New York: I.B. Tauris.

Jaishankar, D. 2011. 'US–India Relations: Can India Step up to the Plate?' *Asian Pacific Bulletin*. 126: 1–2.

Jaishankar, S. 2007. *India and USA: New Directions. Indian Foreign Policy: Challenges and Opportunities*. New Delhi: Foreign Service Institute/Academic Foundation.

Janardhan, N. 2011. 'China, India, and the Persian Gulf', in Kamrava, M. (ed.), *International Politics of the Persian Gulf*. New York: Syracuse University Press.

Jenkins, R. 2003. 'India's States and the Making of Foreign Economic Policy: The Limits of the Constituent Diplomacy Paradigm'. *Publius: The Journal of Federalism*. 33(4): 63–82.

Jerve, A.M. and H. Selbervik. 2009. 'Self-Interest and Global Responsibility: Aid Policies of South Korea and India in the Making'. *Chr. Michelsen Insitute Report*. 9: 1–56.

Jha, N.K. 1989. 'Cultural and Philosophical Roots of India's Foreign Policy'. *International Studies*. 26(1): 45–67.

Jha, P.K. 2011. 'India's Defence Diplomacy in Southeast Asia'. *Journal of Defence Studies*. 5(1): 47–63.

Jha, S.K. 1997. *Indo-Russian Relations*. New Delhi: Gyan Publishing.

Joshi, M. 2005. 'India and the Future of Asia: Arranging a Soft-Landing for Pakistan'. *India and Emerging Asia*: 103–29.

Joshi, N. 2007. 'India's Policy toward Central Asia'. *World Focus*. 28(335/336): 445.

Kamath, P.M. 2005. *India-Pakistan Relations: Courting Peace from the Corridors of War*. New Delhi: Bibliophile South Asia.

Kanwal, G. 1999. 'China's Long March to World Power Status: Strategic Challenge for India'. *Strategic Analysis*. 22(11): 1713–28.

Kapila, S. 2006. 'India–Saudi Arabia: The Strategic Significance of the Delhi Declaration'. *South Asia Analysis Group Paper*. 1734.

Kapila, U. 2009. *Indian Economy since Independence*. New Delhi: Academic Foundation.

Kaplan, R.D. 2009. 'Center Stage for the Twenty-First Century: Power Plays in the Indian Ocean'. *Foreign Affairs*. 88(2): 16–32.

Kaplinsky, R. and D. Messner. 2008. 'Introduction: The Impact of Asian Drivers on the Developing World'. *World Development*. 36(2): 197–209.

Kappel, R.T. 2010. *On the Economics of Regional Powers: Comparing China, India, Brazil, and South Africa*. Germany: GIGA German Institute of Global and Area Studies.

Kapur, A. 1988. 'The Indian Subcontinent: The Contemporary Structure of Power and the Development of Power Relations'. *Asian Survey*. 28(7): 693–710.

Kapur, A. 2006. *India—From Regional to World Power*. Oxon: Routledge.

Kapur, D. 2009. 'Public Opinion and Indian Foreign Policy'. *India Review*. 8(3): 286–305.

Kapur, D. 2009. 'Introduction: Future Issues in India's Foreign Policy: Ideas, Interests and Values'. *India Review*. 8(3): 200–08.

Kapur, S.P. 2005. 'India and Pakistan's Unstable Peace: Why Nuclear South Asia Is Not Like Cold War Europe'. *International Security*. 30(2): 127–52.

Kapur, S.P. and S. Ganguly. 2015. 'India, Pakistan, and the Unlikely Dream of a Nuclear-Free South Asia'. *Global Nuclear Disarmament: Strategic, Political, and Regional Perspectives*: 268–82.

Karat, P. 2007. *Subordinate Ally: The Nuclear Deal and India-US Strategic Relations (Vol. 9)*. New Delhi: LeftWord Books.

Karayil, S.B. 2007. 'Does Migration Matter in Trade? A Study of India's Exports to the GCC Countries'. *South Asia Economic Journal*. 8(1): 1–20.

Karim, M.A. 2009. 'Bangladesh-India Relations: Some Recent Trends'. *Journal of Bangladesh Studies*. 11(2): 35–43.

Karmakar, S., R. Kumar, and B. Debroy. 2008. *India's Liberalisation Experience: Hostage to WTO?* India: SAGE Publications.

Kaul, T.N. 2000. *A Diplomat's Diary (1947–1999): The Tantalizing Triangle–China, India and USA*. New Delhi: Macmillan.

Kavalski, E. 2008. 'Venus and the Porcupine Assessing the European Union–India Strategic Partnership'. *South Asian Survey*. 15(1): 63–81.

Kavalski, E. 2009. *India and Central Asia: The International Relations of a Rising Power*. New York: IB Tauris.

Kavalski, E. 2010. 'An Elephant in a China Shop? India's Look North to Central Asia … Seeing Only China', in *China and India in Central Asia*, US: Palgrave Macmillan, 41–60.

Kavalski, E. 2012. *Central Asia and the Rise of Normative Powers: Contextualizing the Security Governance of the European Union, China, and India*. USA: Bloomsbury Publishing.

Kavalski, E. 2014. 'The Shadows of Normative Power in Asia: Framing the International Agency of China, India, and Japan'. *Pacific Focus*. 29(3): 303–28.

Kavalski, E. 2016. 'The EU–India Strategic Partnership: Neither Very Strategic, Nor Much of a Partnership'. *Cambridge Review of International Affairs*. 29(1): 192–208.

Kaye, D.D. 2005. *Rethinking Track Two Diplomacy: The Middle East and South Asia*. The Hague: Netherlands Institute of International Relations Clingendael.

Keay, J. 2011. *India: A History. Revised and Updated*. New York: Grove/Atlantic, Inc.

Kemp, G. 2012. *The East Moves West: India, China, and Asia's Growing Presence in the Middle East*. Washington, D.C.: Brookings Institution Press.

Kerr, P.K. 2012. 'US Nuclear Cooperation with India: Issues for Congress'. *Current Politics and Economics of South, Southeastern, and Central Asia*. 21(1/2): 131–92.

Keukeleire, S. and B. Hooijmaaijers. 2014. 'The BRICS and Other Emerging Power Alliances and Multilateral Organizations in the Asia-

Pacific and the Global South: Challenges for the European Union and Its View on Multilateralism'. *JCMS: Journal of Common Market Studies.* 52(3): 582–99.

Khan, M. 2009. *Towards Better India-Bangladesh Relations. IDSA Strategic Comments.* New Delhi: IDSA.

Khan, M.N. 2001. 'Vajpayee's Visit to Iran: Indo-Iranian Relations and Prospects of Bilateral Cooperation'. *Strategic Analysis.* 25(6): 765–79.

Khan, Y. 2007. *The Great Partition: The Making of India and Pakistan.* New Haven and London: Yale University Press.

Khan, Z. 2013. 'The Changing Dynamics of India-Pakistan Deterrence'. *Pakistan Horizon.* 66(4).

Khan, Z. and A. Khan. 2016. 'The Strategic Impasse over India's Doctrinal Restructuring'. *The Washington Quarterly.* 39(1): 139–57.

Khan, Z. and R. Waseem (n.a.). 'South Asian Strategic Paradox: India-Pakistan Nuclear Flux'. *Institute of Strategic Studies Islamabad* (accessed on 21 November 2016) http://www.issi.org.pk/wp-content/uploads/2016/02/Dr.-Zulfqar-Khan-and-Rubina-Waseem-35-No.2.pdf.

Khanna, P. 2005. 'Bollystan: India's Diasporic Diplomacy'. *India as a New Global Leader.* London: Foreign Policy Centre: 16–26.

Khanna, T. 2008. 'Book Review-Billions of Entrepreneurs: How China and India Are Reshaping Their Futures and Yours'. *Latin Trade.* 16(9): 54.

Khanna, V.C. and C.V. Ranganathan. 2000. *India and China: The Way Ahead After 'Mao's India War'.* New Delhi: Har Anand Publications.

Khilnani, S. 1997. *The Idea of India.* New York: Farrar Straus and Giroux.

Khorana, S. and M. Garcia. 2013. 'European Union–India Trade Negotiations: One Step Forward, One Back?' *JCMS: Journal of Common Market Studies.* 51(4): 684–700.

Khripunov, I. and A. Srivastava. 1999. 'Russian-Indian Relations: Alliance, Partnership, or ?' *Comparative Strategy.* 18(2): 153–71.

Khurana, G.S. 2007. 'Security of Sea Lines: Prospects for India–Japan Cooperation'. *Strategic Analysis.* 31(1): 139–53.

Khurana, G.S. 2008. 'India–US Combined Defense Exercises: An Appraisal'. *Strategic Analysis.* 32(6); 1047–65.

Kiely, R. 2015. *The BRICs, US 'Decline' and Global Transformations.* UK: Palgrave Macmillan.

Kienzle, B. 2015. 'The Exception to the Rule? The EU and India's Challenge to the Non-Proliferation Norm'. *European Security.* 24(1): 36–55.

Kimball, D.G., F. McGoldrick, and L. Scheinman. 2008. 'IAEA-Indian Nuclear Safeguards Agreement: A Critical Analysis'. *Arms Control*

Association. 30 (accessed on 2 October 2017) https://www.armscontrol.org/node/3205.

Kissinger, H. 1979. *The Tilt: The India–Pakistan Crisis of 1971, White House Years.* Boston: Little, Brown & Company.

Kondapalli, S. 2010. 'India's Interactions with East Asia: Opportunities and Challenges'. *International Studies.* 47(2–4): 305–21.

Krishnasamy, K. 2001. 'Recognition for Third World Peacekeepers: India and Pakistan'. *International Peacekeeping.* 8(4): 56–76.

Krishnasamy, K. 2010. 'A Case for India's "Leadership" in United Nations Peacekeeping'. *International Studies.* 47(2–4): 225–46.

Krishnasamy, K. and A. Weigold. 2003. 'The Paradox of India's Peacekeeping'. *Contemporary South Asia.* 12(2): 263–80.

Kristensen, H.M. and R.S. Norris. 2012. 'Indian Nuclear Forces, 2012'. *Bulletin of the Atomic Scientists.* 68(4): 96–101.

Kronstadt, K.A. and K. Katzman. 2006. 'India-Iran Relations and US Interests'. *Congressional Research Service, Library of Congress Washington DC* (accessed on 11 June 2016) http://fpc.state.gov/documents/organization/70294.pdf.

Kshetri, N. 2013. 'Chinese and Indian Trade and Investment Links with Sub-Saharan Africa: Institutions, Capabilities and Competitive Advantage'. *International Journal of Technological Learning, Innovation and Development 2.* 6(1–2): 161–89.

Kudo, T. 2012. 'China's Policy toward Myanmar: Challenges and Prospects'. *The Institute of Developing Economies Working Paper*, IDE-JETRO (accessed on 29 May 2014) http://www. ide. go. jp/English/Research/Region/Asia/pdf/201209_kudo.pdf.

Kugiel, P. 2012. 'India's Soft Power in South Asia'. *International Studies.* 49(3–4): 351–76.

Kumar, A.V. 2010. 'Reforms in the NPT and Prospects for India's Accession: A Situational Analysis'. *Strategic Analysis.* 34(2): 295–308.

Kumar, N. 2013. *India's Global Powerhouses: How They Are Taking on the World.* MA: Harvard Business Press.

Kumar, P. 2015. 'Indian Foreign Policy: Ambition and Transition'. *Contemporary South Asia.* 23(3): 363–4.

Kumar, R. 2008. 'India as a Foreign Policy Actor-Normative Redux', in Tocci, N. (ed.), *Who Is a Normative Foreign Policy Actor? The European Union and Its Global Partners.* CEPS Paperback Series 3: 001–336.

Kumar, R. and S. Kumar. 2010. *In the National Interest: A Strategic Foreign Policy for India.* New Delhi: Business Standard Books.

Kumaraswamy, P.R. 2008. 'India's Persian Problems'. *Strategic Insights* (accessed on 2 October 2017) http://www.nps.edu/Academics/

384

centers/ccc/publications/OnlineJournal/2008/Jul/kumaraswa-myJul08.pdf.

Kumaraswamy, P.R. 2013. 'India's Energy Dilemma with Iran'. *South Asia: Journal of South Asian Studies*. 36(2): 288–96.

Ladwig III, W.C. 2009. 'Delhi's Pacific Ambition: Naval Power, "Look East," and India's Emerging Influence in the Asia-Pacific'. *Asian Security*. 5(2): 87–113.

Laïdi, Z. 2012. 'BRICS: Sovereignty Power and Weakness'. *International Politics*. 49(5): 614–32.

Lal, R. 2006. *Understanding China and India: Security Implications for the United States and the World*. United States: Greenwood Publishing Group.

Lall, M. 2006. 'Indo-Myanmar Relations in the Era of Pipeline Diplomacy'. *Contemporary Southeast Asia*: 424–46.

Lall, M.C. 2001. *India's Missed Opportunity*. Aldershot: Ashgate Press.

Lall, M. C. 2008. 'India-Myanmar Relations—Geopolitics and Energy in Light of the New Balance of Power in Asia'. *ISAS Working Paper*. 29. Singapore: ISAS.

Lall, M. 2009. 'India's New Foreign Policy: The Journey from Moral Non-Alignment to the Nuclear Deal'. *The Geopolitics of Energy in South Asia*. Singapore: *ISEAS*: 27–50.

Latif, A. 2007. *Between Rising Powers: China, Singapore, and India*. Singapore: Institute of Southeast Asian Studies.

Lee, L. 2011. 'The Indian Nuclear Energy Programme: The Quest for Independence', in *Nuclear Energy Development in Asia*. UK: Palgrave Macmillan, 68–97.

Lee, L. 2014. 'Myanmar's Transition to Democracy: New Opportunities or Obstacles for India?'. *Contemporary Southeast Asia: A Journal of International and Strategic Affairs*. 36(2): 290–316.

Lema, R. and A. Lema. 2012. 'Technology Transfer? The Rise of China and India in Green Technology Sectors'. *Innovation and Development*. 2(1): 23–44.

Lesage, D. and T. Van de Graaf (eds). 2015. *Rising Powers and Multilateral Institutions*. UK: Palgrave Macmillan.

Li, M. 2009. 'Sino-Indian Energy Politics'. *The Geopolitics of Energy in South Asia*, Singapore: Institute of Southeast Asian Studies: 152–61.

Lieber, R.J. 2014. 'The Rise of the BRICS and American Primacy'. *International Politics*. 51(2): 137–54.

Lo, V.I. and M. Hiscock. 2014. *The Rise of the BRICS in the Global Political Economy: Changing Paradigms?* UK: Edward Elgar Publishing.

Loomba, A. 2009. 'Of Gifts, Ambassadors, and Copy-cats: Diplomacy, Exchange, and Difference in Early Modern India'. Cherry, B. and G. Sahani (eds). *Emissaries in Early Modern Literature and Culture: Mediation, Transmission, Traffic: 1550–1700*. Surrey: Ashgate Publishing Ltd.

Lounev, S.I. 2002. 'Russia and India: Political Cooperation in the Sphere of Global, Regional and Bilateral Relations'. *China Report*. 38(1): 109–11.

Luce, E. 2010. *In Spite of the Gods: The Rise of Modern India*. USA: Anchor.

Lyon, R. 2010. *The India-China Relationship: A Tempered Rivalry?* Australia: Australian Strategic Policy Institute.

Madan, T. 2010. 'India's International Quest for Oil and Natural Gas: Fueling Foreign Policy?'. *India Review*. 9(1): 2–37.

Mahrenbach, L. 2013. *The Trade Policy of Emerging Powers: Strategic Choices of Brazil and India*. UK: Palgrave Macmillan.

Malhoutra, M. 2007. *India: The Next Decade*. New Delhi: Routledge.

Malik, J.M. 1998. 'India Goes Nuclear: Rationale, Benefits, Costs and Implications'. *Contemporary Southeast Asia*: 191–215.

Malik, M. 2003. 'The Proliferation Axis: Beijing-Islamabad-Pyongyang'. *The Korean Journal of Defense Analysis*. 15(1): 57–100.

Malik, M. 2003. 'The China Factor in the India-Pakistan Conflict'. *Parameters*. 33(1): 35–50.

Malik, M. 2012. 'China and India Today: Diplomats Jostle, Militaries Prepare'. *World Affairs*. 175(2): 74–84.

Malik, J.M. 1994. 'Sino-Indian Rivalry in Myanmar: Implications for Regional Security'. *Contemporary Southeast Asia*: 137–56.

Malik, J.M. 1995. 'China-India Relations in the Post-Soviet Era: The Continuing Rivalry'. *The China Quarterly*. 142: 317–55.

Malone, D.M. 2000. 'Eyes on the Prize: The Quest for Nonpermanent Seats on the UN Security Council'. *Global Governance*. 6(1): 3–23.

Malone, D. 2004. *The UN Security Council: From the Cold War to the 21st Century*. USA: Lynne Rienner Publishers.

Malone, D.M. 2005. 'The High-Level Panel and the Security Council'. *Security Dialogue*. 36(3): 370–2.

Malone, D.M. 2006. *The International Struggle over Iraq: Politics in the United Nations Security Council*. Oxford: Oxford University Press.

Malone, D. 2011. *Does the Elephant Dance?: Contemporary Indian Foreign Policy*. UK: Oxford University Press.

Malone, D.M. and R. Chaturvedy. 2009. 'Impact of India's Economy on Its Foreign Policy since Independence'. *Asia Pacific Foundation of Canada* (accessed on 1 December 2016) http://www.asiapacific.ca/sites/default/files/Indian__Economic__and__Foreign__Policy.pdf.

Manapatra, C. 2005. 'The United States and the Asian Powers', in Sharma, R.R. (ed.), *India and Emerging Asia*. Delhi: SAGE Publications.

Mannully, Y.T. 2008. 'US–India Nuclear Cooperation and Non-Proliferation'. *Nuclear Law Bulletin*. 2008(2): 9–26.

Mansingh, S. 1984. *India's Search for Power: Indira Gandhi's Foreign Policy, 1966–1982*. California: SAGE Publications.

Mansingh, S. 1994. 'India-China Relations in the Post-Cold War Era'. *Asian Survey*: 34(3): 285–300.

Markey, D. 2009. 'Developing India's Foreign Policy "Software"'. *Asia Policy*. 8(1): 73–96.

Mathur, S. 2005. *Voting for the Veto: India in a Reformed UN*. London: Foreign Policy Centre.

Mattoo, A. and H. Jacob. 2010. 'Shaping India's Foreign Policy: People'. *Politics and Places*. New Delhi: Har Anand Publications, 23–45.

Mattoo, A. and R.M. Stern. 2003. *India and the WTO*. Washington, D.C.: World Bank Publications.

Mawdsley, E. and G. McCann. 2010. 'The Elephant in the Corner? Reviewing India-Africa Relations in the New Millennium'. *Geography Compass*. 4(2): 81–93.

Mawdsley, E. 2014. 'Public Perceptions of India's Role as an International Development Cooperation Partner: Domestic Responses to Rising "Donor" Visibility'. *Third World Quarterly*. 35(6): 958–79.

Mazumdar, A. 2011. 'India's Search for a Post-Cold War Foreign Policy Domestic Constraints and Obstacles'. *India Quarterly: A Journal of International Affairs*. 67(2): 165–82.

Mazumdar, A. 2012. 'India's South Asia Policy in the Twenty-First Century: New Approach, Old Strategy'. *Contemporary Politics*. 18(3): 286–302.

Mazumdar, A. 2014. *Indian Foreign Policy in Transition: Relations with South Asia*. London and New York: Routledge.

McDermott, R.F. 2013. *Sources of Indian Tradition: Modern India, Pakistan, and Bangladesh (Vol. 2)*. New York: Columbia University Press.

McDonnell, T. 2013. 'Nuclear Pursuits: Non-P-5 Nuclear-Armed States, 2013'. *Bulletin of the Atomic Scientists*. 69(1): 62–70.

McDuie-Ra, D. 2009. 'Vision 2020 or Re-Vision 1958: The Contradictory Politics of Counter-Insurgency in India's Regional Engagement'. *Contemporary South Asia*. 17(3): 313–30.

McMahon, R.J. 1996. *The Cold War on the Periphery: The United States, India, and Pakistan*. New York: Columbia University Press.

Medcalf, R. 2008. 'Australia-India Relations: Hesitating on the Brink of Partnership'. *Asia Pacific Bulletin*. 13(3): 1–2.

Mehta, P.B. 2009. 'Still under Nehru's Shadow? The Absence of Foreign Policy Frameworks in India'. *India Review*. 8(3): 209–33.

Menon, S. 2009. 'Hostile Relations: India's Pakistan Dilemma'. *Harvard International Review*. 31(3): 14–18.

Meredith, R. 2008. *The Elephant and the Dragon: The Rise of India and China and What It Means for All of Us*. New York: WW Norton & Company.

Michael, A. 2013. *India's Foreign Policy and Regional Multilateralism*. UK: Palgrave Macmillan.

Michel, D. and A. Pandya. 2009. *Indian Climate Policy: Choices and Challenges*. Washington, D.C.: Henry L. Stimson Center.

Mishra, A.D. and G. Prasad. 2003. *India and Canada: Past, Present & Future*. New Delhi: Mittal Publications.

Mishra, R.K. 2005. 'India–Pakistan: Nuclear Stability and Diplomacy'. *Strategic Analysis*. 29(1): 101–30.

Misra, A. 2004. 'Indo–Pakistan Talks 2004: Nuclear Confidence Building Measures (NCBMs) and Kashmir'. *Strategic Analysis*. 28(2): 347–51.

Mistry, D. 1999. 'Diplomacy, Sanctions, and the US Nonproliferation Dialogue with India and Pakistan'. *Asian Survey*. 39(5): 753–71.

Mistry, D. 2004. 'A Theoretical and Empirical Assessment of India as an Emerging World Power'. *India Review*. 3(1): 64–87.

Mistry, D. 2006. 'Diplomacy, Domestic Politics, and the US-India Nuclear Agreement'. *Asian Survey*. 46(5): 675–98.

Mistry, D. 2014. *The US–India Nuclear Agreement: Diplomacy and Domestic Politics*. India: Cambridge University Press.

Mitra, S. 2012. 'The Dialectic of Politics and Law and the Resilience of India's Post-Colonial Governance: Ultima Ratio Regum?'. *Verfassung und Recht in Übersee/Law and Politics in Africa, Asia and Latin America*: 131–56.

Mitra, S.K. 2001. 'War and Peace in South Asia: A Revisionist View of India–Pakistan Relations'. *Contemporary South Asia*. 10(3): 361–79.

Mitra, S.K. 2003. 'The Reluctant Hegemon: India's Self-Perception and the South Asian Strategic Environment'. *Contemporary South Asia*. 12(3): 399–17.

Mitra, S.K. 2012. *Politics in India: Structure, Process and Policy*. USA and Canada: Routledge.

Mohan, C.R. 2003. *Crossing the Rubicon: The Shaping of India's New Foreign Policy*. USA: Viking by Penguin Books India.

Mohan, C.R. 2006. 'India and the Balance of Power'. *Foreign Affairs*. 85: 17–32.

388

Mohan, C.R. 2007. 'India's Neighbourhood Policy: Four Dimensions'. *Indian Foreign Affairs Journal*. 2(1): (n.a.).

Mohan, C.R. 2009. 'The Re-Making of Indian Foreign Policy Ending the Marginalization of International Relations Community'. *International Studies*. 46(1–2): 147–63.

Mohan, C.R. 2010. 'Rising India: Partner in Shaping the Global Commons?'. *The Washington Quarterly*. 33(3): 133–48.

Mohan, C.R. 2012. 'India's Foreign Policy Transformation'. *Asia policy*. 14(1): 108–10.

Mohanty, M. 2010. 'China and India Competing Hegemonies or Civilizational Forces of Swaraj and Jiefang?'. *China Report*. 46(2): 103–11.

Montgomery, E.B. and E.S. Edelman. 2015. 'Rethinking Stability in South Asia: India, Pakistan, and the Competition for Escalation Dominance'. *Journal of Strategic Studies*. 38(1–2): 159–82.

Moorthy, R., H.K. Sum, and G. Benny. 2015. 'Power Asymmetry and Nuclear Option in India–Pakistan Security Relations'. *Asian Journal of Scientific Research*. 8(1): 80–94.

Mudiam, P.R. 2003. 'The India–Pakistan Dispute over Jammu and Kashmir and the United States'. *Global Change, Peace & Security*. 15(3): 263–76.

Mukherjee, R. 2014. 'The False Promise of India's Soft Power'. *Geopolitics, History, and International Relations*. (1): 46–62.

Mukherjee, R. and D.M. Malone. 2011. 'From High Ground to High Table: The Evolution of Indian Multilateralism'. *Global Governance*. 17(3): 311–29.

Mukherji, R. and S.S. Kale. 2009. 'Introduction: India, Sixty Years on'. *India Review*. 8(1): 1–3.

Muni, S.D. 1991. 'India and the Post-Cold War World: Opportunities and Challenges'. *Asian Survey*. 31(9): 862–74.

Muni, S.D. 1993. 'India and Its Neighbours: Persisting Dilemmas and New Opportunities'. *International Studies*. 30(2): 189–206.

Muni, S.D. 2000. 'India in SAARC: A Reluctant Policy-Maker', in Hettne, B., A. Inotai, and O. Sunkel (eds), *National Perspectives on the New Regionalism in the North (Vol. 2)*, 108–31.

Muni, S.D. 2003. 'Problem Areas in India's Neighbourhood Policy'. *South Asian Survey*. 10(2): 185–96.

Muni, S.D. and I.A. Lodhi. 2010. *The Emerging Dimensions of SAARC*. India: Cambridge India.

Muni, S.D. 2009. *India's Foreign Policy: The Democracy Dimension with Special Reference to Neighbours*. India: Cambridge.

Muni, S.D. and C.R. Mohan. 2004. 'Emerging Asia: India's Options'. *International Studies*. 41(3): 313–33.

Muni, S.D. and C.R. Mohan. 2005. *India's Options in a Changing Asia*. New Delhi: SAGE Publications.

Murthy, C.S.R. 2010. 'Assessing India at the United Nations in the Changing Context'. *International Studies*. 47(2–4): 205–23.

Murti, B. and R.S. Zaharna. 2014. 'India's Digital Diaspora Diplomacy: Operationalizing Collaborative Public Diplomacy Strategies for Social Media'. *Exchange: The Journal of Public Diplomacy*. 5(1): 3–29.

Mullen, D.R. 2013. 'India's Development Assistance: Will It Change the Global Development Finance Paradigm', in *Causes, Consequences & the Role of Law Conference*. Gießen and New York: University School of Law.

Murthy, C.S. 2011. *India as a Non-Permanent Member of the UN Security Council in 2011–12*. Germany: Friedrich-Ebert-Stiftung.

Myint-U, T. 2011. *Where China Meets India: Burma and the New Crossroads of Asia*. Great Britain and USA: Macmillan.

Naaz, F. 2001. 'Indo-Iranian Relations 1947–2000'. *Strategic Analysis*. 24(10): 1911–26.

Naaz, F. 2005. *West Asia and India: Changing Perspectives*. New Delhi: Shipra Publications.

Nafey, A. 2008. 'India and the G8', in Cooper, A.F. and A. Antkiewicz (eds), *Emerging Powers in Global Governance: Lessons from the Heiligendamm process*. Canada: Wilfrid Laurier University.

Nag, B. and A. Nandi. 2006. 'Analysing India's Trade Dynamics vis-à-vis SAARC Members Using the Gravity Model'. *South Asia Economic Journal*. 7(1): 83–98.

Naidu, G.V.C. 2004. 'Whither the Look East Policy: India and Southeast Asia'. *Strategic Analysis*. 28(2): 331–46.

Naik, M.K. 2016. 'Trends in India-Bangladesh Relations'. *PARIPEX-Indian Journal of Research*. 4(7): 85–9.

Nanda, P. 2003. *Rediscovering Asia: Evolution of India's Look-east Policy*. New Delhi: Lancer Publishers.

Narang, V. 2013. 'Five Myths about India's Nuclear Posture'. *The Washington Quarterly*. 36(3): 143–57.

Narang, V. and P. Staniland. 2012. 'Institutions and Worldviews in Indian Foreign Security Policy'. *India Review*. 11(2): 76–94.

Narlikar, A. 2007. 'All That Glitters Is Not Gold: India's Rise to Power'. *Third World Quarterly*. 28(5): 983–96.

Narlikar, A. 2011. 'Is India a Responsible Great Power?' *Third world quarterly*. 32(9): 1607–21.

390

Narlikar, A. 2013. 'Negotiating the Rise of New Powers'. *International Affairs*. 89(3): 561–76.

Narlikar, A. 2013. 'India Rising: Responsible to Whom?' *International Affairs*. 89(3): 595–614.

Narlikar, A. and A. Narlikar. 2014. *Bargaining with a Rising India: Lessons from the Mahabharata*. UK: Oxford University Press.

Natarajan, K. 2014. 'Digital Public Diplomacy and a Strategic Narrative for India'. *Strategic Analysis*. 38(1): 91–106.

Nayan, R. 2010. 'The NPT and India: Accommodating the Exception'. *Strategic Analysis*. 34(2): 309–21.

Nayar, B.R. 1998. 'Political Structure and India's Economic Reforms of the 1990s'. *Pacific Affairs*: 335–58.

Nayar, B.R. 2001. *India and the Major Powers after Pokharan II*. New Delhi: Har Anand Publications.

Nayar, B.R. and T.V. Paul. 2003. *India in the World Order: Searching for Major-Power Status*. UK: Cambridge University Press.

Nayyar, D. 2010. 'China, India, Brazil and South Africa in the World Economy: Engines of Growth?' *Southern Engines of Global Growth*. 1: 9–27.

Nelken, D. 2005. 'Signaling Conformity: Changing Norms in Japan and China'. *Mich. J. Int'l L.* 27: 933–72.

Norling, N. and N. Swanström. 2007. 'The Shanghai Cooperation Organization, Trade, and the Roles of Iran, India and Pakistan'. *Central Asian Survey*. 26(3): 429–44.

Nzomo, M. 2014. 'Foreign Policy and Diplomacy in India–East African Relations'. *Insight on Africa*. 6(2): 89–111.

Ogden, C. 2009. 'Post-Colonial, Pre-BJP: The Normative Parameters of India's Security Identity, 1947–1998'. *Asian Journal of Political Science*. 17(2): 215–37.

Ogden, C. 2010. 'Norms, Indian Foreign Policy and the 1998–2004 National Democratic Alliance'. *The Round Table*. 99(408): 303–15.

Oldenburg, P. and M. Bouton. 2002. *India Briefing: A Transformative Fifty Years*. Delhi: Aakar Books.

Ollapally, D. 2011. 'India: The Ambivalent Power in Asia'. *International Studies*. 48(3–4): 201–22.

Ollapally, D. and R. Rajagopalan. 2011. 'The Pragmatic Challenge to Indian Foreign Policy'. *The Washington Quarterly*. 34(2): 145–62.

Onderco, M. 2015. *Iran's Nuclear Program and the Global South: The Foreign Policy of India, Brazil, and South Africa*. UK: Palgrave MacMillan.

Pachauri, R.K. 2001. 'On Track with Teheran: Shift in India's West Asia strategy'. *The Times of India*. 19: (n.a.).

Pan, C. 2014. 'The "Indo-Pacific" and Geopolitical Anxieties about China's Rise in the Asian Regional Order'. *Australian Journal of International Affairs.* 68(4): 453–69.

Panagariya, A. 2008. *India: The Emerging Giant.* Oxford/New York: Oxford University Press.

Panda, J.P. 2013. 'Competing Realities in China–India Multilateral Discourse: Asia's Enduring Power Rivalry'. *Journal of Contemporary China.* 22(82): 669–90.

Panda, R. 2011. 'India–Republic of Korea Military Diplomacy: Past and Future Projections'. *Journal of Defense Studies.* 5(1): 16–38.

Pande, A. 2011. *Explaining Pakistan's Foreign Policy: Escaping India.* London and New York: Taylor & Francis.

Pande, S. 2013. 'India Should Work with Like-Minded Countries'. *Indian Foreign Affairs Journal.* 8(3): 277–84.

Pant, G. 2008. *India, the Emerging Energy Player.* New Delhi: Pearson Education India.

Pant, H. 2008. *Contemporary Debates in Indian Foreign and Security Policy: India Negotiates Its Rise in the International System.* New York: Palgrave Macmillan.

Pant, H.V. 2004. 'India and Iran: An "Axis" in the Making?'. *Asian Survey.* 44(3): 369–83.

Pant, H.V. 2005. 'India's Nuclear Doctrine and Command Structure: Implications for India and the World'. *Comparative Strategy.* 24(3): 277–93.

Pant, H.V. 2007. 'India and Bangladesh: Will the Twain Ever Meet?'. *Asian Survey.* 47(2): 231–49.

Pant, H.V. 2007. 'A Fine Balance: India Walks a Tightrope between Iran and the United States'. *Orbis.* 51(3): 495–509.

Pant, H.V. 2009. 'Looking Beyond Tehran: India's Rising Stakes in the Gulf'. *India's Growing Role in the Gulf.* 41.

Pant, H.V. 2009. 'Indian Foreign Policy Challenges: Substantive Uncertainties and Institutional Infirmities'. *Asian Affairs.* 40(1): 90–101.

Pant, H.V. 2009. *Indian Foreign Policy in a Unipolar World (Vol. 2).* India: Routledge.

Pant, H.V. 2009. 'A Rising India's Search for a Foreign Policy'. *Orbis.* 53(2): 250–64.

Pant, H.V. 2011. 'India's Relations with Iran: Much Ado about Nothing'. *The Washington Quarterly.* 34(1): 61–74.

Pant, H.V. 2011. *The US-India Nuclear Pact: Policy, Process, and Great Power Politics.* New Delhi: Oxford University Press.

Pant, H.V. 2013. 'India–Russia Ties and India's Strategic Culture: Dominance of a Realist Worldview'. *India Review*. 12(1): 1–19.

Pant, H.V. 2013. *India's Changing Afghanistan Policy: Regional and Global Implications*. USA: Strategic Studies Institute.

Pant, H.V. 2014. 'India and the Middle East: Before and After the Arab Spring', in Mason, R. (ed.), *The International Politics of the Arab Spring*. US: Palgrave Macmillan.

Pardesi, M.S. 2015. 'Is India a Great Power? Understanding Great Power Status in Contemporary International Relations'. *Asian Security*. 11(1): 1–30.

Pardesi, M.S. and S. Ganguly. 2007. 'The Rise of India and the India–Pakistan Conflict'. *Fletcher F. World Affairs*. 31: 131–46.

Pasha, A.K. 1999. *India and West Asia: Continuity and Change*. Delhi: Gyan Sagar Publications.

Pasha, A.K. 2006. *India and Turkey, Past and Emerging Relations*. Delhi: Academic Excellence.

Pasha, A.K. 2007. 'India and West Asia', in Sisodia, N.S. and A.K. Behuria (eds), *West Asia in Turmoil: Implications for Global Security*. New Delhi: Academic Foundation.

Pasha, A.K. 2008. 'US Invasion of Iraq and Indo-Iraq Relations'. *Jadavpur Journal of International Relations*. 11(1): 181–212.

Pasha, A.K. 2010. 'New Directions in India's Role in West Asia and the Gulf'. *International Studies*. 47(2–4): 333–46.

Patel, S. and T. Uys. 2013. *Contemporary India and South Africa: Legacies, Identities, Dilemmas*. India: Routledge.

Paul, T.V. 2006. 'The US-India Nuclear Accord: Implications for the Nonproliferation Regime'. *Int'l J.* 62: 845–66.

Paul, T.V. and M. Shankar. 2007. 'Why the US–India Nuclear Accord Is a Good Deal'. *Survival*. 49(4): 111–22.

Pattanaik, S.S. 2005. 'Internal Political Dynamics and Bangladesh's Foreign Policy towards India'. *Strategic Analysis*. 29(3): 395–426.

Pattanaik, S.S. 2010. 'India's Neighbourhood Policy: Perceptions from Bangladesh'. *Strategic Analysis*. 35(1): 71–87.

Pattanaik, S.S. 2012. 'India's Afghan Policy: Beyond Bilateralism'. *Strategic Analysis*. 36(4): 569–83.

Pattnayak, S.R. 2007. 'India as an Emerging Power'. *India Quarterly: A Journal of International Affairs*. 63(1): 79–110.

Paudyal, G. 2014. 'Border Dispute between Nepal and India'. *Researcher: A Research Journal of Culture and Society*. 1(2): 35–48.

Perkovich, G. 2003. 'Is India a Major Power?' *Washington Quarterly*. 27(1): 129–44.

Perkovich, G. 2003. 'The Measure of India: What Makes Greatness?' *Seminar New Delhi Mayika Singhi*: 56–64.

Pham, J.P. 2007. 'India's Expanding Relations with Africa and Their Implications for US Interests'. *American Foreign Policy Interests*. 29(5): 341–52.

Pham, J.P. 2011. 'India in Africa: Implications of an Emerging Power for AFRICOM and US Strategy'. *Strategic Studies Institute* (accessed on 0 October 2017) http://www.dtic.mil/dtic/tr/fulltext/u2/a539047.pdf

Plagemann, J. and S. Destradi. 2015. 'Soft Sovereignty, Rising Powers, and Subnational Foreign Policy-Making: The Case of India'. *Globalizations*. 12(5): 728–43.

Pradhan, B. 2004. 'Changing Dynamics of India's West Asia Policy'. *International Studies*. 41(1): 1–88.

Pradhan, S.R. 2008. *India, GCC, and the Global Energy Regime: Exploring Interdependence and Outlook for Collaboration*. New Delhi: Academic Foundation.

Pradhan, S. 2010. 'India and the Gulf Cooperation Council (GCC): An Economic and Political Perspective'. *Strategic Analysis*. 34(1): 93–103.

Pradhan, P.K. 2011. 'GCC-Iran Rivalry and Strategic Challenges for India in the Gulf'. *Indian Foreign Affairs Journal*. 6(1): 45–57.

Pradhan, P.K. 2013. 'India's Relationship with Saudi Arabia: Forging a Strategic Partnership'. *Strategic Analysis*. 37(2): 231–41.

Prasad, B. 1962. *The Origins of Indian Foreign Policy: The Indian National Congress and World Affairs, 1885–1947*. Calcutta: Bookland Pvt. Ltd.

Prys, M. 2012. *Redefining Regional Power in International Relations: Indian and South African Perspectives (Vol. 1)*. New York: Routledge.

Purushothaman, U. 2010. 'Shifting Perceptions of Power: Soft Power and India's Foreign Policy'. *Journal of Peace Studies*. 17(2 and 3): 1–16.

Purushothaman, U. 2012. 'American Shadow over India–Iran Relations'. *Strategic Analysis*. 36(6): 899–910.

Quadir, F. 2013. 'Rising Donors and the New Narrative of "South–South" Cooperation: What Prospects for Changing the Landscape of Development Assistance Programmes?' *Third World Quarterly*. 34(2): 321–38.

Quinlan, M. 2000. 'How Robust Is India-Pakistan Deterrence?'. *Survival*. 42(4): 141–54.

Racine, J.L. 2008. 'Post-Post-Colonial India: From Regional Power to Global Player'. *Politique Étrangère*. 5: 65–78.

Raghavan, S. 2009. 'A Coercive Triangle: India, Pakistan, the United States, and the Crisis of 2001–2002'. *Defense Studies*. 9(2): 242–60.

Raghavan, S. 2010. *War and Peace in Modern India*. Ranikhet: Palgrave Macmillan.

Rai, A.K. 2003. 'Diplomacy and the News Media: A Comment on the Indian Experience'. *Strategic Analysis*. 27(1): 21–40.

Rajain, A. 2005. *Nuclear Deterrence in Southern Asia: China, India and Pakistan*. India: SAGE Publications.

Rajamani, L. 2009. 'India and Climate Change: What India Wants, Needs, and Needs to Do'. *India Review*. 8(3): 340–74.

Rajan, M.S. 1993. 'India's Foreign Policy: The Continuing Relevance of Nonalignment'. *International Studies*. 30(2): 141–50.

Rajiv, S.S.C. 2011. 'India and Iran's Nuclear Issue: The Three Policy Determinants'. *Strategic Analysis*. 35(5): 819–35.

Rajiv, S.S.C. 2012. 'The Delicate Balance: Israel and India's Foreign Policy Practice'. *Strategic Analysis*, 36(1): 128–44.

Ramamurthi, T.G. 1997. 'Foundation of India's Africa Policy'. *Africa Quarterly*. 37(1–2): 27–41.

Ramana, M.V. 2007. 'Nuclear Power in India: Failed Past, Dubious Future' (accessed on 16 November 2016) www.npec-web.org/Frameset.asp.

Ramana, S. 2012. 'The Pakistan Factor in the India–Iran Relationship'. *Strategic Analysis*. 36(6): 941–56.

Ramazani, R.K. 1998. 'The Emerging Arab-Indian Rapprochement: Towards an Integrated US Policy in the Middle East?'. *Middle East Policy*. 6(1): 45–62.

Rana, S. 1970. 'The Changing Indian Diplomacy at the United Nations'. *International Organization*. 24(01): 48–73.

Rana, K.S. 2002. 'Inside the Indian Foreign Service'. *Foreign Service Journal*. 80: 28–36.

Rana, K.S. 2004. 'Economic Diplomacy in India: A Practitioner Perspective'. *International Studies Perspectives*. 5(1): 66–70.

Rana, K.S. 2008. *Asian Diplomacy: The Foreign Ministries of China, India, Japan, Singapore, and Thailand*. Washington, D.C.: Johns Hopkins University Press.

Rana, K.S. 2008. 'Regional Diplomacy and India–China Economic Relations'. *China Report*. 44(3): 297–306.

Rana, K.S. 2009. 'India's Diaspora Diplomacy'. *The Hague Journal of Diplomacy*. 4(3): 361–72.

Rana, K.S. 2010. 'India's Diplomatic Infrastructure and Software: Challenges for the 21st Century'. *Strategic Analysis*. 34(3): 364–70.

Rana, K.S. 2014. 'Diplomacy Systems and Processes Comparing India and China'. *China Report*. 50(4): 297–323.

Randol, S. 2008. 'How to Approach the Elephant: Chinese Perceptions of India in the Twenty-First Century'. *Asian Affairs: An American Review.* 34(4): 211–88.

Ranganathan, C.V. 2011. 'Response to India's Look East Policy'. *Foreign Policy Research Centre Journal.* 8: 8–10.

Ray, J.K. 2013. *India's Foreign Relations, 1947–2007.* UK and New Delhi: Routledge.

Reddy, Y.Y. 2007. *Emerging India in Asia-Pacific.* New Delhi: New Century Publications.

Rehman, I. 2009. 'Keeping the Dragon at Bay: India's Counter-Containment of China in Asia'. *Asian Security.* 5(2): 114–43.

Riedel, B. 2008. 'South Asia's Nuclear Decade'. *Survival.* 50(2): 107–26.

Robbani, G. 2016. 'India as a Global Power: Capability, Willingness, and Acceptance', in *Global and Regional Leadership of BRICS Countries.* Switzerland: Springer International Publishing.

Rothermund, D. 2008. *India: The Rise of an Asian Giant.* New Haven, CT: Yale University Press.

Rotter, A.J. 2000. *Comrades at Odds: The United States and India, 1947–1964.* New York: Cornell University Press.

Routray, B.P. 2011. 'India-Myanmar Relations: Triumph of Pragmatism'. *Jindal Journal of International Affairs.* 1: 301–21.

Roy, M.S. 2011. 'Strategic Importance of Turkmenistan for India'. *Strategic Analysis.* 35(4): 661–82.

Roy-Chaudhury, R. 2014. 'India: Gulf Security Partner in Waiting?'. *Adelphi Papers.* 54(447–8): 225–46.

Rubinoff, A.G. 1991. 'The Multilateral Imperative in India's Foreign Policy'. *The Round Table.* 80(319): 313–34.

Rusko, C.J. and K. Sasikumar. 2007. 'India and China: From Trade to Peace?'. *Asian Perspective*: 99–123.

Sachar, B.S. 2003. 'Cooperation in Military Training as a Tool of Peacetime Military Diplomacy'. *Strategic Analysis.* 27(3): 404–21.

Sachdeva, G. 2010. 'The Reconstruction in Afghanistan: The Indian and Chinese contribution', in Laruelle, M., J. Huchet, S. Peyrouse, and B. Balci (eds), *China and India in Central Asia: A New 'Great Game'?* USA: Palgrave Macmillan, 173–94.

Sagar, R. 2009. 'State of Mind: What Kind of Power Will India Become?' *International Affairs.* 85(4): 801–16.

Sakhuja, V. 2012. 'India and Myanmar: Choices for Military Cooperation'. *Indian Council of World Affairs, Issue Brief* (September 2012): 1–9.

Saksena, K.P. 1996. 'India's Foreign Policy: The Decision making Process'. *International Studies.* 33(4): 391–405.

Sardesai, D. and R. Thomas. 2002. *Nuclear India in the Twenty-First Century*. New York: Palgrave Macmillan.

Sasikumar, K. 2009. 'India's Debated Nuclear Policy'. *India Review*. 8(3): 375–84.

Satia, P. 2007. 'Developing Iraq: Britain, India and the Redemption of Empire and Technology in the First World War'. *Past & Present*. 197(1): 211–55.

Sawhney, A. and R. Kumar. 2008. 'Rejuvenating SAARC: The Strategic Payoffs for India'. *Global Economy Journal*. 8(2): 1–17.

Schmidt, J.D. 2014. 'India China Encroachment and Positioning in Southeast Asia', in *India in the Contemporary World*. India: Routledge.

Schmidt, J.D. 2015. 'India's Rise, the European Union and the BRICS: An Uneasy Relation', in Rewizorski, M. *The European Union and the BRICS*. Switzerland: Springer International Publishing, 121–40.

Scott, D. 2007. 'Strategic Imperatives of India as an Emerging Player in Pacific Asia'. *International Studies*. 44(2): 123–40.

Scott, D., 2008. 'The Great Power "Great Game" between India and China: 'The Logic of Geography'". *Geopolitics*, 13(1): 1–26.

Scott, D. 2008. 'Sino-Indian Security Predicaments for the Twenty-First Century'. *Asian Security*. 4(3): 244–70.

Scott, D. 2009. 'India's "Extended Neighborhood" Concept: Power Projection for a Rising Power'. *India Review*. 8(2): 107–43.

Scott, D. 2011. *Handbook of India's International Relations*. London: Routledge.

Scott, D. 2013. 'India's Role in the South China Sea: Geopolitics and Geoeconomics in Play'. *India Review*. 12(2): 51–69.

Selth, A. 1996. 'Burma and the Strategic Competition between China and India'. *The Journal of Strategic Studies*. 19(2): 213–30.

Sen, T. 2003. *Buddhism, Diplomacy, and Trade: The Realignment of Sino-Indian Relations, 600–1400*. USA: University of Hawaii Press.

Sen, T. 2006. 'The Yuan Khanate and India: Cross-Cultural Diplomacy in the Thirteenth and Fourteenth Centuries'. *Asia Major*. 299–326.

Sengupta, D., D. Chakraborty, and P. Banerjee. 2006. *Beyond the Transition Phase of WTO: An Indian Perspective on Emerging Issues*. New Delhi: Academic Foundation.

Sethi, M. 2000. 'Indo-Russian Nuclear Cooperation: Opportunities and Challenges'. *Strategic Analysis*. 14(9): 1757–61.

Shah, S.K. 2015. *India and China: The Battle between Soft and Hard Power*. India: Vij Books India Pvt Ltd.

Shakoor, F. 1997. 'Recasting Pakistan-India Relations in the Post-Cold War Era'. *Pakistan Horizon*. 50(4): 75–92.

Sharma, A. and D. Bing. 2015. 'India–Israel Relations: The Evolving Partnership'. *Israel Affairs*. 21(4): 620–32.

Sharma, S.D. 2009. *China and India in the Age of Globalization*. USA: Cambridge University Press.

Shaw, T.M. 2015. 'From Post-BRICS Decade to Post-2015: Insights from Global Governance and Comparative Regionalisms'. *Palgrave Communications*. 1(14004): 1–6.

Sheth, D.L. 1995. 'Democracy and Globalization in India: Post-Cold War Discourse'. *The Annals of the American Academy of Political and Social Science*. 540(1): 24–39.

Sidaway, J.D. 2012. 'Geographies of Development: New Maps, New Visions?' *The Professional Geographer*. 64(1): 49–62.

Siddiqui, A. 2007. *India and South Asia: Economic Developments in the Age of Globalization*. USA: M.E. Sharpe.

Siddiqi, M. 2006. *India & SAARC Nations*. New Delhi: Maxford Books.

Sidhu, W.P.S. 2004. *Evolution of India's Nuclear Doctrine*. Delhi: Centre for Policy Research.

Sikri, R. 2007. *India's Foreign Policy Priorities in the Coming Decade. ISAS Working Paper, 25*. Singapore: Institute of South Asian Studies.

Sikri, R. 2009. *Challenge and Strategy: Rethinking India's Foreign Policy*. India: SAGE Publications.

Singh, A., 2012. 'Emerging Trends in India–Myanmar Relations'. *Maritime Affairs: Journal of the National Maritime Foundation of India*. 8(2): 25–47.

Singh, A. 2009. 'The India-Canada Civilian Nuclear Deal: Implications for Canadian Foreign Policy'. *International Journal*. 65(1): 233–53.

Singh, K.G. 2004. 'India and the Europe Union: New Strategic Partnership'. *South Asia Analysis Group Paper*. 1163: (n.a.).

Singh, M. 2003. *India and Tajikistan: A Perspective for the 21st Century*. New Delhi: Anamika Publishers.

Singh, M. 2013. 'Japan–India Parliamentary Friendship League and International Friendship Exchange Council'. *PMO*, Tokyo. 28.

Singh, N. 2012. 'How to Tame Your Dragon: An Evaluation of India's Foreign Policy toward China'. *India Review*. 11(3): 139–60.

Singh, S. 2008. 'India–China Relations Perception, Problems, Potential'. *South Asian Survey*. 15(1): 83–98.

Singh, S. and S.S. Rahman. 2010. 'India-Singapore Relations: Constructing a "New" Bilateral Relationship'. *Contemporary Southeast Asia: A Journal of International and Strategic Affairs*. 32(1): 70–97.

Singh, S.K. 2007. 'India and West Africa: A Burgeoning Relationship'. *Chatham House Africa Programme/Asia Programme, Briefing paper, AFP/ASP BP*. 7(01).

Sinha, A. and J.P. Dorschner. 2010. 'India: Rising Power or a Mere Revolution of Rising Expectations'. *Polity*. 42(1): 74–99.

Sinha, A. and M. Mohta. 2007. *Indian Foreign Policy: Challenges and Opportunities*. New Delhi: Academic Foundation.

Sinha, Mrinalini. 2006. *Specters of Mother India: The Global Restructuring of an Empire*. North Carolina: Duke University Press.

Six, C. 2009. 'The Rise of Postcolonial States as Donors: A Challenge to the Development Paradigm?' *Third World Quarterly*. 30(6): 1103–21.

Smith, G. 2010. 'Australia and the Rise of India'. *Australian Journal of International Affairs*. 64(5): 566–82.

Smith, J.M. 2013. *Cold Peace: China–India Rivalry in the Twenty-First Century*. UK: Lexington Books.

Sokolski, H., J. Stephenson, P. Tynan, M.V. Ramana, Z. Mian, A.H. Nayyar, R. Rajaraman, C.D. Ferguson, R. Speier, and G. Perkovich. 2007. *Gauging US-Indian Strategic Cooperation*. Pennsylvania, USA: Army War Coll Strategic Studies Institute Carlislie Barracks.

Solomon, H. 2012. 'Critical Reflections of Indian Foreign Policy: Between Kautilya and Ashoka'. *South African Journal of International Affairs*. 19(1): 65–78.

Southerland, M., I. Koch-Weser, and A. Zhang. 2015. 'China-India Relations: Tensions Persist Despite Growing Cooperation'. *Current Politics and Economics of Northern and Western Asia*. 24(1): 35.

Squassoni, S. 2006. 'India and Iran: WMD Proliferation Activities'. *Library Of Congress Washington DC Congressional Research Service* (accessed on 12 January 2016) http://oai.dtic.mil/oai/oai?verb=getRecord&meta dataPrefix=html&identifier=ADA479100

Sridharan, K. 2006. 'Explaining the Phenomenon of Change in Indian Foreign Policy under the National Democratic Alliance Government'. *Contemporary South Asia*. 15(1): 75–91.

Srinivasan, T.N. 2004. 'China and India: Economic Performance, Competition and Cooperation: An Update'. *Journal of Asian Economics*. 15(4): 613–36.

Staniland, P. 2008. 'Explaining Civil-Military Relations in Complex Political Environments: India and Pakistan in Comparative Perspective'. *Security Studies*. 17(2): 322–62.

Stephen, M.D. 2012. 'Rising Regional Powers and International Institutions: The Foreign Policy Orientations of India, Brazil and South Africa'. *Global Society*. 26(3): 289–309.

Stephen, M.D. 2014. 'Rising Powers, Global Capitalism and Liberal Global Governance: A Historical Materialist Account of the BRICs Challenge'. *European Journal of International Relations*. 20(4): 912–38.

Stewart-Ingersoll, R. and D. Frazier. 2010. 'India as a Regional Power: Identifying the Impact of Roles and Foreign Policy Orientation on the South Asian Security Order'. *Asian Security*. 6(1): 51–73.

Stobdan, P. 2008. 'India and Kazakhstan Should Share Complementary Objectives'. *Strategic Analysis*. 33(1): 1–7.

Stone, R. 2006. 'India Struggles to Put Its Nuclear House in Order'. *Science*. 311(5759): 318–19.

Stuenkel, O. 2012. 'India's National Interests and Diplomatic Activism: Towards Global Leadership'. *India: The Next Superpower*. LSE IDEAS London School of Economics and Political Science: 34–8.

Stuenkel, O. 2015. *The BRICS and the Future of Global Order*. London: Lexington Books.

Subramaniam, P. 2009. 'India and the CTBT: Renewing the Debate'. *Department of International Studies*, Stella Maris College, Chennai (accessed on 21 November 2016) http://www.ipcs.org/article_details.php?articleNo=2876.

Sullivan, K. 2014. 'Exceptionalism in Indian Diplomacy: The Origins of India's Moral Leadership Aspirations'. *South Asia: Journal of South Asian Studies*. 37(4): 640–55.

Suri, N. 2011. 'Public Diplomacy in India's Foreign Policy'. *Strategic Analysis*. 35(2): 297–303.

Suryanarayana, P.S. 2016. *Smart Diplomacy: Exploring China-India Synergy*. New Jersey: World Century Publishing Corporation.

Swami, P. 2006. *India, Pakistan and the Secret Jihad: The Covert War in Kashmir, 1947–2004*. London and New York: Routledge.

Sypott, K. 2015. 'India's Military Modernisation: Assessing the Impact on India's Relative Power and Foreign Relations'. *Culture Mandala: The Bulletin of the Centre for East-West Cultural and Economic Studies*. 11(2): 1–18.

Talbott, S. 2010. *Engaging India: Diplomacy, Democracy, and the Bomb*. Washington, D.C.: Brookings Institution Press.

Taneja, N., S. Ray, N. Kaushal, and D.R. Chowdhury. 2011. 'Enhancing Intra-SAARC Trade: Pruning India's Sensitive List under SAFTA'. *Indian Council for Research on International Economic Relations* (ICRIER).

Taneja, N. and A. Sawhney. 2007. 'Revitalising SAARC Trade: India's Role at 2007 Summit'. *Economic and Political Weekly*. 42(13): 1081–4.

Tay, S. 2010. 'Interdependency Theory: China, India, and the West'. *Foreign Affairs*. 89(5): 138–43.

Tayal, S.R. and S.K. Mishra. 2012. 'India and the Republic of Korea: A Growing Strategic Partnership'. *Indian Foreign Affairs Journal*. 7(3): 321–30.

Taylor, I. 2012. 'India's Rise in Africa'. *International Affairs*. 88(4): 779–98.

Taylor, I. 2014. *Africa Rising? BRICS-Diversifying Dependency*. England: Boydell & Brewer Ltd.

Thakur, R. 1997. 'India in the World: Neither Rich, Powerful, Nor Principled'. *Foreign Affairs*. 76(4): 15–22.

Thakur, R. 2011. 'India and the United Nations'. *Strategic Analysis*. 35(6): 898–905.

Thakur, R. 2014. 'How Representative Are BRICS?' *Third World Quarterly*. 35(10): 1791–808.

Thakurta, P.G. and S. Raghuraman. 2007. *Divided We Stand: India in a Time of Coalitions*. India: SAGE Publications.

Thornton, W.H. and S.H. Thornton. 2006. 'The Price of Alignment India in the New Asian Drama'. *Journal of Developing Societies*. 22(4): 401–20.

Thussu, D. 2013. *Communicating India's Soft Power: Buddha to Bollywood*. New York: Palgrave Macmillan.

Tocci, N. and I. Manners. 2008. *Who Is a Normative Foreign Policy Actor?* Brussels: Centre for European Policy Studies.

Touhey, R. 2007. 'Canada and India at 60: Moving beyond history?' *International Journal*. 62(4): 733–52.

Toukan, A. and A.H. Cordesman. 2011. *The Iranian Nuclear Challenge: GCC Security, Risk Assessment, and US Extended Deterrence*. Washington, D.C.: Center for Strategic and International Studies.

Tripathi, A. 2011. 'Prospects of India Becoming a Global Power'. *Indian Foreign Affairs Journal*. 6(1): 58–69.

Trivedi, R. 2008. *India's Relations with Her Neighbours*. India: Gyan Publishing House.

Twining, D. 2008. 'India's Relations with Iran and Myanmar: "Rogue State" or Responsible Democratic Stakeholder?' *India Review*. 7(1): 1–37.

Twining, D. and R. Fontaine. 2011. 'The Ties That Bind? US–Indian Values-Based Cooperation'. *The Washington Quarterly*. 34(2): 193–205.

Upadhyaya, P. 2008. 'Peace and Conflict: Reflections on Indian Thinking'. *Strategic Analysis*. 33(1): 71–83.

Vajpayee, A.B. 2002. *India's Perspectives on ASEAN and the Asia-Pacific Region (Vol. 21)*. Singapore: Institute of Southeast Asian Studies.

Van Eekelen, W. 2015. *Indian Foreign Policy and the Border Dispute with China*. Netherlands: Brill.

Van Schendel, W. 2002. 'Stateless in South Asia: The Making of the India–Bangladesh Enclaves'. *The Journal of Asian Studies*. 61(01): 115–47.

Vanaik, A. 2008. 'Post Cold War Indian Foreign Policy'. *Seminar New Delhi*. 581: 68.

Varma, L. 2009. 'Japan's Official Development Assistance to India: A Critical Appraisal'. *India Quarterly: A Journal of International Affairs.* 65(3): 237–50.

Varma, S.N. 2002. 'India and Australia towards Forging a Dynamic Relationship', in Gopal, D. (ed.), *Australia in the Emerging Global Order: Evolving Australia-India Relations.* Delhi: Shipra Publications.

Vieira, M.A. and C. Alden. 2011. 'India, Brazil, and South Africa (IBSA): South-South Cooperation and the Paradox of Regional Leadership'. *Global Governance.* 17(4): 507–28.

Virk, K. 2013. 'India and the Responsibility to Protect: A Tale of Ambiguity'. *Global Responsibility to Protect.* 5(1): 56–83.

Vittorini, S. 2015. 'Indian Foreign Policy: Ambition and Transition'. *Commonwealth & Comparative Politics.* 53(2): 224–6.

Vom Hau, M., J. Scott, and D. Hulme. 2012. 'Beyond the BRICs: Alternative Strategies of Influence in the Global Politics of Development'. *European Journal of Development Research.* 24(2): 187–204.

Wadhva, C.D. and Y.P. Woo. 2005. *Asian Regionalism, Canadian and Indian Perspectives.* New Delhi: APH Publishing.

Wagner, C. 2005. 'From Hard Power to Soft Power? Ideas, Interaction, Institutions, and Images in India's South Asia Policy'. *Heidelberg Papers in South Asian and Comparative Politics.* 26: 1–16.

Wagner, C. 2010. 'India's Gradual Rise'. *Politics.* 30(1 suppl): 63–70.

Wagner, C. 2010. 'India's Soft Power Prospects and Limitations'. *India Quarterly: A Journal of International Affair.* 66(4): 333–42.

Wang, V.W.C. 2011. '"Chindia" or Rivalry? Rising China, Rising India, and Contending Perspectives on India-China Relations'. *Asian Perspective.* 35(3): 437–69.

Wagner, D. and G. Cafiero. 2014. 'Can China and India Coexist in Myanmar?'. *Asia Pacific Bulletin.* 250: 1–2.

Warburg, G.F. 2012. 'Nonproliferation Policy Crossroads: Lessons Learned from the US-India Nuclear Cooperation Agreement'. *The Nonproliferation Review.* 19(3): 451–71.

Wastler, B. 2010. 'Having Its Yellowcake and Eating It Too: How the NSG Waiver for India Threatens to Undermine the Nuclear Nonproliferation Regime'. *BC Int'l & Comp. L. Rev.* 33: 201–18.

Weerakoon, D. 2010. 'The Political Economy of Trade Integration in South Asia: The Role of India'. *The World Economy.* 33(7): 916–27.

Weiss, L. 2007. 'US-India Nuclear Cooperation: Better Later than Sooner'. *Nonproliferation Review.* 14(3): 429–57.

Weiss, L. 2010. 'India and the NPT'. *Strategic Analysis.* 34(2): 255–71.

Wilkins, D.B. and M. Papa. 2013. 'The Rise of the Corporate Legal Elite in the BRICS: Implications for Global Governance'. *BCL Rev.* 54: 1149–84.

Willis, J.M. 2009. 'Making Yemen Indian: Rewriting the Boundaries of Imperial Arabia'. *International Journal of Middle East Studies.* 41(01): 23–38.

Wilson, J.D. 2015. 'Resource Powers? Minerals, Energy and the Rise of the BRICS'. *Third World Quarterly.* 36(2): 223–39.

Winters, A. and S. Yusuf. 2007. *Dancing with Giants: China, India, and the Global Economy.* Washington, D.C.: World Bank Publications.

Wulf, H. 2013. *India's Aspirations in Global Politics; Competing Ideas and Amorphous Practices.* Germany: Institute for Development and Peace, University of Duisburg-Essen.

Wulf, H. 2014. *Is India Fit for a Role in Global Governance?* Germany: Centre for Global Cooperation Research.

Yazdani, E. 2007. 'The Dynamics of India's Relations with Iran in the Post-Cold War Era: A Geo-Political Analysis'. *South Asia: Journal of South Asian Studies.* 30(2): 351–68.

Yuan, J.D. 2007. 'The Dragon and the Elephant: Chinese-Indian Relations in the 21st Century'. *Washington Quarterly.* 30(3): 131–44.

Zahirinejad, M. 2013. 'Iran and India: The Need for Constructive Re-Engagement'. *Strategic Analysis.* 37(1): 29–33.

Zhao, H. 2007. 'India and China: Rivals or Partners in Southeast Asia?'. *Contemporary Southeast Asia: A Journal of International and Strategic Affairs.* 29(1): 121–42.

Ziring, L. 1978. 'Pakistan and India: Politics, Personalities, and Foreign Policy'. *Asian Survey.* 18(7): 706–30.

Index

About the Author

Rajendra M. Abhyankar served in the India Foreign Service for 37 years as India's Ambassador to the European Union, Belgium, and Luxembourg. Since 2012, he has been teaching at the School of Public and Environmental Affairs, Indiana University, Bloomington. In other roles, Abhyankar has been director at Centre for West Asian Studies, Jamia Millia Islamia, Delhi (2005–09); director and adviser at Asia Foundation, San Francisco for their India Programme (2005–11); and president at the Hinduja Foundation, Mumbai (2006–09). He is chairman of the Kunzru Centre for Defence Studies and Research, Pune, a private think tank on defence, security, and foreign affairs. He is the author of six books, one of which is a novel based in Sri Lanka. He contributes frequently to national dailies and is currently working on his latest book on the Syrian tragedy. He is multilingual and speaks French, Italian, Greek, Turkish, Arabic, Sanskrit, and three Indian languages.